"True to his unique contribution to missiology, in this final contribution Paul Hiebert has opened our understanding of worldview at a depth yet unexplored. *Transforming Worldviews* begins with a thorough examination of the concepts of worldview, moves on to cultural and philosophical analysis, follows with sound biblical reflection, and ends with a call to transformation. This promises to be a classic in the study of missions. It is Hiebert at his best!"

—**Doug McConnell**, Fuller Theological Seminary

"In this remarkable study, one of the leading missionary anthropologists of the past half century provides the most comprehensive and thorough treatment currently available of worldview and its relation to Christian faith. The culmination of a lifetime of intercultural ministry and reflection, *Transforming Worldviews* is a magisterial work that will shape discussions in missiology and theology for years to come. Indispensable for anyone interested in issues of faith and culture."

—**Harold Netland**, Trinity Evangelical Divinity School

"What a holy passage it is to walk once more with our brother Paul Hiebert by means of these pages, to hear his wisdom distilled, his last word and testament to those who are trying to love God's world in our time. Theory and practice, cultural patterns and missiological issues—there is plenty to provoke our thinking for a long time to come."

—**Miriam Adeney**, Seattle Pacific University

"This book is vintage Hiebert, pulling together in a single volume his seminal thinking on the cultural dynamics of Christian conversion. Drawing on a lifetime of learning, thinking, and writing on the subject, this work augurs to be the standard text on worldview for years to come. The book brims with insights into the cultural and theological 'what' and 'how' of being 'no longer conformed to this world, but transformed by the renewing of our minds.' Written with the clarity and originality of thought that put Hiebert's writings at the forefront of twentieth-century missiological thought and practice, this volume is an apt tribute to the life and work of its extraordinary author, who went to his eternal home on March 11, 2007."

—**Jonathan J. Bonk**, Overseas Ministries Study Center;
editor, *International Bulletin of Missionary Research*

Transforming WORLDVIEWS

An Anthropological Understanding of How People Change

Paul G. Hiebert

B

Baker Academic

a division of Baker Publishing Group

Grand Rapids, Michigan

Published by Baker Academic
a division of Baker Publishing Group
P.O. Box 6287, Grand Rapids, MI 49516-6287
www.bakeracademic.com

Printed in the United States of America

Library of Congress Cataloging-in-Publication Data
Hiebert, Paul G., 1932–2007
    Transforming worldviews : an anthropological understanding of how people change /
Paul G. Hiebert.
        p.   cm.
    Includes bibliographical references (p.   ) and index.
    ISBN 978-0-8010-2705-5 (pbk.)
    1. Missions—Theory. 2. Missions—Anthropological aspects. 3. Christianity and other religions. 4. Religion and culture. 5. Philosophy. 6. Ideology. I. Title.
    BV2063.H468 2008
    266.001—dc22   2007048743

Scripture quotations labeled Message are from *The Message* by Eugene H. Peterson, copyright © 1993, 1994, 1995, 2000, 2001, 2002. Used by permission of NavPress Publishing Group. All rights reserved.

Scripture quotations labeled NIV are from the HOLY BIBLE, NEW INTERNATIONAL VERSION®. NIV®. Copyright © 1973, 1978, 1984 by International Bible Society. Used by permission of Zondervan. All rights reserved.

Scripture quotations labeled NRSV are from the New Revised Standard Version of the Bible, copyright © 1989, by the Division of Christian Education of the National Council of the Churches of Christ in the United States of America. Used by permission. All rights reserved.

Scripture quotations labeled RSV are from the Revised Standard Version of the Bible, copyright 1952 [2nd edition, 1971] by the Division of Christian Education of the National Council of the Churches of Christ in the United States of America. Used by permission. All rights reserved.

Scripture quotations labeled TNIV are from the HOLY BIBLE, TODAY'S NEW INTERNATIONAL VERSION®. TNIV®. Copyright © 2001, 2005 by by International Bible Society. Used by permission of Zondervan. All rights reserved.

Contents

Figures

Introduction

The Christmas pageant was over, or so I thought. In the South Indian village church, young boys dressed as shepherds staggered onto stage, acting dead drunk, to the delight of the audience. In that region shepherds and drunkards are synonymous. When the angels appeared from behind a curtain, however, they were shocked sober, and the moment of hilarity passed. The wise men came to the court of Herod seeking directions, and the star led them to the manger where Mary, Joseph, the shepherds and wise men, and the angels gathered around the crib of baby Jesus. The message has gotten through, I thought. Then, from behind the curtain, came Santa Claus, the biggest boy in class, giving birthday gifts to all. I was stunned. What had gone wrong?

My first thought was "syncretism." The village Christians had mixed Christianity and Hinduism. Then I realized this was not the case. The missionaries had brought both Christ and Santa. So why was I disturbed? Clearly the message of Christ's birth had gotten through. So too the message of Santa, the bearer of gifts. The problem was that the villagers had mixed what in my mind were two different Christmases. One centered on Christ. In it the climate was warm, the trees palms, the animals donkeys, cows, and sheep, and the participants were Mary and Joseph, shepherds, and wise men. The other centered on Santa. In it the climate was cold, the trees evergreen, the animals rabbits, bears, and above all reindeer, and the participants were Mrs. Claus and elves. So what had gone wrong? Somehow the message the missionaries had brought was garbled. The pieces were all there, but they were put together wrong. To understand this mix-up we must ask, what is the gospel and what changes must take place when one becomes a Christian?

Can a nonliterate peasant become a Christian after hearing the gospel only once? Imagine, for a moment, Papayya, an Indian peasant, returning to his village after a hard day's work in the fields. His wife is preparing the evening meal, so to pass the time he wanders over to the village square. There he notices a stranger surrounded by a few curiosity seekers. Tired and hungry, he sits down to hear what the man is saying. For an hour he listens to a message of a new god, and something he hears moves him deeply. Later he asks the stranger about the new way, and then, almost as if by impulse, he bows his head and prays to this god who is said to have appeared to humans in the form of Jesus. He doesn't quite understand it all. As a Hindu he worships Vishnu, who incarnated himself many times as a human, animal, or fish to save humankind. Papayya also knows many of the other 330 million Hindu gods. But the stranger says there is only one God, and this God has appeared among humans only once. Moreover, the stranger says that this Jesus is the Son of God, but he says nothing about God's wife. It is all confusing to him.

Papayya turns to go home, and a new set of questions floods his mind. Can he still go to the Hindu temple to pray? Should he tell his family about his new faith? And how can he learn more about Jesus—he cannot read the few papers the stranger gave him, and there are no other Christians within a day's walk. Who knows when the stranger will come again?

Can Papayya become a Christian after hearing the gospel only once? Our answer can only be yes. If a person must be educated, have an extensive knowledge of the Bible, or live a good life, the good news is only for a few. But what essential change takes place when Papayya responds to the gospel message in simple faith? Certainly he has acquired some new information. He has heard of Christ and his redemptive work on the cross and a story or two about Christ's life on earth, but his knowledge is minimal. Moreover, what he knows is shaped by his cultural beliefs. Papayya cannot pass even the simplest tests of Bible knowledge or theology. If we accept him as a brother are we not opening the door for "cheap grace," syncretism, and a nominal church? If we tell him to wait and learn more, we drive him away. What must take place for a conversion to be genuine?

When we seek to win people to Christ, we look for some evidence of conversion. Our first tendency is to look for changes in behavior and rituals. This was true in missions in the nineteenth century.[1] Many missionaries looked for evidence that people were truly converted, such as putting on clothes; giving up alcohol, tobacco, and gambling; refusing to bow to ancestors; taking baptism and communion; and attending church regularly. Such changes are important as evidence of conversion, but it became clear that these did not necessarily mean that underlying beliefs had changed. People could adapt their behavior to get jobs, win status, and gain power without abandoning their

---

1. Change in behavior was central to Catholic missions after the sixteenth century. Francis Xavier baptized converts who could recite the Lord's Prayer, the twelve articles of the short Catholic creed, and the Ten Commandments. Catholic theology does not make the sharp distinction between beliefs and behavior, between forms and meanings in symbols, that Protestant theology does. Consequently, behavioral transformation is seen as transforming beliefs.

old beliefs. They could give Christian names to their pagan gods and spirits and so "Christianize" their traditional religions.

In the twentieth century, Protestant missionaries began to stress the need for transformations in people's beliefs. People had to believe in the deity, virgin birth, and death and resurrection of Christ to be saved. They had to repent inwardly of their sins and seek the salvation Christ was offering to those who believe. Right beliefs were seen as essential to Christian conversion, and missions set up Bible schools and seminaries to teach orthodox doctrine.

It is becoming increasingly clear, however, that transforming explicit beliefs is not enough to plant churches that are faithful to the gospel. People often say the same words but mean different things. Underlying explicit beliefs is a deeper level of culture that shapes the categories and logic with which people think and the way they view reality. For example, Jacob Loewen, missionary to the Waunana in Panama, asked leaders in the young church what they liked most about becoming Christians. Some said it was the peace that it brought to the people, who traditionally were at war with their neighbors. Others said that it was the worship and fellowship in church services that they enjoyed. Pushed further, they finally admitted that what they appreciated most was the new "power words" that Christianity had brought them. Loewen asked them to explain what they meant, and one man said, "When you want to harm an enemy, you sit right in front of him in the prayer meeting so that when you turn around to kneel and pray he is right in front of you. Then you say, 're-demp-tion,' 'sal-va-tion,' and 'amen,' and the person will get sick." In a South Indian village, all the Christians painted big white crosses on their houses. I thought this was a good witness to their new faith, but they explained that the cross was a powerful sign to defend them from the evil eye. In both cases people had reinterpreted Christianity as a new and more powerful form of magic that enabled them to gain success and harm enemies through right formulas. Such reinterpretations of Christianity into an essentially pagan understanding of reality are not uncommon. We see it in Simon's misunderstanding of Peter and John's prayer (Acts 8:14–24). In fact, it is one of the most common and greatest dangers in the church.

Conversion to Christ must encompass all three levels: behavior, beliefs, and the worldview that underlies these. Christians should live differently because they are Christians. However, if their behavior is based primarily on traditional rather than Christian beliefs, it becomes pagan ritual. Conversion must involve a transformation of beliefs, but if it is a change only of beliefs and not of behavior, it is false faith (James 2). Conversion may include a change in beliefs and behavior, but if the worldview is not transformed, in the long run the gospel is subverted and the result is a syncretistic Christo-paganism, which has the form of Christianity but not its essence. Christianity becomes a new magic and a new, subtler form of idolatry. If behavioral change was the focus of the mission movement in the nineteenth century, and changed beliefs its focus in the twentieth century, then transforming worldviews must be its central task in the twenty-first century.

Here it is important to differentiate between conversion as personal transformation and conversion as corporate transformation. Leading individuals to faith in Jesus Christ is the evangelistic dimension of mission. People come as they are, with their histories and cultures. We cannot expect an instant transformation of their behavior, beliefs, and worldviews. It is important, therefore, to disciple them into Christian maturity. This includes a transformation not only in the way people think and behave but also in their worldviews.

Conversion must also be corporate. The church in each locale, as a community of faith, must define what it means to be Christian in its particular sociocultural and historical setting. It must take responsibility for defining and keeping biblical orthodoxy, and it must do so by defining how Christianity is different from its pagan surroundings. This is the faithfulness side of mission. The apostle Paul is clear; we are to live in this world but not to be of the world. He uses terms such as *sarx*, *archeon*, and *eon* to refer to the contexts in which we live. Too often we understand these terms as referring to a fallen world from which we should flee. But even when we withdraw into Christian colonies, we take the "world" with us. We cannot simply outlaw sin and thereby live in holy communities. The flesh, the world, and the age are what we are in now. They are good because humans were created in the image of God and can create cultures and societies that are good. Governments are God-ordained because they help keep order in a fallen world. But the flesh, the world, and the age are also fallen and sinful. Fallen humans create fallen systems that do evil. The fundamental characteristic of the flesh, the world, and the age is not that they are good or evil—they are both—it is that they are temporary. They stand in contrast to the kingdom of God, which is eternal, totally righteous, and good. The process of maintaining true faith in this world and age is ongoing, for each generation must learn to think biblically about being Christian in its particular context.

How can worldviews be transformed? Before answering this question, we must explore further the nature and operations of worldviews.

1

The Concept of Worldview

The concept of worldview has emerged during the past two decades as an important concept in philosophy, philosophy of science, history, anthropology, and Christian thought. It is one of those fascinating, frustrating words that catches our attention. Its ambiguity generates a great deal of study and insight, but also much confusion and misunderstanding. There is no single definition agreed upon by all. At best we can examine the history of the concept along with some of the definitions and theories that have emerged. We can then develop a model that helps us understand the nature of our mission as Christians in the world.

Origins of the Concept

The concept of worldview has several roots. One is in Western philosophy, where the German word *Weltanschauung* was introduced by Immanuel Kant and used by writers such as Kierkegaard, Engels, and Dilthey as they reflected on Western culture.[1] By the 1840s it had become a standard word in Germany. Albert Wolters notes:

> Basic to the idea of Weltanschauung is that it is a point of view on the world, a perspective on things, a way of looking at the cosmos from a particular vantage point. It therefore tends to carry the connotation of being personal, dated, and

1. David K. Naugle (2002) gives an excellent history of the concept in Western philosophy.

private, limited in validity by its historical conditions. Even when a worldview is collective (that is, shared by everyone belonging to a given nation, class, or period), it nonetheless shares in the historical individuality of that particular nation or class or period. (1985, 9)

In the nineteenth century, German historians turned from the study of politics, wars, and great persons to the study of ordinary people. Because they could not examine the lives of every individual or event, they focused their attention on whole societies, looking for broad cultural patterns. For example, Jacob Burckhardt in his *Civilization of the Renaissance in Italy* sought to explain such diverse things as festivals, etiquette, folk beliefs, and science in Renaissance Italy in terms of one paramount theme, individualism. Oswald Spengler traced how cultures selectively borrowed traits from other cultures and how they reinterpreted these traits commensurate with their own underlying worldviews. For example, he showed how the Egyptians had a "deep" concern for time. They kept detailed records of past events and built large monuments for the dead to remind people of their great past. The Greeks, on the other hand, had a "shallow" concept of time and lived essentially in the present. Their historians argued that no important events had occurred before their age. They were interested not in past history but in the structure and operation of the world around them. Wilhelm Dilthey explained different periods of history in terms of their *Zeitgeist*, or "spirit of the times."

From the perspective of history, this examination of everyday human activities raised new questions. How do cultural patterns emerge, how do they spread from one region to another, and why do some die out while others persist for centuries and millennia? For example, the cultures of the West were deeply shaped by the Greco-Roman world from which they emerged. They are shaped more by Greek than by Hebrew and Indian philosophies, and more by Roman than by Confucian concepts of law and social order. The German historians used the term *Weltanschauung* to refer to the deep, enduring cultural patterns of a people.

Another root of the concept is found in anthropology. Anthropologists empirically studied peoples around the world and found deep but radically differing worldviews underlying their cultures. The more they studied these cultures, the more they became aware that worldviews profoundly shape the ways people see the world and live their lives.[2] They found that some cultures have similar traits, while others are radically different from one another. This led to the theory of cultural cores and diffusionism, which held that cultural patterns often spread from one group of people to another. Franz Boas, Robert Lowie, Edward Sapir, and especially A. L. Kroeber used diffusionism to develop the idea of cultural areas made up of societies that share common culture complexes. This notion generated the idea that each culture has a basic configuration, or *Volksgeist*.

2. For excellent studies on African cosmologies, see Forde 1954.

As anthropologists studied different cultures more deeply, they found that below the surface of speech and behavior are beliefs and values that generate what is said and done. They became aware of still deeper levels of culture that shaped how beliefs are formed—the assumptions that people make about the nature of things, the categories in which they think, and the logic that organizes these categories into a coherent understanding of reality. It became increasingly clear that people live not in the same world with different labels attached to it but in radically different conceptual worlds. This growing awareness led to investigations of deep culture and the use of words such as "ethos," "zeitgeist," "cosmology," "cosmos within," "outlook on life," "world event," "world metaphor," "world order," "world theory," "world hypotheses," "world making," "world picture," "cultural core," "root paradigms," "collective unconscious," "cultural unconscious," "plausibility structure," "the whole universe seen from the inside view," and "worldview."

Like the other words in this list, "worldview" has many problems associated with it. First, because of its roots in philosophy, it focuses on the cognitive dimensions of cultures and does not deal with the affective and moral dimensions, which are equally important, nor with how these three dimensions of being human relate to one another. Second, it is based on the priority of sight or view over hearing or sound. All cultures use both sight and sound, but in most, sound is the dominant sensory experience. Spoken words are more immediate, relational, and intimate than printed ones. Written words are impersonal, detached from specific contexts, and delayed. Scripture says that in the beginning God spoke and the world came into being. In many societies spoken words have the powers of magic and curse or blessing. A third problem with the term is that it applies both to individuals and to communities. A. F. C. Wallace notes that while individuals have their own "mazeways," the dominant worldview in cultures is shaped greatly by power and the social dynamics of the community (1956). Despite these problems, we will use the term "worldview" because it is widely known and because we lack a better, more precise term. We will, however, define the concept as we use it in this study as the "fundamental cognitive, affective, and evaluative presuppositions a group of people make about the nature of things, and which they use to order their lives." Worldviews are what people in a community take as given realities, the maps they have of reality that they use for living.

Because this study is done in the theoretical framework of anthropology, it is important to trace some of the roots of the concept in that discipline.

History of the Concept in Anthropology

The concept that gave birth to the idea of worldview in anthropology was that of "culture." Early anthropologists used the term "civilized." They placed human societies on a scale ranging from "primitive" to "civilized," from prelogical to logical. Franz Boas and his successors rejected this ranking of societies as ethnocentric and arrogant. They introduced "culture" for the different sets of beliefs and practices of any people, beliefs and practices that make sense to the people who live in them. As they studied other cultures deeply, they realized that there were many standards by which to compare the lifeways of different people, and that no one is superior to the others in all or even most measures.

Franz Boas and his disciple, A. L. Kroeber, were largely responsible for introducing the concept of "culture" into American anthropology. By "culture" they meant the patterns of learned beliefs and behavior that order human activities. Clark Wissler, one of Boas's students, used the concept to map distinct culture areas among North American Indians by looking at deep, underlying similarities and differences between tribes. Implicit in this view was the notion that a culture is not a random assortment of traits but an integrated coherent way of mentally organizing the world. In other words, an underlying "pattern" or "configuration" "gives to any culture its coherence or plan and keeps it from being a mere accumulation of random bits" (Kroeber 1948, 311). Moreover, culture has depth. While surface traits may change rapidly, certain deep, underlying patterns persist for long periods of time. This view was summed up by Edward Sapir, another of Boas's students, who defined culture as a "world outlook" that embraced in a single term "those general attitudes, views of life, and specific manifestations of civilization that give a particular people its distinctive place in the world. Emphasis is put not so much on what is done and believed by a people as on how what is done and believed functions in the whole life of that people, on what significance it has for them" (Sapir 1949, 11).

Ruth Benedict

One of the earliest anthropologists to look deeply at the integrating structures beneath explicit culture was Ruth Benedict, a student of Boas and a novelist-turned-anthropologist. She argued that cultures are not simply collections of traits and that an underlying pattern links traits into a coherent whole. Therefore, cultural traits should be understood in the light of a culture in its entirety. In her classical study of three cultures, *Patterns of Culture* (1934), she sought to understand their underlying "ethos" or spirit, by first looking at the whole rather than the parts.

Drawing on her earlier work as a novelist and poet,[3] she used three Greek mythical figures to characterize the tribes. The Zuni of New Mexico, she said,

3. Benedict drew on gestalt psychology and Oswald Spengler's examination of Western cultural configurations in *The Decline of the West*, which contrasts the Apollonian view of humans of the classical Greek world and the Faustian view of the modern world. She also draws on

are Apollonian in nature. They stress an ordered life, group control, emotional reserve, sobriety, self-effacement, and inoffensiveness above all other virtues. They distrust individualism. They have priests who perform rituals as these have always been done.

The Kwakiutl of Vancouver Island are the opposite. They value violent, frenzied experiences to break out of the usual sensory routine and express personal emotions with great abandon, seeking ecstasy through fasting, torture, drugs, and frenzied dance. In their ceremonies the chief dancer goes into a deep trance, foams at the mouth, trembles violently, and is tied up with four ropes to keep him from doing damage. The most sacred Kwakiutl cult was the Cannibal Society, whose members ate the bodies of ritually killed slaves. Benedict labeled them Dionysian after a hero in Greek mythology. They accumulated enormous amounts of subsistence goods and destroyed them to demonstrate their wealth, gain prestige, and shame their rivals.

The Dobuans of Melanesia are different from the other two. Their highest virtues, Benedict noted, are hostility and treachery. They practice sorcery, and if anyone has a good crop of yams, it is assumed he performed sorcery against those whose yams did not grow well. The Dobuans live in a state of perpetual fear of one another and, Benedict argues, regard this as normal. Alan Barnard notes, "So, what is normal for the Zuni is not normal for the Kwakiutl. What is normal in Middle America is not normal for the Dobuans, and vice versa. In Western psychiatric terms, we might regard the Zuni as neurotic, the Kwakiutl as megalomaniac, and the Dobuans as paranoid. In Dobu paranoia is 'normal'" (2000, 104).

Benedict sought to give us a "feel" of different cultures in terms of deep affective themes that shape people's view of the human order.

Mary Douglas

Mary Douglas explored the relationship between cultural beliefs about purity and pollution, two poles along a continuum (1966). She points out that cleanliness has as much to do with order as with hygiene. Dirt is anything that is out of place in the cultural classification system. She writes,

> Shoes are not dirty in themselves, but it is dirty to place them on the dining table; food is not dirty in itself, but it is dirty to leave cooking utensils in the bedroom or food bespattered on clothing; similarly, bathroom equipment in the drawing room; clothing lying on chairs; outdoor-things in-doors; upstairs things downstairs; under-clothing appearing where over-clothing should be, and so on. (1966, 48)

Nietzsche's studies of Greek tragedy in which he differentiates between the Dionysian culture, which pursues meaning in existence through excessive emotional experiences and the illuminations of frenzy, and the Apollonian culture, which distrusts all this and stresses moderation and order through self-control.

In some cultures, such as India, concepts of purity and pollution define the moral order. Sin is not the breaking of impersonal laws, nor the breaking of relationships, but defilement. Restoration to righteousness calls not for punishment prescribed by laws, nor reconciliation with those one has offended, but for purification rites that restore the moral order.

Later Douglas explored the relationship between individual actions and cultures (1969). She postulates two axes to examine this: grid and group. By grid she means cultural freedom and constraint. Low-grid people have the freedom to interact with others as equals. To be high-grid is to be constrained by strong, sharply defined cultural norms that must be obeyed. By group she means people doing things together (high group) or acting as autonomous individuals (low group). Combined, these form a two-dimensional grid that helps us understand different types of situations, individuals, and even cultures.

Edward Sapir and Benjamin Whorf

Before Boas's work, it was thought that all languages were essentially alike. Their words used different sounds but referred to the same things. Their underlying grammars were the same. Benjamin Whorf showed that this is not the case. Edward Sapir and Benjamin Whorf argued that people who speak different languages have different ways of looking at the world. In other words, there are many different forms of thought, each associated with a particular language that embodies its way of seeing reality. They pointed out that so-called primitive languages, such as Hopi, are more sophisticated in some ways than English.

Robert Redfield

Robert Redfield is another anthropologist who has made a major contribution to our understanding of worldviews (1968). He was influenced more by British social anthropologists, such as Bronislaw Malinowski, than by American cultural anthropologists like Boas. Malinowski had written, "What interests me really is the study of the native, his outlook on things, his *Weltanschauung*, the breath of life and reality which he breaths and by which he lives. Every human culture gives its members a definitive vision of the world, a definite zest of life" (1922, 517).

Redfield was concerned with the question, what are the universal ways in which all people look outward on the universe? He defined worldview as "that outlook upon the universe that is characteristic of a people. . . . It is the picture the members of the society have of the properties and characters upon their stage of action. . . . [Worldview] attends specifically to the way a man, in a particular society, sees himself in relation to all else. It is that organization of idea which answers to a man the questions: Where am I? Among what do I move? What are my relations to these things? . . . It is, in short, a man's idea of the universe" (1968, 30, 270).

Redfield focused his attention on the cognitive dimensions of culture, arguing that while humans see the world differently from one another, they all live in the same world, and they all must deal with certain worldview universals. These, he said, include conceptions of time, space, self, other humans, the nonhuman world, notions of causality, and universal human experiences such as birth, death, sex, and adulthood.

Redfield's goal was to compare worldviews and formulate a general worldview theory. His universal cognitive categories are helpful because they provide us with a grid to study all worldviews. These categories also enable us to compare these worldviews and to build larger ethnological theories regarding the nature of worldviews in general.

Redfield's model has it limitations. Because it focuses on the cognitive dimensions of cultures, it has no place for feelings and values. Moreover, it defines themes in outside, or etic, categories that the anthropologist imposes, like a cookie cutter, on all worldviews. There is little room for other themes that might emerge from the study of different cultures. Furthermore, it is descriptive and has no criteria for evaluating cultures or prescribing remedies for cultural evils.

Redfield's model has another major weakness: it is based on a synchronic or structuralist view of culture that disregards both social and cultural change. It views worldviews as abstract, static systems removed from the discourse of everyday life and historical times. Redfield viewed these systems as harmonious, functioning wholes in which the forces of culture work toward homeostasis. All change is seen as inherently pathological and destructive. The model cannot deal with the fact that all cultures are constantly changing, are full of internal conflicts, and lack full integration. Nor does Redfield deal with or explain changes that take place throughout history.

Finally, Redfield's model is mainly descriptive. It has no place for corporate sin and structural evils. It offers no guidelines for those who wish to change cultures and worldviews to help people caught in poverty, oppression, and sin.

Michael Kearney

Michael Kearney developed Redfield's worldview from the perspective of Marxist ideology. He defines the worldview of a people as "their way of looking at reality. It consists of basic assumptions and images that provide a more or less coherent, though not necessarily accurate, way of thinking about the world" (1984, 41). Like Redfield, Kearney argues that all humans live in a real world and that this, together with the way human senses work, gives a common shape to all worldviews. In other words, all worldviews must have some connection to external realities. Hence, Kearney argues, all humans must deal with invariant features or themes of reality to live in this world.[4] To determine

---

4. Kearney recognizes that humans use rational processes to integrate these features into structural wholes, but he argues that this logical integration is secondary to empirically based

these universals, which can be used to compare worldviews, Kearney draws on Redfield's themes. First, a person must acquire an understanding of *self*, of who one is in the world. This must be defined over against *others*. The latter include other humans, animals, nature, spirits, gods, and anything that is "not-self." Second, a person must have some notion of the *relationships* between the self and these others. For example, in some societies, people see themselves as parts of larger communities made up of groups of people, or of nature, or of the universe, and speak of "corporate identity," "responsibility," and "shame at letting the group down." In the West, people view themselves as autonomous individuals and speak of "freedom," "the inalienable rights of individuals," "self-fulfillment," and "the guilt of breaking an impersonal moral law."

Kearney's third universal theme is *classification*. To make sense of their worlds, people must classify their perceived realities into taxonomies and organize these into larger domains. In doing so, they name the "realities" with which they must deal, whether material objects, living beings, invisible spirits, or cosmic forces. His fourth theme is *causality*. People seek to explain their experiences in terms of causes and effects. Their explanations are based on observations of nature and the use of common sense.

Finally, all people have notions of *space* and *time*. The former includes not only images about geographical space but also sacred, moral, and personal space, as well as concepts of other worlds, heavens, and hells. The latter includes notions of past, present, and future; how these relate to one another; and which is most important.

Kearney's model, like that of Redfield, is essentially static. There is little place for change and conflict as essential elements in human life and no way to evaluate cultural systems as good or evil.

Morris Opler

Morris Opler presented a more dynamic model of worldviews (1945). He rejected Benedict's reduction of an entire culture to a single dominant pattern. Like Redfield, he introduces the notion of multiple "worldview themes"—deep assumptions that are found in limited number in every culture and that structure the nature of reality for its members. He points out that while cultures share similarities, each is unique in fundamental ways. People sense that there is a different "feel," "spirit," or "genius" to a particular way of life. Worldview themes, he argues, emerge within a culture and must be discovered by studying how the people themselves look at the world. Understanding these themes and the interrelationships between them is the key to discovering the underlying worldview.

---

themes. In this he rejects the notion of R. G. Collingwood and other mentalists, who argue that worldviews are largely mentally shaped views of reality. Ironically, Kearney builds his model by means of logical plausibility rather than empirical studies.

Figure 1.1

GROUP AND INDIVIDUAL AS WORLDVIEW THEMES

Group-Oriented Societies	Individual-Oriented Societies
• People are born into extended families in which they live their entire lives.	• Everyone grows up to look after himself/ herself and organize nuclear families.
• Identity is based on birth and the place a person occupies in the group.	• Identity is based on individual achievement.
• Children learn to think in terms of "we."	• Children learn to think in terms of "I."
• Harmony should always be maintained and confrontations avoided.	• Speaking one's mind is a characteristic of an honest person.
• Violating the norms leads to a sense of shame and loss of face for self and group.	• Violating the norms leads to a sense of guilt and loss of self-respect.
• Relationships between boss and worker are seen in moral family terms. The boss is responsible for the overall well-being of his worker.	• Relationships between boss and worker are governed by contracts based on voluntary exchange and mutual advantage.
• Hiring and promotion must take kinship and friendships into account.	• Hiring and promotion should be based purely on skills and rules of selection.
• The relationship is more important than the task. People should not be fired.	• The task is more important than the relationship. People can readily be fired.

Source: Adapted from Hofstede 1994, 67.

Opler defines a theme as a "postulate or position, declared or implied, and usually controlling behavior or stimulating activity, which is tacitly approved or openly promoted in a society" (1945, 198). Themes find expression in many different areas of cultural life. An example of a theme is the American focus on the individual person as the basis of society. This is reflected in the importance given to individual freedom, self-fulfillment, human rights, and laws granting personal ownership of property (fig. 1.1).

Themes vary in their importance. Some are found in many areas of life and elicit strong public reactions when violated. Others are minor and influence only limited areas of the culture. Dominant themes are often encoded in formal rituals that prescribe the details of behavior and etiquette and highlight their importance. Minor themes may be less visible but no less important in shaping everyday life. Furthermore, nonmaterial expressions of a theme are generally more elusive than its material manifestations.

Opler argues that no culture can survive if it is built around only a set of themes, for each theme pulls the culture to the extreme. Counterthemes therefore emerge as limiting factors that keep themes from becoming too powerful and destroying the culture. For example, individualism is a strong theme in mainstream American culture, but carried to the extreme, it leads to loneliness and narcissism. Parents would not care for their children, communities for their people, or the nation for its citizens. Consequently, people organize families, join clubs and churches, elect leaders, and obey the laws of the society to build a sense of community. When themes run into conflict with counterthemes, most Americans side ultimately with the autonomy and rights of the individual. A husband or a wife can divorce the other without the consent of the other, children can leave their parents when they are grown to live with their spouses, and people can complain when the government interferes too much in their lives.

Opler critiqued Redfield's model of static themes, which are integrated into a larger configurational whole. He argued that in any worldview there are conflicting themes and counterthemes and that cultures constantly change as the interplay between dominant themes and counterthemes and among dominant themes shifts over time.

The interplay of themes and counterthemes has important implications for our understanding of culture. What is loosely called "structure" in society and culture is not fixed rules and patterns of learned behavior blindly imitated but the interrelationship and balance of themes and counterthemes worked out by people in specific situations. This view sees culture as mental guidelines and principles that are used in social relationships but that are re-created or modified in every social transaction. For instance, when Americans shake hands, they reinforce a behavior ritual of greeting. But individuals may begin a new form of greeting, and in time the culture may change.

Themes and counterthemes should not always be seen as opposites but as poles—often mutually reinforcing—along a continuum. Either alone would make society impossible; each is in tension with the other, a tension that is never resolved. In such cases, reality cannot be divided into black and white categories; instead it moves between shades of gray as one theme or the other gains dominance.

Themes and counterthemes are linked in complex ways to form a more or less coherent worldview, but no worldview is fully integrated. All have themes that are in tension with one another in the larger configuration that makes up the whole.

One strength of Opler's model is its emic approach to the study of cultural themes. Themes are discovered by analyzing a culture from the viewpoint of its people, not by imposing themes on a culture from without. Another strength of Opler's model is its dynamic nature. Most worldview models see worldviews as integrated, harmonious, and static. Opler sees cultures as arenas in which different groups in a society seek to impose their views on others. Power and conflict are intrinsic to the model. For example, the rich view the world differently than the poor, and minority groups differently than those in positions of dominance and power. Moreover, worldviews are constantly changing as the surrounding world changes. This view assumes that conflicts are normal—not necessarily good but always present—in a society. It accounts for culture change as the balance of power shifts from one group to another and from one cultural segment to another. For instance, as Hispanics grow in number and strength in Los Angeles, they influence the dominant worldview of the region.

A second strength of Opler's model is that it fits with our current understanding of organic systems. Most other models look at cultures as mechanistic systems in which change is bad, while stasis and sharp boundaries are good. We will examine the difference between mechanical and organic systems later.

Opler's model focuses on the evaluative dimension of culture. While he does not distinguish between cognitive and evaluative themes, most of his examples put values and judgments at the heart of a culture. His model enables us to the see the effects of sin and evil on worldviews. It recognizes that conflicts and power struggles are endemic to all societies, and that different segments of a society seek to oppress the others for their own advantage. It makes us aware, too, that worldviews are often ideologies that those in power use to keep others in subjection. Worldviews both enable us to see reality and blind us from seeing it fully.

A weakness of Opler's model is that each worldview is presented as an autonomous entity, having its own unique set of themes and counterthemes; thus there is no easy way to develop broader theories of worldview through systematic comparisons. Another is that he does not take into account the affective, or feeling, dimension of a culture. Finally, Opler's model is synchronic. It examines the way worldviews are structured but does not look at the historical changes that have taken place in specific worldviews.

E. A. Hoebel

Like Opler, E. Adamson Hoebel postulated that cultures are organized on the basis of multiple themes or fundamental assumptions about the way the world is put together (1954). He sees these themes as forming a logically coherent, structured whole. As a leader in the field of legal anthropology, he differentiates between "existential postulates" (which deal with the nature of reality, the organization of the universe, and the ends and purposes of human life) and "normative postulates" (which define the nature of good and evil, right and wrong).

For Hoebel, the underlying integration of worldviews is based on a rational structure. He argues that different themes are not randomly associated but related to one another in logical ways. This means not that they are totally logical, but that internal logical contradictions lead to cognitive dissonance and attempts to resolve the tension.

W. J. Ong

W. J. Ong points out that the word "worldview" itself reflects a worldview, namely, the modern worldview that gives priority to sight over sound (1969,

637). He notes that in most traditional societies sounds are regarded as more important than sight. Such societies lack writing and store their information orally in stories, proverbs, songs, and catechisms. These societies are generally small and are highly immediate, personal, and relational. For people, sounds are immediate because they must be in active production in order to exist at all. Words are spoken in the context of specific relationships, and they die as soon as they have been said. Communication is, therefore, a flux of immediate encounters between humans and other beings and is full of emotions and personal interests. Spoken words are also powerful. The right sounds can cause rain to fall and enemies to fail. Other sounds, such as drumming and shouting, protect people from evil spirits.

Sounds point to the invisible and speak of mystery. In the jungle, the hunter hears the tiger before he sees it; a mother hears a noise at night and is warned of an enemy attack. It is not surprising, therefore, that sounds lead people to believe in spirits, ancestors, gods, and other beings they cannot see. Sight, conversely, carries little sense of mystery and leaves little room for what is not seen. Ong argues that the fundamental views of reality in oral communities are radically different from those of literate societies and proposes that we use the term "world event" instead of "worldview."

Stephen Pepper

Stephen Pepper postulates that worldviews, which he calls world hypotheses, draw on deep, or root, metaphors to organize their understandings of the world (1942). People often use objects of everyday experience as analogies for understanding complex realities. For example, the apostle Paul speaks of the church as a body with Christ as its head. Arnold Toynbee talks of civilizations as if they were living beings. He speaks of their birth, maturation, ill-health, decay, and death. Pepper outlines four fundamental metaphors that he believes shape worldviews. One of these is the organic metaphor, which sees the world and ultimate realities as living beings. Another is the mechanistic metaphor, which looks at the world as an impersonal machine, like a watch, run by invisible forces operating according to fixed laws. We will discuss these in depth later.[5]

Clifford Geertz

Clifford Geertz differentiates between worldview and ethos. He defines worldview as a people's "picture of the way things, in sheer actuality, are, their concept of nature, of self, of society. It contains their most comprehensive ideas of order." A people's ethos, on the other hand, is "the tone, character,

---

5. Pepper also includes "formalism" and "contextualism" as root metaphors. Neither of these is used later, so they are not discussed here.

and quality of their life, its moral and aesthetic style and mood; it is the underlying attitude toward themselves and their world that life reflects" (1973, 303). He notes, "Religious belief and ritual confront and mutually confirm one another; the ethos is made intellectually reasonable by being shown to represent a way of life implied by the actual state of affairs which the worldview describes, and the world-view is made emotionally acceptable by being presented as an image of an actual state of affairs of which such a way of life is an authentic expression" (303).

Geertz argues that although we can distinguish between worldview (cognitive assumptions) and ethos (affective and evaluative assumptions), the two are fundamentally congruent in that they complete each other and lend each other meaning. The nature of good and evil is widely seen as rooted in the very nature of reality—good being the way reality is meant to be.

Talcott Parsons, Edward Shils, Clyde Kluckhohn

In a high-level seminar, leading sociologists, psychologists, and anthropologists developed a systems approach to the study of humans. Talcott Parsons, Edward Shils, Clyde Kluckhohn, and their associates concluded that humans—societies and persons—have three dimensions: cognitive, affective, and evaluative (Parsons and Shils 1952). They put the evaluative at the core because it judges the cognitive to determine what is true and false, the affective to determine what is beautiful and ugly, and itself to determine right and wrong. Furthermore, the evaluative dimension of thought makes decisions that lead to actions.

Parsons and his associates outline six evaluative dimensions that they claim are universal. Each dimension is a continuum from one polar theme to the other. For example, they postulate a continuum of cultures extending from those in which the autonomous individual, personal freedom, and self-fulfillment are highly valued, to those in which the group, collective interests, and corporate responsibility are most important. On the emotional level, cultures range from those that stress self-control, moral discipline, and renunciation of desires (Hopi, Protestant ethic, and monasticism) to those that celebrate immediate self-gratification and abandonment of moral and social rules (Kwakiutl, hippies, Hindu tantrics). We will examine these six evaluative themes in more detail in the next chapter.

A Model

We need a model before we can examine specific worldviews. As a preliminary definition, let us define "worldview" in anthropological terms as "the foundational cognitive, affective, and evaluative assumptions and frameworks a group of people makes about the nature of reality which they use to order

Figure 1.2
THE DIMENSIONS OF CULTURE

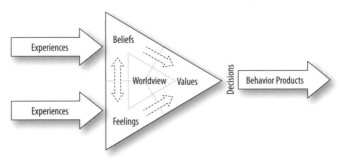

their lives." It encompasses people's images or maps of the reality of all things that they use for living their lives. It is the cosmos thought to be true, desirable, and moral by a community of people.

We will use Opler's model of themes and counterthemes to analyze worldviews, but we will modify it in significant ways. First, we will draw on the insights of Parsons, Shils, Kluckhohn, and their colleagues in speaking of the three dimensions of worldview: cognitive, affective, and moral, which we distinguish for analytical purposes. In reality all three operate simultaneously in human experiences. People think about things, have feelings about them, and make judgments concerning right and wrong based on their thoughts and feelings (fig. 1.2). The moral includes people's concepts of righteousness and sin and their primary allegiances—their gods. We will examine these three dimensions more fully in the next chapter.

To permit comparison and theory building, we can begin with Redfield's seven categories, not as etic categories imposed on a worldview but as suggestive themes that can be explored in a culture. In doing so, we need to let the worldview we are examining determine the nature and place of time, space, self and other, nonhumans, causality, and common human experience in it. We can also use the themes and counterthemes we find in one culture to see if there are similar themes and counterthemes in other worldviews. For example, Americans assume that the world around them is real, orderly, and predictable, and that they can experience it with a measure of accuracy by means of their senses. They therefore take the material world seriously. If we look at how orthodox Hindus view the material world, we find that for them the natural world has no ultimate reality. It is maya—a world of subjective experiences, a transitory, ever-changing creation of our minds. In such a chaotic, unpredictable world, meaning and truth can be found only in oneself, in the deep, innermost experiences of the self. On the other hand, we find hierarchy to be an important theme in Indian culture. People belong to castes that are ranked according to their ritual purity. Turning to the American worldview, we find a stress on the equality of all humans. In reality a great deal of hierarchy exists in the West as

Figure 1.3

WORLDVIEW THEMES AND CULTURAL ANALYSIS

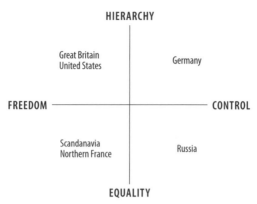

well, but it is not held up as the ideal. Such comparisons of themes and counterthemes in two or more worldviews can help us explore each more deeply and to compare and make generalized theories regarding worldviews.

The value of understanding worldviews in terms of themes and counterthemes is seen in the work of Emmanuel Todd (1987). Todd, a Dutch demographer, examines European worldviews in terms of two intersecting worldview dimensions: that of freedom–control and of hierarchy–equality (fig. 1.3). He notes that Scandinavia and northern France stress equality and freedom but allow for a measure of control to achieve equality. Germany, on the other hand, values order and control and affirms hierarchy as a consequence. Britain and the United States value freedom above all else and accept a great deal of hierarchy, despite their affirmation of the equality of all people. Russia affirms equality and uses high control to achieve it. This analysis helps us understand some of the tensions between democracy, socialism, Marxism, and fascism.

So far, we have a synchronic model of worldviews that helps us understand how people view the structure of the world. We need to add a diachronic dimension to see how people look at the human story. These views are generally embedded in a people's myths. Unfortunately the word "myth" in popular use has come to mean fiction and fantasy. In its technical, scientific sense, it means the grand narrative in which history is embedded, the narrative by which the history and the stories of human lives are interpreted. In other words, myths are transcendent stories believed to be true that bring cosmic order, coherence, and sense to the seemingly senseless experiences, emotions, and ideas in the everyday world by telling people what is real, eternal, and enduring.[6]

---

6. Postmodern critiques charge that all metanarratives are suspect and oppressive because they work on the unconscious. We argue that without authoritative metanarratives, people have no sense of place or purpose in the universe and are alienated from one another and reality.

Robert Antoine observes, "Myths are not lies or second hand 'unscientific' approaches, but a sui generis and irreplaceable method of grasping truths which otherwise would remain closed to us. 'The language of a myth is the memory of the community,' of a community which holds its bonds together because it is a 'community of faith'" (1975, 57).

Care must be taken not to reduce myths to intellectual discourses that answer questions of "why" and "wherefore." They transcend pure rationality and science because they speak of things that people may not directly perceive and of mysteries and infinite realities they cannot fully comprehend. Myths look beneath the surface world at what is really going on in this world. They are the language not only of thought but also of the imagination. They speak of eternal truth, which transcends time, in contrast to empirical truth, which is time- and language-bound. They give people a sense of meaning, not in terms of abstract analysis, as does Western thought, but by drawing them into grand narratives that give meaning to their lives by explaining the past and the present and pointing to the future. In myths people see not truth but reality, because truth is always about something, but reality is what truth is about (Lewis 1960, 66).[7]

To understand a worldview, therefore, it is essential to study both the synchronic and the diachronic themes and stories. In our study, we may focus on one or the other, but we need to keep both in mind to understand the worlds in which people live.

But worldviews are more than visions of life. Brian Walsh and J. Richard Middleton argue that "a vision of life, or world view that does not actually lead a person or a people into a particular way of life is no world view at all. Our world view determines our values. . . . It sorts out what is important and what is not, what is of highest value from what is less. . . . It thus advises how its adherents ought to conduct themselves in the world" (1984, 54). Worldviews are not foundational ideas, feelings, and values, but "worlds" that are inhabited—what Peter Berger calls "sacred canopies" that provide a cover of protection for life under which making homes, shaping communities, and sustaining life can take place (1967).

Functions of Worldviews

Taken together, the assumptions underlying a culture provide people with a more or less coherent way of looking at the world. As Clifford Geertz points out, worldviews are both models *of* reality—they describe and explain the nature of things—and models *for* action—they provide us with the mental blueprints that guide our behavior (1973, 169). Models influence human

---

7. C. S. Lewis became a Christian after a long debate with J. R. R. Tolkien over the nature of myth. Both wrote classic myths that give us deep insights into the story of the gospel.

actions, but the two are not the same. Our behavior is determined not only by our norms and ideals but also by the conflicting forces and changing circumstances that pressure our everyday lives. Furthermore, mental blueprints do not account for idiosyncratic variations.

Worldviews serve a number of important cultural and social functions. First, as Brian Walsh notes (2006, 244–45), worldviews are our plausibility structures that provide answers to our ultimate questions: Where are we (what is the nature of the world)? Who are we (what does it mean to be human)? What's wrong (how do we account for evil and the brokenness of life)? What is the remedy (what is the path from brokenness and insecurity to a life that is whole and secure)? They do so by providing us with mental models of deeply ingrained assumptions, generalizations, or pictures and images that shape how we understand the world and how we take action. They are the foundations on which to build our systems of explanation and supply rational justification for belief in these systems. In other words, if we accept our worldview assumptions, our beliefs and explanations make sense. The assumptions themselves we take for granted and rarely examine. As Geertz notes, worldviews provide us with models or maps *of reality* that structure our perceptions of reality, but we use them as maps *for living*. In other words, they provide us with the mental blueprints that guide our behavior. Worldviews emerge out of our interaction with the world—individually and corporately. Culture is external to the individual.

Second, our worldview gives us emotional security. Faced with a dangerous world full of capricious and uncontrollable forces and crises of drought, illness, and death, and plagued by anxieties about an uncertain future, people turn to their deepest cultural beliefs for comfort and security. It is not surprising, therefore, that worldview assumptions are most evident at births, initiations, marriages, funerals, harvest celebrations, and other rituals that people use to recognize and renew order in life and nature. Our worldview buttresses our fundamental beliefs with emotional reinforcements so that they are not easily destroyed.

Third, our worldview validates our deepest cultural norms, which we use to evaluate our experiences and choose courses of action. It provides us with our ideas of righteousness and sin and with ways to deal with them. It shapes our perception that this is the way it is and this is the way it ought to be. It also serves as a map for guiding our behavior. Worldviews serve both predictive and prescriptive functions.

Fourth, our worldview helps to integrate our culture. It organizes our ideas, feelings, and values into a more or less unified view of reality. Although there are indeed themes and counterthemes and compartmentalization into different domains of our experiences, our worldview gives us a sense that we live in one world that makes sense to us.

Fifth, as Charles Kraft observes, our worldview monitors culture change (1979, 56). We are constantly confronted with new ideas, new behavior, and new products that come either from within our society or from without. These may introduce assumptions that undermine our cognitive order. Our worldview helps us select those that fit our culture and reject those that do not. It also helps us to reinterpret those we adopt so that they fit our overall cultural pattern. For example, villagers in South America began to boil their drinking water, not to kill germs but (as they saw it) to drive out evil spirits. Worldviews, therefore, tend to conserve old ways and provide stability in cultures over long periods of time.

, Finally, worldviews provide psychological reassurance that the world is truly as we see it and a sense of peace and of being at home in the world in which we live. People experience a worldview crisis when there is a gap between their worldview and their experience of reality.

We will now examine some of the fundamental characteristics of world-views.

2

Characteristics of Worldviews

Before we use our model to study and compare specific worldviews, we need to examine the fundamental structure of worldviews more fully. We will look first at the synchronic and then the diachronic structures of worldviews. There is a danger in this approach because it can lead to the belief advanced by Plato that absolute reality is a static structure devoid of transition, and that change is a matter of appearance. For him, mathematics belong to changeless eternity (Whitehead 1938, 93). Following Ferdinand Eisenstein, Alfred North Whitehead, Ludwig von Bertalanffy, and others, we now see human systems, including cultures and their worldviews, as organic, dynamic systems in a state of constant flux and change, so that any attempt to define them at a given moment is only an approximation. We must realize that ultimately meaning in our lives is found not in an understanding of our human structures, but in our human stories. But we cannot separate the synchronic and the diachronic approaches. In reality both are part of one whole. It is for analytical purposes that we divide them, because of the limitations of our human minds. We will look at the synchronic and the diachronic nature of worldviews simply as heuristic devices that enable us as finite humans to study realities that are far too great and complex for us to comprehend.

We need, also, to study the role of worldviews as they shape and are shaped by our views of human history.

Synchronic Structures

Although worldviews, as amorphous wholes, are hard to examine, they do share common characteristics that we can examine.

Depth

One characteristic of worldviews is captured by such terms as "core culture" and "deep structure."[1] These terms convey the idea that worldviews underlie the more explicit aspects of culture. It is helpful here to think of a culture as having several levels. On the surface are the visible elements such as cultural products and patterns of behavior, including speech. Below these are myths and rituals—enacted cultural dramas—that give expression to the conscious beliefs, feelings, and values of the culture. They are charters for defining and establishing deep cultural themes and social norms that the people see as indispensable to the preservation of their culture and society. Below myths and rituals are systems of beliefs that encode our cultural knowledge. Finally, below these systems of beliefs are the unseen structures underlying the entire explicit culture—the worldview (fig. 2.1). Edward T. Hall writes,

> There is an underlying, hidden level of culture that is highly patterned—a set of unspoken, implicit rules of behavior and thought that controls everything we do. This hidden cultural grammar defines the way in which people view the world, determine their values, and establish the basic tempo and rhythms of life. . . . One of the principle characteristics of PL [primary level] culture is that it is particularly resistant to manipulative attempts to change it from the outside. The rules may be violated or bent, but people are fully aware that something wrong has occurred. In the meantime, the rules remain intact and change according to an internal dynamic all their own. (1983, 6–7)

The word "depth" can be misleading. As used here it does not mean foundationalism, the notion that worldviews are the foundations on which cultures are built. This implies a one-way causality, that worldviews determine the shape of the surface cultures. In fact, causality goes both ways. Changes occur regularly in the explicit levels of a culture. New technologies, such as cars and the Internet, emerge, and these transform the underlying worldviews. Similarly, on the explicit level of beliefs, people become Christians but it often takes years, even generations, before the worldview of their church is transformed. People going abroad encounter new cultures and ways of viewing the world and are forced, at the worldview level, to deal with others and otherness. As we will see, worldview transformations can occur, but generally do so to maintain congruence with the changes taking place in surface

---

1. The concept of "depth" has emerged in several fields. In structural linguistics, Ferdinand de Saussure (1916), Romane Jacobson, and Noam Chomsky (1986) looked below the conscious linguistic phenomena to study their deep, unconscious infrastructure. In psychology, Sigmund Freud examined the power of the unconscious ego in shaping human behavior. In anthropology, Claude Levi-Strauss (1978) investigated the unconscious components of kinship systems and the thematic underpinnings of myths. All of these efforts examine deep, underlying systems that enable humans to create languages and cultures.

Figure 2.1

LEVELS OF CULTURE

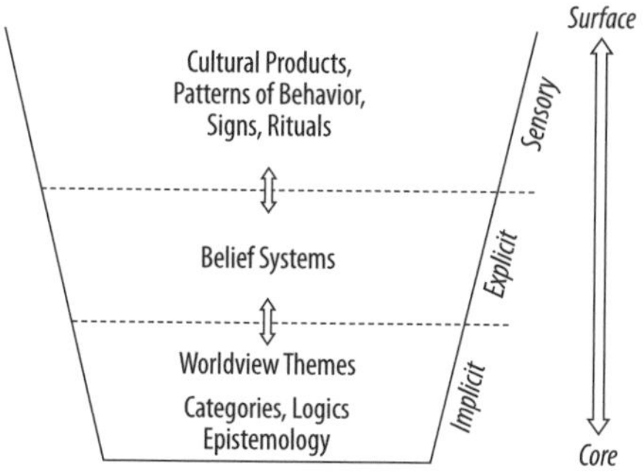

culture. Worldviews often act more as keepers of tradition than as initiators of new worlds.

CATEGORY FORMATION

Looking at depth raises the question of whether there are levels of depth within a worldview itself. Several are discernible. Fundamental to any culture is the creation of categories or sets. These can be formed in different ways.

Digital and Analogical Sets

At a fundamental level, worldviews are based on the way people form mental categories (Hiebert 1994, 107–36). Some worldview themes are built primarily on digital or "well-formed," clearly delineated Cantorian sets with a finite number of categories in a domain. The result is the law of the "excluded middle"—members cannot belong to two sets at the same time. Digital sets are associated with propositional logic, Euclidian geometry, and Cantorian algebra. Objects in such bounded sets are seen as uniform in their essential characteristics. Their differences and uniqueness are of little importance. Thus everything can be analyzed into constituent components, and everything can be taken apart and put together in terms of these components.

Other worldviews, such as those in India, are built on analogical,[2] or "fuzzy," sets that have an infinite number of steps between in and out and between one set and another. For example, classical Western music is based on seven notes and five half notes, and singers pride themselves on a clearly articulated scale when they sing. In Indian classical music, based on fuzzy sets, there are sixty-four steps between *sa* (do) and *ri* (re), and sixty-four between *ri* (re) and *ga* (me). If the player needs more, he can subdivide these microsteps further.

2. The term "analogical" is used in two distinct ways, which creates considerable confusion. In terms of logic it concerns analogies. In set theory it refers to analogical sets, as opposed to digital sets.

The result is that musicians slide from one note to the other, rather than jump from one step to another. Slides and quivering notes, not precise scales, are the beauty of the song.[3] Fuzzy sets lead to "fuzzy logic," "fuzzy algebra," and "fuzzy geometry."[4]

An example of the difference between well-formed and fuzzy sets is seen in the ways people perceive so-called human races. Most North Americans use well-formed sets and classify people as "white," "black," "Hispanic," and so on. There is no place in their worldview for intermediate positions. During the slave era, people with one black and three white grandparents were regarded as "black" and known as "quadroons"; those with one black and seven white great-grandparents were regarded as "black" and called "octoroons." Everyone was either "white" or "black." Those who think in terms of fuzzy sets perceive races as shading from one to the other with no sharp lines dividing them. There are "whites," "blacks," "Hispanics," "white-blacks," "Hispanic-whites," "black-Hispanics," "black-white-Hispanics," and many other combinations.

All cultures use both well-formed and fuzzy sets. The difference lies in which is more fundamental to the thinking of the people. Modernity is based primarily on digital sets. Roads are marked by curbs and lanes, pictures are framed, and the sciences begin by creating taxonomies, a practice already seen in Aristotle's organization of living things into genus, species, and subspecies (although Plato was right when he noted that there are no clear boundaries between species or, for that matter, most things). An American in the market asks for "an apple." She may qualify it with adjectives such as half ripe, fully ripe, or green, which are fuzzy categories. In India a person may ask for "a half ripe," because he wants to eat something tomorrow and does not care what kind of fruit it is. He does not want something that is ripe now but will be rotten tomorrow, or green and uneatable tomorrow. When the merchant asks what kind of half ripe, he says that an apple or orange or banana half ripe will do. Here the fuzzy category, half ripe, is the noun, and orange, apple, and banana are adjectives modifying the noun.

Intrinsic and Relational Sets

Another difference in category formation involves what defines a set—why are members assigned to this set and not to another? Some categories are

3. After listening to Indian music with its slides and glides, Westerners often ask when the performers are "going to hit a note." They are listening for precise scales, which to Eastern ears sound mechanical and wooden.

4. Fuzzy sets were first discussed by L. A. Zadeh (1965). For a discussion of fuzzy logic see H. Zimmerman (1985). The term "fuzzy" is misleading. In mathematics, numbers have four levels of increasing power: nominal, ordinal, interval, and ratio. Well-formed sets are interval and lead to interval logic. Fuzzy sets are ratio and give rise to ratio logic. This is the difference between algebra and calculus. Analogical mathematics is more powerful than digital mathematics, because it deals with an infinite set of categories.

defined on the basis of the intrinsic characteristics of the members. In English an "apple" is an apple because of what it is. All apples share the same characteristics. These are intrinsic sets—members are members of the set because of what they are in themselves. In modern cultures intrinsic sets are dominant. The world is seen as made up of discrete, autonomous categories. This person is a "male," "adult," "drives a Mercedes," and "has a PhD."

In most traditional cultures, extrinsic or relational sets are dominant.[5] This middle-aged woman may have a doctorate, but that is secondary to the fact that at home and in the community she is the wife of Peter, the daughter of John and Mary, and the mother of Sarah. In other words, her identity is defined not primarily in intrinsic terms but in terms of who or what she is related to. In many cultures, this feeling of relatedness extends far beyond humans to the land on which one was born and on whose crops one is fed, the animals one raises, and the spirits of the neighborhood. A person can be a person only by belonging to a community and a place, hence the proverb, "I belong, therefore I am."

All cultures use both intrinsic and extrinsic categories. Intrinsic, digital sets are foundational in the sciences, with their extensive taxonomies of particles, chemicals, plants, animals, diseases, and other domains of knowledge. They are also the basis for creating order in life: streets have curbs, lanes, stoplights, and center barriers. Driving is regulated by impersonal rules. Houses are clean when the borders between categories are sharp and things are in their proper place. In India fuzzy relational sets are fundamental. Streets are arenas where driving is done by negotiating relationships with all the other players—trucks, cars, motorcycles, rickshaws, pedestrians, cows, dogs, and chickens. Meetings begin not at an abstract set time but when enough people are present to start. Paint that drips on the floor does not make the floor "dirty."

The use of intrinsic and extrinsic sets leads to two different logics. In intrinsic sets, the observer is outside the picture, unrelated to the people or objects he is studying. He seeks objective, impersonal data that he can process using abstract, algorithmic logic. To remain objective, he must set aside his own feelings and morals, since these are subjective and contaminate the findings. In relational sets, the observer is in the picture and must understand his place in it, for that shapes what he observes. He cannot "bracket" his feelings and morals, for these are essential components of any relationship. Relational knowledge breaks down the barrier between cognitive knowing and affective and moral knowing.

The use of relational categories calls for thinking in terms of relational logic rather than abstract, analytical logic. The Greeks, with their stress on the

---

5. The intersection of well-formed and fuzzy, and intrinsic and extrinsic sets leads to four ways to create categories. The implications of this phenomenon for evangelism and church planting are explored in Hiebert 1994, 107–36.

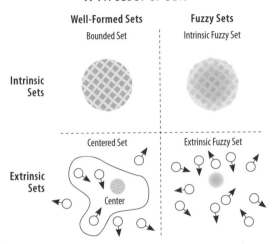

Figure 2.2
A TYPOLOGY OF SETS

autonomous individual, developed abstract, algorithmic logic in their search for universal theories based on impersonal facts. For them knowledge was "knowledge about" reality—detached and impersonal. The Hebrews stressed relationships and relational knowledge of others in the particularities of life. To "know" another was to know that person in relationship, intimately and personally, not abstractly and objectively. They saw the world not simply as a mechanical system of empirical objects in logical connection but as an organic body of personal relations and responses, a living and evolving community of creativity and compassion. This knowledge draws us into personal response and accountability in learning to know another.

If we combine digital and fuzzy sets and intrinsic and extrinsic sets, we have four fundamental ways in which to order our world. It is important to remember that all cultures use these different ways even though the emphases vary from culture to culture (fig. 2.2).

Folk and Formal Taxonomies

All cultures use folk taxonomies in everyday life. These are high-context and concretely functional in nature. They seek to tell us not about the intrinsic nature of things but about their place in everyday life. They communicate *about* entities and organisms with persons who already know culturally significant properties of the organisms being discussed. For example, folk taxonomies often differentiate between leaves, nuts, and game that can be eaten and those that cannot, or between raw and cooked.

Formal taxonomies, commonly used in science and philosophy, are low-context, highly abstract categories. They are designed to tell us about the underlying nature of reality and differentiate between categories in the same domain. Although they appear to communicate a great deal about the organism and set being discussed, in fact they communicate little because in most cases only the describer has seen the organism, and no one with whom he is communicating shares his understanding of it (Hall 1977, 122).

SIGNS

One important worldview issue is the relationship of categories and other signs to reality (Hiebert 1989). One view is that signs, such as the word "tree," point to objective realities. Consequently, sentences can convey objective truth. As we will see later, this view was essential to modern science, based as it was on a positivist epistemology that required precise symbols and words to express truths corresponding exactly with reality. Considerable effort was made to overcome the "fuzziness" and ambiguities of ordinary signs. Precise meanings require precise words and mathematics, or the meanings are lost.

A second view is that signs, such as words, are cultural constructs that shape the way people see the world. In other words, people from different cultures order their experiences differently, even though they live in the same world. As we will see, linguists such as Ferdinand de Saussure (1916) argued that signs do not point to objective realities. They evoke subjective images in the mind. Consequently, there is no way to fully determine whether what we say is true. It is simply how we see things, not what they objectively are. Conceptual categories become arbitrary creations of the mind, and cultures become isolated islands of meaning between which there can be no real communication. People in other cultures interpret what we say in terms of their own cultural categories, and there is no way to test whether their ideas correspond with ours.

A third view, espoused by Charles Peirce (1955), is that signs point to external realities and evoke subjective images in the mind. They are the bridges by which we know the world outside. In other words, signs are triadic: they have the sign form (the word "tree"), the objective reality to which they refer (trees in the outside world), and the subjective images the signs create in the mind (mental category "tree"). Here the correspondence is not like that of a photograph, whose claim to truth is a one-to-one correspondence to reality. Rather, it is like a map of reality. In other words, the correspondence is complex and varied. At some points a map must correspond exactly to reality, or the map is useless. Maps are also focused, claiming to be true in some aspects and not in others. A road map does not have all the buildings or trees on it—to add everything would make it useless. Maps also reveal hidden realities not visible to the eye. For example, a political map colors one country green and another yellow. This does not mean that the countries are these colors. It means that one territory belongs to one country and the other to another. Finally, maps and blueprints must be complementary. A builder needs different blueprints for the structure, the electrical wiring, and the plumbing. But the wiring and the plumbing blueprints must fit the structural blueprint. One does not want wiring and pipes running through the middle of rooms.

The relationships between external realities and internal images mediated by signs vary greatly.[6] In some the link is arbitrary. Young parents in the West name their children on the basis of personal choice. Most words used in everyday discursive speech are essentially arbitrary. In English we look at a tree and say "tree." We could have said "chettu" or "preta." There is no essential ideographic link between the word "tree" and the objects we call trees. Once we have agreed in our community to call this object a tree, however, the link becomes one of social and historical, not private, definition. It is passed down from generation to generation and is no longer arbitrary. I may try to change it, but my efforts are meaningless if I cannot get the community to accept the changes.

Discursive language is the basis of most verbal communication. We use it to talk about the ordinary things of life—things we can see and experience directly. We change it easily as new words are coined to represent new realities we observe or create and concepts we need to express.

In some signs the link between the external and the internal world is not arbitrary. For example, iconic symbols link the two by means of visual and oral similarities. On a computer the images of printers, arrows, files, and magnifying glasses let the user know what function each button has. Similarly, many street signs and lane lines communicate without words. In many ways icons are easier to use in multilingual settings because they communicate by images, not by letters and words.

There are a few signs in which the sign and the reality are one. For example, when a minister or justice of the peace says, "I now pronounce you husband and wife," he is not just communicating information. His words are performative. They change the legal status of the bride and groom. A moment earlier, either can call the marriage off with no legal consequences. After the pronouncement, the couple has to go through a legal divorce to undo the marriage.

Understanding these three types of signs is particularly important in dealing with religious matters, such as prayers and rituals. Protestants tend to see the Lord's Supper as helping believers to remember and reflect on the death of Christ. Some Orthodox churches see it as more iconic in nature. The bread and wine do not literally become the body and blood of Christ, but they are much more than arbitrary symbols. Other churches regard the Eucharist as

---

6. Here we will use Peirce's definitions of signs. For him signs are the overarching category of forms that represent some reality, real or perceived. Signs divide into symbols, icons, and indexes. In symbols the connection between sign and reality is socially constructed and arbitrary. Examples would be the English alphabet and most words. In icons there is a resemblance between the sign and reality. Most icons are polysemic and multivalant. Examples are the icons on a computer screen: a picture of a printer, an arrow, a folder. Indexes convey meaning not about the object itself but about its place in a larger order of things. Examples would be ordering files alphabetically and using the Library of Congress method of classifying books.

transformative. The bread and wine become, in fact, the literal body and blood of Christ. At the worldview level, it is important to remember that different cultures use different types of signs in different ways, and often our misunderstanding of their practices, such as magic and witchcraft, has as much to do with their and our understanding of the nature of the signs involved as with the beliefs behind them.

Finally, we need to distinguish between parametric and nonparametric signs. Parametric signs, such as most ordinary words, refer directly to perceived realities. Nonparametric signs communicate meanings, feelings, and values that cannot be reduced to discursive signs. They point beyond themselves to mysteries, feelings, and moral judgments that cannot be reduced to words. For example, a young man may give his fiancée a bouquet of flowers to show her that he loves her. These must be special flowers, not a bunch of dandelions. He is not simply saying, "Here are some plants for you"; through the flowers he is communicating deeper feelings of affection. Similarly, rituals such as baptism point beyond the immediate experience to mysteries that cannot be reduced to words. All we can do is use ordinary signs and say, "Do not take this literally." To do this we often embody our communication in rituals.

Logics

At a higher level, although people use different logics in different contexts, one or another of these is seen as foundational and given more credence. For example, modernity places great trust in algorithmic or propositional logic. Other logics are seen as less exact and trustworthy. In other cultures, analogical or relational logics are viewed as more important (Wilson 1970).

Abstract, Algorithmic Logic

One logical system, and the one underlying most of the sciences, is abstract, algorithmic logic. It is abstract because it creates concepts such as "molecule," "atom," "electron," "wave," and "string" in which the relevant features of certain prototype phenomena have been abstracted from the irrelevant features. For example, one does not ask about the "color" or "smell" of a molecule, which is often depicted as a spherical ball located in space and time. The process is an attempt to formulate general theories that apply to increasingly larger domains of experience.

Algorithmic logic begins with basic, foundational units of analysis: atoms, persons, stars. It seeks impersonal mechanistic formulas that describe the behavior and interaction between these parts. This is why it (using digital sets) can best be done by computers programmed to process the bits of information in terms of given formulas.

One of the limitations of abstract, algorithmic logic is that it reduces very diverse realities into a few highly abstract categories. It treats humans as a single category and overlooks their infinite variety. Another limitation is that it is hard to link the high-level abstractions to the particularities of real life. We are told not to lie, but when is it lying and when is it "coloring the facts" in everyday living?

Analogical Logic

Algorithmic logic works with intrinsic digital sets. It does not work with analogical, or "fuzzy," sets, or with relational sets. For example, mathematics based on digital sets, which is the basis for modern algebra, cannot give a precise answer to the question of what is two-thirds of pi because neither the number two-thirds nor pi can be reduced to digital numbers. We can provide close approximations but never exact answers.

In recent years new forms of mathematics have emerged, including "fuzzy sets," "fuzzy algebra," "fuzzy logic," and "fuzzy management" (Zadeh 1965; Grint 1997). The term "fuzzy" is misleading because fuzzy logic is neither imprecise nor sloppy. In fact, it is more powerful and precise than digital algorithmic logic because it deals with much higher levels of complexity. It does not reduce the world to binary oppositions and machine logic. It is based on analogical or ratio sets that have an infinite number of points between zero and one and between one and two.[7] It challenges the Aristotelian binary logic that has come to dominate modernity, which divides everything into good and bad, right and wrong, truth and lies, life and death, 0 and 1—a dualism that shapes the way we see the world. Keith Grint writes, "Effective management depends upon taking the *right* as against the *wrong* decision, having analysed the data *correctly* rather than *incorrectly,* after considering *both sides* of the argument. Good management is really concerned with good *boundary* management: decide which side of the boundary something should fit into, and the rest is easy. Such 'formal' logic underlies most of the contemporary mathematics" (1997, 10).

Digital categories and the formal analytical logic based on them are precise and may help us cope with the complexity of the real world by reducing it to a finite number of sets, but it does not fit much of reality. Few categories in the real world are digital in nature. Currently research is being done on fuzzy intrinsic sets and on "fuzzy" logic.

Topological Logic

Another form of logic is topological or analogical logic. Here we examine complex realities by comparing them with realities we already know. Robin

---

7. Numbers have four levels of power: numeral, ordinal, interval, and ratio. Numeral numbers state sheer numbers that do not need to refer to the same kinds of things. One woman has four pets, another woman one—but the four are four cats, and the one is one leopard. Ordinal numbers show sequence, but with no uniform interval. In a race the first and second to cross the finish line may be seconds apart, the third may be minutes later. Interval numbers are discrete and have a uniform distance between them. Ratio numbers are the most complex and refer to numbers along an infinite continuum.

Horton writes, "In evolving a theoretical scheme, the human mind seems constrained to draw inspiration from analogy between the puzzling observations to be explained and certain already familiar phenoma [*sic*]. . . . Whether we look amongst atoms, electrons and waves, or amongst gods, spirits and entelechies, we find that theoretical notions nearly always have their roots in relatively homely everyday experience, in analogies with the familiar" (1970, 146).

Topological logic is powerful because it draws on the imagination and generates mental explorations. We compare A with B: in some ways A and B are the same, and in some ways they are different. But analogies invite us to explore unexamined areas where we are not sure if the analogy holds.

Analogy is foundational to the formation of categories. The world we experience is infinitely varied. No two trees or persons are exactly alike. We use analogy to create mental categories by noting common patterns and overlooking other characteristics as irrelevant. For example, a person is a human even if he or she is tall or short, has one hand or two, speaks Spanish or English. Whitehead notes, "The procedure of rationalism is the discussion of analogy. . . . The development of civilized [we would add all] thought can be described as the discovery of identities amid diversity" (1938, 98).

Analogy is foundational to modern law. Although our general belief is that the law is a set of known rules applied by a judge, legal rules are in fact generalizations. They are never clear, nor are there any simple formulas with which to apply them to the variety of particular cases to which they apply. Edward Levi writes, "The basic pattern of legal reasoning is reasoning by example. It is reasoning from case to case. It is a three-step process described by the doctrine of precedent in which a proposition descriptive of the first case is made into a rule of law, and then applied to the next similar situation. The steps are these: similarity is seen between cases; next the rule of law inherent in the first case is announced; then the role of law is made applicable to the second case" (1949, 2).

At higher levels, analogy helps us understand strange and complex realities by comparing them with things that we understand. Thus early physicists viewed atoms as miniature solar systems; Christians understood God as a living being, using humans as their metaphor; and Indian villagers saw *ammas*, or capricious, territorial local spirits, as female humanlike beings.

Horton notes that the deep analogies used by cultures profoundly shape the way people view their world (1970, 147). As we will see later, modernity tends to use impersonal root metaphors. Its complex, rapidly changing world is made up largely of inanimate things, and the modern mind seeks explanation largely in impersonal analogies. This is why many people find themselves less at home with their fellow humans than with things. In traditional cultures, where the human scene is central and being less at home with people than with things is unimaginable, analogies draw naturally from people and their relations—in other words from personal root metaphors. On this level, one fundamental difference between modernity and most traditional cultures is the difference in the root metaphors they use in their explanatory quests.

Stephen Pepper introduces the idea of root metaphors, metaphors that form the foundations on which worldviews are built (1942). We will use two, organic and mechanistic, that are found in all cultures. The organic root metaphor sees living beings, particularly human beings, as its foundational analogy. Pepper notes, "To take man, everything about him, his body, his shape, his actions, his expressions, his motives, his emotions, and everything else about man that appeals to man's fancy, as the source of explanation of everything in the world: what could be more to man's taste, or seem more natural" (1942, 120). This gives rise to a world full of life and living beings—gods, spirits, humans, animals, plants, even the earth itself—as living in relationship to one another. The mechanistic root metaphor sees the machine, such as a watch, or, more recently, the electromagnetic field, as the ultimate model for understanding all things.

These two metaphors lead to two kinds of knowledge: interpersonal and impersonal. In an organic world, to intimately know another human involves not only outside observations but a hermeneutical process that enables one to understand the inside being of the other. Here we are learning to know and be known, and to relate to others who are like ourselves—not just as objects but as subjects in their own right. This interpersonal knowledge involves more than simple material observations. It involves understanding minds as well as brains, understanding persons as humans. Interpersonal knowledge extends also to our relationship with God and other spirit beings. In a mechanistic worldview, the knower is outside the machine, looking at it objectively. He has detached knowledge about it, although, as Michael Polanyi notes, even such knowledge involves the active participation of the knower—she is not simply a passive receptor of the information she processes (1962). The organic metaphor looks for underlying order but is not formulaic in nature. It uses qualitative analysis to discern that order. The mechanistic metaphor looks for formulas based on impersonal natural "laws" and uses quantitative methods to test its hypotheses.

Another difference between these root metaphors concerns certainty. Mechanistic worldviews value algorithmic or propositional logic. An algorithmic process, if carried out correctly, generates the right answer. Examples are propositional, mathematical, and computer logics. A mathematical formula is precise because it can be manipulated to generate the right answer. But algorithmic logic works only if the data is precise and complete. In much of life, we must make decisions based on approximate and incomplete data. As Eisenstein noted, as far as the laws of mathematics refer to reality, they are not certain; as far as they are certain, they do not refer to reality (Schroeder 1991, 139).

Relational Logic

A fourth kind of logic is relational, or concrete functional, logic. We, as modern people, see fundamental reality in terms of self-contained intrinsic categories. A rose is a rose because it shares intrinsic characteristics with other roses. The premise of modern science is the development of extended taxonomies and subtaxonomies of different domains of the world: physical, biological, social, cultural, spiritual, and so on.

In much of the world, people define reality at the deepest level in relational terms. This man is the husband of Lois, father of Mary and John, and grandfather of Susan and Mark. As the oldest male, he is head of his clan and an elder in the village council. Relational categories lead to concrete, functional logic, just as intrinsic categories lend themselves to highly abstract, analytical logic.

The significance of this shift can be seen in how fundamental modern categories compare with those of many traditional societies around the world. Most people in nonmodern societies think in relational, functional categories. A person is the mother of Mary, the cousin of the chief, or the friend of John. She or he is a woman or a man, but that is secondary to the person's relational identities. A. R. Luriia illustrates this in his study of the Kirghiz of Central Asia (1976). He showed people a picture of three adults and one child, and asked them which of these does not belong to the others (fig. 2.3). Most modern people say the "child," because the child is not an "adult." The Kirghiz said that the first person is the father, the second is the mother, and they need children, so the child is part of the family. The third adult must be an uncle, and he can be eliminated from the set. When shown a picture of a hatchet, a log, a hammer, and a saw, modern people eliminate the log because it is not a "tool." The Kirghiz, however, argued that with a log they could make a fire if they had a hatchet or a saw. One young man said, "The saw will saw the log and the hatchet will chop it into small pieces. If one of these things has to go, I'd throw out the saw. It doesn't do as good a job as a hatchet." When Luriia suggested that the hammer, saw, and hatchet were tools and so belonged together, another Kirghiz said, "Yes, but

Figure 2.3

RELATIONAL LOGIC

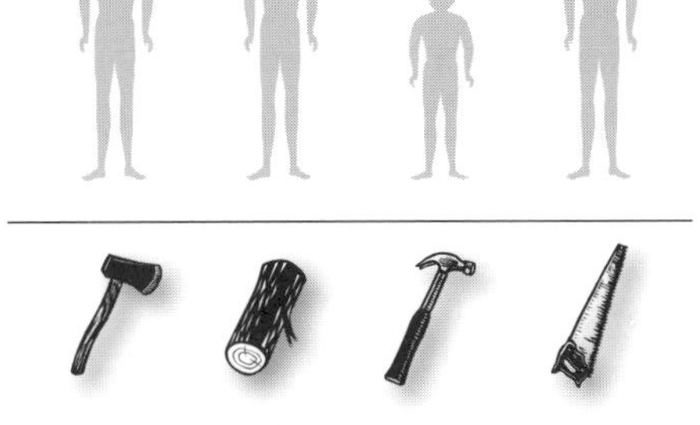

even if we have tools, we still need wood—otherwise we can't build anything."
Moreover, the hammer is useless because there are no nails.

Wisdom

On another level we speak of wisdom. When we examine realities and mysteries too complex to be reduced to words, numbers, and algorithms, we need evaluative logic or wisdom that can make considered assessments based on the knowledge at hand, the factors involved, and a comparison with previous experiences. This is the kind of knowledge stressed in organic worldviews. The logic of wisdom is found in proverbs, parables, riddles, and literature. It is the foundation for British and US legal systems, which are based on precedent cases, not simply on legal formulations, and use inference, parallels, and precedent (Tiénou and Hiebert 2006).[8] In wisdom there is no simple formula that produces the right results. Decisions must be based on a profound understanding of the present situation and on past experience. Questions of truth, feelings, and values are taken into account, as well as the objective facts and subjective perceptions of the participants. Alternative solutions must be considered. For every proverb there is a counterproverb: "A stitch in time saves nine," but "Haste makes waste."

The difference between algorithmic and evaluative logic can be seen in answering this question: what is the best road to take from the Sears Tower in Chicago to O'Hare Airport? Algorithmic logic can measure and show us the shortest route, or even the route that would take the least time given distances and speed limits, but it cannot tell us which is the "best" route to take if by "best" we mean the route that will get us there fast, safe, and with the least stress. This answer must take into account the time of day, weather, construction, and accidents. The experienced taxi driver listens to traffic reports, talks over the radio to other drivers, and draws on his knowledge of backstreets to get his clients to O'Hare fast. He uses what we call "wisdom," which draws on algorithmic logic but looks more widely in making informed judgments based on the knowledge at hand.

All cultures use abstract, analytical, topological, and evaluative logics, but they often value one over the other, particularly at the level of formal analysis conducted by religious, philosophical, and scientific experts.[9] In most societies relational knowledge is the dominant theme. They use mechanistic categories to deal with matters such as gathering food and building houses, but more important are interpersonal categories in the community and in hunting animals. In modernity the mechanistic conception of the world is dominant. This was the

8. Unlike French law, which is based on the Napoleonic Code applied through algorithmic logic to specific cases, British law is based on the corpus of laws and comparison with precedent cases: stare decisis.

9. Paul Radin has shown that in small tribal societies, sometimes thought to be "primitive," there are philosophers and scientists who reflect on the deeper questions of reality (1927).

view of the Ionian philosophers culminating in Democritus, and later advocated by Galileo, who argued that mechanical properties of things alone are primary, and that other properties are derivative or secondary (Polanyi 1962, 8).

CAUSALITY

When striving for a good life, and when misfortunes occur, most people do not stand by in despair and do nothing. They strive to ensure success and overcome crises. The first step is to find the right belief system to explain the situation. Once they have done this, they then can diagnose the case and select the proper treatment.

Most cultures have a "toolbox" of different belief systems that they use to explain what is happening (Hiebert, Shaw, and Tiénou 1999, 133–74). Some of these involve beings such as humans, spirits, demons, *jinn, rakshasa, nats,* and God. These explanation systems include shamanism, witchcraft, soul loss, ancestors, and moral judgments. Others concern impersonal powers, such as magic, astrology, fate, luck, pollution, and biophysical factors.

Philosophical or formal religions and sciences seek to find true causalities and use abstract analytical thought to do so. Ordinary people are more concerned about healing and success than about explanation systems and often use several different explanation systems and treatments at the same time, most of which reside at the folk level, hoping that one of them will work. If the systems they use do not work, they are willing to try others. If these other systems do not work either, the people may appeal to formal explanations as a last resort—it is fate, or God's will, or the inevitable process of nature.

Most people differentiate between immediate and second and third levels of explanation. When the lights in a room suddenly go out, we might speculate that the bulb has burned out, a fuse has blown, or the wiring has short-circuited. Investigation shows that the gracious woman of the house has turned off the light switch. Further investigation shows that her husband, seated on the sofa reading a mystery novel, asked her if she would mind turning off the light for him, and that he did not want the light because he wanted to save on the electricity bill and recent surgery prevented him from getting up himself.

THEMES AND COUNTERTHEMES

On a higher level, Morris Opler (1945), Robert Redfield (1968), and others use the concept of themes to examine worldviews. Stephen Pepper (1942), Jacques Ellul (1964), Peter Berger and his associates (Berger, Berger, and Kellner 1973), and others use root metaphors in much the same way. We will use worldview themes and root metaphors as the framework for examining worldviews throughout this study.

Opler's model is particularly helpful. He defines a cultural theme as "a postulate or position, declared or implied, usually controlling behavior or stimulating activity, which is tacitly approved or openly promoted in a society" (1945,

198). He notes that there are a limited number of such themes in any culture. Opler goes further. He observes that no culture and no worldview is static and totally integrated. There are always tensions and conflicts. These he explains, in part, by introducing the idea that there are themes and counterthemes in any worldview. Themes are dominant, but if pushed to the extreme, they destroy a society. For example, the individual and the group stand in tension to each other. A strong group orientation leads to the suppression of the individual, but extreme individualism leads to the death of the society. Similarly, as we have already seen, there are tensions between freedom and order, and between equality and hierarchy. As Opler recognizes, in most cases themes and counterthemes are poles on a continuum. Differences between worldviews are often one of emphasis. In some cultures one is dominant; in another the other is stressed. The tension leads to constant change and movement as different individuals and groups seek to impose their views on society. As we will see later, cultures and their worldviews are better seen as organic, ever-changing systems rather than as static, harmonious systems in which change is bad.

Epistemological Assumptions

On yet another level are the epistemological assumptions a culture makes about the nature of reality and human knowledge (Hiebert 1999). An example is the fundamental difference between the modern materialistic realism, which assumes a real, material world outside our perceptions of it, and Hindu idealism, which assumes that the world outside is maya, or an illusion created in the mind. Most Americans assume that the world around them is real, orderly, and predictable, and that they can experience it with a measure of accuracy by means of their senses. They therefore take the material world seriously. Many Hindus see ultimate reality as existing inside the person. The external world is a sum of subjective inner experiences—a transitory, ever-changing creation of our minds. It has no ultimate reality. It is maya, or virtual. In such a chaotic, unpredictable world, meaning and truth can be found only in oneself, in the deep, innermost experiences of the self. Sensory experience and rational analysis are illusory and cannot be trusted. Consequently, true reality cannot be discovered by empirical experiments and analysis, but must come as inner flashes of insight, which ultimately show us that even we do not truly exist as separate individuals but are parts of one ultimate cosmic energy field.

Implicit

Because worldviews are deep, they are generally unexamined and largely implicit. Like glasses, they shape how we see the world, but we are rarely aware of their presence. In fact, others can often see them better than we ourselves do. To shift metaphors, they are like the submersed portion of an iceberg, which keeps it afloat but is unseen.

An example of implicit structure is language. When we speak, we think of the ideas and feelings we want to express. We do not stop to think about the ways we make sounds with our mouths, the particular sounds our culture uses to form words, or the ways we string words together to form sentences. In fact, if we stop to examine the phonetic and morphological structures of our speech, we forget the message we intended to communicate. When we learn another language, we simply use the sounds of our language to vocalize their words because we assume that all languages use the same vowels and consonants we do. It comes as a shock when we find that other languages make sounds differently: that there are four different *t*'s and four different *d*'s in Telugu, and that changing the tones in Chinese words totally changes their meanings. We can learn new vocal habits by explicitly examining how sounds are made in another language. If we fail to do so, although we may learn to speak the new language, we will do so with a heavy accent.

We are similarly largely unaware of our own worldview and how it shapes our thoughts and actions. We simply assume that the world is the way we see it, and that others see it in the same way. In the West, we assume that there is a real world outside our bodies, that time is linear and moves from past through the present to the future, and that freedom is an unquestioned good. In other cultures, time repeats itself in endless cycles with no beginning or end, and conformity to the group is of highest value. It is this implicit nature of worldviews that makes it so hard to examine them. They are what we use to think with, not what we think about. Edward Hall notes, "The cultural unconscious, those out-of-awareness cultural systems that have as yet to be made explicit, probably outnumber the explicit systems by a factor of one thousand or more. Such systems . . . apply to the formative and active aspects of communication, discourses, perception . . . , transactions between people, and the action chains by which humans achieve their varied life goals" (1977, 166).

We become conscious of our worldviews when they are challenged by outside events they cannot explain. Immigrants, refugees, bicultural children, and others caught between conflicting worldviews are also made conscious of their own deep assumptions.

Worldviews can also be made visible by consciously examining what lies below the surface of ordinary thought. As we will see, this surfacing of worldview assumptions is an important part in discipling new converts. This is true for converts seeking to live Christlike lives in a modern-postmodern world as well as for converts from Hinduism and Islam.

Constructed and Contested

Human knowledge consists of mental constructs, models that help us make sense of experience. To be useful, they must correspond, more or less adequately, to reality. They are not copies of reality but isomorphic models among which experience can enable us to choose. Over time they become progressively adequate (Piaget 1970, 15; Rossi 1983, 10–11). We create alternative models and choose one over the other on the basis of fit, adequacy, and usefulness.

Knowledge of the physical world is based on empirical experiences, but it involves abstract reflections on those experiences that are different from the objects themselves. This abstraction does not simply record empirical data on the blank slates of our minds or discover what already exists in external reality, which therefore cannot produce a new reality, as empiricism argues, for then there would be no "explanation" or "understanding" of the data, only a passive copy of reality. In other words, the mind does not stay inactive. It does not merely reflect reality. It reacts to it and works its knowledge of it into a system. It seeks to integrate all experiences, past and present, into an ideological system according to mental processes that are culturally shaped. Nor are these mental processes predetermined in the individual prior to experience, as idealists argue. Rather, knowledge systems involve processes of reflection entailing a reorganization of thought. This reorganization occurs through the application of mental processes (such as category formation and logic), the formation of alternative models, and the selection of certain models over others after evaluation. Over time the systems become progressively more adequate. In short, culture is not the mere sum of sense data. It is comprised of the gestalts, or configuration of sense data plus memory, concept formation, verbal and other symbolic elements, conditioned behavior, and many other factors.

Worldviews are also contested. As Michel Foucault observes, because worldviews are human creations, different groups in a society have vested interests in advancing those that privilege them (1980). Knowledge is power, and the powerful seek to preserve their vested interests by controlling the dominant worldview. They silence subordinate views and seek to enculturate immigrant communities, who are a threat to their view of the world. This tension between social groups explains, in part, why worldviews are constantly changing.

More or Less Integrated Systems

Worldviews are more or less integrated mental constructs. Knowledge is not the sum of bits of information.[10] It is the system of interpretation that emerges out of the relationships between pieces and gives meaning to the whole. Worldviews are about pattern and see the whole as greater than the sum of the parts. In other words, worldviews are paradigmatic in nature and

10. N. Troubetzkoy, the founder of structural linguistics, shifted linguistic analysis from the study of conscious linguistic phenomena to the study of their unconscious infrastructure. In doing so he focused on the underlying structural nature of language. Instead of focusing on units, he examined the relationships between units and introduced the concept of *system* into linguistics.

Figure 2.4
THE CONFIGURATIONAL NATURE OF KNOWLEDGE

Observational Data   Interpretation A   Interpretation B

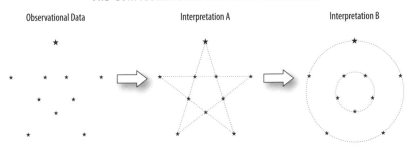

demonstrate internal logical and structural regularities that persist over long periods of time.[11]

An example of the paradigmatic or configurational nature of knowledge is seen in figure 2.4. Most people looking at the dots try to give them meaning by organizing them into a larger "pattern" that links the dots together and so gives them "meaning." Some see a "star," others two "circles." Do the stars or circles exist in reality, or are they created by the mind of the beholder? The answer is both. Individual observers interpret the dots as a star, or as two circles. However, they would not see a star or circles if the dots were not arranged such that they can be interpreted in these ways. If the dots were placed randomly on the page, observers would conclude that there is no order in their arrangement. It is the configurational nature of knowledge that gives meaning to uninterpreted experiences by seeing the order or the story behind them. Configuration gives to knowledge a coherence that makes sense out of a bewildering barrage of experiential data entering the mind. It helps people get a "picture" of reality.

Generativity

Worldviews are generative. They are not specific instances of human speech and behavior. They generate speech and behaviors. On the surface, human activities are infinitely varied. We go to stores and buy goods without thinking about the rules that regulate economic behavior in our society. We watch a football game on television and know what is going on. This is possible because the bewildering variety of social and cultural phenomena we experience can be rendered intelligible by explaining them in terms of certain elements and by the rules that regulate the relationships between them.

A good illustration of generativity is the game of chess. Each game is different, but behind all games are certain givens. There are thirty-two pieces,

11. Thomas Kuhn (1970) introduced the concept of paradigm to the study of human knowledge systems. Margaret Masterman (1970) and Ian Barbour (1974) elaborated on the nature and functions of knowledge paradigms.

each with its own characteristics. There are rules governing how pieces can be moved and what constitutes a victory. Players develop strategies based on these givens. These givens enable participants to play an almost infinite number of games, each of which is different, but all of which conform to the underlying structural order.

Another example of generativity is language. We say sentences that have never been said before, and listeners understand them. This is possible because we can generate an almost infinite number of sentences using the sounds, words, and rules of the language. A third example is computer programs. Using one program, players can take part in any number of different games or drive wildly around race tracks with a different race each time they play. Worldviews are the elements and rules of a culture that generate cultural behavior.

Dimensions of Worldview

As we have seen, cultures are made up of three interacting dimensions: ideas, feelings, and values. Worldviews, the foundations on which cultures are built, have these same dimensions. We will look at each of these and then at their interaction with one another.

COGNITIVE THEMES

Worldviews have a cognitive dimension. This dimension includes the deep assumptions about the nature of reality shared by the members of a group. It includes the mental categories and logic people use for thinking and the cognitive themes and counterthemes that underlie the culture. It provides a culture with the fundamental mental structures people use to define and explain reality. For example, Christians speak of God, angels, demons, sin, and salvation. By the latter they mean eternal life with God in heaven. Hindus speak of *devas* (gods), *rakshasas* (demons), *karma* (the cosmic law of good and evil that punishes and rewards gods, humans, and animals and determines their future lives), *samsara* (the cycle of rebirths), and *moksha* (salvation). By the latter they mean deliverance from endless life and merger back into the cosmic whole. The Tiv of Nigeria speak of God, ancestors, spirits (good and bad), and life force. They attribute many diseases to witches. Without shared beliefs, communication and community life are impossible.

Time

Robert Redfield points out that one cognitive theme found in all societies is a sense of time (1968). People experience repetition—some things repeat themselves, such as the cycles of days, moons, seasons, and life. They also experience nonrepetition—some things happen before others, and some things appear and do not reappear.

Although all people experience repetition and sequence, they organize these differently in their worldviews of time (fig. 2.5).[12] For instance, we in the West assume that time is linear and uniform. It runs like a straight line from a beginning to an end. Moreover, it can be divided into uniform intervals, such as centuries, years, days, minutes, seconds, and nanoseconds. Edward Hall writes, "As a rule, Americans think of time as a road or a ribbon stretching into the future, along which one progresses. The road has segments or compartments which are to be kept discrete ('one thing at a time'). People who cannot schedule time are looked down upon as impractical" (1959, 28).

Figure 2.5
SOME WORLDVIEWS OF TIME

1. Uniform linear time
   - has a beginning and an end
   - all units are of equal duration and value
   - is nonrepetitive, does not repeat itself
   - tells a unique story
   - is modern scientific time

2. Cyclical time
   - repeats itself in cycles of life, seasons, years
   - has no beginning and no end
   - is renewed by return to origins in a "rebirth" or new beginning (e.g., New Year's rites)
   - is commonly associated with agricultural societies and a fertility cycle

3. Pendular time
   - oscillates, moving forward and backward
   - moves slower and faster
   - comes to dead stops

4. Critical event time
   - is linear, has a beginning and an end
   - involves different types of time with different value and duration
   - is measured by a sequence of events (e.g., breakfast time, work time, sleep time)

5. Dream time
   - involves leaving time and entering the eternal Now, in which dead, living, and unborn all unite
   - involves reentry into time
   - is commonly associated with rituals and altered states of consciousness

12. Ludwig von Bertalanffy argues, contra Kant, that the categories of space, time, number, causality, ego, and so on are not given once and for all as a priori concepts valid for every rational being, but are products of long and tortuous cultural development (1981, 97).

Time viewed this way is unidirectional and irreversible. English speakers use tense in verbs—past, present, or future—and so locate the statement along a time line. Sir Isaac Newton wrote, "Absolute, true, and mathematical time, of itself, and from its own nature, flows equably without relation to anything external."[13] Despite Einstein's theory, which holds that time is a dimension of the universe and relative to the observer, that different observers may experience the sequence of events differently, that time for you need not be the same as time for me, and that reality embraces past, present, and future, most modern people still see time as an absolute clock by which the universe operates.

Uniform linear time is compatible with a mechanistic worldview, with notions of progress and evolution, and with an orientation to the future. This view emerged in the Middle Ages with the invention of the clock.[14] The clock disassociates time from human experience and thereby nourishes the belief in an independent, fourth dimension of the universe that can be mathematically measured in terms of uniform sequential intervals. The clock has made us into timekeepers, and then time-savers, and now time-servers. Lewis Mumford notes that the popular concern with timekeeping and scheduling followed the mass production of watches in the middle 1800s. Today scheduling and punctuality are essential to organizing transportation and production in an industrial society. Mumford writes, "The clock, not the steam-engine, is the key machine of the modern industrial age" (1934, 14). In many societies, wearing a watch is one of the signs that the person is modern.

This shift to clock time has profoundly shaped modernity. Neil Postman writes, "With the invention of the clock, Eternity ceased to serve as the measure and focus of human events. And thus, though few would have imagined the connection, the inexorable ticking of the clock may have had more to do with the weakening of God's supremacy than all the treatises produced by the philosophers of the Enlightenment" (1985, 11–12).

Other cultures, such as those of ancient Greece and China, interpret time as operating in cycles. Still other cultures see time as oscillating like a pendulum. In many societies, the process of time is not seen as linear, going in the same direction, or cyclical, going round and round. Rather it is experienced as the oscillation of opposites: day and night, summer and winter, drought and flood, life and death. The past has no long duration. All past is equally past. It is simply the opposite of now. In this view, time moves at different rates, goes backward and forward, and sometimes stops altogether. Psychologically we experience time in this way. A good movie is over without our awareness that several hours have passed, a boring lecture drags on forever, and sometimes time seems to stop altogether.

13. Cited by Alfred Crosby (1997, 93). For a discussion of modern scientific views of time, see Hawking 1988.

14. Ironically this took place in monasteries, where clocks were invented to regulate the daily schedules of the monks.

Another view of time is event time. Here events are viewed as distinct units, each of which has its own beginning, process, and end. For example, time for the Nuer, an African tribe in Sudan, is related to the familiar processes of caring for cattle and doing domestic chores. E. E. Evans-Pritchard writes, "The daily timepiece is the cattle clock, the round of pastoral tasks, and the time of day and the passage of time through a day are to a Nuer primarily the succession of these tasks and their relationship to one another" (cited in Kearney 1984, 103).

John Mbiti maintains that traditional African time separates events into those that occurred in the past (*zamani*) and those that are taking place right now or are about to take place (*sasa*). Time, therefore, has a long-ago past used in story form to retell past calamities, a recent past of months and years of events remembered, a present, and the present anticipation of an indefinite future. It is not hard for us to understand event time, because we often plan our "free time" according to our daily activities. We think of the church service as an "event" with a beginning, activity, and an end. When it is over, we enter "meal time" or "go for a picnic time." Then there is "rest time" or "watch the football game time." We plan to go grocery shopping after we are finished at the doctor's office.

Morris Opler's concept of themes and counterthemes makes clear that no culture is controlled by one concept of time. One may be dominant in the culture, but other perceptions of time operate in different spheres of life. For example, in the United States business and industry operate by linear clock time, but patients must wait until the doctor is ready to see them. Clock time dominates the work week, but free time takes over on the weekend.

People perceive the passage of time in different ways. Traditional Chinese culture was oriented primarily to the past. The people looked to it as the model for the present and as the primary source of information on how to build a good society, the issue that concerned them most. Modern people see the passage of time as divided into the past, the present, and the future, and place great emphasis on planning and engineering a better future. Today an increasing number of people are becoming present oriented. They want immediate experiences and do not want to delay gratifying their desires. Other worldviews divide time into two parts: past and present. The future does not "exist" in the real sense. It is only the anticipation of things to come that they experience now, in the present. The future is unreal, uncertain, and intangible.

An illustration of how worldview differences influence our daily lives is given by Edward Hall (1959). Americans, for instance, place a premium on punctuality and define being "on time" as from five minutes before to five minutes after the set time (fig. 2.6). If someone arrives fifteen minutes after the appointed hour, an apology is expected, but a detailed explanation is not needed. Arrival more than fifteen minutes after the appointed time needs an apology and a credible excuse. In traditional Arabia, only servants are expected

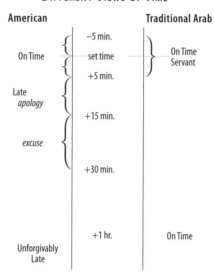

Figure 2.6

DIFFERENT VIEWS OF TIME

to show up at the set time, and then as an act of obedience. The proper arrival time for men of equal rank, who want to show their independence and social status, is roughly an hour after the set time. Only after an additional half hour are they considered "late."

There is no confusion when two Americans or two Arabs agree on a meeting time, because they share the same assumptions about what it means to "be on time." But when an Arab and an American arrange a meeting, confusion often results. The American arrives "on time" at the set hour, the Arab "on time" an hour later. The American is frustrated at having to wait and complains that Arabians lack a sense of time, and the Arab is perplexed by the subservient behavior of the American, who arrived, as he sees it, an hour early. It is important to remember that Americans have different and complex concepts of punctuality for different occasions, which often confuses foreigners in the United States. To see this, one need only compare differences in concepts of punctuality for doctors' appointments, picnics, formal dinners, and work.

Space

All humans have mental maps of the world around them. In the Middle Ages, the earth was seen by Christians in the West as an island (Orbis Terrarum), made up of Europe, Asia, and Africa, with the holy city of Jerusalem in the center[15] and God in control. This sacred space was surrounded by a

---

15. In 1459 Fra Mauro made a world map in which Asia was so large that it pushed Jerusalem out of the center. He explained, "Jerusalem is indeed the center of the inhabited world

dark, inhuman, evil void of the deep waters. Europeans had many stories of monsters: giants, ogres, and satyrs who were seen as the embodiments of evil forces or as "the descendants of Cain." Such creatures were to be killed.

This view of geography as sacred space is widespread around the world. For Muslims the center of the world is Mecca. For Hindus the gods reside in the mountains. As Raja Rao notes, for Indian villagers the major geographical features around them have mythological stories associated with them: "There is no village in India, however mean, that has not a rich *stala-purana*, or legendary history, of its own. Some god or godlike hero has passed by the village—Rama might have rested under this pipal-tree, Sita might have dried her clothes, after her bath, on this yellow stone, or the Mahatma himself, on one of his many pilgrimages through the country, might have slept in this hut, the low one, by the village gate. In this way the past mingles with the present, and the gods mingle with men" (1967, vii).

In such societies, space is more important than time. Time separates past from present. Space brings them together. This land was bought by our ancestor who is now buried under the tree. In Palestine we can sit at Jacob's well: four thousand years ago—but right here—Jacob dug the well. Two thousand years later—but right here—we can touch the well where Jesus talked with the Samaritan woman. It is modernity that shifts the priority to time over space.

Understandings of local space, too, vary from culture to culture. In South India, villagers believe that walls project power auras ten to twenty feet beyond the end of the wall in the direction it points. If this power strikes a nearby wall at a weak point, it will cause that wall to crack. Houses are usually built on an imaginary nine-feet-by-nine-feet grid, and walls are strong at the intersection points of the grid. If the neighbor's house is not built on the same grid, one's house can cause his house to crack. It is important, therefore, in building a house to make sure that one's walls are built on the same grid as the neighboring houses.

The concept of space as homogeneous and extending uniformly in all directions in which events take place emerged in Europe after AD 1250 when mapmakers began making charts for voyages beyond sight of land. By the fourteenth century, Ptolemy's idea of treating the earth's surface as neutral space and imposing a grid on it had spread throughout Europe. In time, local grids were integrated into a global grid of meridians. By the sixteenth century Giordano Bruno would write, "There is a single general space . . . which we may freely call Void: in it are innumerable globes like this one on which we live and grow; this space we declare to be infinite, since neither reason, convenience, sense-perception nor nature assign to it a limit" (cited in Crosby 1997, 105).

---

latitudinally, though longitudinally it is somewhat to the west, but since the western portion is more thickly populated by reason of Europe, therefore Jerusalem is also the center longitudinally if we regard not empty space but density of population" (cited in Crosby 1997, 57).

But this homogeneous space was essentially secular. There was no place for God or sacred space in it. The shift to secular space can be seen in Western art. Alfred Crosby writes, "Medieval artists were sure that the rank of their subjects was more important than the actual shape of their faces, the color of their eyes, or the way their arms set into their shoulders. Artists often indicated significance by the most obvious means: by size, making the protagonists— Christ, the Virgin Mary, emperors—relatively large and locating them dead center. Unimportant people and things were small and fitted in along the edges or wherever there was an open patch" (1997, 168). Renaissance artists, however, were more concerned with accurate spatial perceptions through the use of "vanishing points" and converging orthogonals than with deeper messages. Realistically portraying nature and space became an end in itself.[16] Artists sought to present a picture of reality as if viewed in a single instant by a single human eye (Crosby 1997, 191).

In the early modern age, space on earth was measured in terms of local geographic features. For example, early American colonists used a survey method known as "meets-and-bounds," or the "indiscriminate" system, to demarcate their lands. A field would be bounded on two sides by a river and a road and on the third by a line that met the river at its fork and joined the road at the crest of the hill. When towns were planned, streets were laid according to the main topographical features in the area, such as rivers, valleys, or railroad tracks.

As the frontier expanded westward, the use of local reference points to measure space proved inadequate at sea and in long-distance land travel. Global reference points were needed to enable travelers to move over long distances and to arrive at their destinations. Imagine, for example, traveling across the United States using only local township maps that do not connect to the maps of neighboring communities. A new way of orienting space known as the "Township-and-Range" system emerged using the North and South poles and the equator as the reference points. These provided a worldwide grid that enabled people to locate every point on earth in its relationship to all other points on earth. This system made ocean navigation and transcontinental flying possible.

In the United States, the shift from local reference points to global reference points to locate positions on earth took place in the early nineteenth century. This shift had a profound influence on the ways fields and cities were laid out (fig. 2.7). In the eastern states, such as Pennsylvania and Maine, roads followed the paths of least effort for the traveler. They were not laid out in a checkerboard fashion, and they were not "square" to the world. Midwestern

16. What we mean by "realistic" is geometrically accurate, a picture of nature as the eye sees it. In contrast, traditional Muslim pictures are exquisitely decorated surfaces without an illusion of real depth, and Chinese landscape paintings, which do offer an impression of great depth, do not have a fixed point of view (Crosby 1997, 190).

Figure 2.7
WORLDVIEWS AND THE ORDERING OF SPACE

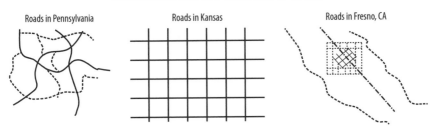

roads and fields were laid out north and south, and east and west, often on one-mile grids. Cities, too, felt the impact of the change. Fresno, California, was originally laid out parallel to the railroad tracks that ran down the San Joaquin Valley, northwest to southeast. When meridians and longitudes were introduced, the new streets were laid out north-south and east-west. Considerable confusion arose where the two grids collided downtown. Similar shifts in street grids took place in many other US cities when one worldview theme was replaced by another.

The modern stress on individualism has influenced the American perception of space. Fields are divided into farms, and each farmer lives on his or her own farm. Town blocks are divided into individually owned lots and houses, and even in the house, certain rooms are seen as belonging to certain family members. In many parts of the world, farmers live together in small hamlets for companionship and safety and walk to their fields.[17]

Organic/Mechanistic

As we noted earlier, Stephen Pepper writes of root metaphors, two of which, mechanistic and organic, have been widely used to analyze worldviews (Ellul 1964; Berger, Berger, and Kellner 1973; Dijksterhuis 1986). Because these are fundamental to most worldviews, we will use these as theme and countertheme in our analysis of cultures.

Individual/Group

All people have a perception of their own self. Indians have three selves: personal, social (determined by the caste into which one is born), and cosmic. The cosmic self is like a drop of water blown off the waves of Brahman, the impersonal ocean of cosmic power and being. So long as it floats in the air, it

17. George Jennings points out that most of the Protestant missionaries sent out from the United States from 1890 to 1950 came from Midwest farms. Abroad they carried their midwestern spatial mentality with them. They divided the lands up by denominations using the principle of comity. They divided their denominational territories into "fields," and assigned one missionary family to each field. Most missionaries in rural areas lived alone on their compounds and saw one another at missionary gatherings held two or three times a year for fellowship and business.

can say "I." In the end it falls back into the ocean and continues to exist, but no longer has unique identity. It is merged into the cosmic force field.

All people belong to groups. They are part of families, clans, clubs, ethnic groups, and institutions. This corporate identity provides them a place within their society.

As we saw earlier, societies differ in the priority they give to the group versus the autonomous individual. In group-oriented societies, people find their identity in their relationships to others and their place in society. For example, in Japan the related self is most important. The autonomous self should be empty. In contrast, modernity stresses the autonomous self. The individual self is the center of a person's identity; his or her group self is less important. Alexis de Tocqueville, in describing American culture after his extensive travels in the United States in 1831, distinguished between selfishness or egoism and individualism. He wrote:

> Selfishness is a passionate and exaggerated love of self, which leads a man to connect everything with himself, and to prefer himself to everything in the world. Individualism is a mature and calm feeling, which disposes each member of the community to sever himself from the mass of his fellows, and to draw apart with his family and his friends; so that, after he has thus formed a little circle of his own, he willingly leaves society at large to itself. . . . Individualism, at first, only saps the virtues of public life; but in the long run it attacks and destroys all others, and is at length absorbed in downright selfishness. (1863, 119–20)

Group/Others

All people belong to human groups and differentiate between "us" and "them." This we-they differentiation underlies most distinctions within social systems, whether based on ethnicity, class, gender, age, or association. In totemic societies "we" may be extended to include certain animals and plants in certain human groups.

Finally, all people have a conception of the nature of human beings and differentiate between humans and nonhumans—between humans and animals, trees, stars, and certain kinds of spirits. Most traditional small-scale societies see humans as part of nature and posit relationships, even kinship, between humans, animals, plants, and spirits; but they note the differences between human and not-human. For example, the native people of the Ituri forest distinguish four ranks of living beings: people, pygmies, chimpanzees, and other animals. Europeans in the sixteenth century regarded themselves as civilized, and Africans and Native Americans as savages and subhumans, which justified enslaving them. In the eighteenth century these "others" became primitives and aboriginals—people like us but behind us in the evolution of civilization. Now they are often labeled natives—like us but different.

This World/Other Worlds

Many cultures see this world in which humans live as the only cosmos. For example, in modern secular science there are no otherworldly beings, no heavens and hells. In many cultures, this universe is filled with beings and forces. There are humans, animals, plants, and even the earth, which is seen as Mother because she gives birth to so much life. The sky is full of sky gods, rain gods, a sun god, a moon god, and impersonal planets, all of which are part of this world and interact with earthbound creatures. Other cultures believe in other, parallel universes distinct from this one. The Greeks believed in seven heavens and seven hells.

An estimated two-thirds of tribal societies believe in a high God who lives outside this universe. He is the Creator but as we will see later, in many cultures he became angry with humans and left, leaving them on their own. The Hebrews put God outside the physical universe but acknowledged his constant involvement with humans throughout history. In Hebrew thought God was all-important. The Greeks believed in a universe in which order was natural without any reference to God at all. When he did intervene in this universe, it was exceptional and extraordinary. In Greek thought, God was unnecessary.

Other Themes

So far we have used Redfield's categories to begin the investigation of themes and counterthemes in different worldviews. It is important to remember, however, that these are only preliminary heuristic devices, and that we will discover most of the themes in a specific worldview by a careful analysis of the culture of which it is a part. Because these themes will differ markedly from one culture to another, we cannot list them, but must remember that they are central to the study of any worldview. Examples of such worldview themes will be given in chapters 5 through 10.

AFFECTIVE THEMES

Worldviews also shape deep feelings of joy and sorrow, fear and revulsion, and awe and worship. They influence people's tastes in music, art, dress, food, and architecture as well as the way they feel toward one another and about life in general. These affective assumptions underlie the notions of beauty, style, and aesthetics found in a culture. For example, in cultures influenced by Theravada Buddhism, life is equated with suffering. Even joyful moments create suffering, for one realizes that they will come to an end. There is, therefore, little use in striving for a better life here on earth. By contrast, in the United States after World War II, many people were optimistic. They believed that with hard work and planning they could achieve a happy, comfortable existence during their lifetime. Powerful, pervasive, and long-lasting affective themes act as a wall, protecting beliefs from attacks from within and without by providing emotional support to their truthfulness.

Figure 2.8
AFFECTIVE TYPES IN AMERICAN PROTESTANT WORSHIP SERVICES

	High Church	Evangelical Church	Charismatic Church
Dominant mood	mystery, awe, holiness	peace, order, hope	ecstasy, power, action
Extreme mode	asceticism, monasticism	piety, mysticism	thrill, frenzy
Building	cathedral	church	meeting hall
Forms of expression	rituals, chants, liturgy, candles, procession, high order	preaching, hymns, testimonies, silence, meditation	prophecy, choruses, dance, clapping, healing
Posture	kneeling, prostration	bowing, standing, sitting	raised hands, uplifted heads
Focus	God the Father	God the Son	God the Holy Spirit
Central message	creation, order, providence of God	sin, redemption, presence of God	helplessness, illness, power of God
Central story	cosmic history	human history	personal story

Different affective themes are expressed in different ways. In high Christian churches, the dominant emotions are awe and wonder in the presence of great mystery expressed in high rituals. In many "low" Protestant churches, feelings of peace and calm are evoked by means of meditation and orderly preaching. Many charismatics seek ecstasy through dance, music, and rhythm (fig. 2.8). In short, religions vary greatly in the emotions they value and the ways these emotions are expressed.

On the one hand, scholars and leaders who stress the preaching of cognitive truth in church services and downplay the importance of feelings in worship tend to overlook the importance of feelings in the lives of ordinary people. They push to get work done and fail to see the emotional distress caused by their actions. People often leave the church with their heads full and their hearts empty. Most people make religious decisions on the basis of emotions and experience as much as on the basis of rational argument. On the other hand, stressing affectivity alone leaves people with their hearts full and their heads empty. Both cognition and affectivity are vital to religious life.

EVALUATIVE THEMES

Evaluative or normative assumptions give rise to the social and moral order in a culture. They include such notions as virtues, standards, morals, and manners. These in their own turn provide the standards people use to make judgments, including their criteria for determining truth and falsehood, likes and dislikes, and right and wrong. For instance, in North America it is worse to tell a lie than to hurt people's feelings. In other cultures it is more important to encourage other people, even if it means bending the truth. In North

America sexual immorality is one of the greatest sins. In South Asia losing one's temper is the worst offense. In medieval Europe clergymen valued reflection, character, wisdom; noblemen valued courage, bravery, chivalry, elegance, and show; and merchants valued efficiency, precision, and particularity (Crosby 1997, 230).

Moral Order

Robert Redfield notes the distinction between cultures in which morality is at the center of the worldview, and those where it is marginal. He observes that in most band, tribal, and peasant societies, humans live in a universe that has moral significance. Humans and nonhumans are bound together by relationships, and right relationships are the basis of morality. Morality is based on duty and ethical judgment. This sense of morality is violated when relationships are broken, as is seen in the definitions of sins in Japan during the Engi era (fig. 2.9).

In these group-oriented societies, violation of norms leads to a deep sense of shame, and the greatest punishment is ostracism. People do not see or talk to the shunned person, and eventually he or she repents or leaves. Redfield writes:

> In the primary worldview Man and Not-Man are bound together in one moral order. The universe is morally significant. It cares. What man sees out there, that which is not himself and yet in which he somehow participates is a great drama of conduct. . . . The universe is spun of duty and ethical judgment. Even where the Not-Man acts not as man should act, where the supernaturals are unjust or

Figure 2.9

A CLASSIFICATION OF SINS IN JAPAN DURING THE ENGI ERA

(FOUND IN THE 70 VOLUMES OF *THE LITURGY OF GREAT EXORCISM AND PURIFICATION*)

Heavenly Sins (sins against the cosmic order):
1. *ahanchi*: to break down the divisions between rice fields
2. *mizoume*: to break the water path of the rice fields
3. *shikimaki*: to sow seed in plots already sown by others
4. *tikihagi*: to flay a sacred horse alive
5. *kusohe*: to urinate or defecate at a sacred place

Earthly Sins (sins against the community):
1. *ikihadatachi*: to murder or injure a person
2. *shihadatachi*: to desecrate the body of the dead
3. *kokumi*: to be a crookback
4. *onogahaha okaseru tsumi*: to have sexual intercourse with one's mother
5. *onoga ko okaseru tsumi*: to have sexual intercourse with a woman and her daughter
6. *kemono okaseru tsumi*: to have sexual intercourse with an animal
7. *takatsu kami no wazawai*: to be struck by lighting

(Minoru Hayashi)

Figure 2.10
IMAGES OF MORAL ORDER

Focus	legal order	right relationships	cleanliness
Sin	breaking the law	breaking relationships	defilement
Response	guilt	shame	repugnance
Salvation	punishment, restore moral order	forgiveness, reconciliation, restore relations	washing, purification, restore cleanliness
Image	righteousness	shalom, peace	holiness, purity
Example	United States	Japan	India

indecent, the conduct of these gods is thought about according to the morality that prevails on earth. The universe is not an indifferent system. It is a system of moral consequences. (1968, 112)

This unity of humans with nature is broken in urban and modern societies. Redfield notes, "Man comes out from the unity of the universe within which he is oriented now as something separate from nature and comes to confront nature as something with physical qualities only, upon which he may work his will. As this happens, the universe loses its moral character and becomes to him indifferent, a system uncaring of man. The existence today of ethical systems and of religions only qualifies this statement; ethics and religion struggle in one way or another to take account of a physical universe indifferent to man" (1968, 114).

In modern societies laws are based on impersonal norms established by the culture. They hold the autonomous individual accountable to these laws. Personal violation of them leads not to a sense of shame but rather to one of guilt. Other societies equate morality with purity, and violations lead to a sense of defilement and pollution (fig. 2.10).

Heroes and Villains

Evaluative standards determine in each society what an ideal man and woman look like, what constitutes a good marriage, and how people should relate to one another and to strangers. At the deepest level, evaluative assumptions determine fundamental allegiances—the gods people worship, the goals for which they live. During the past century North Americans have placed a high value on technology and material goods, and business is their central activity. Their status is determined largely by their wealth, and their culture is focused on economic themes. The skylines of modern American cities are dominated by bank and insurance buildings. In the Indian countryside, on the contrary, people place a high value on religious purity, and the greatest honor is given to members of the priestly caste. Their culture is organized around religious themes, and temples are the centers of their villages. Medieval towns, with their kings, vassals, lords and knights, and bishops focused on power, conquests, and religion. Castles and cathedrals were their dominant structures.

Parsons's Evaluative Themes

Talcott Parsons and his colleagues outline seven moral dimensions that they believe exist in all societies (fig. 2.11). Like Morris Opler, they arrange each of these along continua from one pole to the other. As Ruth Benedict noted, societies range from those that express emotions publicly to those that keep emotions under control. A second theme concerns a person's identity. In some societies a person has identity only as a member of a group; in others the person is seen as an autonomous individual. A third theme involves a continuum from this-worldly mindedness to an other-worldly orientation. For example, in medieval Europe the dominant concerns involved God, divine judgment, and eternal salvation. Young men and women were encouraged to enter monasteries and to deny themselves the pleasures of this world. Cathedrals and monasteries were thriving centers of cultural life. A great shift took place in the Renaissance, when the focus of life turned to this world and a good life of comfort, success on earth, and self-fulfillment. Consequently science, technology, business, and entertainment flourished.

A fourth evaluative theme in Parsons's list concerns valuing what a person achieves as opposed to what one acquires through birth, such as royalty, ethnicity, and heritage. In much of North America people are valued by what they do, the education they get, the money they earn, the power they control. Through these achievements they can rise in the social order. These factors, however, cannot get them into blue-blood society. This comes only through birth, marriage, and admission into the social circles of the elite. In England those born into noble families are seen as upper class and tied to royalty. In India the caste into which a person is born determines his or her marriage partners, occupation, place of residence, and status in life. Personal achievement operates only in restricted areas within this larger social system.

The fifth dimension of values in Parsons's model is that of diffuseness versus specificity. This is harder to grasp. By diffuseness Parsons and his colleagues mean societies that take whole contexts into account in dealing with social activities. In a sense these societies see things "holistically" and consider all factors in determining actions. For instance, in an African village, when patients line up to see the doctor, the chief is put at the front of the line even when he comes later than the others. In Indian village panchayats, both the accuser and the defendant are on trial for breaking the peace. In discussing the case, the elders take into account the character of the persons involved, the history of their previous behavior in the village, their caste ranking, their education and wealth, and all the extenuating circumstances in which the dispute arose. Societies characterized by specificity, on the other hand, focus

Figure 2.11

EVALUATIVE NORMS AT THE WORLDVIEW LEVEL

1. Emotional Expression	vs.	Emotional Control
• seek gratification of senses and desires • permissive • examples: Kwakiutl, modern consumer culture, tantricism		• delayed gratification, renunciation • disciplinary • examples: Hopi, Protestant ethic, monasticism
2. Group Centered	**vs.**	**Individual Centered**
• collective interests • corporate responsibility and decisions • examples: Bunyoro, tribalism		• individual interests • personal fulfillment and decisions • examples: Kapauku, modernity
3. Other-World Oriented	**vs.**	**This-World Oriented**
• stress other worldly gain • examples: medieval Europe, Buddhism		• stress this worldly gain • examples: modernity, postmodernity
4. Emphasize Ascription	**vs.**	**Emphasize Achievement**
• relations based on one's birth • value attributes • example: caste system in India		• relations based on one's achievements • value performance • example: class system in United States
5. Focus on Whole Picture	**vs.**	**Look at Specific Details**
• take broad context into account • example: Indian village *panchayat* cases		• take only narrow context into account • example: US court cases
6. Universalist	**vs.**	**Particularist**
• treat everyone alike • stress universal truths, laws, grids • push for standardization • universal, absolute theories • absolute ethics • examples: Judeo-Christianity, modernity		• treat each person on basis of his or her ascribed role, status, and situation • stress uniqueness of each situation • value uniqueness and diversity • adaptation to situational context • situational ethics • examples: Hinduism, postmodernity
7. Hierarchy Is Right	**vs.**	**Equality Is Right**
• see people as intrinsically unequal • give privileges to the superior • patron-client relationships • example: Indian caste society		• see people as intrinsically equal • hold everyone equal in rewards/ punishment • contractual relationships • example: Scandinavian societies

Source: Adapted from Parsons and Shils 1952.

only on the specific issues at hand. For the most part the US courts exclude character and extraneous factors in discussing cases and determine judgments solely on the basis of those considerations prescribed by law, not the attitudes of the community in general.

Another value underlying many societies concerns the tension between hierarchy and equality. In traditional Indian culture, hierarchy is recognized as not only real but also good. A person's status is based on what he or she has done in his or her previous life. Therefore, to be born low is a form of punishment for past sins. To improve the circumstances of the lowborn is to cut short their punishment and cause them to be reborn again in a lowly state. The result is a caste system that ranks all people according to a hierarchy based on purity and pollution. In contrast, Scandinavia stresses equality and seeks to reduce the difference between rich and poor, men and women, old and young. England and the United States affirm the equality of all persons but, in fact, allow a great deal of hierarchy as manifested in the limiting of equality to theoretical equal opportunity, not to equal housing, wealth, education, and medical care. We must also examine how the sets of values in a culture relate to one another. For example, many people in the United States affirm equality but value freedom more highly. Consequently, when the two conflict, equality is sacrificed for the sake of freedom.

THREE DIMENSIONS

While different cultures can be located along these continua of themes and counterthemes, it is better to view these poles as they are found in most worldviews. In one culture, while one pole may be the dominant theme, some people in the society may in fact uphold the countertheme. In another culture, the opposite pole may be dominant and the other subordinate or countercultural. Moreover, the balance between themes and counterthemes in a culture can also vary between public and private life.

Together, cognitive, affective, and evaluative assumptions provide people with a way of looking at the world that makes sense out of it, that gives them a feeling of being at home, and that reassures them that they are right. This worldview serves as the deep structure on which they construct their explicit belief and value systems and the social institutions in which they live their daily lives.

Diachronic Characteristics

Humans are storytellers. Everyday knowledge is piecemeal and disconnected. To find meaning in life, people tell stories that give meaning to this world by showing us that it is a drama—a mystery, a romance, a tragedy, or a comedy.

Narrative knowing is different from critical, analytical knowing (Camery-Hoggatt 2006). Rational analysis is based on hard, objective evidence and logical, discursive analysis and creates abstractions from concrete reality. Stories, on the other hand, are based on both imaginative and rational analysis and deal with the complexities of human experience that cannot be probed by the rational mind alone; they include contradictions, compromise, conflict, and crisis. They affirm that narrative knowing is real knowledge involving real truth and falsehood. Rational analysis focuses on cognitive knowing, but rationality unchecked by virtue and beauty leads to ugliness and evil. Narratives combine rationality and imagination and the cognitive, affective, and evaluative dimensions of life in a single whole. Jerry Camery-Hoggatt writes:

> Where rational discourse defines truth in terms of accuracy and verifiable propositions, storytelling encompasses those terms, but places them within a wider setting that includes fidelity, integrity, courage, discovery, empathy, and sometimes the negative emotions of fear, anger and hatred. Rational discourse aims for logical coherence, clarity of exposition, simplicity of language . . . and the rigorous clarification of ambiguity. Narratives move in the other direction: they develop and exploit ambiguity and multivalence; they time the delivery of information to create suspense, to surprise, or to entrap their listeners into fresh perspectives on the human condition. (2006, 461)

Stories are not meaningless farce. They bring scattered pieces together and fuse them into a meaningful whole. Eugene Peterson writes, "Learning stories isn't the same as learning the multiplication tables. Once we've learned that three times four equals twelve, we've learned it and that's that. It's a fact that doesn't change. The data is stored in our memory for ready access. But stories don't stay put; they grow and deepen. . . . The stories keep releasing new insight in new situations. As we bring new experience and insight to the story, the story gathers that enrichment in and gives it back to us in fresh forms" (1997, 36–37).

At the core of worldviews are foundational, or root, myths, stories that shape the way we see and interpret our lives. For modern people, myths carry the idea of fictitious stories that are not true but are only imagined; or they are prelogical primitive philosophies that premodern people took to be true "once upon a time" and used to allay their fears by projecting these onto mysterious beings; or they are fundamentally no different from legends and fables.

In anthropology, the term takes on technical meaning. A myth is the overarching story, bigger than history and believed to be true, that serves as a paradigm for people to understand the larger stories in which ordinary lives are embedded. Myths are paradigmatic stories, master narratives that bring cosmic order, coherence, and sense to the seemingly senseless experiences, emotions, ideas, and judgments of everyday life by telling people what is real, eternal, and enduring. Robert Antoine observes, "Myths are not lies or second-hand 'unscientific' approaches, but a *sui generis* and irreplaceable method of grasping truths which otherwise would remain closed to us. 'The language of myth is the memory of the community,' of a community which holds its bonds together because it is a 'community of faith'" (1975, 57).

Myths are "a narrative resurrection of a primeval reality, told in satisfaction of deep religious wants, moral cravings, social submissions, assertions, even practical requirements" (Malinowski 1926, 19). A people's mythology serves as a cultural repository of truth, feelings, and morals functioning to validate their belief systems. Myths codify and communicate beliefs, express the deepest feelings, and define and enforce morality. They are not idle tales, but hard-working, active forces. They are not intellectual explanations or artistic imagery, but charters of life and moral wisdom.

Myths give meaning; they look beneath the surface at what is really going on in this world. They are archetypes of human existence, told in story form by common folk who are not philosophers to give meaning to their lives and expression to the deep emotional and moral stresses they face. Human stories change, but myths abide and give life. By speaking indirectly of things otherwise too difficult for humans to hear, they force people to discover meaning by active imagination and thought until the truths dawn on them. Myths speak of eternal truth transcending time in contrast to empirical truth, which is time- and language-bound.

Myths are also moral charters, setting forth what is acceptable and unacceptable in the society. They define and illustrate good and evil in the stories of heroes and evildoers.

Finally, myths tell people about the community to which they belong, their place in it, and the moral order of the society. To be part of a people is to be a part of their story. Rollo May writes, "Our powerful hunger for myth is a hunger for community. . . . To be a member of one's community is to share in its myths, to feel the same pride that glows within us. . . . The outsider, the foreigner, the stranger is one who does not share our myths" (1991, 45).

In this technical sense, the exodus in the Old Testament is both history and myth. Historically it happened. Mythologically it became the story the Israelites used to interpret their history. Whenever they were in trouble, they looked back to the exodus and attributed their problems to their sins and rejection of God. What they needed to do, therefore, was to repent and turn to the Lord, and he would deliver them just as he had done in the time of Moses.

Root myths, like root metaphors, are important elements in worldviews (fig. 2.12). In Hinduism, humans live in human time, gods in god time, and animals in animal time. What to humans is a lifetime is but a moment in the lives of the gods. Many myths have gods reborn on earth, living a whole lifetime, and returning to the realm of the gods—all in the blink of an eye in heavenly time. Vishnu, one of the great Hindu gods, lives for one hundred divine years—or

Figure 2.12
WORLDVIEW FOCI

Root Metaphors	Root Myths
• synchronic	• diachronic
• structure of reality	• story of reality
• understand how reality operates	• give meaning to reality

3.15 trillion human years. Each night he sleeps twelve hours and dreams the world, which undergoes one thousand cycles of four eras each. Each day he awakes, and the world ceases to be.

Mircea Eliade notes that the ancient Hebrews viewed time as linear (1975). They had a strong sense of history, seeing it as a series of events ordered in a larger sequence beginning with creation and progressing through the birth of Moses, the exodus, the period of the judges, the era of the kings, and the exile in Babylon.[18] Not only were these events part of a story told in history, but history itself was part of a cosmic drama. The Hebrews were interested in ordering these not along a uniform-linear timeline of impersonal dates but in an unfolding story or plot in which events marked different stages in their relationship to God.

For early Christians, too, history was real, not in terms of the passage of impersonal chronological time but in terms of an unfolding cosmic drama written in history. They divided history into two periods—from the beginning to the incarnation, and from Christ's first coming to his final return. In the Middle Ages historians in Europe were not concerned with dates. "Time, beyond the individual life span, was envisioned not as a straight line marked off in equal quanta, but as a stage for the enactment of the greatest of all dramas, Salvation versus Damnation" (Crosby 1997, 28).

The Jewish emphasis on finding meaning in history has also shaped modern worldviews, including Christianity, Marxism, and capitalism. Marxism sees humans as beginning in an idyllic world of tribal communities characterized by equality and mutual care. Human history has been one of decline as oppressive social and cultural systems have dehumanized people. What is needed is a revolution and a restoration of the ideal state. Capitalism, on the other hand, sees humans starting in a primitive or backward state, and history as growth. This concept of time underlies modern ideas of development and progress.

Combining synchronic and diachronic analyses, we have a model for studying worldviews (appendix 1). We will use this model to study specific

18. Mircea Eliade argues that the view that meaning is found in real history, which has a "story" or "plot," originated with the Hebrews and that it has shaped the worldviews of Christians, Muslims, Marxists, and Western secularists (1975). It stands in sharp contrast to the worldviews of Hinduism and Buddhism, in which no sharp distinction is made between history and legend.

worldviews after we examine the relationship of worldviews to cultural and social systems.

Missiological Implications

Christians must take the worldviews of other people seriously, not because they agree with them, but because they want to understand the people they serve in order to effectively share with them the good news of the gospel. Worldviews are not merely imaginary pictures created by a community to unite its members and keep them in line. Most people maintain that their beliefs are more than useful fictions. For them their worldviews declare the way things really are and are true in an ultimate sense.

It is important to understand the worldviews people have that are based on their experiences, assumptions, and logics. A phenomenological description of their world is not enough. It is equally important to compare different religions to develop metacultural grids that facilitate understanding and evaluation of different religions. Such comparisons provide invaluable insights into the nature not only of different religions but also of the religious longings of the human heart.

Finally, it is important to study worldviews to transform them. Too often conversion takes place at the surface levels of behavior and beliefs; but if worldviews are not transformed, the gospel is interpreted in terms of pagan worldviews, and the result is Christo-paganism.

3

Worldviews in Human Contexts

A study of worldviews must examine not only their nature but also their place in the larger contexts of human life. To do so, we must begin with *phenomenology*, with in-depth studies of humans and their contexts in order to understand them and the ways they see their worlds. But how do we do this?

As we have seen, two main streams of human analysis have emerged: synchronic and diachronic. The former looks at the structure of reality through a slice of time, examining the parts and how these relate to one another. Its strength is that it sees the underlying structure of human beings—that which is common to them all, and how it operates to make life possible. For example, humans are studied by physicists, chemists, biologists, psychologists, sociologists, anthropologists, and systematic theologians. Each brings his or her perspective and throws light on the full nature of being human. But synchronic studies have their limitations. They must put aside the fact that humans are in time and constantly changing. They present their theories as ahistorical universals that apply to all humans. These theories also tend to be highly abstract and hard to apply to the particularities of everyday life. In a sense, these theories are helicopter views of humans, seeing them in general terms and overlooking the uniqueness of each individual. Moreover, with specialization, these theories are isolated into different research traditions with little attempt to develop an integrated theory that draws insights from them all.

A second approach to the study of humans is diachronic. Here time is the central variable. The focus is on the story of each individual, community, and nation, and how they fit into one comprehensive human history. The strengths of this approach are twofold: we recognize humans as real people with all their particularities and idiosyncrasies, and we hear the stories that give meaning to their lives. The weakness is that the insights of synchronic studies are less easily articulated.

Both synchronic and diachronic analyses are necessary to understand humans. These perspectives are not competing but complementary. When one is in focus, however, the other is out of focus, making it difficult to keep both in mind as we look through the lens of one or the other.

Integrating Multiple Perspectives

How can we draw on the insights of different, potentially complementary, ways of studying people? First we will examine synchronic approaches, their components, and how they are organized into larger models. Then we will look at humans diachronically: at the stories of their personal, corporate, and human histories.

Reductionism

The simplest way to integrate different synchronic perspectives (physical, biological, psychological, social, cultural, and spiritual) is through reductionism, which reduces all insights to a single level of analysis. Religious truths are reduced to cultural beliefs, cultural beliefs to social constructs, societies to aggregates of individual humans, humans to animals, animals to chemical reactions, chemical reactions to atomic particles, atomic particles to quantum particles. In the end, everything, including humans, is epiphenomenal.

This way of integrating knowledge, however, is self-defeating. Ludwig von Bertalanffy writes, "Regarding this theory, I am in fundamental disagreement, not because of . . . metaphysical prejudices, but because the theory does not fit the facts. . . . Human beings (and organisms in general) are not stimulus-response machines, as the theory presupposes" (1981, 15). Since ultimately human scientists are studying themselves, they and their theories are nothing more than strings vibrating in different patterns.

A particularly devastating application of reductionism involves science and theology. One form is scientific reductionism (fig. 3.1). This is common among non-Christian scientists who reject the claims of Christianity. Some argue that Christianity is a useful fiction that holds societies together. Others see it as a harmful opiate justifying oppressive social systems. Many regard Christianity as a human construct having little to do with claims of truth. One of the fundamental assumptions on which many scientific theories are built is that science is true and religion is not. This leaves God outside our everyday worlds and undermines our faith in God. Few Christians would consciously

Figure 3.1

**A REDUCTIONIST APPROACH
TO INTEGRATION**

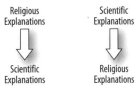

admit to such reductionism, but its influence can be seen in Christian thought and life.

A second form of reductionism is theological reductionism (fig. 3.1). Some Christians reject scientific knowledge altogether. They attribute all human problems, such as illnesses, to spiritual causes and refuse to seek answers in science, for fear that science will lead them astray. Others are willing to make use of scientific knowledge because it is helpful but do not seriously examine the conceptual foundations on which it is based.

There is a real danger in such theological reductionism. First, a measure of mental dishonesty inheres in it. On the one hand, most of us are willing to use what the sciences have to offer—modern medicine, cars, television, airplanes, computers, cell phones, communication theories, counseling insights, and knowledge of human societies. On the other hand, we are unwilling to give credit where it is due for these advances in human knowledge and technology. Second, and more seriously, in using the ideas and the products of the sciences for practical purposes, we unwittingly bring its assumptions into our thinking. It is not uncommon, for example, to find Christians who express faith in Scripture but who live their lives on the basis of pragmatism and materialism.

Stratification

A second way to integrate different perspectives of humans is compartmentalization—what Clifford Geertz calls the "stratigraphic method." The validity of each system of thought is accepted, but each is assigned to a different compartment (fig. 3.2).

Many people, including theologians such as Friedrich Schleiermacher, argue that the sciences are matters of fact and truth. Religion, they say, is a matter of feelings—it provides people with meaningful transcendent experiences. Some, such as Immanuel Kant, argue that religion is a matter of morality—it provides people with values that regulate their behavior and make corporate life possible. Most Christians reject this view. They hold that Christianity is about facts and truth as well as feelings and morality.

Modernity imposes another stratigraphic dualism on us. As Lesslie Newbigin points out, in the West science is seen as public truth (1989). All students,

Figure 3.2

A Stratigraphic Approach to the Study of Humans

including those in Christian schools, must study mathematics, physics, chemistry, and the social sciences. Religion, however, is seen as a matter of personal truth, as a matter of faith, not of facts and experimental verification. No classes on Christianity, Islam, or Hinduism are required. In fact, they cannot be taught as truth in public schools. While this compartmentalization enables people of different disciplines and religions to live peacefully together, it undermines their convictions that their beliefs are part of the greater truth. Christian "beliefs" are left to govern Christians at home, while scientific "truth" rules their public lives.

Compartmentalization in a more subtle form finds wide acceptance in Christian circles. Many Christians affirm Christian truth with regard to the gospel and supernatural matters such as sin, salvation, miracles, and prophecies, but they use scientific theories to explain and respond to immediate "natural events" such as illnesses, technology, and business decisions. This leads to an other-worldly Christianity and to the secularization of everyday life. It also produces a sharp distinction between evangelism, which is seen as a spiritual matter, and social ministries such as healing and education, which are left to the sciences. A recent variation of this dualism is to use theology to define the gospel but to use the methods of the social and business sciences to grow churches. This approach fits the Western worldview with its emphasis on human control, planning, pragmatism, problem solving, and "doing something."

Reducing Christianity to emotions, values, private opinions, or supernatural truth secularizes large areas of our lives. If we preach Christ but turn to secular sciences for answers to our everyday problems, we lose sight of him. Although we are busy planning and working, there is little of God in what we do. Scripture is clear: God created both the heavens and the earth, including humans, and he continues to be constantly involved in both.

Integration

A third approach to bringing together different perspectives in the study of humans is to integrate them into a single theory. Ideally we would like a grand unifying theory that incorporates all knowledge into one system of explanation. In reality, this is impossible because we are finite humans and cannot simultaneously comprehend the infinite complexity and full story of God and this universe. At best, our theories are partial explanations of reality. It is also true that we live in human cultures that shape how we think and live. We cannot occupy a position outside societies and cultures. Even our attempts to develop metacultural grids are themselves formulated in the symbols and thought patterns of particular cultures.

To bring different perspectives together, we must recognize that each focuses on certain aspects of human beings and, of necessity, leaves out many others. The analogy of maps helps us understand the nature of human knowledge. To understand a city we need several maps, each of which tells us some truth about it. We need maps of roads, political jurisdictions, sewage and electrical systems, building zones, and so on. It is impossible to chart all the facts about a city on one map. Similarly, to describe human realities we need different maps, including theology, anthropology, sociology, psychology, biology, chemistry, and physics. Each contributes to our understanding of the whole. None is complete in itself.

Another useful analogy is blueprints. To construct a house we need different blueprints diagramming different parts of the building: structure, wiring, plumbing, and landscaping. The analogy of blueprints is apt because there is one master blueprint that presents the basic structure of the house. As Christians we hold that this master blueprint is a biblical worldview that helps us see the big picture of reality presented in Scripture and in nature. This blueprint begins with the God of the Bible and includes the reality of an orderly creation, humans shaped in the image of God, the fall, redemption through the death and resurrection of Christ, and eternal life in him. The fullest expression of this worldview is found in the New Testament and in the teachings of Jesus. Theology, science, and the humanities chart the details and applications of this worldview. When they conflict, we must reexamine both our different understandings as well as our worldview to seek a resolution.

The blueprints of the same house must be complementary, that is, the information they provide must fit together without contradiction. For example, the electrical blueprints should not show wires running where the structural blueprint shows no wall. In complementarity we take the theories of each discipline seriously with regard to its own context, the questions it asks, the data it collects, and the methods it legitimates. But we must also check to see that they are congruent with other theories.

SYSTEMS

In recent years, systems approaches have emerged as a powerful model for studying complex realities. The pioneer of this approach was Ludwig von Bertalanffy (1968). Since its introduction the concept has undergone

Figure 3.3
LINEAR AND SYSTEMS CAUSALITY

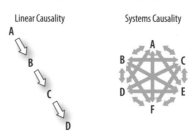

elaboration and critique and now provides a well-developed theory of complex organizations. Systems theory is now used to understand such complex fields as ecology, psychology, life, the military, and institutional organizations.

What is a system? Howard Brody and David Sobel give a good definition: "A system is an organized set of components regarded as a whole consisting of interdependent parts. The parts can be replaced by similar parts without severely disrupting the system, but alteration of the organization among the parts will disrupt the system. Each system can be a part of another higher-level system. A hierarchical pattern of systems can be formed to represent the living systems" (1979, 3).

Systems see causality as multidirectional. Both reductionist and stratigraphic approaches to integration are based on linear logic. A causes B, which in turn causes C. To integrate different parts we need a systems view of causality. A can cause B and C, but B and C can also cause A (fig. 3.3). The three are related, and change in any one of them affects the other two. Bertalanffy writes, "You cannot sum up the behavior of the whole from the isolated parts, and you have to take into account the relations between the various subordinated systems and the systems which are super-ordinated to them in order to understand the behavior of the parts" (1968, 68).

In systems, no one variable is the underlying cause for change. Social changes can lead to cultural, psychological, and biological changes. But changes originating in culture will bring about changes in social organization, personality types, and material culture. Similarly, spiritual transformations will affect social, cultural, and other dimensions of human life.

Multidirectional causality often leads to feedback loops in which changes in one variable cause changes in other variables which, in turn, affect the original variable. There are basically two types of feedback: a negative feedback to return the system to its previous equilibrium and a positive feedback to stimulate growth and maturation. Each hierarchical level has its specific information patterns. Moreover the information flow is not limited to a hierarchical level. It may influence the adjacent levels and even jump to influence widely spaced levels.

Figure 3.4
A SYSTEMS APPROACH TO THE STUDY OF HUMANS

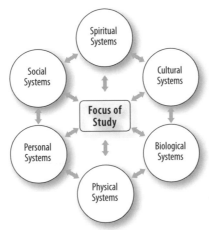

There are two characteristics of systems. First, the whole is greater and different from the sum of its parts. Single components cannot be properly understood apart from their place in the system. Indeed, complex living systems cannot be understood as the sum of their parts but must be understood in terms of the ways parts and subsystems function, particularly the way they continually change their relationship to one another and to the system—and to the environment around them. The intriguing element in this systems view is that all living things and all their subsystems are spontaneously active.

Second, systems are frequently structured such that individual members are systems at the next lower level. The resulting hierarchical structures combine systems into ever-higher levels of order. At the highest level are what some call a "system of systems" (fig. 3.4).

MECHANICAL AND ORGANIC SYSTEMS

Systems can be divided into two broad types: mechanical and organic. Examples of the former are complex machines, such as cars and computers. These are closed systems based on the notion of equilibrium or stasis for which the threat of disruption derives primarily from external forces.[1]

1. Talcott Parsons and Edward Shils (1952) and other leading scientists used a general systems approach in their studies of people, but like the early social and cultural anthropologists, they used a mechanistic approach to systems, which led them to see social and cultural systems as harmonious and static. This weakness should prompt us not to reject a system-of-systems approach but rather to look at humans in terms of organic systems—systems that are characterized by constant tension and conflict within and between subsystems and that are constantly changing.

Living systems, on the other hand, are open systems. Examples of the latter are living beings such as cells, organs (e.g., liver, heart), and organisms (e.g., plants, animals, humans). These also include larger systems made up of living beings, such as an ant colony or a beehive. In human systems these larger systems include groups, organizations, societies, and, ultimately, the global human web. The boundaries within and between living systems are often fuzzy or "leaky." We will focus here only on living human systems (fig. 3.5).

Living systems share several characteristics. First, in contrast to healthy mechanical systems, which are static and in which most changes are signs of malfunction, everything alive is in constant disequilibrium and change. No living system is stable for long. Change may be good or bad, but equilibrium is a form of death. This quality of change is remarkably similar among an unexpected array of living things ranging from simple cells to humans, corporations, nation-states, global systems, and the earth. Systems may change any time their contexts change. The contrast can be seen by way of illustration. Airplanes are flying machines. In flight they essentially remain unchanged. Birds are flying beings. In flight they constantly change their wings, feathers, and body shape to adjust their flight. Planes impersonally consume jet fuel. Birds digest their food and convert it into the many different compounds needed to keep them alive and in flight.

Second, changes in organisms are systemic. They can be initiated in any of the parts or systems, and these affect other systems or the system of systems as a whole. A feedback loop is the defining property of nonlinear systems. Living systems do not simply run; they change. In this view, the living beings in a system are not simply mechanical parts or objects controlled by the system; they are active parts in shaping the whole. The result is a focus not only on the system but also on the individuals that constitute it. This introduces moral issues because it treats the parts as living beings, not as inanimate objects.

Third, change in living systems results from their changing relationships with their environments. "Living systems are continuously exchanging matter, energy, and information with their environments and must periodically adapt their inner activities to accommodate changes in the environment. Environment is simply and relatively defined as everything outside the boundaries of the system" (Brody and Sobel 1979, 7).

Finally, new components introduced into a system are normally reinterpreted within the framework of the system. For example, when pills were first introduced to Papua New Guinea tribal people, they saw these as new and more powerful forms of magic.

LEVELS OF SYSTEMS

In looking at living systems, we can examine different levels of organization. Human organs are made up of different cells, each of which is born, lives,

Figure 3.5
MECHANISTIC AND ORGANIC SYSTEMS

Mechanistic	Organic
• are static; change is bad; new improved models replace old	• are dynamic; growth and change are normal
• are driven by linear causality; change begins at one point and affects other areas	• are driven by multidirectional causality; change begins at different places
• age, develop hardening of the categories, grow rigid, die	• reproduce, regenerate, transform themselves, or die
• examples: old corporations, bureaucracies with top-down management, communication that must flow up through channels	• examples: new corporations, flexocracies with bottom-up feedback loop, communication that can jump levels
• are managed by engineering and control	• are managed by building vision, relationships, teams, and ownership

serves its function in the whole system, and dies. Organs, in turn, can be seen as subsystems within the human biophysical body. Similarly the physical, biological, psychological, and spiritual parts of a human interact to form a whole person. But people are not autonomous beings. They are products of and contribute to corporate human systems: social systems that organize them into societies and cultural systems that encode their beliefs, feelings, and values. To this we need to add spiritual systems, for humans are spiritual realities and therefore relate to angels and fallen angels, and to God, the source of all creation.

Ultimately, in exegeting humans it is important that we take a system-of-systems approach that avoids reductionism and stratigraphic approaches to the study of humans and also avoids the denial of spiritual realities. We must recognize that the boundaries are "leaky" within and between living systems. We must realize that change can be initiated in any of the systems or subsystems and that such changes affect all other human systems. Moreover, we must differentiate, when changes take place, between cause and symptoms. For example, biological problems can cause disruption in our family (social system) and eventually force us to reexamine our theological explanations (cultural system) and our prayer life (spiritual system). Similarly, living in known sin can cause biological, social, and cultural symptoms. Often in examining humans individually and corporately, it is difficult to find the root cause for the changes and thus easier merely to treat symptoms with the hope that the problem will go away.

On the one hand, human systems are influenced by changes in the outside environment. Climate changes can radically alter the social, cultural, and personal lives of people in a society. On the other hand, changes in human systems affect the outside environmental systems, for instance, through deforestation and urban spread.

The systems approach is not the full answer, since there is always the tendency to stratify the system under examination. Economists treat economics as foundational and define human well-being ultimately in economic terms. Sociologists define it in terms of social health. Christians are in danger of defining it in spiritual terms. A true system-of-systems approach must rank priorities of human well-being, but in doing so also recognize the contribution that all systems make toward achieving that state.

In our analysis of worldviews, we will focus on cultural and social systems, although these must also be seen in their relationship to the physical, biological, psychological, and spiritual systems of which they are a part.

Worldviews and Cultural Systems

Worldviews are part of cultures. They are the substructures on which cultures are built. It is important, therefore, to examine the relationship between the deep and the surface structures of a culture. As we noted earlier, it is helpful to look at culture as having three dimensions—cognitive, affective, and evaluative. We begin by examining the cognitive structures of a culture.

Cultural Knowledge

Larry Laudan provides a helpful model of cultural knowledge (1977, fig. 3.6 of this volume). He notes that human minds work on several levels of

Figure 3.6
LEVELS OF CULTURAL KNOWLEDGE

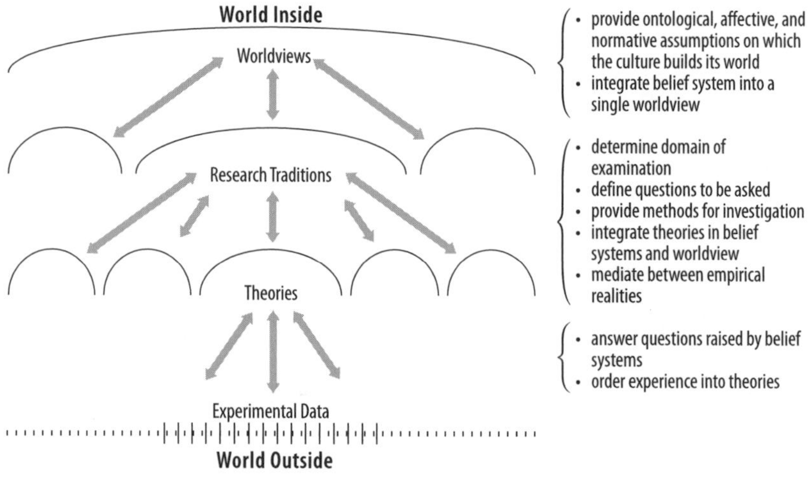

abstraction. Understanding these is crucial to understanding worldviews and their relationship to explicit cultural beliefs and practices.

MATERIAL CULTURE

On the surface, culture is manifest in the material world. People make clothes, make tools, build houses, farm the land, cook food, and fly planes. These cultural products display the knowledge of the people and often manifest deep assumptions about the nature of reality. For example, Brian Walsh shows how houses reflect worldview assumptions (2006).

PATTERNS OF BEHAVIOR

A second obvious manifestation of culture and worldview are the patterns of behavior that people in a society share: how they greet one another, how they drive, how they cook their food, how they divide labor in the society, and how they relate to one another and to strangers who enter their communities. It is not incidental behavior that concerns us here but the behavioral patterns prescribed by the community.

SIGNS

Our knowledge of the world around us is rooted in an unending flow of experiences, each of which is unique. To make sense of these (given the limits of our brains), we need to reduce them to a limited number of categories, so we create words that lump a great many experiences into one. We see many different objects and label them all "trees." We see a great many people, each of whose face is distinct, and call them "humans." It is this ability to generalize and to create languages that enables us to think about the world and decide on courses of action.

In addition to words, we create a great many other signs to experience and communicate the world in which we live. A sign is anything that stands for something else in the minds of the users. We use facial expressions to communicate feelings, lines to create lanes on roads, bells to announce worship, and perfumes and flowers to speak of love. As humans, we experience and comprehend reality mediated through words, gestures, drawings, and other signs that link our experiences to images in our heads. We live in the webs of signs that we create to sort and comprehend our world. Mary Douglas describes the process:

> As perceivers we select from all the stimuli falling on our senses only those which interest us, and our interests are governed by a pattern-making tendency. . . . In a chaos of shifting impressions, each of us constructs a stable world in which objects have recognizable shapes, are located in depth, and have permanence. In perceiving we are building, taking some cues and rejecting others. The most acceptable cues are those which fit most easily into the pattern that is being built

up. . . . As time goes on and experiences pile up, we make a greater and greater investment in our systems of labels. So a conservative bias is built in. It gives us confidence. At any time we may have to modify our structure of assumptions to accommodate new experience, but the more consistent experience is with the past, the more confidence we can have in our assumptions . . . by and large anything we take note of is pre-selected and organized in the very act of perceiving. (1966, 36–37)

Signs reduce a great many experiences into a single category so that human minds can grasp them. Signs are building blocks that enable humans to construct mental worlds of reality as they perceive it. They use these inner worlds to live in the external world and to manipulate it. In their minds they think of their house and drive to it. They mentally picture a purple cow, so they paint their cow purple. In short, it is this ability to create signs that enables us as humans to think and communicate with one another about the world in which we live. Signs are not isolated units. They are parts of larger systems. In English we speak of the color "red." This belongs to our taxonomy of colors: red, orange, yellow, green, blue, and violet. So when we say an object is "red," we are also saying it is not orange, yellow, green, blue, or violet. Different cultures create different taxonomies,[2] and as we will see later, these taxonomies reflect and reinforce the underlying worldviews. To understand worldviews as parts of cultural systems, it is important to study the signs people use to reflect their beliefs, feelings, and values because in doing so we learn to understand the mental worlds of the people who use them.

RITUALS

At the heart of cultural behavior are rituals. They range from simple rites such as shaking hands, bowing, or embracing, to fiestas, New Year's celebrations, fairs, festivals, weddings, masked dances, pilgrimages, banquets, memorial days, and sacred rites. Modern people commonly regard rituals as harmless interludes or discount them as meaningless performances. But rituals play a central role in most societies. They are multilayered transactions in which speech and behavior are socially prescribed.

On one level, rituals maintain social order in human communities by enacting the norms that order relationships between people as they form families, groups, communities, and societies. On another level, they give visible expression to the deep cultural norms that order the way people think, feel, and evaluate their worlds. They give public expression to the moral

2. Taxonomies related to the material world are not totally arbitrary and relative to one another. Berlin and Kay (1969) have shown that cultures follow the same sequence in categorizing colors, and Wick Miller and Eugene Hunn have shown that different cultures agree in the general taxonomy of birds and plants. Signs communicate images in the mind, but many of them also refer to objects in the real world.

order that people believe was created by the gods, defined by the ancestors, or instituted by the culture's heroes when they taught people to be civilized and human. Because rituals dramatize in visible form the deep beliefs, feelings, and values of a society, they are of particular importance in studying worldviews.

MYTHS

At the heart of cultures are deep myths, the cosmic narratives that explain how reality came into existence through events that took place in primordial time, often resulting from the acts of supernatural beings. In the modern world, the word "myth" carries the idea of fictitious stories, which are not true but only imagined. In anthropological terms they are transcendent stories believed to be true, which serve as paradigms people use to understand the bigger stories in which ordinary lives are embedded. They are the master narratives that bring cosmic order, coherence, and sense into the seemingly senseless experience, emotions, and ideas in the everyday world by telling people what is real, eternal, and enduring.

Myths look beneath the surface world at what is really happening in this world. They are the language not only of thought but of the imagination. They speak of things too hard for humans to bear by telling them these things indirectly, forcing people to discover their meanings by active imagination and thought until the truths "dawn" on them. It is because root myths are archetypes of human existence, told in story form, that they are so important in our attempts to understand worldviews.

BELIEF SYSTEMS

In cultures, signs are used to organize mental theories, which are limited, low-level explanatory systems that seek to answer specific questions about a narrow range of reality. They do so by linking perceptions, concepts, notions of causality, logical comparisons, and the like to form explicit understandings of reality. For example, some people attribute illnesses to viruses and bacteria; others to the anger of ancestors; others to curses, broken taboos, and witchcraft; and still others to fate or bad karma. All are logical explanations for reality as perceived by people in a particular context. They are alternative explications for the same set of questions—in this case, Why do people get sick? The theories themselves may reside on different levels of generality, with broader theories subsuming more limited ones.

Theories are imbedded in higher-level systems of knowledge. Thomas Kuhn calls these "paradigms," Peter Berger talks of "fields of consciousness," and Larry Laudan refers to them as "research traditions." We will label them "knowledge systems." Knowledge systems are generally made up of at least three key components: (1) a set of beliefs about what sorts of entities and processes make up the domain of inquiry; (2) a set of questions worth asking;

and (3) a set of epistemic and methodological norms about how the domain is to be investigated, how theories are to be tested, and how data are to be collected. Knowledge systems serve important functions in the generation of theories. They indicate what is uncontroversial background knowledge to people in that tradition, identify portions of theories that are in difficulty and need modification, establish rules for the collection of data and testing of theories, and challenge theories that violate the foundational assumptions of the tradition (Laudan 1996, 83–84).

An active knowledge system is generally made up of a family of theories, some of which are mutually consistent while other, rival theories are not. What these theories have in common is that they seek to answer the same questions and can be tested and evaluated using the methodological norms of the research tradition. The sciences, for example, physics, chemistry, biology, medicine, and sociology, are belief systems. In theology, the disciplines of systematic theology and biblical theology are belief systems. Everyday American belief systems include auto mechanics, electrical engineering, cooking, football, classical music, and farming. Knowledge systems guide thought processes and enable people to focus on experience and formulate theories to help them solve the problems of life and pursue their goals. In so doing, they help give meaning to life.

WORLDVIEWS

As Laudan (1977) and Kuhn (1970) point out, at the highest level of abstraction, belief systems and a great deal of common-sense knowledge are loosely integrated into a larger worldview. A worldview is the most fundamental and encompassing view of reality shared by a people in a common culture. It is their mental picture of reality that "makes sense" of the world around them. This worldview is based on foundational assumptions about the nature of reality, the "givens" of life, and clothes these belief systems with an aura of certainty that this is, in fact, the way reality is. To question worldviews is to challenge the very foundations of life, and people resist such challenges with deep emotional reactions. There are few human fears greater than a loss of a sense of order and meaning. People are willing to die for their beliefs if these beliefs make their deaths meaningful.

INTERCONNECTIONS

To understand the role of worldviews in cultural systems, it is important to study their relationship to belief systems, theories, and symbols. It is important to show the link between explicit theories and practices and the larger knowledge systems in which they are embedded. It is easy to listen to what people say and look at what they do and then to describe their culture in terms of specific beliefs and practices, such as those associated with auto mechanics, cooking, physics, and religion. But this misses the point that specific beliefs and doctrines are part of larger knowledge systems that seek to make sense out of life. It is important to study the questions, data, and methods that lie behind specific theories. For example, it is important to know not only why people believe a person is spirit-possessed but also what they believe about possession in general: what are its manifestations, when and why does it occur, what are the possible remedies, and how does it relate to other beliefs? Knowledge systems legitimate key questions, data, and methods of analysis that are answered through explicit beliefs.

Next, it is important to show how knowledge systems are embedded in worldviews and how they relate to one another. Worldviews provide the fundamental assumptions about the nature of reality and of right and wrong that belief systems use to build their theories. Worldviews also mediate between belief systems when conflicts arise. For example, in the West, the tension between science and religion cannot be resolved simply by reconciling the two on the level of specific theories, such as those related to the origins of humankind. Integration can occur only when both are embedded in a single worldview that mediates their disagreements.

Cultural Feelings and Values

Most research to date has focused on the cognitive dimension of cultures and worldviews. It is important to keep in mind that the affective dimensions are equally important in shaping the way people live their lives. Here too there are levels. On the surface, feelings are manifested through material objects and behavioral patterns, which are often shaped by people's worldviews. On a deeper level, affectivity is expressed in signs, rituals, and belief systems. Different societies have different ways of dealing with joy, sorrow, anger, hatred, and love. We will examine this dimension in more detail as we look at specific worldviews.

The third dimension of culture is morality, the judgments people make about right and wrong, righteousness and sin. Like the cognitive and affective dimensions, these judgments are manifest at all levels of culture, from cultural products and behavior patterns to signs, rituals, and belief systems. We will also consider worldview moral themes as we examine specific worldviews.

Worldviews and Social Systems

Cultural worldviews are social creations, produced and sustained by communities of people in order to understand and live in their world. For example, Americans have created many words to describe different kinds of motor vehicles, because these play an important role in their lives. At a deeper level, the introduction of cars has profoundly shaped the way Americans now see the world. Similarly, the invention of computers is changing not only the words but also the worldviews of young people around the world.

Human societies live in different worlds, both external and perceptual, so their worldviews are often radically different. For example, the Nuer live close to nature as horticulturalists. Their sense of time is shaped by the passing of seasons and the cycles of birth, maturation, and death. They also reckon time in terms of socially constructed events such as moving camp, weddings, festivals, and raids (Evans-Pritchard 1940, 104). Like many tribal and agricultural societies, they shape their concepts of time more by the daily, monthly, and annual changes of nature than do modern industrial societies. The latter, with their electric lights, furnaces, air conditioners, and windowless offices, are largely insulated from environmental influences and seasonal cycles. They are driven more by socially constructed concepts of time such as hours, weeks, months, centuries, and millennia.

Because people in a society more or less share the same worldview, they can communicate with one another. Individuals may have their own mental maps, but social life is possible only if they share common languages, beliefs, and worldviews. Moreover, they use their shared signs, beliefs, and worldviews in every social transaction, though in doing so they reinforce or change this shared culture.

It is important to remember that worldviews are intertwined with social systems. The powerful use them to justify the oppression of the poor, and the poor to justify rebellion. For example, high-caste Hindus explain and justify the suffering of the low-caste poor by attributing it to sins the poor committed in previous lives. Worldviews reflect social class, ethnicity, religions, and other corporate identities and shape these identities. Well-to-do Americans attribute their high status to their race, intelligence, or work, and often blame the poor for being lazy. In churches and schools there often are debates over ideology, debates that are frequently rooted in worldview differences. Considerable energy is expended and other activities suffer until these differences are resolved.

The interplay between worldviews and social systems is apparent when norms are broken. When this occurs, individuals and groups in the society devise strategies to impose what they believe to be the norms on the group. Each side wants the other to play the game according to its rules. In short, worldviews shape behavior, but when behavior is breached, social power plays attempt to impose particular worldviews on the community.

Worldviews and Other Systems

Cultures with their worldviews are linked to other systems, which they shape and which shape them. We cannot go into detail here regarding these contexts in which worldviews operate, but we must keep them in mind to understand the place of worldviews in human activities.

One of these is the personal system. Each human can be studied as a system, and each person has some understanding of the world in which he or she lives. Personal experiences play an important role in the way each individual tailors the worldview learned from his or her culture. Generally, these variations are minor. For a society to exist, there must be a large measure of consensus on worldview essentials, but individuals may be permitted to hold their own views on certain things.[3] Worldviews are also shaped by the physical and biological systems in which they are found. People living in cold climates face problems and develop knowledge systems different from those living in tropical or desert environments. Urbanites tend to develop different worldviews than their country cousins (Hiebert 1999).

We must also take spiritual systems seriously. Satan seeks to blind people by keeping them bound by false ideologies, and God seeks to open their minds to the truth. On one level, spiritual warfare is a battle between and for worldviews.

It is important to remember that change can begin in any one of the systems. The effects of this change spread throughout the whole system of systems. No one system is the prime mover, the root cause for change. Changes in the social system affect the spiritual, cultural, psychological, biological, and physical systems to which they are linked. But changes may be initiated in the cultural system, which in turn affect the other systems. Thus it is often hard to determine where specific changes originated because their effects are seen throughout the whole macrosystem. Just as in the case of the human body, where the often invisible cause of an illness may be biological, psychological, physical, social, cultural, or spiritual, the visible symptoms are manifest in other subsystems.

History

Finally, we must keep in mind that worldviews exist in and are deeply shaped by their historical contexts. The West has been deeply shaped by Greco-Roman and Hebrew worldviews, China by Confucius and Buddha, and Latin America by Iberian, African, Aztec, and Mayan worldviews. A full system-of-systems approach must see worldviews as being shaped by and shaping an ever-changing world (fig. 3.7).

3. There is discussion on "open" and "closed" societies. In the former, people are encouraged to look at things in alternative ways. In the latter, little deviance from the society's views is permitted. This phenomenon can be observed in families. Some parents demand that their children conform to their beliefs. Others provide their children a frame of reference but encourage them to think for themselves.

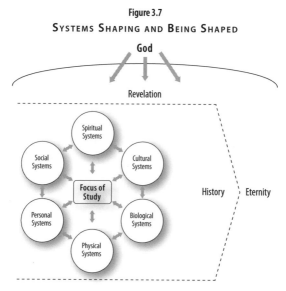

Figure 3.7
SYSTEMS SHAPING AND BEING SHAPED

Cultures and societies exist in time and are constantly re-created by the people in their social transactions. People learn their worldviews from their parents and their communities. It is primarily ideas from the past, therefore, that shape those of the present. But people can and do change their worldviews through changes in their surrounding worlds and changes in their own ways of thinking. We will examine worldview change later.

4

Methods for Analyzing Worldviews

People from different cultures disagree not only on explicit beliefs but also on the basic assumptions they use to organize their conceptual worlds. Can they ever really understand one another? What methods can they use when they try to do so? Suppose, for example, that a person in a different society tells us that his illnesses are caused by demons and that he has actually seen them. What are we to make of it?

Obviously we must avoid the ethnocentric temptation to judge the person and conclude that he is ignorant and foolish without first trying to understand him in terms of his own cultural concepts and values. But the answer to our question is not so simple. In trying to understand another culture, the outsider can observe human behavior and products but cannot see beliefs and worldviews. These can be inferred only from the acts and comments of the people. There may be no informant who will, or even can, verbalize the worldview of the culture, for it exists largely implicitly in the minds of the people. If an anthropologist must depend on inference to arrive at abstract conclusions, what do we mean when we say that person *knows* something about that culture?

Moreover, anthropologists themselves carry their own sets of assumptions. Should they examine other cultures in terms of these assumptions ("etic" analysis) or in terms of the culture's own concepts and values ("emic" analysis)? Both etic and emic models are useful, but the questions remain: Can an anthropologist, given his own cultural biases, ever really understand another culture in its own terms? And even if he does so, can he effectively communicate it to others who have not lived in-depth in that culture?

This problem of understanding can be illustrated by looking at the concepts of maya, karma, and dharma, which are basic to Indian thought. Can we translate these accurately into English? No English word has exactly the same meanings or the same emotional and moral associations as any one of these Indian words. To be accurate, we should use those Sanskrit terms themselves. If we carry this thinking to the extreme, we can understand and describe a culture only in terms of its own language and sociocultural context, but this makes cross-cultural communication and understanding virtually impossible. Each culture then remains a conceptual island, and, at best, we can only move from one to another but never build a bridge of understanding between them.

Clearly, our understanding of another culture is only approximate, just as *its* model of the world around it is approximate. But this does not mean we have no understanding of it at all. Careful study can give us a great many insights into another culture, and as we develop new methods for learning about the thinking and conceptual processes of others, these approximations should become more accurate and easier to verify.

The problem of cross-cultural comparison will be solved only as we formulate concepts and methods of investigation that are increasingly free from the biases of any single culture. The process is a tedious one, for our biases are deep-seated. Nevertheless, considerable progress has been made along this line in the field of anthropology.

Worldviews are largely implicit. How then can we study them? There is no easy answer to this question, nor are our conclusions always right. As we study a people's culture, we must infer their basic assumptions from their explicit beliefs and practices. We look for similarities and patterns that seem to run like a thread through a wide range of cultural products and practices, and for beliefs that make sense out of them. We examine the language to discover the categories the people use in their thinking. We study their symbols and their rituals, such as festivals and rites of birth, marriage, and death, which often reveal their deepest understandings of reality.

We often discern the basic assumptions underlying another culture more clearly than those underlying our own. We learn our primary culture as children and thereafter take its assumptions for granted. Other cultures, however, are strange to us, so we look for their foundations in order to understand them. Similarly, foreigners often see our assumptions more clearly than we do, and we need to listen to what they say about us. Our initial reaction is often to reject their observations as overly critical. On further reflection, however, we often find them to be true. We also see our own culture more clearly when we return from living in another setting. Entering another culture forces us to develop a measure of detachment from our own, as well as a metacultural frame that is outside both cultures and translates between them. When we return "home," we see it through new eyes.

Methods for Analyzing a Worldview

There is no overarching set of methods for discovering worldviews; rather, several methods can be used. It is best to triangulate the findings of any one method with those produced by other methods. In the end, uncovering worldviews is often as much an art as a science. As Peter Berger and his associates point out, "Our methodological caveats are thus made not in a stance of assertive self-confidence but in an attitude of (if we may coin a psychology-of-science term) cognitive nervousness. We recommend the same nervousness to everyone else concerned with this problem" (Berger, Berger, and Kellner 1973, 5).

Ethnosemantic Analysis

One powerful method for discovering worldviews is to study the words people use and how these words are grouped into larger semantic sets and domains. Languages encode and shape the categories and themes of the worldviews of their native speakers. Studying them opens the door into the way people think because words are one of the primary ways in which people communicate their inner thoughts. The assumption here is that words are important indicators of cognition. We must, therefore, study people's language to learn how they see their world. The danger is that we constantly translate their terms into English and in so doing, miss the worldview implicit in their language. We need to lay aside the totalizing power of English, realizing that it has shaped our own understandings of reality.

Signs such as words are always related to members of the same set. Thus to say "red" is also to say "not yellow, green, blue, or violet." Ethnosemantic analysis focuses on the internal ordering of groups of words, such as nouns and verbs, to discover the folk taxonomies and domains of people in order to describe the cultural knowledge, rules, and norms that account for appropriate types of behavior in specific contexts and in general. Such behavioral norms are often detected when they are breached, and people gossip or act to enforce the norms. Drawing from the study of cognitive structures, analysts seek to discover the worldview themes and conceptual framework underlying these ethnosemantic structures (Werner and Schoepfle 1989). This assumes a certain formal logical relationship between different semantic domains.

The nature and power of ethnosemantic analysis can best be seen by way of illustration. People from different cultures were asked to group a set of English words into larger domains and to explain why they grouped the words they way they did (fig. 4.1).

Figure 4.1
An Ethnosemantic Test

rock	angel	woman
lion	tree	sand
man	cow	God
bush	fish	girl
demon	deer	whale
Mickey Mouse	virus	troll

One young Masai from Kenya grouped the words as follows (fig. 4.2). He put "man," "lion," and "whale" together and said that they were all rulers: man ruled society, lion the jungle, and whale the sea. He put "woman," "girl," and "cow" together. In Masai culture, when a man wants to get married, he must give the bride's parents a large number of cows. Early anthropologists called this "bride price," but this designation was a total misunderstanding. The man is not buying the bride. Later anthropologists called it "progeny price" because the young man can marry the woman before he gives all the cows, but her children belong to her father until the agreed number of cows is given. This too is incorrect. Women and cows are valued most highly in Masai society because they give birth to life. When a man gives cows to his prospective father-in-law, he is giving the most valuable gift he can give in exchange for the gift of the woman to his extended family. The larger the number of cows he gives, the more the young man values the marriage, so he seeks to give as many as possible.[1] In order to gather ten or twenty cows, he works and raises some, his father contributes several, and his uncles, cousins, and brothers add a few. The father-in-law keeps some of the cows given as an expression of gratitude for giving his daughter to the young man, and the rest he distributes to his brothers, sons, and others in the extended family.

Figure 4.2
Masai Domains

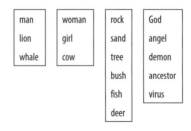

---

1. This, of course, is the ideal. In reality a man tries to give fewer cows for a wife, but the underlying premise is the same: life-givers are exchanged as gifts.

This web of gift exchanges shows the value of women in the community and provides them with a great measure of security, for a woman has the cows to provide for her necessities if her husband leaves her. If a man tries to divorce his wife, all his male relatives upbraid him for being a bad husband, because they don't want to have to give the cows back. If the young woman wants to leave her husband, her female relatives all admonish her to be a better wife. In Masai culture divorce rates are low.

The young Masai put rock, sand, tree, bush, fish, and deer together. He said that these belong to no one until they are taken by someone. A fish or a bird belongs to the person who catches it. Similarly, the fruit on trees and bushes is free for the taking. No one can own them. Finally, he grouped God, angels, demons, ancestors, and viruses together and said that these all can kill humans.

Indian Hindus taking the same test do not group the words in larger domains. They arrange the words along a hierarchy of life (fig. 4.3). One worldview assumption is that all life is one. Different units of life, such as gods, humans, animals, plants, and rocks, are fragments of this life. Some beings, such as gods, angels, and demons, have more life and purity and rank higher on the scale. Other beings, such as animals, plants, and rocks, have less life and are defiled, and rank lower on the ladder. Humans are in the middle. They too are ranked along a hierarchy of purity and pollution. At the top are the

Figure 4.3
HINDU VIEW OF LIFE

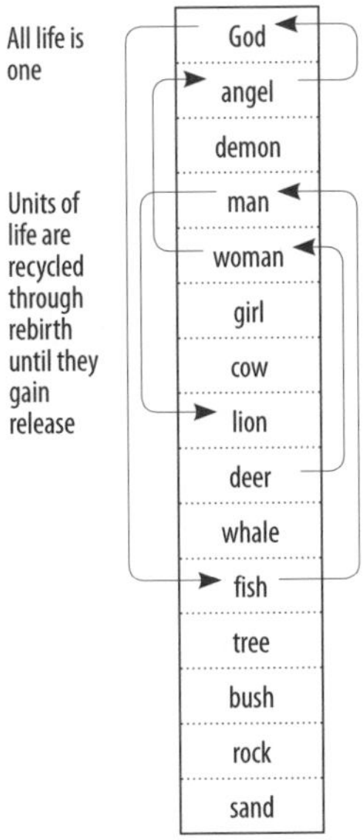

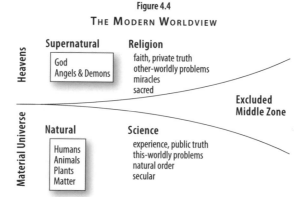

Figure 4.4

THE MODERN WORLDVIEW

Brahman priests. Below them are the warrior castes, the merchant castes, and the worker castes. At the bottom are the untouchables, who are seen as very polluted and thus outside the pale of normal society.

When people die, they are reborn higher or lower on the ladder, depending on their lives. Those who keep the caste order and do good are reborn as angels or even gods. Those who disrupt the social order and do evil are reborn as animals to suffer for their misdeeds. Salvation means to be released from this endless cycle of lives and to merge back into the cosmic life.

Modern people, in general, group the words into domains and larger realms based on intrinsic, digital categories (fig. 4.4). Most make a fundamental distinction between supernatural and natural realities. They put God, angels, and demons into the former and the remaining real beings into the latter. Mickey Mouse and trolls are excluded as fictional characters. They divide the natural world into domains of humans, animals, plants, and matter. The difference between plants and matter is that between life and no life; the difference between animals and plants is that between life that moves around and eats other life and life that stays still and gets eaten; and the difference between humans and animals is that between beings that have a soul or create elaborate cultures and those that do not. There are disagreements between those influenced by science, who put whales together with land animals because they are mammals, and common folk who put whales with fish as a subcategory of animals. Although all Westerners do differentiate between different kinds of life, they do not all agree on how many kinds there are.[2]

---

2. Christians see the fundamental distinction as the presence or absence of an eternal soul. Secular scientists have sought to define the difference in terms of the ability to make tools, use language, create culture, or think abstractly, none of which has been a satisfactory norm. Many scientists argue that there is no essential difference between humans and animals and remove the line between them. The question of whether a line separates humans from animals is the fundamental worldview debate between secular scientists and Christians.

Figure 4.5
ETHNOSEMANTIC ANALYSIS

Worldview themes
Higher-level domains
Domains
Categories

This comparison of how people from different cultures organize a list of words helps us see how ethnosemantic analysis—the study of how words are organized into larger systems of thought—can help us uncover deep worldview themes. The analysis begins with an examination of the meanings associated with words. It then examines how the words are grouped into domains and how the domains relate to one another. It is particularly helpful in uncovering the emic order that people impose on the world.

The ethnosemantic method for examining worldviews was pioneered by Edward Sapir and Benjamin Whorf, who argued that language and its categories filter our perceptions of reality, shape our beliefs, and organize our understanding of the world. The method has been developed in detail by James Spradley (1980) and by Oswald Werner and G. M. Schoepfle (1989), who examine words and other symbols to determine the categories, taxonomies, and domains in a culture and the logic linking them together into cognitive systems that reveal underlying worldviews.

Spradley outlines one method of ethnosemantic analysis (fig. 4.5). The first step is to gather words or categories into a domain. For example, we can gather words related to religious beliefs, or to farming, or to family ties. These can be elicited from observing events, or by asking questions such as, what kinds of X are there? or what kind of thing is X? By this means we can chart a cultural domain. Sometimes word associations are used to elicit folk taxonomies. The informant is asked to say a number of words he or she associates with a particular category. For example, we can ask what the characteristics of a "good man" or a "good woman" are. The second step is to order the categories and domains into a hierarchy of domains of increasing levels of generalization. This mapping of domains is known as componential analysis, from which it is then possible to deduce some of the basic worldview themes of a culture (Werner and Schoepfle 1989).

Spradley lists eight steps in using ethnosemantic methods to uncover worldview themes (fig. 4.6). One example of ethnosemantic analysis is the examination of the levels of "friendship" among the Igede of West Africa (fig. 4.7).

Sentence Completion

Closely related to ethnosemantics and domain analysis is the method of sentence completion. Sentence-completion tests provide insights into a people's concepts of themselves and their purposes, opportunities, and values. For

Figure 4.6
ETHNOSEMANTIC METHODS FOR DISCOVERING WORLDVIEWS

Ethnosemantics seeks to discover worldview themes by examining words to determine the categories, domains, and taxonomies people use in ordering their worlds. J. Spradley lists eight techniques that can be used in the process.

- Immerse yourself in the culture.
- Gather a cultural inventory, i.e., a collection and transcript of data collected.
  - Make a list of cultural domains: a domain is a major subsystem of a group's acquired knowledge.
  - Make another list of suspected but still unidentified domains. It helps to examine other kinds of objects, events, acts, actors, activities, goals, ways to achieve things, ways to avoid things, ways to do things, places for things, places for doing things, stages in activities, stages in events, etc.
- Analyze the components of folk domains.
- Identify the way a domain is organized, such as the steps or stages involved.
- Construct a schematic of the culture scene, demonstrating in graphics the relationship to domains.
- Identify the universal themes that become apparent in the relationship of domains. (Examples include social conflict, cultural contradictions, informal techniques of social control, acquisition and maintenance of status.)
- Make a written summary of the culture scene.
- Compare this scene with other scenes in the same culture and with other scenes in other cultures.

Source: Adapted from Spradley 1980.

Figure 4.7
FRIENDSHIP TERMS OF THE IGEDE

(each level has several subcategories)
unresponsive friendship (*oligwuh ojwugwume*)
friendship with outsider (*oligwu olabadoweh*)
casual friendship (*oligwuh ochakala*)
ritual friendship (*oligwuh oliyaka*) "age mates"
supportive friendship (*oligwuh odubwo*) "helper"
intimate friendship (*oligwuh olikeje*) literally "liver-friend"

example, in studying the characteristics of a "good" or an "evil" person, we can ask questions such as: "They praise him because he . . ." "If she is a true friend, she . . ." "He is a good person because he always . . ." "She is a bad/evil person because she . . ." "He gets angry with his friends/relatives if . . ." "Her relatives reject her because she . . ."

Sentence-completion tests can also help us understand the strategies people use in living their lives. For example, we can ask questions such as: "If she is in difficulty, she . . ." and "If he is afraid, he should . . ." Such images of the self, the group, and the world are incorporated by individuals in the group as fundamental assumptions about the nature of reality and the action strategies people should use in living in that world.

Analysis of Other Signs

Steve Moon (1998) has expanded the ethnosemantic method to include other cultural signs, such as food, dress, buildings, modes of transportation, and cultural products such as pens, watches, cars, computers, music, and art. He collected various cultural signs in Konya, Turkey, and organized them into larger clusters on the basis of their common association in the minds of the people. He then examined the underlying worldview themes that emerged out of the comparison of these cognitive domains (fig. 4.8).

Figure 4.8

WORLDVIEW DOMAINS IN KONYA, TURKEY

Modern Turkey	Orthodox Islam	Sufi Islam
Cultural signs		
• shopping mall	• mosque	• dervish hall
• movie theater	• madrasa	
• posters of movie stars	• posters of Khomeini	• posters and poems of Rumi
• statues of Ataturk		
• women in jeans, T-shirts	• women in *hijab*	• women with scarves
• fast-food shops: hot dogs, hamburgers, Western food	• falafel	
• modern literature, magazines	• Qur'an	• writings of Sufi saints
Worldview themes		
• secularism	• religious orthodoxy	• mystical religious experiences

Analysis of Rituals

Rituals are culturally structured dramas that are stylized, regularly repeated, dramatically structured, authoritatively designated, and intrinsically valued (V. Turner 1974). They communicate the deep beliefs, intense feelings (awe, sorrow, loyalty, tenderness, respect, and attraction), and values (ideal person, central moral issues) of a society through formal symbolic codes. They re-create the social, cultural, personal, and cosmic order necessary for human life by making cosmic norms explicit in visible forms.

As we have already seen, underlying everyday social and cultural life are deep structures that enable people to think, feel, and judge the world around them. Their deep beliefs organize their experiences; their deep feelings help them experience and make sense of what is beautiful and ugly, aesthetically desirable and undesirable; and their deep morals enable them to judge between good and evil. Rituals bring to the surface and reinforce through reenactment the largely invisible foundations of their societies and cultures—in other words, their worldviews. They show how things should be. They provide people with models of what it means to be fully human, fully male or female, or fully a person of God. For example, in an American church wedding, the bride is dressed in white and the groom in formal attire. They treat each other with the greatest love and respect and pledge to live only for the other. They are courteous to their new in-laws. A few months later at home alone, things are often different. The new husband and wife argue, ignore each other, and want their own way. Why then the poetic talk of love and self-sacrifice in the marriage ceremony? Here the ritual not only publicly establishes a new relationship between them, that of a married couple, it also states the society's ideals for marriage, what a marriage should really look like. The fact that no one consistently lives up to the ideals does not make the ideals irrelevant. Without deep beliefs, feelings, values, and ideals, no truly human society is possible.

Rites fall broadly into three types, each of which casts light on different worldview themes. The first are rites of intensification, sometimes called rites of restoration or renewal. They publicly affirm the existing social and cultural order, which becomes blurred and forgotten in ordinary life. In a sense, they are like housecleaning. As people live in their homes, the homes become dirty. Dust settles on the shelves, food is spilled on the floor, clothes are left lying on the chairs, and rugs are soiled. Periodically, the family stops and cleans things up. Rites of restoration act as social and religious housecleaning rituals, restoring meaning and order to a world that is falling into chaos and meaninglessness.

Rites of transformation mark transitions in the life of individuals and groups. They include life-cycle rites such as birth, initiation, marriage, and death; cycles of the year, such as New Year, seed-planting time, and harvest; and religious pilgrimage, such as the stations of the cross. They are like remodeling one's house. To do so one must first tear down the old and go through a period of chaos before the new is completed. Rites of transformation, such as conversion, make lasting worldview changes possible in short, intense periods of time.

Rites of re-creation help people rebuild their world when the old world has been totally destroyed. This is like rebuilding a city after a tsunami, when there is nothing left to salvage. In many traditional societies, the present world cannot be repaired. It must be re-created by a ritual reenactment of the original creation. If this is not done, the world will fall into chaos and darkness. In some cultures, the annual New Year's festival is such a ritual, re-creating a world that has run down.

Because rituals visibly reenact the deepest beliefs, feelings, and values of a people, they are a vital key to understanding their worldview.[3] In studying

3. For an excellent example of the analysis of rituals for discovering worldviews, see Meade 2005.

rituals, we begin by collecting data through observation and participant observation. We observe the different parts of the ritual, the participants, their roles and relationships to one another, the speech acts, music, actions, ritual objects, and symbols. We study the structure of space (drawing maps is one way) and note how it is used. We keep a time line and look for the sequence of events or story in the ritual. We look at the social and cultural contexts and the events leading up to and following the event—the total ritual field. We gather native accounts: collect written texts and folklore texts, and interview select informants and specialists in the ritual.

The second step in ritual analysis is interpreting the data—finding meaning in the ritual. Here we begin by analyzing key symbols and their meanings in the rite and comparing these with the meanings associated with these symbols in other cultural settings. For example, blood is often a key symbol in rituals, but it also has significant meanings in other cultural settings. The third step is to look at the symbols in terms of their larger symbolic domains to note binary oppositions, linkages, and redundancies.

We then examine the ritual process as a whole, studying the types and phases of ritual transition, affirmation, and affliction. Here we note characteristics such as separation, liminality, and aggregation and the role of the ritual in the overall sociocultural life of the people. Finally, we look for the deep worldview themes, which are often brought to the surface, made visible, and reaffirmed in rituals.

Analysis of Folklore and Myths

In seeking to understand the diachronic themes of worldviews, it is essential to study people's folklore and myths (Dundes 1965). Myths are the broader stories that people take to be true about the ultimate nature of things. They provide the paradigms—the cookie cutters—that help people understand their cosmology, human history, and biographies by showing them the fundamental "plot" or "story line" in which they live. Myths provide people maps of their origins and destinies.

Myths often provide the fundamental themes that underlie a culture. Myths grapple with the inherent contradictions of human life and seek to resolve them by moving them to ever-higher levels of structural abstraction until they lose their tensions (Levi-Strauss 1984).

One approach to the study of myths is to look for the themes that run through them. For example, in Western romances, "falling in love" and marrying despite many oppositions is a common theme. In the Indian epics (*Mahabharata, Ramayanam*), the stories of the gods (Puranas) present cosmic battles between good and bad gods and good and bad kings, surrounded by courtiers, armies, and bodyguards. Often the enemies belong to the same families. Most have wives and children who are also caught up in the battles.

Myths enable people to explore the contradictions in their lives—the tensions between good and evil, love and hate, acceptance and rejection—and show them that something lies beneath the surface of the visible, audible world. They communicate something that is "just as real, maybe even more real, than what we're seeing, and hearing and touching" (Peterson 1997, 38). Myths help make sense of a confusing and often fearsome world. They integrate and validate the reality in which people live.

In studying myths, it is important to study not only the stories known by everyone but also those told in specific communities, the local folk myths. For example, in a South Indian village, the Komati caste keeps a sense of its identity by telling the story of its patron goddess, which is written in small pamphlets sold in the bazaar. It tells of a beautiful young Komati virgin who lived some three hundred years ago. The local king saw her and ordered that she be prepared as his bride when he returned a week later. She agonized over the marriage. If she married the king she would be queen, but she would also have defiled her caste by marrying outside it. She decided caste purity was more important, so when the king came to wed her, she jumped into a big, fiery pit, from which she rose as a spirit seen by all. She is now the patron goddess of the Komati caste. Although 102 leaders of family lineages in the caste jumped into the pit with her, leaders of the other 612 gotras did not. In time, the caste split between the "Jumpers" and the "Didn't Jumpers." The former are of higher rank because their leaders were willing to sacrifice their lives for caste purity, and now they won't marry Didn't Jumpers. The underlying tension is that between caste purity and royal prerogative with a luxurious life. The resolution is that the former is more important than the latter.

Wisdom Literature

One of the important ways to discover worldview themes is to examine the wisdom traditions of a people: their songs, proverbs, aphorisms, poetry, riddles, parables, and stories (Dundes 1965). In oral societies, these are the storehouses in which the deep beliefs, feelings, and morals of the society are preserved and communicated from generation to generation.

Wisdom traditions look at the paradoxes of human life: the tensions between birth and death, joy and sorrow, riches and poverty, love and hate, good and evil. In doing so, they focus on the important issues in a culture and reaffirm the core themes and counterthemes of its worldview.

Narrative Analysis

A primary way people make sense of experience is to put it into narrative form. This is particularly true of difficult life transitions and traumas. People create plots from disordered experiences and give them meaning by going beyond historical events into their deeper understanding of the world's story and their place in it (Riessman 1993).

Narrative analysis studies the first-person accounts of people's experiences to see how they impose order on the flow of experiences in order to make sense of the events and actions in their lives. How people view life determines what is included or excluded from their stories, how events are plotted, and what they are supposed to mean. Individuals interpret and construct past events in their personal narratives to claim identities and construct lives. "How individuals recount their histories—what they emphasize and omit, their stance as protagonists or victims, the relationship the story establishes between teller and audience—all shape what individuals can claim of their own lives. Personal stories are not merely a way of telling someone (or oneself) about one's life; they are the means by which identities may be fashioned" (Rosenwald and Ochberg 1992, 1).

People create autobiographical narratives that they use to understand and explain their lives. These stories are typically woven into a community of life stories, which together help us understand the deep structures of the nature of life itself.

Aesthetic Culture

In studying the affective themes of worldviews, it is important to examine aesthetic culture such as art, music, bardic performances, theater, dance, drama, films, and magazines. Too often we incorrectly assume that small-scale oral and peasant societies have little in the way of entertainment or artistic expressions. Most of these societies have many art and musical forms that are used in varying contexts to express different emotions. For example, there are often songs of lament, of war, of joy and celebration, and of worship. In Indian villages we find several different forms of bardic and theatrical performances used to entertain people.

Evaluative Ideals

Normative themes can be identified by studying a culture's heroes and villains. For example, in China great men are sages who bring wisdom and reconciliation to the society. In Hindu cultures, heroes are the sadhus, or holy men, who stand above the turmoil of life and meditate with inner peacefulness (such as Mahatma Gandhi and Sadhu Sundar Singh). In Muslim cultures they are the ayatollahs and mullahs, religious leaders who proclaim the word of God. In Christian cultures they are the saints, church leaders (pope, bishops), and evangelists (Billy Sunday, Dwight Moody, Billy Graham). In modernity they are scholars, political heads of state, business tycoons and entrepreneurs, and top entertainers (sports, movie, and TV personalities, pop singers, and musicians). In Western movies the heroes are sheriffs and cowboys, the villains bandits and Indians. In Hinduism, the hero is Rama. His foe is Ravana.

Key Informants

In any society, certain individuals become known as specialists in their fields: the best potter, the best singer, the best doctor. There are also those known for their wisdom. As Paul Radin points out, these are the native philosophers, found in all societies (1927). Because worldviews are, in one sense, the philosopher's approach to reality, Robert Redfield writes, "The outsider waits. He listens to hear if one or many of the natives have themselves conceived an order in the whole. It is *their* order, *their* categories and *their* emphasis on this rather than that which the student listens for. Every worldview is made of the stuff of philosophy, the nature of all things and their interrelations, and it is the native philosopher whose ordering of the stuff to which we, the outside investigators listen" (1968, 88). It is the people's foundational cognitive, affective, and normative conceptions of reality that is their worldview. The outsider must withhold his suggestions for systematizing the whole until he has heard from the people.

Thick Descriptions

Clifford Geertz pioneered the idea of interpretive anthropology using the method of "thick description" (1983). Thick description involves analyzing particular sociocultural events to understand how the people themselves see and interpret them and to help us understand these ways of seeing reality. One danger is to see other peoples as strange and primitive, as not like us. The other is to see them as just like us and to overlook the differences. Interpretive anthropology seeks to build bridges of understanding that help us translate and bring understanding between different cultures and worldviews. This method involves a deep social and cultural analysis of specific human settings or dramas to understand the cognitive, affective, and evaluative meanings associated with them and to see how these meanings are shaped by their social systems.

Cases

Fundamental to much of anthropological research is the gathering of data on specific cases. Cases are specific social events that have a beginning, process, and an end. Each performance of a ritual is a case. So too is the life of each individual, which, on earth, begins with birth and ends with death. So too is a legal case, which begins with some disturbance of the community peace and order and ends when the case is resolved. In fact, many human situations can be studied as cases.

In studying cases to discover their underlying order and deep meanings, we gather a number of cases in the same domain. For example, we can collect several cases involving disputes and their resolutions through community law. After considering the surface events and the explanations given by the people, we look for deep principles that reveal the people's deep understandings of justice and the means to achieve it. One anthropologist writes, "Play with the data: unless you change and become like little children you will never enter into the kingdom of research."

The first level of the analysis of cases is phenomenology, or detailed analysis of the situation. Here the purpose is to explore and understand particular situations. We do this by looking for patterns in the case or cases and for predictability. In time, in observing many cases, patterns normally appear that help us understand the nature of the case and develop hypotheses about causes and effects in it. In description we can also compare different cases as long as they are comparable, and we can develop neutral categories for comparison.

The second step is to move beyond description to explanation in terms of theories. Here also we generate additional hypotheses for further study. In diachronic analysis we trace the causes for changes over time. For example, we can study the history of a person, a country, or a community. Our aim is to understand why things have happened the way they did. In synchronic analysis we scrutinize the dynamics of complex systems in order to understand how they work. For example, we examine how village rituals function or how conflicts are resolved. We can also begin to formulate general comparative theories. For example, we may want to compare funeral rituals in several different societies or different economic systems.

Deep Philosophical Analysis

Philosophical studies of the deep beliefs of a people give insights into their worldview. Examples of such studies are *Sources of Indian Tradition*, edited by William Theodore De Bary (1958); *African Worlds: Studies in the Cosmological Ideas and Social Values of African Peoples*, edited by Daryll Forde (1954); and *The Indian Mind*, edited by Charles Moore (1967).

Cross-Cultural Comparisons

One powerful heuristic tool for unearthing worldviews is the comparison of cultures to find matching or contrasting themes. This is most easily done with etic themes imposed on all cultures—such as Robert Redfield's themes of time, space, person, other, and causality. These set themes force the observer to examine areas of the culture relevant to the theme and to formulate a worldview of that theme. A more difficult approach is the study, as an initial step, of emic themes emerging out of the study of different cultures. Because each culture is different, themes from one culture cannot always be compared directly with those of another. In these cases a dialogue between worldviews can help provide bridges of understanding and comparison. For example, culture A may have themes 1, 2, 3, and 4. Culture B may have themes 1 and

4 parallel to the themes in culture A, but also themes 5 and 6. One can then ask what in culture B compares to themes 2 and 3 in culture A, and what in culture A compares with 5 and 6 in culture B. This comparison provides a heuristic device to guide us in looking for similarities and contrasts in areas that may not have been consciously explored in either culture. This "dialogue" between worldviews can help us find parallel sets of themes in two cultures. The process can be extended to three or more cultures (fig. 4.9; for a specific example, see appendix 2).

Figure 4.9
CROSS-CULTURAL COMPARISON OF WORLDVIEW THEMES

Culture A			Culture B	Culture C
Theme 1	<—	comparison —>	Theme 1 <— —> ?	
Theme 2	<—	—>	?	—> Theme 2
?	<—	—>	Theme 3 <— —> Theme 3	
Theme 4	<—	—>	Theme 4 <— —> Theme 4	

Comparisons enable us not only to understand particular worldviews but also to understand shifts taking place in worldviews over time. For example, they help us understand what happens to the worldviews of people who become Christians, and to examine whether deep conversion has indeed taken place. They also help us understand intercultural communication and miscommunication. Both areas are critical in our mission outreach around the world.

We now turn our attention to the study of specific worldviews.

5

Worldviews of Small-Scale Oral Societies

Throughout history, small-scale societies have been the basic form of human social organization. These include what social scientists call bands and tribes.[1] It is impossible to do justice to the great number of worldviews found in these societies. At best, we can examine a few themes that are common to many of them, themes that are difficult for modern people to understand. The purpose of this study is not to examine the many thousands of so-called traditional societies but to help modern people understand them better. One problem we face today is the lack of understanding by the modern world of these societies and cultures, which have been the basis of human existence for most of history.

Fundamental presuppositions about the nature of reality underlie the cultural knowledge of band and tribal societies. Although there is considerable variation in these worldviews, some generalizations can be made that apply to most of them. Studying them can help us not only to make sense of their cultures but also to see the worldview we in our own turn bring with us when we minister among them.

1. In some parts of the world "tribe" has become a pejorative term, implying that tribal peoples are primitive because they are not "modern." The problem is not with the word "tribe" but with the word "modern," for any term referring to societies that are not modern are by definition less civilized. These connotations are survivals of the theory of cultural evolution.

Cognitive Themes

We will here look at some worldview themes and counterthemes common to many band and tribal societies. There are differences between bands and tribes, but there are also commonalities that we can explore.

Organic and Holistic

The worlds of small-scale societies are alive and dynamic. Humans are part of a world full of living beings and invisible forces. In such a world, life is not divided into segments such as religion, science, and humanities; public and private domains; social, economic, political, and legal spheres. This holistic worldview is at the heart of all life and affects everything we do: how we eat, whom we marry, how we plant seeds, and where we are buried.

BEINGS AND FORCES

In small-scale societies, the earth that seems lifeless brings forth life in bewildering array—it is the mother of all life. Everywhere one looks there are grasses, bushes, trees, and flowers of many kinds. A multitude of insects breaks the silence of the night. This world is populated with fish, birds, and animals; humans, ancestors, and the unborn; as well as spirits of mountains, rivers, the sky, and the earth, and of sickness and prosperity. There is often a high god who created the earth and its abundance of life but who is now in the heavens. These creations all spring from the earth, which is the lifeblood of the community.

All forms of life live in the same space. A village and its surrounding forest and plains are inhabited by living beings of many kinds: humans—living, deceased, and unborn—witches and ghosts; spirits of trees, rivers, fields, and mountains; spirits of disease and power; animals, birds, fish, insects, and plants. All these beings live together, experiencing love, mutual alliances, rivalries, anger, and jealousy. Rocks, hills, and the earth with its fertility are alive and share the same vital life force and the same world (fig. 5.1). In such a world, no distinction is made between supernatural and natural. All forms of life are interrelated. Plants and animals are experienced as kin, totems, and spiritual helpers, and the forces of nature are seen in terms of the balance of medicine, witchcraft, and various powers.

In many small-scale societies, people believe in a Great Spirit or high god who lives in the heavens and who is uninvolved in the everyday affairs of humans. According to many myths, he created humans, who offended him in some way, prompting him to abandon them.

All beings, including humans, are earthbound. They form their own communities and interact with one another in everyday life. Like humans, animals and spirits are neither good nor evil—they are both. If humans placate spirits, the latter are generous and bless humans with children, health, good crops,

Figure 5.1

<small>TRIBAL WORLDVIEW</small>

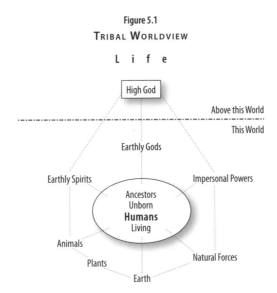

and long lives. If humans neglect or offend them, they are vindictive, bringing diseases, drought, barrenness, and failure in the hunts.

The world is also full of impersonal powers: magic, mana, medicines of many kinds, evil eye, evil mouth, luck, forces of nature, and astrological influences. All matter is animated by the energy of the universe. Certain mountains or forests or rivers are places of power where individuals go to meditate and have more intense experiences of the spirit world and to gain spiritual power. Others, such as burial sites, are often avoided because people fear being attacked by malevolent spirits and powers. To use these impersonal powers for personal advantage, people turn to magic, divination, astrology, and their knowledge of nature, which provide them with formulaic rituals and practices enabling them to control these forces; or they go to specialists, such as magicians, shamans, and astrologers, who control these forces.

<small>HUMAN CENTERED</small>

Tribal worldviews, for the most part, are human centered. The universe is alive with gods, spirits, and nature beings of many kinds, but it is the ancestors, the living members of the society, and their unborn progeny who are center stage. It is the common life they share—as a family, as a lineage or a clan, and as a tribe—that must be preserved by supplicating, coercing, or bribing the surrounding gods and powerful but capricious spirits.

People in many tribal societies see themselves not as separate, autonomous individuals but as part of an endless stream that flows from parent to child and from generation to generation (fig. 5.2). The same blood, the same life that they received from their first ancestors, runs through the veins of everyone

Figure 5.2

THE LINKAGE OF LIFE

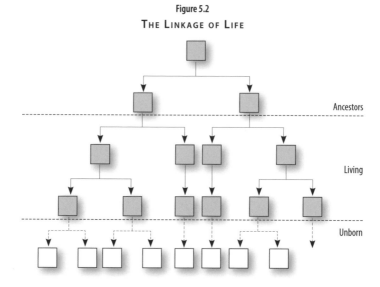

who belongs to the same lineage, clan, and even tribe. Regarding the Akan of West Africa, J. B. Danquah writes, "The Great Ancestor is the great father, and all men of the blood of that ancestor are of Him, and are of one blood with all other men created of His blood and breath. Life, human life, is one continuous blood, from the originating blood of the Great Source of that blood" (1965, 28).

Individuals are important only because they are interconnecting nodes in the larger webs of kinship. Their well-being is dependent on the kin group's well-being, and their life has meaning only as it is shared. The most important obligation of the people, especially the leaders, is to protect and nourish this life. To be an autonomous individual is to be as good as dead.

The tie between parent and child is seen as much more than biological. It is primarily social and spiritual. Not only do children receive their bodies from their parents, but they also acquire their personalities, social identities, and spirits from this flow of life. Consequently, the righteousness of the parents brings blessings to their children, and the sins of the parents bring punishment on their children and their children's children (cf. Exod. 20:5–6).

In the flow of the river of life there are older and younger people: grandparents, parents, children, and grandchildren. The younger generation is responsible for providing the older generation with food by working their fields, performing manual services, and showing them respect and deference in every way. In return, the older generation blesses the younger people, provides them with counsel, and shares its inheritance with them. For example, among the Mende of Sierra Leone, if a son leaves home without permission, the father may curse him. "When the son runs into misfortune, he may return home repentant. He goes first to his mother, who takes him to his father with a gift of rice, fowl, and money. He sits or kneels at his father's feet, holding the father's right foot with his right hand. The father prays a prayer of forgiveness and blesses his prodigal son who has returned home. Disobedience on the part of a son . . . is a grave offense, bringing the most serious consequences, and the sin can only be expiated in a ritual way" (Little 1954, 122).

Ancestors play a central role in human life. Spirit beings fall broadly into two categories: ancestral and nonancestral. Ancestors are the spirits of deceased members of the community. It is widely believed that a person survives after death and that his surviving personality goes to the land of the dead. Animals and grain may be provided for the journey, and money and personal articles are buried with the body, which the deceased person uses to greet the spirits and to demonstrate his earthly position and rank to them. The dead need relatives to perform these funeral rites, because failure to carry out the rites condemns the person's spirit to remain on earth and haunt it.

The relationship between the living and the dead is commonly expressed in a series of rituals in which immediate ancestors increasingly progress toward the realm of more distant ancestors and finally into the great body of nameless ancestors. Ancestors are frequently supplicated at times of plowing, seed planting, and harvesting crops to assure their blessings. Special offerings are made when someone dreams of an ancestor, or there is illness or misfortune in the family because ancestors are angry and want to be fed. It is widely believed that ancestors can help the living and intercede on their behalf with the gods.

The third group of humans is the unborn. If there are no children, the family dies out and the ancestors are forgotten. It is important, therefore, to preserve tribal lands so that the unborn have something when they come. In the southwestern United States, developers sought to buy land from a Native American tribe to build a shopping mall. The elders said they would need to discuss it with the tribe as a whole. They decided they could not sell it. The living and the ancestors were in favor of selling, for it would help the living get rich, but the unborn said that if the land was sold, they would have nothing when they came.

In some tribes, the river of life not only links humans into lineages, clans, and tribes; it is also extended to include animals and sometimes even plants. A particular lineage or clan may be associated with a particular species of animal and/or plant in what is known as totemism. One common myth is that the first ancestor had three children; the first child was a human and became the founder of the Tiger Clan; the second was an animal and the progenitor of tigers; and the third was a plant, the ancestor of tiger lilies. The webs of life extend to include all of nature.

GROUP ORIENTATION

Small nomadic bands are generally characterized by an emphasis on the freedom of the individual but in the context of relationship to others, that is, in group-based or intimate interpersonal relationships rather than through formal roles and institutions. The accumulation of wealth, arrogance, boasting, competition, the desire for status, the tendency to lord it over others, and all behaviors that cause strife are condemned. There is a strong ethic of humility. A successful hunter takes care to avoid giving the impression that he wants or expects special honor or privilege. Among the Algonquin of Canada, for instance, a successful hunter gives most of the kill to others. When two men hunt, each tries to jockey the other into killing a moose, while making sure the moose does not get away.

This ethic of humility is closely tied to a value of sharing. Greatness lies not in accumulating wealth but in the ability to share with others, and to do so without taking credit for it. A leader is not one who demands honor but one who leads while making others feel good.

In horticultural societies, human life finds its ultimate expression in the community more than in the autonomous individual. Few themes in tribal worldviews are more difficult for modern people to understand than this group-centeredness. Most modernists take it for granted that all people see themselves as autonomous, individual humans. Self-reliance, personal achievement, individual choice, and inalienable individual rights are unquestionably good in their minds. Group-oriented people, however, need unity, blending, fuzziness, and mystery. They need to be surrounded, not to be alone. They are horrified by that which divides and separates. The sorcerer is the loner.

In most small horticultural societies, people see groups as the important units of society—families, lineages, clans, bands, and tribes. Individuals exist only in and for the groups. As long as their group exists, they cannot die, for they are remembered as ancestors. Their existence is tied to the unity and well-being of their group. Personal wants are subordinate to the needs of the group. Group loyalty, self-effacement, self-sacrifice, sharing, and hospitality are cardinal virtues. Self-centeredness, hoarding, stinginess, and bringing shame on one's group by one's own behavior are sin. In such a world, life takes on great meaning. D. Zahan writes, "The cosmos does not constitute a fixed, cold, and mute world. On the contrary, it is a world charged with meanings and laden with messages, a world which 'speaks.' Thus man finds in his surrounding a partner with whom he can enter into communication, with which he must in fact maintain an almost constant dialogue if he wants to be informed about himself" (1979, 81).

Harmony is essential to group life, but it is precarious and threatened by the conflicts and uncertainties of everyday life. Change, therefore, is often viewed as a threat. Social controls and community rituals play an important part in creating and enhancing harmony. They provide every person a place within the group and prescribe their behavior. They affirm the importance of the community in the life of the people.

In group-centered, present-centered, particularist societies, relational categories are the basis for living. Women are first mothers, then wives, daughters, elders, chiefs, and ancestors in relationship to specific people. That they are females is secondary. Moreover, the categories are often fuzzy. Outsiders who intermarry with members of such societies progress through stages of belonging to the group.

Many signs in oral societies are symbols pointing to realities and evoking images in the mind.[2] But important signs, such as a person's name, are often seen as icons in which the sign not only refers to the person but also shapes the person's personality. To name a child Brave Eagle is to give the child the characteristics of the eagle. When a person takes on a new identity, as in initiation into adulthood or conversion to another religion, he or she is given a new name. For example, people in the Old Testament were given new names when they entered new relationships with God (Gen. 17:5; 32:28; Num. 13:16). To say a person's name is to invoke his or her presence. It is often taboo for commoners to say the name of the chief, wives to use the names of their husbands, and the living to utter the names of the dead.

In a world conceived as full of life, maintaining harmonious relationships with other living beings is essential to life. The Eskimo pours fresh water into the mouth of the seal he has caught because it was tired of saltwater and so let itself be caught. The farmer makes an offering to the earth, asking for forgiveness for the pain he inflicts in planting the seed. The pastoralist blesses his cattle so that they will bear young.

Because relationships must constantly be negotiated, it is impossible for humans to fully plan their lives. A man may agree to meet a friend the next morning, but if at the last moment relatives stop by, the ancestors demand food, his cow has a calf, or the spirits harass him, it may be afternoon before he can come. People learn to live in the ever-changing flux of relationships in everyday life.

Shame plays a more important role in group-oriented communities than does guilt. When people fail, they feel ashamed that they have let down their group, their ancestors, and their gods. They feel less a sense of guilt at having personally broken some universal moral law. In fact, there may be little awareness of such laws. All important norms are group norms.

Shame is also tied to success and honor. A group-oriented student is ashamed when the teacher asks her to stand up because she has the best grade in the class. This makes her stand out from the group. Shame is a dynamic that pressures people to conform to their group and so maintains harmony and peace.

Closely tied to shame is the value placed on reconciliation and saving face. Wrongdoers are punished, but in the end they must be restored to everyday

2. Here we are following Charles Peirce's theory of signs, which holds that all signs are triadic: there is a form, a reality to which it points (external or objective dimension), and the image it evokes in the mind (subjective dimension). In other words, signs mediate between the outside world and the inside world of the mind. Peirce also divides signs into indexes, symbols, and icons.

life in the community. If they are not allowed to have some sense of human dignity, they carry resentments that destroy relationships and keep matters from being settled. Consequently, after a person has made restitution, there is often a ritual of reconciliation to put the past behind and reincorporate the person into the group. The greatest punishment in these societies is to be banned and shunned. A person who does not submit to the group's decision is ostracized. He continues to live in the village, but everyone treats him as nonexistent. This is a far greater punishment than being put in jail.

Fertility

Fertility is important in an organic worldview. Reproduction is essential for the continuation of life. The fertility cycle shapes people's view of time. Crops are planted, harvested, and replanted. Animals and humans have their rounds of birth, marriage or mating, and death. Rituals are performed at these points to ensure fertility in nature and humans. Prayers are offered to game that is killed so that its relatives are not offended and will allow themselves to be taken in a hunt. Water is poured on the ground to slake its thirst and to encourage it to provide a bountiful harvest. Dances are performed to ensure good rains. Seed and fields are blessed, and the first fruits of harvest are offered to the ancestors, spirits, and gods in thanks. In pastoral societies, rituals are performed to safeguard the reproduction of animals.

Equally important are rites that guarantee fertility among humans. There are few evils so great as barrenness, which is often seen as the curse of a witch or as a sign that gods or ancestors are angry. Consequently, there are many rituals associated with marriage, pregnancy, and birth, rituals to make women fertile and to safeguard them and infants during the dangerous months surrounding birth, when they are particularly vulnerable to malevolent beings and forces. Equally important are other life-cycle rites that mark the other major transitions in life: initiation into adulthood and transformation into an ancestor.

Space and Time

For people in traditional small societies, the earth is the place where the living, the ancestors, and God meet. For modern people, the earth is a raw, passive fact, the object of exploitation and economic and industrial profitability.

Land

At the heart of tribal life is mother earth, the basis of life. The earth provides the food that keeps people alive and the world in which they live. The land is also where the ancestors are buried. Its important features tell the stories of their lives. "Here is where Great Chief Big Hawk defeated the enemy in battle." "That tree was planted over the grave of our great-grandfather who

saved the people from drought." "Over there is where our ancestors now live."
Brian Walsh writes,

> If "where we are" is the land that we experience as our mother, a world of
> profound harmony in which animals, plants, stars, moon, sun, and wind are
> amongst "all my relations," and we find our fundamental identity (answering
> the "who we are" question) in being children of the land, kind to the animals
> and members of a clan, then the home making will require that we maintain
> this sensitive balance amongst the relations. Human homes cannot be divorced
> from animal homes, nor should they be constructed in a way that renders our
> animal kin homeless. (2006, 245)

Walsh notes that the use of space in villages in small-scale societies reflects
the social order. The location and size of houses mark the leaders, the elders
of clans, and the common folk. Forest lands and fishing rights on streams
belong to different clans. The organization of houses is culturally influenced
and reflects deep worldview assumptions. Certain parts of the house and the
village are the domain of the women, other parts of the men.

Houses and land become homes when they become storehouses of personal and corporate memories shaped and stored by myths and founding
stories. "This room is where our ancestors and unborn live." "That bow and
arrow were carved by my grandfather when I was initiated into manhood."
History and grounding myths are not recorded on printed pages, but tied to
geographic sites and told and retold by parents to their children as they pass
these places.[3]

Time separates people from different generations, but space brings them
together. A certain ancestor lived more than a hundred years ago, but he built
this very house. In a sense Christians understand this religious view of space
when they walk the roads of Palestine. We sit at the well that Jacob dug; we
walk in the garden of Gethsemane and remember that this is where Jesus walked
the night before his crucifixion. Space brings the past into the present.

Above all, land is important because it is sacred. It belongs to the gods, who
gave it to the people, who protected it from great enemies. We see this in the
Old Testament when the Hittites, the Philistines, the Moabites, and other tribes
equated their gods with their people and their lands. Land in these societies is
not a commodity that people can buy and sell. It belongs to the lineages and
tribe, which allocate its use to their members. If there is extra land, strangers
may be given permission to use it until the people need it. In return, the strangers

---

3. Brian Walsh observes that the relocation of people, such as the Native Americans, destroys
their cultures, and their social order disintegrates because they are taken from their lands so
richly tied to their stories and placed in standardized housing that has no stories or memories
for the people (2006). Elie Wiesel writes, "Ultimately, one might say that the opposite of homes
is not distance but forgetfulness. One who forgets, forgets everything, including the roads leading homeward" (quoted in Walsh 2006, 246).

are expected to give gifts of appreciation and return the land on request, for it belongs not only to the living but also to the living dead and the unborn.[4]

In many small horticultural societies a sharp distinction is made between the geographic worlds of men and of women. For example, among the Lele of Southwest Congo, men are associated with the forest and women with the village and surrounding fields (Douglas 1954). The prestige of the forest is great. God gave it to the Lele as the source of all good and necessary things, the sacred medicines, and above all the hunt and meat. Good meat, like antelope and wild pig, comes from the forest. Goats, dogs, and rats, which are found around the village, are considered unclean. Men hunt in the forest using weapons and sacred medicines, boasting that they can work all day in the forest without feeling hungry. The forest is the source of all good things, but it is also a place of danger, not only for women but often for men as well. A tree may fall on their heads, they may twist an ankle or cut themselves with a knife, but these events derive from their own moral status. If women enter the forest, it endangers the whole village.

Women are associated with the homes, the village, and the grasslands, where they clear small fields and plant maize, manioc, and raffia palm trees. They cook the meat the men bring home from the hunt, but they cannot climb trees to draw palm wine or weave and sew raffia clothes. These are men's tasks. Women draw water, gather firewood, cultivate fishponds in the marshy streams, cultivate salt-yielding plants, and prepare salt from the ashes.

In parts of Papua New Guinea, women live in the village, raise crops, and care for children. Men hunt game. At night men gather in the men's longhouse for fellowship and to plan the important things of life—politics, future hunts, and raids on neighboring villages. Occasionally they visit their families, but men's lives center around the longhouse.

Time

For the most part, people around the world are concerned about life here and now. They seek meaning in this existence and want a good life on earth. They are faced with the problems of daily life such as diseases, droughts, floods, and sudden death. When food is available, all eat exuberantly. When it is gone, people bear the pangs of hunger with fortitude, just as other creatures do. They offer sacrifices to the spirits and use magic to influence nature. In the end, however, they are aware that they are dependent on the spirits and forces of nature for their lives.

Life focuses on event time, not clock time. Everyday events are loosely correlated with the cycles of night and day and the seasons of the year. People

---

4. Native Americans let early European immigrants settle on their land and accepted trade goods and money as gifts of appreciation. When they asked settlers to return the land, the settlers called them "Indian givers," because the settlers thought they had bought the land.

order their lives on the basis of specific events, such as planting and harvesting, and birth, marriage, and death. Time is not a commodity to be bought and sold or something that can be measured or that runs out. Moreover, many events are part of larger cycles of day and night and seasons of the year. For example, it is now work-in-the-field time. We will work for a while, and we will continue to work some more. The present event, therefore, has past, present, and future in it. When we finish working in the field, it will be feed-the-animals time. Now work-time is totally in the past. Later it will be eat-the-evening-meal time, sleep-time, and then work-in-the-field time again. Life, too, is marked by cycles of birth, initiation into adulthood, marriage, and death. Individuals come and go, but from the perspective of the group, life continues, constantly renewing itself through offspring.

The past is not sharply distinguished from the present. People do not think of having a history that stretches out linearly behind them. Rather the past is the timeless storehouse of ancestors and traditions—the stories told today of those still remembered. Likewise, the future is seen as an extension of the present. People do not think much about the distant future. The view of time might be described as the present event with past, present, and future in it (in a church service, past-present-future are part of the event), the recent past, and the present anticipation of the near future.

Because time endlessly repeats itself, there is often little sense of a long-term history as a progression of events leading to some future culmination. The important stories are those of the high god and of the origins of the tribe, which are past. Present events have little lasting importance, and few group-oriented societies keep track of histories and biographies. For most, land and space are more important than time and history.

One important exception to this ahistorical view of time is the Israelites in the Old Testament. For them, Israel's history was closely tied to the cosmic history of God's acts and therefore assumed great significance. Moreover, their personal biographies took on meaning because these were part of Israel's history.

This does not mean that traditional people have no interest in ultimate realities beyond death. Paul Radin notes that there are philosophers in all societies who struggle with the greater issues of life and seek the high god who lies beyond the immediate world of local gods, spirits, and ancestors (1927).

Orality

W. J. Ong observes that most bands and tribes are oral societies (1969). Their worlds are built more on sound than sight. Such worlds are highly immediate, personal, and relational. Words are spoken in the context of specific relationships and die as soon as they have been said. Communication is a flux of immediate encounters between humans full of emotions and personal interests. It is only with the advent of recording machines that sounds can be preserved.

As noted in chapter 1, sounds point to the invisible and speak of mystery and therefore lead people to believe in beings that they cannot see. Sounds are widely thought to be powerful and sacred. To say the right sounds is to cause things to happen. Ong notes, "Sound signals the present use of power, since sound must be in active production in order to exist at all" (1969, 637). The right sounds can cause rain to fall. Other sounds, such as drumming and shouting, protect people from evil spirits.

Oral communication is highly relational. It takes place in specific contexts, is spoken to a particular audience or person, and focuses on particular messages. It communicates paramessages, such as feelings and moral judgments, through tone of voice, gesture, facial expressions, and standing distances. It requires listening and responding as well as remembering. It invites moral judgment and response.

In oral societies, knowledge is stored in the forms of stories, parables, songs, aphorisms, proverbs, riddles, poems, creeds, and catechisms that can be easily remembered. It is also stored in rituals that are living reenactments of primordial events. Regarding oral societies, Neil Postman writes,

> When a dispute arises, the complainants come before the chief of the tribe and state their grievances. With no written law to guide him, the task of the chief is to search through his vast repertoire of proverbs and sayings to find one that suits the situation and is equally satisfying to both complainants. That accomplished, all parties are agreed that justice has been done, that truth has been served. You will recognize, of course, that this was largely the method of Jesus and other biblical figures who, living in an essentially oral culture, drew upon all of the resources of speech, including mnemonic devices, formulaic expressions and parables, as a means of discovering and revealing truth. (1985, 18)

Proverbs, parables, and sayings are not supplementary to logical argument. They are the substance of thought itself, the storehouses of wisdom.[5]

Particularism

Small-scale societies have a particularist view of reality. In contrast to modern people, who look for abstract universal laws that apply equally to all humans (whether these laws be scientific, legal, or moral), tribal people focus on the particularity of each event. Each tribe has its own gods and ancestors who

5. Postman notes that in literate societies, proverbs are relegated to teaching children. Judges and lawyers, university professors, and pastors do not regard proverbs as relevant responses to disputes. They depend on written materials to define and organize the method of finding truth. In the academic world the published word has greater prestige and authenticity than the spoken word.

live on its soil. Each recognizes that other tribes have other gods and ancestors and do not try to convert them to its own beliefs. In fact, it is impossible for others to adopt a tribe's beliefs without becoming a part of its society through marriage or adoption.

When wars arise, each tribe calls on its gods and ancestors for help, and victories and defeats are attributed to their power. For instance, the Philistines and other tribes thought Israel's God was the God of the hills, because that is where the Israelites lived (1 Kings 20:23–28). In contrast, Jehovah declared himself to be not a territorial god but the God of the universe.

This focus on particularity can be seen in everyday events. When the chief shows up at a modern hospital, the doctor expects him to stand in line like everyone else, whereas his people expect him to go to the head of the line because he is more important.[6] The missionary doctor charges everyone the same for medicines. The people expect the rich to pay more for the same treatment. The particulars of each case must be taken into account to determine how a person should act.

Particularism extends to identities. People of one's own tribe are humans. Those of other tribes are not fully human. The word the people use for foreigners is often "subhumans," and they can be treated as such.

Concrete Functional Logics

All humans depend on human reason, but different cultures use different logics to order their thoughts. For example, modern, educated elites value abstract analytical thought based on intrinsic, digital categories. They believe that the principles of logic they discover are universal or true for all people everywhere. Traditional group-oriented societies do use abstract reasoning in specific situations, but their fundamental logic is concrete-functional, based on relational, often fuzzy, categories.

FUNCTIONAL LOGIC

As we noted earlier, A. R. Luriia found that the Kirghiz of Central Asia, when presented with pictures of people and objects, grouped two adults with a child rather than with a third adult and chose two wheels and pliers rather than putting three wheels together. They argued that with two wheels and pliers, they could make a cart. Besides, what would they do with three wheels? They needed either two or four. He found them unwilling to depend only on abstract, propositional logic and intrinsic sets. Luriia told a Kirghiz man, "Cotton grows only in warm, dry places. In England it is cold and it rains all the time. Can cotton grow there?" The man replied, "I don't know. I've heard of England, but I don't know if cotton grows there." When Luriia repeated

---

6. Of course, presidents, prime ministers, and heads of state in the modern world do not stand in line in hospitals, airports, or supermarkets.

the syllogism, another man replied, "I don't know. . . . If it's cold it won't grow, while if it's hot, it will. From your words, I would have to say that cotton shouldn't grow there. But I would have to know what spring is like there, what kinds of nights they have" (1976, 111).

This does not mean people in oral societies are incapable of abstract propositional thought. Placed in schools where this form of thinking is taught, they soon learn to think this way. In everyday life, however, they think of things in concrete contexts, not in terms of abstract intrinsic categories. Thus they are often accused by modern people of having only a primitive mentality. The inaccuracy of this judgment becomes clearer when we realize that we ourselves do not use abstract logic of this type in our everyday lives. If we have too many people to fit in our car, do we leave the child because she "does not belong with the adults"?

Logic of Magic

Broadly speaking, magic is the control of this-worldly forces, such as mana, by the proper use of chants, amulets, and rituals. It does not involve supplicating spirit beings in the hope that they will respond. People believe that saying the right formulaic sounds causes rain to come or protects them from diseases or evil spirits. In this sense, magic is more akin to the logic of modern science than that of religion.

Our modern temptation is to see magic as meaningless, as childish fantasies and prelogical thought. But the logic of magic gives meaning to and control over people's existence by creating a harmonious world in which everything is connected to everything else, and events in one part of the world cause changes in other parts. This connectedness is based not on biophysical connections alone but on assumed transphysical realities underlying the world.

Sir James Frazer noted two laws that underlie magical thinking (1922). The first is the "law of sympathy," or homeopathy—the principle that "like produces like." For example, a shaman pours water to produce rain, and a magician makes a doll resembling his enemy and sticks pins into it, causing the enemy to become ill and die. Similarly, the crowd at a football game leans toward the goal line trying to help their team make a touchdown. The second is the "law of contagion," the principle that things that have once been in contact continue ever after to act on each other. For instance, the magician may do magic on a piece of clothing, a fingernail clipping, or a strand of hair from a victim, causing that person to grow weak; a wife may secretly perform magic on her husband's food if she suspects that he is having an affair; or a young man may cast a spell on a young woman to make her fall in love with him.

The use of magic is essentially pragmatic—if something seems to work, then keep on doing it until it no longer does. There is little need to explain why things work, only to know that they do.

Magic is amoral; it can be used for good or for evil. In fact, what is good in the eyes of the one performing the magic may be destructive to the person on the receiving end. Most magic is used to benefit people, particularly when it is practiced by the community. A shaman or medicine man performs rituals for a family, a village, or a tribe to control the weather, prevent diseases, assure victories in battle over enemies, punish deviants, and bring prosperity. Practiced individually and secretly, however, magic is often used for selfish and evil ends. A man seeks to gain advantage over a neighbor using "waste-away" magic. He curses a rival to kill him or casts a love spell on a woman to compel her into an illicit relationship.

Affective Themes

Little study has been done on affective themes in band and tribal societies. As we noted earlier, Ruth Benedict, drawing on her prior work as a novelist and poet, used three Greek mythical figures to describe the deep affective themes of different cultures. The Zuni of New Mexico stress emotional reserve, sobriety, self-effacement, and inoffensiveness. The Kwakiutl of Vancouver Island seek violent, frenzied experiences to break out of the usual sensory routine and express personal emotions with great abandon, seeking ecstasy through fasting, torture, drugs, and frenzied dance. The dominant emotions of the Dobuans of Melanesia are hostility and treachery, and the people live in a state of perpetual fear of one another.

Small-scale societies are rich in aesthetic culture. Songs, dance, painting, body decorations, clothes, dramas, house decorations, and storytelling give expression to the deep feelings of the people. Unfortunately, given our modern stress on truth and our neglect of feelings and morals in the academic community, this aesthetic culture is little understood. It is vital that ministers and missionaries research affective themes in the cultures in which they serve, for feelings as much as ideas determine the way people live.

Evaluative Themes

A world of interpersonal relationships is a moral world. Impersonal forces such as gravity and fire do not sin. Sin in group-oriented societies involves a break in relationships between humans, ancestors, gods, spirits, animals, and nature. The consequence is a loss of peace and a breakdown of community. Reconciliation is the restoration of relationships and harmony.

In a relational world, high value is placed on sharing and taking responsibility for those in one's group. Great people are not those who keep what they have for themselves but those who share freely with those in need.

Ancestors play an important role in maintaining moral standards in bands and tribes. They punish faults and reward good with peace, health, and fertility. Witchcraft, too, shapes people's sense of morality. It provides them an avenue to blame others for their misfortunes and to absolve themselves.

Diachronic Themes

As we have seen, myths are an indispensable part of the lives of oral people. They give meaning to the universe, express the people's deepest feelings, and define their moral order. Myths store information in ways that are easily remembered—they are told and retold on many occasions.

Origin Myths

Origin myths, which explain how the world came into existence, are the most universal kind of myth. They often tell of gods and goddesses who created the earth or gave it existence through their death and dismemberment. Others describe the origin of the first humans and explain how they came to suffer and die. Other origin myths describe how humans acquired fire, bows and arrows, and houses, and how they came to domesticate plants and animals.

Separation Myths

Separation myths are also widespread. They explain how humans lost their pristine state in paradise and came to suffer toil and separation from God. According to the Nuer cattle herders of southern Sudan, the sky and the earth were originally connected by a rope attached to the Tree of Creation by which humans first entered the world. Every day people climbed down the rope from the sky to obtain their food. When people died on earth, they ascended to the sky via the rope for a short time and were rejuvenated. The Nuer have different versions explaining how the rope was severed, making death a permanent human condition. In one, a girl descended from the sky with some companions to get food on earth. She met and had sexual relations with a young man. He had originally come from the sky, but he had spent his entire life on earth, never reascending. When it was time for the girl to return, she refused, declaring her love for the young man. Her companions ascended to the sky and cut the rope, severing forever the means for immortality. Consequently, the people are now separated from Kwoth, the high god, not because of sin, but because of an impetuous young girl and her vindictive companions.

The Dinka of the Sudan believe that in the beginning Nhialic, the high god, and humans were close friends, and people climbed up to the sky by a rope. There was no death or illness, and a minimum of labor was required to produce food. But the sky was close to the earth, so humans had to be careful not to strike Nhialic when planting and pounding the millet. One day a woman using a long-handled hoe to plant millet raised it upward and struck Nhialic. He was angry and withdrew far from earth. Thereafter people had to labor for food and suffer sickness and death. In another version, the woman used a long pole to pound the millet and struck Nhialic seated above her.

Culture Heroes

Many myths in small-scale societies tell of mythic figures who live between the world of humans and that of the gods, and who in ancient days turned people into full humans by teaching them culture. Typically these cultural heroes brought fire that turned raw meat into food and melted rocks into metal. They introduced language, agriculture, and techniques for brewing beer and baking bread. They taught people arts, crafts, laws, ceremonies, and social organization. They were the link between the original sacred realm and the mundane world of ordinary human life. Culture heroes also defeated monsters and other evil forces threatening human existence. Often in the end, however, these culture heroes, like the gods, became offended with human ineptness and left humans to their own devices.

Catastrophes

Myths of cosmic cataclysms are widespread. Some occurred in the past, some recur periodically, and some are expected to lead to the end of the world or to a new creation in the future. Stories of floods are common. Other cosmic catastrophes include earthquakes, conflagrations, falling mountains, and plagues. Often these are caused by the anger of the gods because of the sins of human beings. In many of these myths of calamities, most humans are killed, and only a few survivors remain to repopulate a virgin earth, now purified of previous evils. Judgment is followed by order and morality.

In some apocalyptic myths, judgment will take place in the future, and the world will cease to exist. In a myth of the Caroline Islands, Aurepick, the Creator's son, will submerge the island with a cyclone when he sees that the chief no longer has any concern for his subjects. The Nigritos of the Malay Peninsula believe that Kavei, an evil god, will destroy the earth and all its inhabitants when people no longer obey him (Eliade 1975, 56–57). In these myths the destruction is final.

Other myths tell of a destruction followed by the re-creation of an earthly paradise in which the dead will rise, and sickness and the old earth will be abolished. The Choctaw Indians and the Eskimo of North America believe that the world will be destroyed by fire, but that the spirit of humans will return, reclothed with flesh, to inhabit their traditional lands. Underlying these myths is the belief that the world is degenerating, and that destruction and re-creation are needed to restore the cosmic order.

In many eschatological myths, creation, degeneration, and destruction are followed by re-creation, degeneration, and destruction in an endless cycle of time. In Judeo-Christian cosmology the final judgment occurs once. Time is not circular but linear and irreversible. In it human history begins in sacred history and ends in sacred history. The belief in an imminent end of present human history and the coming of Christ was strong during the persecutions of the early church, but receded after Christianity became the official religion of the Roman Empire.

Millenarianism is widespread in tribal societies around the world today and is often the result of the encounter of traditional worldviews with Christianity. These include the Melanesian cargo cults, the Native American Ghost Dance movements, and many of the African and Chinese independent churches. Frequently these non-Western millenarian movements look for a day when the local people will obtain all the material goods—the "cargo"—that Western peoples seemingly have. This will transpire, they say, only through cosmic cataclysms in which God will give them what is rightly theirs and punish the colonialists who are rich because they have stolen the goods God sent to them.

When people from small-scale societies come to Christ, it is important that their conversion touch all levels of their culture and society, and that it be corporate as well as personal. If conversion takes place at the conscious levels of culture but not at the worldview level as well, the result is Christo-paganism—a syncretism in which the forms of the gospel are present, but the heart of it is missing.

Our study here is not a definitive or exhaustive study of the worldviews of small-scale societies. Rather, it is an all-too-simple model that needs more study, but it can help us examine the specific worldview of the people we serve. Hopefully it also makes us aware of how distant our modern and postmodern worldviews are from people in traditional societies and from a biblical worldview. As we will see later, in many ways tribal worldviews are closer to Scripture than those of the modern missionaries who come to serve in these societies.

6

Peasant Worldviews

During early human history most people lived in small-scale societies. Today, more than two billion peasants live in more than a million villages. These rural communities form the backbone of the great civilizations of China, India, Europe, Russia, as well as in many parts of North and South America.

There is great diversity among peasant societies and worldviews. Peasants live in low, hot, flat coastal areas, and in high, cold, rugged mountains. They are rural cultivators, using animals to plow, and many irrigate their fields. They raise animals for work and food.

Peasants live in two worlds. On the one hand, they are poor, subsistence-oriented, rural people living in relatively isolated communities. They care most about what is going on in their families, fields, and villages. On the other hand, they are tied to the world outside their communities. They are subject to outside governments and markets; taxation, military conscription, and market forces intrude on their everyday concerns.

Eric Wolf (1955) makes a useful distinction between closed and open peasant communities. The former are more inward-looking than the latter. Closed communities tend to produce basic grains for food rather than commercial crops and are more isolated from the cultural, historical, and political life of the larger social and national systems in which they live. Open communities have more economic, political, and cultural ties to the outside world. The influences of the outside world are more direct and more important in the everyday lives of the peasants. Today Coca-Cola, transistor radios, fertilizers, and sewing machines are found in many peasant villages.

Cognitive Themes

Given the great diversity in peasant societies, it is difficult to speak of a "peasant worldview." A few common themes, however, do emerge. Such themes, rather than providing answers, can serve as preliminary heuristic tools to think more deeply about the specific peasant communities we serve.

Small Bounded Community/State

Peasant communities are microcosmic systems embedded in larger socio-cultural systems. For the most part they are self-subsistent and self-contained. Agriculture and aquaculture are the primary bases for life. Like horticultural-ists, most peasants are people of the land. As a result, the theme of fertility and a focus on crops and the rhythm of the seasons play a central role in the people's minds. So too do concerns with power and with pragmatic solutions to the concrete problems of everyday life.

These similarities to tribal worldviews, however, mask a fundamental shift in how land is perceived. In most tribes, land belongs to God and is given to tribes, clans, and lineages for use. It cannot be bought or sold. The opposite is true in most peasant societies: land ultimately belongs to the state. Individuals may own it, but the state can tax it and confiscate it through the right of eminent domain. Furthermore, individuals can buy and sell land. Land is an economic commodity rather than a divine heritage.

This shift leads to worldview differences between peasants and the rulers of the state. The peasants are close to the land and look to it for their sustenance; the rulers consider land to be a political and economic means of exploitation for personal or national gain. If their control of the land and the peasants is lost, the state dies. Consequently, ruling bodies must maintain armies to defend their land, attack other states to expand their own territories, and dominate their peasants to prevent insurgency.

Community/Individual

Peasant villages are communities with a strong sense of identity and com-pleteness. Villagers sense that they are part of a community greater than the sum of its members. They are locals, homegrown, who see their villages as their bounded, microcosmic world, where they hope to live out their lives from the cradle to the grave. Most members have little desire to leave and enter the big, dangerous world outside. In their village they know how to live and have a sense of security and identity.

COMMUNITY AS ONE WHOLE

The village is made up of the land and its inhabitants. This includes people, but it often also includes the ancestors; local earthbound spirits; animals; plants, such as ancient trees associated with historic memories; particular hills and rivers; and distinct sacred sites, such as the tomb of a saint or a temple housing gods known for certain powers. These all reside in the traditional, often sacred boundaries that separate them from neighboring villages. Local spirits have no power beyond these boundaries. Here rites involving relationships between villages are performed.

The sense of community in small-scale societies is based on the intimate knowledge its members have of one another and their shared sense of local history. Gossip spreads news; festivals unite the community in corporate rituals; and markets bring farmers together with village craftsmen, religious and political leaders, and beggars. Robert Redfield writes:

> The people of a band or a village or small town know each of the other members of that community as parts of one another; each is strongly aware of just that group of people, as belonging together: the "we" that each inhabitant uses recognizes the separateness of that band or village from all others. Moreover, to the member of the more isolated band or village the community is a round of life, a small cosmos; the activities and institutions lead from one into all the others so that to the native himself the community is not a list of tools and customs, it is an integrated whole. (1989, 10)

Such a way of thinking does not break the community into parts that are put together. The whole is more real and greater than the sum of the parts. In other words, the community functions as an organic, not a mechanistic, system.

Integration in peasant communities varies greatly. In China, Native North America, and other parts of the world, the community is socially and culturally fairly homogeneous: members usually share language, ethnicity, religion, and community rituals, and there may even be shared kinship relationships. In other peasant communities, such as villages in South India, integration is not achieved through a strong sense of belonging to one group or one kind of people. Here the same village often has Muslims, Hindus, and Christians. Hindus are divided into touchable castes and untouchable castes. Gypsies and other transient castes live within village boundaries as very distinct cultural enclaves different from the others. Moreover, village Indians are strong individualists at heart. Integration here is based on the social and cultural systems that unite different kinds of peoples into a whole based on interdependence for the sake of mutual survival. The Brahmans—the Hindu priests—maintain relationships between the village and the high gods. The high Sudras are the farmers, the lower Sudras the weavers, potters, laundrymen, barbers, and toddy tappers, as well as magicians and priests to the local spirits. The untouchables are the field laborers and sweepers who keep the village public places clean, including removing the carcasses of dead animals. Integration is based not on a shared sense that all are one kind of people, but on a realization that as different kinds of people they form a larger organic community in which each caste must play its part if the community is to survive.

Small communities have a strong sense of corporate identity. Members are homegrown people who are born and raised in the village, people whose stories are known and who are linked to particular families and lineages and to the village as a whole. Those people are "us."

There may be minority enclaves in a village, but they are local residents and so part of the community as a whole. In a South Indian village these enclaves would include Muslims, who live in separate *palems*, or sectors, have their own culture and religion, and their own social system. Such enclaves also include the Gypsies, who live in separate *tandas*, or hamlets, adjacent to the village and have their own culture, social organization, and gods and who are neither Hindu nor Muslim.

Outsiders

Although individuals and groups of people who come from outside and pass through the village may participate in its life, they remain "others" or "them." Most commonly, they are people from neighboring villages. They may be connected with the village through marriage, trade, and politics, but they are not members. In many ways the relationships combine tensions of friendship and rivalry, as villages compete and ally with one another in regional life.

In South Indian villages these outsiders may be hunting and gathering people from the nearby forest who come to trade forest goods for food and clothing. They also include traditional itinerant caste men such as bards, minstrels, members of drama teams, entertainers, and religious specialists and holy men, all of whom are part of the tradition of the country. They visit the village on regular rounds and are hosted during their stays, but they are not part of the village (Hiebert 1971).

In most of the world, outsiders include government officials who come from the cities that are the centers of nation-states to collect taxes and to enforce law and order. Government agents, such as police officers and revenue collectors, may be stationed in the village, but they too are outsiders—treated with due respect, but with distance. To inform the police of misconduct in the village is to violate one's loyalty to the village and face the threat of being ostracized from the community.

Another group of outsiders are traders and businessmen who come regularly to the weekly markets to buy and sell goods to local craftsmen and merchants and to lend money to local moneylenders.

Yet another group is that of the religious leaders who come from the centers of high religion in the city. They include the Muslim mullahs, the Hindu priests and holy men, the Christian bishops, and the Shinto priests.[1] In many parts of the world, they are highly honored, even revered. They often have more power over local villages than do outside government and business leaders. Religious outsiders also include pilgrims passing through on their way to distant shrines.

Finally, there are total strangers: unknowns who pass through the countryside, foreigners who visit the village as missionaries, and now, tourists and entertainers. They are truly "others," not humans in the sense that locals are.

OUTSIDE WORLD

Beyond the village and its neighboring region is the outside world, the world of cities and nation-states, outside businesses, and centers of high religion. This world is foreign, dangerous, and "other." A power differential exists between macrosystems and microsystems, between the political power and wealth of the centers and of the peasant community, between the literacy of the city and the orality of the village, and between the religious establishments of high, literate religions.

Oral/Literate

One of the inventions that changed human history is writing. Oral societies use pictograms and ideograms, but the creation of logo-syllabic scripts enabled people to express both words and syllables. The characters used were mainly nonpictorial and arbitrary.[2] The written word transformed the way societies were organized. It enabled people to communicate over long distances and to store vast amounts of information that was fixed in time. It gave rise to cities, city-states, nations, and the global world. It also led to the emergence of high cultures over against folk cultures, which are often more oral in nature (fig. 6.1).

Writing divided peasant villages into literate and nonliterate people, but its impact was not what we see in modern cultures. Rather, literate people emerged as classes of specialists such as priests, whose major function was to communicate to and about God, and scribes and secretaries who served the local headmen and rulers, the latter of whom were often nonliterate, in recording historical events and making treaties. Written texts were used by these specialists primarily as a way of storing and recalling information. In practice their primary form of communication with the people was oral. The Brahman priest may use a text, much the way a preacher uses his notes, to

1. Leaders of local religious rites and practices, such as magicians, shamans, spiritists, and priests to the local gods and goddesses, are generally members of the local community, not outsiders.

2. Jack Goody traces the origins of truly alphabetical signs to the Sumerians who inhabited the lower part of Mesopotamia around 3100 BC (1987, 28).

Figure 6.1
ORAL AND LITERATE CULTURES

Oral	Literate
• audial	• visual
• immediate, face-to-face	• mediated, delayed, one step removed
• personal, relational, involves feedback	• impersonal, no feedback
• tied to specific local contexts	• detached from contexts of time and space
• dialogical, transactional	• unidirectional
• multivocal: cognitive, affective, and evaluative	• monovocal: primarily cognitive
• transitory, fluid, short-lived, remembered	• stored, permanent, can be reproduced exactly
• stored in stories, songs, proverbs, poetry, dramas, rituals	• stored on stones, parchments, paper
• believe in invisible, hear it	• believe in what you see, no invisible
• meandering discussions	• linear arguments
• spiral, meandering progression	• linear progression
• concrete functional logic	• linear logic
• affirms subjectivity of knowledge	• affirms objectivity of knowledge
• affirms diversity	• homogenizes

guide his chants, but it is the oral chant, not the written, that has power. When schools were founded, they were religious training centers, such as Muslim madrasas, Hindu *muts*, and Christian monasteries, which prepared people for religious ministries. Education was not a means for individual advancement or a path into the bigger world, but rather provided job security for religious specialists.

In business, literacy is power. When a peasant challenges a merchant regarding a loan, bringing witnesses to say that he borrowed four pots of rice as seed, and the merchant produces a paper on which the amount is recorded as five pots, with the thumbprint of the peasant on it, the merchant wins if the case is taken to courts outside the village.

Literacy in peasant villages is also found among itinerant bards, historians, and philosophers who move from village to village sharing their lore. It is also used in business transactions with the outside world. But oral communication remains the dominant mode of communication in everyday village life, which is built on face-to-face relationships.

Pluralism

Small-scale societies are relatively homogeneous. People in them more or less share the same worldview. In peasant societies, many different social groups coexist, meaning that in the same village, different worldviews are held by different communities. Differences may be religious; for instance, the same

Indian village may have Hindu, Muslim, and Christian enclaves, with Gypsies, tribals, and nomads on the margins. Multiple ethnic groups may also live in the same village, for example, Indian villages with their many castes and Latin American towns with many ethnic immigrants. Culture and worldview differences also exist in communities in which class differences emerge between rich and poor, literate and oral, blue- and white-collar workers, rulers and ruled, and elite and commoner.

At the worldview level, pluralism has profound consequences. People must incorporate into their worldview the fact that there are other worldviews, and that these make sense to other people. Most people affirm the rightness of their own beliefs compared to those of the other groups in their community, but they often emulate the beliefs and practices of the dominant elite in their villages because these elites have high status. A second consequence is that culture and worldview increasingly lose their function as the integrator of peasant societies. There is usually a trade language that everyone uses in public affairs, and people know how they should behave toward members of other groups. But they share a full worldview only with the members of their own group and seek to preserve their own beliefs and identity.

Patron-Client/Market Economy

Many peasants divide economic activities into two conceptual domains. Land, agricultural labor, crops, animals, plows, hoes, and other goods and activities connected with farming are associated with subsistence. These produce the food necessary to keep people alive. Buildings, beds, clothing, baskets, pots, and other nonsubsistence goods are associated with cash and trade. They are not essential to staying alive.

The two domains are kept separate. Subsistence labor is paid not in cash but in grain and other food that workers store to sustain themselves in the future. Other work is paid in money, which is often quickly spent. A farmer may go into debt to build a house, but the moneylender cannot take his land away to pay the debt because land belongs to subsistence, not trade. To take someone's land is to kill that person.

At the center of subsistence activities are patron-client relationships. Patrons are landowners who organize the farming. Their workers, such as the field laborers, iron smiths, carpenters, potters, launderers, barbers, washermen, leatherworkers, and sweepers, are their clients. Clients are expected to provide the essential services needed to produce the crops and maintain the life of the patron. The patron is responsible for the survival and well-being of his workers. In addition to the grain he gives them to keep them alive, he must give them clothes, blankets when they are cold, and places to build their huts. Clients, in turn, have the hereditary right and responsibility to do the work the patron assigns them. In addition to working in the fields and the home, clients must be willing to carry the patron's luggage, help in family weddings and funerals, and fight for him if his rivalries erupt into open violence. This is a system not of economic contracts, which are found in the market economy, but of symbiotic exchanges in which the subsistence needs and social aspirations of all are met through a network of social obligations.[3]

Economic activities in patron-client systems are not calculated in terms of profit and loss or equal and fair exchange. In a year of bad crops, the landlord gets little more than his own subsistence because he must provide enough for his workers to live, whether there is work or not. In good years, the patron makes a handsome profit because he must give the workers little more than a subsistence portion of the crop and small bonus shares. The system provides workers with security in times of want, and patrons with laborers, power, prestige, and occasionally wealth.

The difference between patron-client and market economies can be seen in the rules of borrowing and lending money (fig. 6.2). In market economies, like those of the modern world, the underlying reasons for borrowing are economic. A person borrows money to live or to make more money. In patron-client economies, borrowing strengthens social relationships with the patron. As soon as a person has a patron, he or she borrows to increase the mutual interdependency.

Figure 6.2
RULES FOR LENDING MONEY

Market Economy	Patron-Client Economy
• One borrows for economic reasons.	• One borrows to strengthen an existing relationship.
• One must repay the loan according to agreed terms.	• The borrower does not need to repay the loan until the lender needs the money more than the borrower does.
• One takes the initiative to repay the loan and does so on regular installments.	• The lender must ask the borrower to make payments and then the borrower must make token payments.
• One pays off the loan plus the interest. The goal is financial independence. A person's security lies in having personal wealth.	• Before paying off a loan, the borrower makes a bigger loan. The loan is made not for economic reasons but to build strong patron-client bonds to gain social and economic security—a good patron will care for his clients in times of need.

Modern governments and mission and development agencies rarely understand this separation between subsistence and trade activities. The result has often been devastating to peasants. When the government takes land and

3. For an example of patron-client relationships in Indian villages, see Hiebert 1971.

gives peasants cash for it, moneylenders, relatives, and friends are entitled to a share of that cash. Soon the peasants have neither land nor cash. If the peasants then want to buy land elsewhere, their creditors will first collect their debts, and the peasants' relatives ask for help from those creditors, because those creditors now have money.

Accumulation of Wealth

In villages, accumulation of wealth becomes a dominant value. In tribal societies, wealth is important not as an end in itself but as a means for building relationships and gaining status through sharing. In peasant societies, particularly among the ruling elite, wealth above that needed for livelihood is hoarded because wealth in and of itself is regarded as a measure of status and power. This accumulation of material goods is fostered by the production of agricultural surpluses that make sedentary life possible. Unlike nomadic and seminomadic societies, in which an excess of material goods is a liability, in permanent villages goods are transformed into symbols of social status.

The effect of this switch from sharing to accumulating is far-reaching. The manufacturing of nonessential goods such as jewelry, fine clothing, palatial houses, and other luxuries increases dramatically. The rulers and upper-class elite parade their wealth. They build great palaces, employ large entourages of guards, servants, and attendants, and live in luxury. The difference in wealth in peasant societies is often great. The upper class lives in great luxury, while peasants live on the edge of starvation.

Growing economic and political inequality, compounded with the peasants' awareness of this imbalance, fuels hostility and resentment on the part of the commoners, who then often revolt. Because the peasants lack organizational skills and military technology, these insurrections generally end in appalling bloodshed followed by increased repression.

Formal/Folk Culture

The growing complexity of peasant villages leads to the emergence of the formal culture of the elite over against the folk cultures of the common people. It gives rise to formal science over folk science. For example, in India ayurveda and unani are two highly developed systems of medical science, which stand in contrast to allopathic medicine in the West. The growing complexity and social stratification also give rise to formal religions alongside folk religions. On the formal level, philosophical religions, such as Confucianism, Buddhism, Hinduism, and Christianity, deal with ultimate questions and claim universal truth. In contrast, the everyday life of most villagers is dominated by folk religions that deal with everyday questions and rely on local earthbound spirits, ancestors, witchcraft, magic, evil eye, and other unseen powers to explain and respond to human dilemmas. The emergence of elite culture also leads

Figure 6.3
KEY QUESTIONS OF EACH LEVEL

Formal Religion	• ultimate origin, purpose, and destiny of the universe, society, and self
Folk Religion	• meaning in this life and the problem of death
	• well-being in this life and the problem of misfortunes
	• knowledge to decide and the problem of the unknown
	• righteousness and justice and the problem of evil and injustice
Science	• ordering of human relationships
	• control of nature

to formal literature and arts. Classical music, sophisticated literature, lavishly staged plays and operas, and highly trained musicians are found in the courts of kings, rajas, and sultans. Common people, on the other hand, sing folk songs, use local instruments, tell ordinary tales, and dance local dances.

Formal, elite religion leads to philosophical reflections on the nature of things and to asking ultimate, ontological questions about the origin, purpose, and destiny of the universe, society, and the self. It also leads to specialization and the distinction between formal leaders, such as priests, ministers, and prophets, and the laity. In contrast, folk religions deal with the existential problems of everyday life (fig. 6.3). Their leaders are shamans, witch doctors, magicians, and other people believed to have special powers.

An analytical model can help illuminate the relationship between folk and formal religions at the worldview level. The vertical dimension concerns transcendence. There are three levels: this world seen, this world unseen, and other worlds unseen. The horizontal dimension involves two root metaphors found in all societies: (1) a mechanical metaphor that sees things as inanimate parts of greater mechanical systems, controlled by impersonal forces or impersonal laws of nature; and (2) an organic metaphor in which the things being examined are thought to be alive in some sense, to undergo processes similar to human life, and to relate to one another in ways analogous to interpersonal relationships.

Combing these two dimensions of transcendence and metaphor produces a grid or matrix with which to compare different belief systems (figs. 6.4–6.6). The model creates six sectors, two on each level of the immanent-transcendent scale. Each level deals with different ontological entities. At the bottom are the sciences, belief systems in which people use "natural" explanations to account for empirically perceived phenomena. Natural sciences use mechanical or impersonal analogies, and the humanities use organic or transactional ones. At the top are what are typically called "religions"—belief systems concerned with ultimate cosmic realities: heavenly gods, demons, fate, karma, heaven, and hell. The middle level is difficult for modern people to understand. It deals with the *trans-empirical realities of this world*—with magic, evil eye, earthly

Figure 6.4

INDIAN BELIEF SYSTEMS

	Organic	*Mechanical*
Other Worlds	Brahma, Vishnu, Siva Other high gods Rakshasas, yakshas, other demons	Brahman karma Samsara Dharma
This World Invisible	Goddesses of this earth Capricious spirits Ancestors, unborn	Magic Evil eye Astrology Amulets
This World Visible	Living humans Subhuman beings Animals, plants	Ayurveda and unani medicines Matter

Figure 6.5

BEINGS AND POWERS IN ISLAM

	Beings	*Powers*
Other Worlds	Allah Archangels Angels, devils	Kismet
This World Invisible	Jinn Quarina Zar Aisha Quandisha Ancestors, souls of the dead	Baraka Magic Dhikr Astrology Evil eye Auspicious numbers
This World Visible	Walis, saints Humans Animals, plants	Medicines Natural forces

Figure 6.6

CHINESE BELIEF SYSTEMS

	Organic	*Mechanical*
Other Worlds	Jade emperor (T'ein) Gods, goddesses	Ming Yin, Yang
This World Invisible	Earth gods Spirits, ghosts Mythological beings Ancestors Animal spirits (totems)	Five elements Magic Feng shui Divination Palistry Taboos Luck Auspicious days and numbers
This World Visible	People Animals Plants	Acupuncture Medicines Matter

spirits, ancestors who continue to live in the village, witchcraft, divination, and the like. A study of particular peasant societies reveals a great diversity of folk and formal religions (Hiebert, Shaw, and Tiénou 1999).

Affective Themes

A great deal of study has gone into the analysis of the social systems and the cognitive and evaluative themes of peasant cultures. Less has been done on affective themes.

It is easy to imagine that life in peasant societies consists mainly of hard labor, with little entertainment and excitement. This is far from the truth. Family and community rituals, festivals, and regional fairs bring people together from near and far. There are also many forms of entertainment. In an Indian village there is a constant flow of itinerant bards and minstrels, comic performers, jugglers, animal trainers, circuses, traveling drama troops, and street dramas put on by local associations. One particularly common form of entertainment is the fiesta celebrating important days in the year. These celebrations often last two or three days. More ethnographic study is needed on the affective themes of peasant communities.

Evaluative Themes

We turn now to some evaluative themes underlying the moral order in peasant societies. Although there are many exceptions to these in specific societies, all peasant societies must deal with these issues in one form or another.

Hierarchy

The emergence of social pluralism in peasant villages leads in almost all cases to hierarchy. One or more groups gain wealth, power, and status and rule the village. The other castes, classes, or communities are poor and oppressed. On the state level, a small group of people controls the villages by means of armies and police forces.

The social fact of dominance in most cases leads to a worldview that accepts hierarchy not only as a fact of life but also as right and necessary. A family, village, and state must have a head who has power to rule and maintain order. Disorder is seen as a great evil.

Hierarchy in peasant cultures is often justified by religion. In Indian villages, the hierarchy of castes is seen as divinely ordained. One's standing in it is determined by the good and bad deeds of one's previous lives. To try to break free from the caste system and rise above one's status determined at birth is to invite cosmic judgment on oneself and the community. In medieval

Europe and Russia, rulers were believed to be divinely appointed. In Chinese villages, wealth and power are often seen as the blessings of the gods.

With dominance comes the acceptance of violence as a necessary means of maintaining the social order. The dominant value is maintaining order, and the leaders must maintain it at any cost. To do so they must have police to control the people and armies to hold off enemies. The greatest sin is treason—to reject the authority of the state and its rulers.

Dominance leads in a fallen world to what Christians see as injustice. The powerful exploit the poor rather than care for them. Those with high status do not seek to include those with low status; rather, they despise the lowly and exclude them from their social circles. On the worldview level, this oppression is usually justified by blaming those at the bottom for their plight. They have sinned against the gods, they live impure lives, they have earned their suffering through the misdeeds of their previous lives, or they are less than fully human. Slavery, too, is justified by one means or another as morally right.

Limited Good

Village life is public—everyone and almost everything is known by all. This is conducive to a sense of community and mutual responsibility in times of crisis. The negative side is that intimacy often leads to envy of and gossip about the good fortunes of others, particularly those who belong to another ethnic group or class.

The fact that the village is a small, closed system often leads to a view of reality that George Foster has called the "image of limited good."

> By "Image of Limited Good" I mean that broad areas of peasant behavior are patterned in such fashion as to suggest that peasants view their social, economic, and natural universes—their total environment—as one in which all of the desirable things in life such as land, wealth, health, friendship and love, manliness and honor, respect and status, power and influence, security and safety, exist in finite quantity and are always in short supply, as far as the peasant is concerned. Not only do these and all other "good things" exist in finite and limited quantities, but in addition there is no way directly within peasant power to increase the available quantities. . . . If "good" exists in limited amounts which cannot be expanded, and if the system is closed, it follows that an individual or a family can improve a position only at the expense of others. (1965, 296–98)

Because one person's advance is thought to occur only at the expense of another's, open ambition becomes a threat to other members of the community. Someone's gain implies someone else's loss. A person, therefore, should be content with what he or she has and not strive for more. There is a great deal of gossip about who has gotten what and how he or she acquired it.

Those who do get ahead through enterprise and work are targets of gossip, hatred, and ostracism. In extreme cases, their crops are destroyed at night, and their newly built houses are vandalized. The lesson is clear: do not try to get ahead because to do so you must rob others and they will turn against you.

People jealously guard what they have, including relationships. They zealously guard and cultivate their relationships to powerful individuals and seek to reserve the attention of these patrons for themselves. They assume that the bounty of a generous patron is easily spread thin. They also do not want to admit that they have learned anything from someone else (Pike 1980). To do so means that they are indebted to that person. Consequently, people learn most of what they know by watching and imitating others. There is little formal education.

The notion of "limited good" contributes much to the conservatism of most peasants. People are afraid of their neighbors' response to new ways. This belief also adds to envy and mistrust of one's neighbors and to gossip as a powerful means of social control.

There is one exception to the concept of limited good. Goods that come to a person from outside the system are seen not as a threat to the village but as a windfall. Others feel jealous but not threatened if someone is given a gift from the government, inherits wealth from a distant relative, or finds a pot of gold. Buried treasures are a common theme in peasant societies. They serve as a way of legitimizing wealth. A person can hide his or her savings and then suddenly "discover" a pot of gold. Others may accept this as a blessing from the gods.

Diachronic Themes

Myths are important in peasant life. They are told to children by the grandparents, recounted by bards, reenacted in street dramas, and illustrated in pictures.

Floods and Disasters

One of the most common themes worldwide is that of a catastrophic flood (Kluckhohn 1965, 162). It is particularly widespread in Taiwan, South China, Southeast Asia, and Malaysia. If we add myths about earthquakes, famines, and plagues, "catastrophe" is a nearly universal theme in mythology.

Bandit-Hero

Another common story involves bandit-heroes, such as Robin Hood in England, Janosik in Poland, Pancho Villa in Mexico, Shenka Razin in Russia, and the bandits glorified in Chinese peasant lore. Peasants often protest the harsh conditions of their lives by telling stories about bandit-heroes who openly defy an oppressive social order. These figures are champions of the peasants. They exact revenge, redress wrongs, and claim land for the landless. They restore justice and equality.

Imminent Millennium

Closely related to stories of bandit-heroes are myths of a coming millennium in which the world will be perfect. These may speak of a return to a golden age of justice and equality or of a new age on earth. This new world will come through the judgment of the gods or through peasant revolts. Marxism, with its promise of a new world, found a ready audience in peasant societies.

At times myths of bandit-heroes and imminent millenniums give rise to peasant revolts that are bloody and cruel. The peasant revolts in Europe after the eleventh century, the Taiping Rebellion in China in the nineteenth century, the uprisings of the Spanish anarchists in the same century, and the Mexican peasant revolt of 1917 are examples. E. J. Hobsbawm (1959, 24–25) observes that such myths and revolutions are protests, not against the fact that the people are poor and oppressed, but that they are excessively poor and oppressed. Revolts are not expected to create an equitable world. They can only right wrongs and prove that sometimes oppression can be turned upside down. Beyond that, the hero is merely part of a dream of how wonderful things might be.

Restored Status

A fourth type of myth concerns the fall of a particular group of people in the village from high status and their return to it. For example, most untouchable castes in India have myths showing that they were once high castes and that their current low status is due to the deceitful actions of others or the mistakes of their ancestors. But some day this injustice will be reversed, and they will return to their former privileged position in society.

These stories of fall and rise serve two functions. First, they give dignity to the untouchables, who can claim, at least among themselves, that they are not what they publicly appear to be. Second, they justify actions by the caste designed to raise its social status. As untouchable castes gain power and wealth and take on the symbols and practices of high castes, they can claim that they are not upsetting the social order but instead are restoring it to the original condition.

Given the great number and diversity of peasant societies, no themes or myths hold true for all of them. Our exploration here is primarily to introduce guiding concepts for our study of the worldview of the peasants we serve. Additional in-depth, society-specific studies would help us understand the people and communicate with them more meaningfully.

Villages and Modernity

Traditional, primarily oral, peasant villages have had an uneasy relationship with the outside world of cities and states, where literacy is essential to life. If villages had schools, they were primarily religious schools, preparing religious leaders for special vocations. The coming of colonial rule changed this situation radically. With colonial rule came the values of the Enlightenment. One of these was the education of all people by means of schools established by the government and by missionaries. Jack Goody writes:

> The value of literacy as a means of social and personal advancement was immediately clear. The new conquerors used writing at every stage of the administration of the country; once they had locked away the Maxim guns in their armoury, it was the pen and telegraph that took over. The increasing dependence on written communication manifested itself not only internally, but also in communications with subject peoples. These had to be trained to man the burgeoning bureaucracy and to extend this communication to the people themselves. (1987, 141–42)

Literacy produced a new ladder of mobility and shifted the focus from status based on ascription to that based on achievement. The result was a new set of rewards leading to a new system of stratification, namely, classes based on achievement rather than ethnic groups and castes based on birth. It opened the door for successful individuals to leave the village and operate at the national and even international level. The new elite made sure their children were well educated, and the system of education that opened the door to social mobility now became the means of preserving status.

With modern schooling came modern social systems. The growth of towns and cities, the development of regional economic and political systems based on mass participation, and the growth of media depended on literacy. With schooling also came the modern worldview with its stress on the autonomous individual, the spread of secularism, and the advancement of science as public truth.

The introduction of public schooling for everyone split the population into two halves, one of which was mainly rural, the other mainly urban. There was inevitably a sense of inferiority on the part of the oral population because of the power of literacy in the modern world. Goody writes that "Many of the literates working in the country will be doing so reluctantly, with their eyes on the town and on its life. For literacy achieved through formal education is the main method of self-advancement, of reaching beyond the level of subsistence farming. Indeed, it is not only at the subsistence level that agriculture is considered to provide an inadequate life; the stress on school-learnt values falls elsewhere, in favour of white-collar jobs . . . preferably in an urban setting" (1987, 141).

Writing and recording maps on paper has altered the basic categories of time and space. Peasant life is governed by the cycles of the seasons: plow-fields time, plant-seed time, harvest-crop time. Literacy introduced a sense of chronology: the cycles of weeks, months, and years, which do not always match the seasons.[4] Moreover, it divided the day into hours, minutes, and seconds. Goody notes, "Typically non-literate societies adjust the two (solar and lunar cycles) by a process of fudging; the harvest moon appears when the harvest is ripe. Only literate societies have to wrest the month away from the moon, or the year from the sun" (1987, 132). Writing also introduced a technical sense of history.

Maps changed the way land was measured and recorded. No longer were the reference points the river, the rock buried at the corner, and the old tree down the hill. Such points were now recorded in terms of invisible grids determined by the poles and equator, a global grid that encompassed all earthly space.

We now turn to the rise of modernity and its impact on the world.

4. The seven-day week was based on the planetary cycles of Chaldean astronomy.

7

The Modern Worldview

One of the great worldview shifts in history took place in the seventeenth century with the dawn of modern science and modernity. Modernity is the first truly global culture. "It is a world system and spirit that today both encompasses us as individuals and encircles the globe" (Guinness 1994a, 324).

After the triumph of Christianity in the fourth century, the Western mind was above all else theistic. Virtually without question, all life and nature were assumed to be under the supervision of a personal God whose intentions toward humans were perfect and whose power was unlimited. God was seen as a loving father who nourished his children and guided the course of worldly events according to his wishes. Nature was seen as obedient to his commands and extraordinary interventions in daily life. For Christians, life was the implementation of God's purposes. In such a world, people understood the purpose of history and of their lives, and thus life was meaningful. They did not set out to understand, or presume themselves capable of understanding, the natural world, for it was at every point under the will of God.

After the thirteenth century, the ideas of Aristotle, Plato, and Ptolemy were introduced to Europe by pilgrims returning from the Crusades[1] and by scholars

---

1. Christian and Jewish scholars living in Muslim countries translated Greek philosophical and medical writings into Arabic. Muslim scholars built on these. The first Latin translations of Aristotle were later made from the Arabic, and for more than three hundred years European scholars read Aristotle with the help of the commentaries of Islamic scholars such as Ibn Rushd [Averroës] (Ramachandra 1996, 23).

who studied in the Muslim universities in Spain (Crosby 1997, 56). Charles Malik writes, "If we examine the written history of practically every science and every intellectual discipline we shall find that the original conception of that science or discipline was Greek and almost invariably (mathematics excepted) Aristotelian. . . . Aristotle is at the base of practically half of Western civilization" (1987, 4).

By the thirteenth century the cathedral schools were being displaced by universities, which taught the new paradigm that later became the basis of modernity. This included a focus on understanding the material world through systematic investigation and the use of systematic abstract logic, and faith in human reason. The world was thought to be a coherent, law-abiding system that was intelligible to humans.

The Holy Roman Empire had been in decline since the late Middle Ages, but it was the French Revolution that shattered the sacred foundations of history. The secular state emerged based on rationalism and the will of citizens. Public life was now the realm of reason alone and had no place for a seemingly unknowable God. Religion was relegated to the private sphere of life and seen as imagination, and God ceased to be relevant to public life. A rigidly materialistic, atheistic philosophy of history emerged that reduced the spirit to matter and morals to social constructs defined in terms of material progress.

The eighteenth-century Enlightenment ideals of reason and freedom developed into modernity. Andrew Fix writes:

> In the years between 1650 and 1700 an intellectual transformation of fundamental and far-reaching importance changed the very nature of the assumptions and attitudes upon which European thought had been based for centuries, and in so doing changed the intellectual framework with which educated Europeans understood themselves and their world. . . . Few transformations of worldview have been as decisive and influential as that which changed the religious worldview of traditional Europe into the rational and secular worldview of modern Europe. (1991, 3, 5)

René Descartes initiated the pursuit of objective truth untainted by cultural biases. This he sought to achieve by applying Greek abstract, algorithmic, digital reason to experience. He began his exploration of the world by doubting everything, even his own existence. He trusted only in his reason to provide the answers. Reason became the ultimate judge of what is true, right, and good.

After the eighteenth century the stress on rational and empirical analysis played a major role in the gradual displacement of the traditional medieval worldview. The world was understood as material rather than spiritual, as mechanical rather than teleological. It was a big clock once wound up by the Creator but now running according to natural laws. Fix notes that "the empiricism of Francis Bacon and the mechanistic cosmology of Descartes encouraged a rejection of the principle of intellectual authority in favor of free and rational inquiry and set off a massive cultural and intellectual transformation. The attempt to understand the physical world in terms of reason was followed closely by a desire to understand humankind's relationship to nature, society, and God in similar rational terms" (1991, 7).

Although the term "modern" has a long history, what Jürgen Habermas calls the *project* of modernity came into focus only during the eighteenth century. "That project amounted to an extraordinary intellectual effort on the part of Enlightenment thinkers 'to develop objective science, universal morality and law, and autonomous art according to their inner logic.' . . . The scientific domination of nature promised freedom from scarcity, want, and the arbitrariness of natural calamity" (Harvey 1990, 12).

In the past two centuries modernity has spread around the world and taken different forms in Japan, India, and Latin America. Vinoth Ramachandra observes, "Modernity is the first truly global civilization to emerge in human history. . . . Its impact is felt even in the more remote villages of the world as much as in the universities, commercial centres and government offices of major cities. It is full of paradoxes and ambiguities, bringing in its wake both enormous blessings and terrible sufferings" (1996, 143). Modernity offers a uniform vision of the world and promises, through the scientific domination of nature, freedom from scarcity, want, and calamities.

We need to study the worldview of modernity to understand how it is shaping not only the world around us but also our own ways of thinking. Most readers of this book will have a modern or postmodern worldview.[2]

Cognitive Themes of Modernity

Modernity is complex and varies greatly from culture to culture, but some central themes run through all these manifestations. Here we can examine only a few.

Naturalism/Supernaturalism

Foundational to the emergence of modernity was the reintroduction of Aristotelian dualism into Western thought (fig. 7.1). Europe in the Middle Ages was shaped by the contingent dualism of Creator and creation, in which the former was ultimate reality, dominant, and eternal, and the latter contingent, subordinate, and temporal. The latter was intrinsically tied to the former.

---

2. It hard to think about these assumptions because we so take them for granted that they seem self-evident. E. A. Burtt (1954, 28–31) faults contemporary scientists and philosophers for taking too much of the past for granted, and for not looking at these deeper, determinative worldview assumptions that frame their thinking.

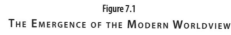

Figure 7.1
THE EMERGENCE OF THE MODERN WORLDVIEW

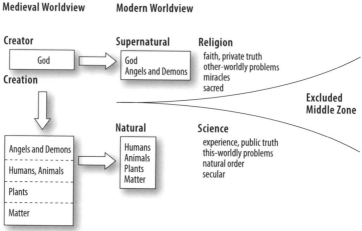

One consequence of this was an "other worldly" orientation in which the worship and service of God were held in high esteem, and making money and earthly comfort were despised. This view also placed angels, both good and fallen, in the realm of creation. Art commonly centered on religious themes, portrayed spiritual realities in visible signs such as halos, and depicted angels and demons as part of the everyday lives of people. Architecture focused on cathedrals often decorated with angels and gargoyles, music on sacred themes, and church rituals on an encounter with a transcendent God and a renunciation of the devil and all his ways.

The introduction of Greek dualism radically altered this view of reality. It separated reality into two largely unrelated realms: supernatural and natural. On the one hand, there is the spiritual realm in which God and other spirit beings live and act. This is the world of religion. On the other hand, there is the natural realm—the material world of science. Nicholas Lash writes:

> In the seventeenth century, for the first time, the term "super" . . . began to connote a realm of being, a territory of existence, "outside" the world we know. With "nature" now deemed single, homogeneous and self-contained, we labeled "super" that "other" world inhabited (some said) by ghosts and poltergeists, by demons, angels, and suchlike extraterrestrials—and by God. . . . By the end of the seventeenth century, "believing in God" had become a matter of supposing that there is, outside the world we know, a large and powerful entity called "God." (1996, 168–69)

The world of science became increasingly secular. The earth of the fifteenth century was seen as an island (Orbis Terrarum) made up of Europe, Asia, and Africa, with the holy city of Jerusalem in the center and God in control. This sacred space was surrounded by the dark, inhuman, evil void of the deep waters. Crossing the seas and discovering new lands radically changed how Europeans viewed the earth. For the first time, the world was seen as a uniform, continuous, secular space covered by continents and oceans. In this new world, "others" were no longer "fallen" and in need of redemption. They were secular humans and could be compared with other humans. In these comparisons they were seen as "barbarians" and "savages." It was the Westerners who explored the world and gave names to and studied "others."

By the late seventeenth century, the realms of heaven and earth were beginning to move apart in the minds of European intellectuals. God became increasingly unreal, and the material universe became the ultimate reality. Many dropped the idea of divine involvement in nature, but kept that of general providence in which God imposes order by means of law. But as Fix notes, "Once the growing sense of separation between man and God had introduced the corrosive force of doubt into peoples' belief in direct divine intervention into the temporal world, it would not be long before this acid attacked the foundations of belief in indirect divine control of the world as well" (1991, 9).

God, angels, and demons were relegated to other worlds and religion to heavenly matters. Nature concerned this world, devoid of resident spirit beings. Reality was seen exclusively in terms of energy and matter, and nature as completely self-contained, self-sufficient, and self-ordering. The supernatural domain was relegated to fanciful beliefs, emotions, and morals. Angelo Rentas writes, "Science has become a universally valid source of knowledge for our culture. The truth claims of science are often taken more seriously than the truth claims of religion or the arts. In practice, scientific truth has become recognized as the only *objective* truth. Science speaks, and most people listen and believe" (2006, 24).

The two domains were seen as autonomous and disconnected. The only crossing of the gulf was divine intervention in the natural sphere through visions, miracles, and other anomalous events that violate the "laws of nature," and the facticity of these was increasingly called into question. Even rituals invested with cosmic and sacred truth were increasingly displaced by public displays that engendered momentary meaning and entertainment. This dualism between natural and supernatural, science and religion, fact and faith, natural laws and miracles, body and spirit dominates the worldview of most ordinary modern people. It relegates religions to matters of personal faith and leads to the secularization of everyday life. Scientism holds that nature constitutes the sum total of reality.

This shift from Creator/creation to supernatural/natural raised deep philosophical questions. If God is in heaven, who is in charge on earth? John Locke argued that humans are the gods of the world, and that they can plan and rule the world through reason, science, and government. This theory led to an emphasis on a rationalization of all areas of life and the development of techniques to engineer a better world. The result was an explosion of technological and managerial innovation that swept through all areas of modern life.[3]

In the end, the naturalistic forms of modernity denied religious transcendence and revelation and affirmed that everything is found in a single, orderly system of nature run by laws. God is the invention of human imagination. Religion is based on blind faith and therefore is irrational. "Appeals to the 'super' at any level were dismissed as superstitions, or at least, 'out of bounds' for academic discussion" (Meneses 1997, 8). The naturalistic worldview holds that the material universe is the sum total of reality. The supernatural does not exist. Philip Johnson writes, "According to naturalism, what is ultimately real is nature, which consists of the fundamental particles that make up what we call matter and energy, together with the natural laws that govern how those particles behave. Nature itself is ultimately all there is. . . . To put it another way, nature is a permanently closed system of material cause and effects that can never be influenced by anything outside of itself—by God, for example. To speak of something as 'supernatural' is therefore to imply that it is imaginary" (1995, 37–38).

Naturalism is the worldview of the dominant cultural systems of Europe and North America. It is the foundation for the scientific academy, education, the legal system, and the news media. As Lesslie Newbigin notes, science became public facts, taught to everyone (1991). Religion became a matter of private faith. The result was the secularization of the domain by the demystification and desacralization of knowledge, a secularism that continues to spread around the world with modernity despite resistance from religious communities. Secularism also understood humans within nature as another animal, albeit one that, paradoxically, transcends nature and can observe and engineer it.

This supernatural/natural dualism led to a number of subthemes and counterthemes.

---

3. Later Jean-Jacques Rousseau would argue that reason cannot save humans, because what is reasonable to one person or group is oppressive or nonsense to other people and groups. He argued that the world can be saved if humans fit into the order of Nature, for Nature has ordered the world from the beginning. Experience and deep emotional identification with nature, not reason, can save us.

Friedrich Nietzsche challenged Rousseau's analysis and argued that nature is not peaceful and harmonious. It is a brutal power struggle in which the strong devour the weak. He posited that human salvation lay in a strong leader with a vision who could motivate and lead the masses of people in creating a new world. In time this new world order would collapse under its own weight, and a new vision would be needed to revitalize human endeavors in world building. Charles Darwin argued that the answer lies in power and competition, and the survival of the fittest leads to progress and development, not destruction, as Charles Lyell believed. At the same time Adam Smith argued for free enterprise and competition, and Herbert Spencer for economic liberalism and against cooperativism and socialism as the road to progress. This philosophy of progress as the product of "nature, red in fang and claw," underlies the modern theories of evolution and capitalism.

This World/Other Worlds

In the Middle Ages Christians saw the world as a place teeming with life. It was full of mystery and majesty and had meaning and purpose. It was a home to be enjoyed, not simply a house in which to live.

In modernity the focus is on this world, not on heaven, hell, or other worlds. This world has increasingly been seen as a material universe built out of lifeless particles—atoms, quarks, and now strings or loops—whose movements can be explained in terms of natural laws that are independent of God. An understanding of these laws can help humans engineer a better world. There is little room for mystery and transcendence. Nonmaterial realities, such as God and spirits, are relegated to matters of faith, not fact. As Max Weber noted, the world has become disenchanted. It is nothing more than a material reality. The sense of transcendence has faded from everyday life. But this has left a difficult problem. In the human sciences, humans are the objects of analysis, but humans are also the subjects doing the analysis. If humans are totally reduced to nature, then there is no room for a knower. As Allan Bloom observes, "We can know everything in nature except that which knows nature" (1987, 77).

Science, the sole reigning, dominant plausibility structure of modernity, focuses on the study of this material world using rational methods. Materialism is the water scientists swim in, the tenet whose falsity is literally unimaginable. In a 1998 survey, Edward J. Larson and Larry Witham found that 90 percent of the members of the National Association of Sciences are materialists. The number rises to 95 percent for biologists. Franklin Harold writes, "We should reject, as a matter of principle, the substitution of intelligent design for the dialogue of chance and necessity; but must concede that there are presently no detailed Darwinian accounts of the evolution of any biochemical system, only a variety of wishful speculations" (quoted in Behe 2005, 18). Michael Behe adds that "the problem is not such explicit and deliberate materialism. The problem is rather socially constructed materialism, spread more by social pressure than by rational argument. The social pressure doesn't have to be overt; it doesn't have to involve ridicule or arm-twisting. It is often just an intellectual climate in which most people do not recognize that their theoretical options have been artificially limited" (2005, 19). Challenging this materialist assumption is seen as heresy supported not by rational argument but by emotional hostility.

The physical sciences, the first of the sciences, examined empirical data and offered explanations of phenomena capable of verification within a materialistic framework. Later the human sciences tried to follow the same path. By definition the sciences limit the scope of their analysis to the world, using materialist explanations. They exclude supernatural and teleological explanations, such as God and human purposes. For many modernists this led to the metaphysical assumption that the world is all there is, and that spiritual realities do not exist. The primary tenant of secularism is that the ultimate good for humans consists in something attainable in this life. Religions are rejected because they hold that the good for humans is not fully obtainable in this life.

Concern for this life rather than eternity led to a stress on physical comfort and material abundance. This is the central message of many advertisements. People are encouraged to drive with soft leather heated seats in air-conditioned comfort with surround sound and shock absorbers that take the bumps out of the road. No one asks where they are going. Given this obsession with the good life here on earth, it should not surprise us that modernity has little place for suffering, sacrifice, or death (Becker 1973).

The shift in focus from other worlds to this world was accompanied by a shift in interest from eternity to the present. Medieval time was embedded in cosmic history. People were important because they were part of the history of the church, which was greater than they. The history of the church took on meaning because it was part of divine history, beginning with God and creation and ending in eternity. Modernity focuses on the present and today's happiness as more important than the story of past generations or the welfare of future generations. It is fascinated not so much with history as with *news*, with the immediate. Newspapers, radio, television, and the World Wide Web inform people instantly as events occur around the world. News becomes entertainment, and breaking the news to others brings honor. This focus on the immediate calls for "instant" answers and gratification.

Human Centered/God Centered

With supernatural/natural dualism came a shift from a theocentric to a human-centered world. Western culture in the Middle Ages was centered on God and his works. Under his reign were human communities, primarily the church, within which people found their identities and homes. Serving the church was highly valued, and cathedrals were the heart of city life.

Modernity replaced this top-down living with a bottom-up world in which autonomous, free humans became the center of the universe and the measure of all things. They were the arbiters of truth. They constructed societies and cultures and were responsible for history. The world became a "picture" that they observed. The result was a shift from a world ordered by God to one engineered by humans. This humanism was articulated by Descartes who wrote, "Now free will is in itself the noblest thing we can have because it makes us in a certain manner equal to God, and exempts us from being his subjects: and so its rightful use is the greatest of all the goods we possess, and further there is nothing that is more our own or that matters more to us" (1991, 326). Ramachandra notes, "Here is expressed the Enlightenment project of self-creation, to carve out a territory that is exclusively one's own possession" (1996, 161).

The shift from theocentrism to humanism is a Copernican revolution that radically changes the way modern humans view the world. The very essence of humans changes because they now are the epicenter of the universe. They are now autonomous subjects that study the world. They can discover the laws of nature and use these to better their lives. It is what they think about God and the world that matters, not what God thinks about them. It is they who determine what is true and what is false. It is not that scientists disproved the existence of God or that most modern people have consciously rejected him. Rather they have relegated him to the "super" sphere—to churches, sacred rituals, miracles, and things science cannot explain, and gradually he has faded from view in everyday life. Not atheism but deism, the notion that God created the world but left it to run according to its own inherent laws, was modernity's initial religious response. People increasingly could live without him because they increasingly were in control of their own destinies. In the end, humans became the essence of reality. The result was secular humanism.[4]

In modern philosophy the place of God in the universe became problematic. At first God was seen as the great creator of the world, which he made to run according to mathematical precision, for without this order it would be incomprehensible. He was also the sustainer of this order. The main exercise of his providential power was to maintain, not interrupt, the exact mathematical regularity. In time philosophers and scientists began to wonder whether the self-perpetuating machine was really in need of a "super" beginning. The only place left for God was in the irreducible fact that there was an intelligible order in things and a need for moral order. But, as E. A. Burtt points out, "The bulk of thinking men, ever and inevitably anthropomorphic in their theology, could hardly sense religious validity in such theistic substitutes. For them, so far as they were considerably penetrated with science or philosophy, God had been quite eliminated from the scene" (1954, 299–300).

In the end, the Enlightenment killed God. For many, like Marx, this was liberation from the moral and social tyranny of religions. Nietzsche replaced this easygoing, self-satisfied atheism with agonized atheism, for he understood the consequences of this liberation. He treated with contempt the "Last Man" who, accepting the news that God is dead, goes on living as though truth and falsehood, right and wrong, and good and evil still make sense. Modern people had lost the sacred canopy that gave meaning and security to human endeavors. They lived in an increasingly meaningless world but insisted that their lives had meaning. Now they were the gods of the world, but these gods

4. The term "humanism" is used in many mutually contradictory ways. For Heidegger and others, humanism is secular—"it designates that philosophical interpretation of man which explains and evaluates whatever is, in its entirety, from the standpoint of man and in relation to man." There is, however, a Christian humanism that regards humans as being at the center of God's creation and as the objects of his love; this humanism, however, is not human centered but God centered.

were gods of power, violence, and cruelty, not of love and benevolence. Rousseau saw the need for religion to give meaning and morality to societies and called for a civil religion in which those who govern appear to be draped in the colors of religion (Bloom 1987, 196).

With human centeredness came the doctrines of liberty and equality, an emphasis on freedom and human rights, and a high value on private ownership of property and on capitalism.

SCIENCE/RELIGION

With supernatural/natural dualism came the separation between science and religion, a distinction not made in most cultures, and the dominance of the former as the encompassing explanation system. This process of secularization has devalued religious institutions, beliefs, and practices and substituted for them those of reason and science.

Initially the materialistic worldview was not secular in orientation, nor did it clash with beliefs in a divine Creator who had set the world in motion and gave orders that creation obeys. Even Locke, a skeptic, admitted that the rationality of the universe and the order of nature were of divine origin. But science introduced scientific rationality and made religions objects of empirical study. In so doing it declared them to be irrational and fictional. If different religions claimed validity in their own right, the ultimate truth of any could be doubted.

Nicholas Lash points out that as science developed, it defined "religion" as a category that represented the "other" over against which it defined itself (1996, 188). Prior to the seventeenth century, "super" was used adverbially or adjectivally to refer to a quality of objects or persons that enabled them to behave in a manner beyond their state, that is, superhumanly. Vinoth Ramachandra notes, "On this understanding, it is only God to whom the term 'super' could *never* be applied. For who or what can elevate the nature of divinity?" (1996, 142).

After the Enlightenment, science characterized religion as that which science was not. Science was objective, rational, empirical, and true for everyone; religions were subjective, emotional, and matters of personal faith. Scientists might disagree on the surface, but underneath they all shared the same worldview, and their work led to progress. They believed that the "scientific domination of nature promised freedom from scarcity, want, and the arbitrariness of calamities. The development of rational forms of social organization and rational modes of thought promised liberation from the irrationalities of myth, religions, superstition, release from the arbitrary use of power as well as from the dark side of our own natures. Only through such a project could the universal, eternal, and the immutable qualities of all of humanity be revealed" (Harvey 1990, 12).

Religious people had fundamental disagreements, and their arguments did not lead to an advancement of knowledge. Science made religions an object of study, dividing them into species and comparing and ranking them along the scale of logic. In so doing, it relegated religions to the world of private beliefs and superstitions and claimed to define truth in the public square. It did not tolerate anything that resisted its domination of the field of knowledge. Conrad Waddington writes, "Science *by itself* is able to provide mankind with a way of life which is, firstly, self-consistent and harmonious, and secondly, free for the exercise of that objective reason on which our material progress depends. So far as I can see, the scientific attitude of mind is *the only* one which is, at the present day, adequate in both these respects. There are many other worthy ideals which might supplement it; but I cannot see that any could take its place as the basis of a progressive and rich society" (1941, 170, italics added).

One consequence of this worship of science is that not only scientific data but also scientific theories are held to be "facts," not mental constructs. This assumption is reinforced by the high degree of specialization in scientific knowledge, which makes it difficult for outsiders to distinguish between fact and mental construct. This view leads ultimately to the belief that the insights of science can help us conquer nature and deliver us from the problems of life.

To understand modernity today, we must understand the role that universities and research centers play in the shaping of modern thought (Malik 1987). The belief that physical realities are the only realities and that science is the way to certain truth has extended itself far beyond the academy into the everyday life of most modern people. Scientism and efforts to find ultimate explanations of human phenomena underlie much of modern thought. This concerted reductionism assumes that all phenomena can be completely understood from the knowledge of their underlying structures and constituent parts. To gain credibility, a discipline must show that it is a science.[5] The result is scientism, which relegates religious, ethical, and aesthetic knowledge to the realm of mere fantasy.

Given a supernatural/natural dualism, it should not surprise us that religion and science are seen by many as two very different and potentially hostile systems of explanation. It is proper for science to study religion. It is of no public importance for religions to study science—science does not need to take their claims of truth seriously. Science, modernity argues, is built on the solid foundations of experience and reason. Religion is based on faith. Science looks for laws that order the material world and are independent of God; religion looks for miracles as evidence of super realities. As science increasingly explains the mysteries of nature, religion is pushed back to smaller domains

---

5. Ironically, many theologians have argued that theology is a kind of science, indeed, the queen of the sciences. Often by this they mean that theology is an orderly, systematic pursuit of knowledge. But today science is much more than this, and in trying to make theology a kind of science we submit it to the questions, methods, and assumptions of science, which are defined not by theologians but by the larger scientific community. As Christians we need to define science as a kind of theology, and not the other way around.

of explanation and becomes increasingly irrelevant. Transcendent spiritual realities, such as God, angels, and demons, are not used to explain earthly events, and the reality of this-worldly spirits and powers such as witchcraft and magic are denied. This has led to a growing secularism that seeks to demystify and desacralize the world around us. For many, science is the ultimate explanation of reality, a new religion.

MATERIALISTIC SECULARISM/HEAVENLY SPIRITUALISM

The triumph of science led to the secularization of thought in all realms of ideas at the same time.[6] Religious beliefs, practices, and institutions that once were central to life were now relegated to its margins. Sacred time and space gave way to secular time and space.

This growing secularism was not a result of a conscious rejection of God and transcendent realities or of scientific proofs of his nonexistence. At first these spiritual realities were used to answer ultimate questions about the origin, purpose, and destiny of the universe and to address matters of morality (Kant's moral laws within), and they were relegated to special rituals set in sacred space and time. Later God was consigned to other-worldly matters or forgotten as a relic of the past. Life became increasingly the purview of science.

This secularization of nature can be seen in understandings of time. In medieval Europe, history was a grand drama with purpose and meaning. Scientific time rejected this. As Burtt notes:

> Time seems to us nothing but a measurable continuum, the present moment alone exists, and that moment is itself no temporal quality but merely a dividing line between the infinite stretch of a vanishing past and the equally infinite expanse of the untrodden future. To such a view it is impossible to regard the temporal movement as the absorption of the future into the actual or present, for there really is nothing actual. . . .
>
> Time as something *lived* we have banished from our metaphysics. (Burtt 1954, 95)

Modern people have lost a sense of time as a dimension in a cosmic drama. Mircea Eliade suggests that modern humans have sought to retain a sense of meaning by reconstructing all of human history, believing that doing so will make sense of the world. But, as he notes, without a cosmic narrative to

6. Originally secularization in Europe emerged as a way to allow for religious pluralism within a nation-state following the religious wars. Instead of religious conformity, the state was now built on the "abstract notion of human rights based on the concept of a universal human nature" (Ramachandra 1996, 159). Harvey Cox (1966), Lesslie Newbigin (1966), and the Lausanne Committee (1980) distinguish between secularization as a liberation from ecclesiastical control, and secularism as a new, closed worldview that functions as a religion. In the West, the sacred society we call Christendom has collapsed.

give them meaning, histories and biographies are reduced to interesting but unimportant stories.

Public Sphere/Private Sphere

In modernity, the division between the "secular" and the "religious" has led to a distinction between public and private spheres of life, and between public and private knowledge (fig. 7.2). Peter Berger and his associates argue that this dichotomy is between "the huge and powerful institutions of the public . . . and the private sphere . . . 'left over,' as it were, by the large institutions" (Berger, Berger, and Kellner 1973, 133). These public institutions are the large corporations, labor unions, government bureaucracies, political parties, and academic institutions that dominate public life. The private sphere involves areas of life where individuals have control, such as families, voluntary associations, and neighborhoods. The result of this divorce is the fragmentation of human consciousness between office and home, and work and play.

Public truth is secular, humanistic, materialistic, and rationalistic, and therefore not subject to moral considerations. It includes science and value-free facts, which are the most highly prized commodities in our culture. Barry Smart writes, "Existing for the most part in the dense, impersonal, or faceless domain of 'the social,' a virtual moral vacuum ordered through legal-rational mechanisms of government, human beings are constituted both as objects of forms of knowledge and the subjects of associated therapeutic, managerial, and bureaucratic technologies which promise the manipulation of human beings into compliant patterns of behavior" (1993, 80).

Private truth is seen as a matter of personal belief and therefore as a matter not of truth and falsehood but of different perceptions of personal truth. Religious truth, feelings, morals, and traditions are relegated to the private

Figure 7.2
SPHERES OF LIFE

Public	Private
• work	• home
• mechanistic order	• organic, relational order
• public control	• personal freedom
• rationalized	• creative freedom
• controlled emotions	• expressed emotions
• hierarchy control	• equality, relational
• management	• therapy
• objective public truth based on facts	• private truth, feelings, values based on faith
• production, profit	• consumption, entertainment
• high church	• low church
• science	• religion

domain, where the operative principle is pluralism and respect for the freedom of each person to choose the value he or she will live by. The one requirement imposed on almost everyone is that one must not impose one's religious or moral truth on others. Religions, including Christianity, are seen as a matter of personal faith without general validity and certainty. The pluralism of religions and denominations, in contrast to the apparent monolithic unity of science, only reinforces the notion that they represent personal opinions, not public truth. Occasionally religions are thought to contribute to the common good, especially where they inculcate the moral sensibility of respect for law and order needed to support the nation-building projects of the state.

Modern and traditional elements coexist in modernity in strange and not always easily recognized ways. This is particularly true in non-Western countries with the rapid expansion of modernity, which has forced peoples to reevaluate their place in the world and generated movements that seek to preserve traditional beliefs and values.

IMPACT ON CHRISTIANITY

Modern Neoplatonic dualism has left many Western Christians with a spiritual schizophrenia. They believe in God and the cosmic history of creation, fall, redemption, final judgment, and new creation. This provides them with ultimate meaning and purpose in life. Yet they live in an ordinary world that they explain in naturalistic terms—one in which there is little room for God. They drive cars, use electricity, and ingest medicines—all products of scientific understandings that reinforce a scientific way of thinking.

This internal tension increases when Christians read the Bible. There they find God at work in human history with no sharp distinction made between super and natural phenomena. The biblical worldview does not fit modern secular explanations that deny spiritual realities.

The consequences of this modern dualism have been destructive to the church. Liberal theologians sought to reduce this tension by explaining the miracles of the Bible in naturalistic terms. Conservative theologians affirmed the reality of miracles but saw these as breaking the laws that govern the world—a position that reinforced the belief that ours is a material world governed by impersonal laws. For both, God largely faded from view in their everyday lives.

In missions this dualism has led to a division between "evangelism" and "social gospel," reinforcing the dualism that led to the secularization of modern societies. For many people, evangelism concerns the super salvation of the soul, and the social gospel involves ministry to human physical needs, such as food, medicine, and education. Missionaries planted churches and built schools and hospitals. They saw their task as Christianizing and civilizing people. The two endeavors were often seen as separate tasks. In much of the world, people welcomed the schools and hospitals that were brought by missionaries and that were based on science, but rejected the gospel and the church. Consequently, modern missions often became a powerful secularizing force.

The relegation of religion to the private sphere increasingly made Christianity a matter of personal faith, not public truth. In the West, the sciences and the humanities were required subjects in both public and private schools, but Christianity could be taught as truth only in private schools. Ultimately, it was science that judged the truth claims of Christianity, not Christianity that judged the truth claims of science.

Modern dualism also led many missionaries to deny the reality of spirits, magic, witchcraft, divination, and evil eye, which were important in the everyday life of the people they served. Young Christians in these communities kept their beliefs in these this-worldly spiritual realities but hid them from the missionaries because the missionaries did not believe in such phenomena. The result was "split-level" Christianity in which young Christians were Christian in public, going to church and reciting the confessions on Sunday, but were traditional religionists in private, turning to magicians, diviners, and shamans during the week (Hiebert, Shaw, and Tiénou 1999). In the West, this relegation of angels and demons to other worlds has often led to a functional denial of their activity in everyday life on earth.

Finally, the public/private split has made many Christians apprehensive about the whole idea of mission. Who are we to say that our truth is superior to the truths by which others live? But the gospel claims simply to be *the truth* for everyone. That is an arrogant assertion, unless it is true.

Mechanistic Root Metaphor/Organic Root Metaphor

The reintroduction of Greek dualism was accompanied by a shift from an organic to a mechanistic view of the world. In the Middle Ages, Europeans saw the world as full of living beings interacting with one another. God created it, and it included angels, humans, animals, and other beings, all relating to one another. The world existed for the sake of humans, and it was immediately present and fully intelligible to their minds. The categories used to understand it were not those of mass, energy, velocity, momentum, material space, and impersonal time, which could be measured, but those of essence, form, beauty, and morality. Alfred Crosby observes, "The old European's universe was one of qualities, not quantities" (1997, 47). Even numbers were associated with qualities. God created the universe in six days because six was the perfect number; ten stood for the law, forty for Lent and Christ's days on earth after the resurrection, and thus, for St. Augustine, "life itself."

The Renaissance introduced a mechanistic view of the world. As scientists such as Galileo, Descartes, and Laplace studied nature, they increasingly argued that the real world is a world of bodies moving in space and time in accord with precise mathematical formulas. The earth was ousted from the center of the heavenly spheres and reduced to a minor planet circling a small star in a universe comprised of a hundred billion galaxies of a hundred billion stars. Newton's laws explained this physical world, which was seen as a perfect machine whose future happenings could be predicted by one who has full knowledge of the position and motion of all the atoms at any given moment. That world can be controlled by those who have full knowledge of how it works.

This shift from an organic to a mechanical root metaphor profoundly changed how people saw the world around them. It was no longer alive and full of personal relationships. Increasingly the universe became an impersonal void filled with lifeless galaxies and stars. Mother earth became lifeless land to be exploited, and, as Le Corbusier observed, houses became mass produced, standardized "machines for living," not homes full of relationships, memories, and personal artistic expression. People who resettled in big housing projects are homeless because they have no memories of those who inhabit that place and few personal relationships with their neighbors.

Alwyn Jones notes the consequences of a mechanistic worldview:

> It allows scientists to treat matter as dead and completely separate from themselves, and to see the material world as a multitude of different objects assembled into a huge machine. . . . Priority . . . is given to the parts over the whole, the presumption being that a knowledge of the whole can gradually be built up from a detailed understanding of the relationship between the parts. The model of reality which emerges from this is a vast machine whose fundamental characteristics can be understood by an analysis of its parts and laws which govern their working. . . . This has led to the "searchlight" effect—of high specialization but not seeing the whole. (1991, 236–40)

One of the generally accepted scientific principles is that understanding of complex phenomena can be accomplished only if they are first reduced to their simplest and most basic elements. General conclusions must be drawn from the particular and not from unanalyzed complex situations.

With a mechanistic worldview came the concept of structure seen as the interrelation of impersonal parts in a common system governed by impersonal codes or rules of functioning. This principle was applied not only in the natural sciences but also in the human sciences, which were increasingly modeled after the natural sciences and their search for objectivity. People became by-products of social, linguistic, and cultural constructs.[7] The "subject" that dominated earlier philosophical traditions was eliminated or decentered. The humani-

---

7. In linguistics this view emerged with the semiotic theory of Ferdinand de Saussure, who argued that language can be analyzed in terms of its present laws of operation without reference to its historical development. He argued that signs point not to objective realities but to cultur-

ties and arts, which were dominant in the Middle Ages, were relegated in the academy to lower status.

Modern humans see the world as one of machines and now computers, and increasingly machines replace humans in factories, bureaucracies, and other institutions. Peter Berger and Thomas Luckmann note that the hallmarks of modernity are factories in which nature is shaped into machines and bureaucracies in which people are reduced to machines to make and market machines (1967). In the end, humans became things—programmed machines, not persons. Lewis Mumford (1934), Stephen Pepper (1942), E. A. Burtt (1954), Jacques Ellul (1964), Peter Berger and Thomas Luckmann (1967), Peter and Brigitte Berger and Hansfried Kellner (1973), and E. J. Dijksterhuis (1986) trace the consequences of this shift to a mechanistic worldview. Rational order, control, efficiency, productivity, and profit become primary values. The result is the commodification and commercialization of much of life.

Foundationalism/Holism

Foundationalism emerged in the twelfth century with the reintroduction of Greek thought from the Arabic and Spanish universities (Finger 1985, 18–21).[8] The central question it posed is, what are the unchanging universals in reality? It held that there are basic unchanging elements, and that if these are known, we can, by putting them together, understand the structure of reality. This foundationalism is seen in Newton, who assumed that everything is composed of basic building blocks and put together like a machine.

Foundationalism led to a reductionist view of humans. They are spiritual beings, but their spirituality can be explained in terms of their cultural beliefs. Their cultural beliefs are constructed by their social community, which itself is made up only of individuals. Human psychological processes can be explained in terms of biochemical processes. Francis Crick, codiscoverer of the structure of DNA, writes, "Your joys and your sorrows, your memories and your ambitions, your sense of personal identity and free will, are in fact, no more than the behavior of a vast assembly of nerve cells and their associated molecules" (1994, 3). But cells and molecules are not the foundation for reality. They are made up of atoms, neutrons, protons, electrons, nutrinos, quarks, and other subatomic particles, which in turn are made up, some think, of strings or loops. The foundation of reality is lifeless matter and energy.

Foundationalism leads to determinism and an engineering approach to reality based on technological solutions. It also leads to the division of the sciences into disconnected disciplines, which creates a division of labor and absolutizes the gap between experts and laity. Physics and astronomy were the

ally created arbitrary images in human minds, where they acquire meaning only with reference to other signs in their domains (Best and Kellner 1991).

8. Foundationalism is based on the resurgence of Platonic realism that gave rise to scholasticism and later the humanistic school of Erasmus and culminated in the Enlightenment school.

first "hard" sciences to emerge. The other natural and human sciences have largely adopted this model of classical physics.

Foundationalism also assumes that ultimate truth is ahistorical and acultural and can be known. It uses the methods of Greek philosophy, namely, digital categories and abstract, algorithmic logic, which are propositional in nature. It rejects all internal contradictions and fuzziness in categories. Its goal is to construct a single systematic understanding of ultimate truth, a grand unified theory that is comprehensive, logically consistent, and powerful. To arrive at objective truth, it separates cognition from feelings and values to prevent the latter from introducing subjectivity into the process.

IMPERSONAL ORDER/INTERPERSONAL RELATIONSHIPS

At the heart of modernity is the quest for order and control and the preoccupation with the elimination or reduction of forms of disorder through the engineering and management of orderliness in modern forms of life. This quest constitutes the archetype for all other tasks, the one that renders all other tasks mere metaphors of itself (Bauman 1991, 4).

Order and control in modernity are rooted in the belief in impersonal mechanistic laws. A. R. Radcliffe-Brown writes, "The postulate of the inductive method is that all phenomena are subject to natural law, and that consequently it is possible, by the application of certain logical methods, to discover and prove certain general laws, i.e., certain general statements or formulae, of greater or lesser degree of generality, each of which applies to a certain range of facts or events" (1958, 7). This concept of law extends to laws that govern nature, social and economic laws that regulate societies, and moral laws that define good and evil.[9] Laws enable humans to order nature. Moral laws are legislated and mechanically applied to order society. Barry Smart notes that this treats "human agents simply as potential, not actual objects of social technologies, that is as puppets or cultural dopes" (1993, 79–80). For Max Weber, the disenchantment, rationalization, and regulation imposed by modernity depersonalizes all areas of human life, undermining the possibility of meaningful and ethical conduct of life. As a result, humans are vulnerable to manipulation and oppression in the impersonal and faceless social domain, "a virtual moral vacuum ordered through legal-rational mechanisms of government, [in which] human beings are constituted both as objects of forms of knowledge and subjects of associated therapeutic, managerial and bureaucratic technologies" (Smart 1993, 80).

The role of God in a mechanistic world became increasingly problematic. The universe was seen as a giant clock—with springs, cogwheels, and hands governed by impersonal forces and laws. Early scientists had assumed God was

---

9. Sociology and economics emerged as scientific disciplines to achieve a degree of rational control over social and economic development (Smart 1993, 43).

the clock maker, who created and maintained the clock because all machines are made by some intelligent being. As the mathematically precise nature of the material world was discovered, the concept of natural laws emerged. These postulate that given the same conditions, the same actions will lead to the same results because the components are seen as continuously interdependent in mathematically predictable ways. In the process, the doctrine of divine providence, in which nature obeys God's orders, was replaced by the concept of autonomous laws. Galileo argued that nature is inexorable, acts only "through immutable laws which she never transgresses," and cares "nothing whether her reasons and methods of operating be or be not understandable by men" (Burtt 1954, 75). L. Febvre and H. Martin note, "Armed with the mighty concept of law, [science] gradually strove to reduce the powers of God. In the first place it strove to establish that, if it was possible to admit the original intervention of a *primum movens*, an initial divine motor, there was in any case no longer room, once the machine was started, for an interventionist God, for his miracles, or even, quite simply, for his Providence" (1984, 459). In the end, Laplace argued we no longer even need the assumption that God is the creator of the universe, since there is no "maker."

In time, interpersonal relationships also became problematic. Objective knowledge is "knowledge about" someone or something, not a personal, intersubjective knowing. Human love is rendered impossible because love, by its very nature, seeks to know another, not in detached, objective ways, but in personal, intimate ways. Human freedom, too, must be rejected because it is the potential for self-commitment based on our limited capacity for reflection. Hope is rendered obsolete because it imagines potential realities beyond what "is." Finally, faith (in an ideal, another person, or God) has no place in human knowledge because it "disappears into the security of invulnerable facts and the capacity to control and manipulate the other. A thing need not, cannot, believe" (Kavanaugh 1981, 44).

One consequence of this belief in a mechanical world ruled by autonomous, impersonal laws is determinism. Nature is a closed system determined by forces that obey laws. Humans do not really have free will. Their experiences of choosing are illusions—their thoughts and actions are forced on them by outside causes, such as child-rearing practices, cultural conditioning, economic determinants, and genetic codes. This view also rejects purpose as a cause for human behavior.

The Greco-Roman concept of a universe ruled by impersonal laws included belief in impersonal moral laws. The Hebrews saw laws as God's commandments, which he gave humans to show them the way things ought to be according to divine intention—the fulfillment of the demands of a relationship, whether this relationship is with other human beings or God. These laws concerned God's covenant relationship with Israel. It was not the goal of the legal process to impose punitive measures. According to Gerhard von Rad,

"There is absolutely no concept in the Old Testament with so central a significance for all the relationships of human life as that of *sdqh* [righteousness, justice]. It is the standard in the Old Testament not only for man's relationship to God, but also for his relationships to his fellows, reaching right down . . . [to] the animals and to his environment . . . for it embraces the whole of Israelite life" (1962, 2:370, 373). Specific laws were perceived as just not because they corresponded to some abstract ethical norms but because they sustained shalom within the community. Punishment served to restore the integrity of the community's life and its relationship with God. In this worldview sin and crime are both corporate and individual.

In Greco-Roman thought laws are impersonal, abstract, universal standards of morality; justice calls for strict punishment of violators, and crime is the violation of these laws.[10] In this view, the task of the judicial system is to maintain law and order by impartially dispensing justice and punishing the offender. The symbol of justice is the blindfolded judge, holding the scales of justice.[11] There is little room for love, mercy, forgiveness, and the restoration of the offender into the community.[12]

In this view, rules and procedures must be established if society is to function. Nepotism, favoritism, and other relational factors should be rejected in organizing governments and bureaucracies. Human relationships are secondary and can be rightly conducted only when laws are obeyed. For example, lying is wrong, not because it undermines a relationship, but because it violates a universal moral law. The offender is guilty of breaking the law and must be punished, even if the punishment destroys relationships and harms innocent people. Modernity defines justice as living within the law, not as living in harmony with others.

10. The Greco-Roman concept of law has deeply shaped the view that God is duty bound to punish sinners and uphold the moral law. If he overlooked breaches of universal law, the world would fall into sin and chaos. This view sees moral law as existing apart from God and in some cases leads to the idea that God is moral because he keeps the moral laws—an idea present in Hinduism and other Indo-European worldviews. This view of law also led to emphasis on the punitive-retributional understanding of the cross to the exclusion of other understandings of salvation, including forgiveness and restoration of fellowship and cleansing from defilement.

11. In contrast to Greek views of law, Christians are called to live under the "law of Christ" (Gal. 6:2), but this is the law of love, not a code of legislation. Christians should understand justice as a power that heals, restores, and reconciles rather than kills.

12. Western Christians have imbibed deeply of this belief in the rule of law. Sin is seen as primarily the breaking of divine laws, and salvation as forgiveness from divine punishment, rather than sin as breaking our relationship with God and following another god, and salvation and reconciliation as restoration of fellowship with God. For many the law seems to be higher than God—God is righteous because he keeps the divine moral law that governs the universe. This view that the moral law transcends God is at the heart of the Hindu worldview in which the gods are subject to the judgment of karma and must be reborn as humans, animals, or plants as judgment when they sin, which they frequently do.

The rule of impersonal law also gives rise to abstract structures for ordering human activities, such as governments, armies, factories, and schools. These are defined in terms of impersonal statuses and roles ordered like parts in a machine. In these institutions, people are like cogs in a machine, each carrying out a specialized task. The result is specialization, institutionalization, and trust in experts. The processes are constantly reviewed to improve them. There is no final order, no stable structure. Ultimately this rule of impersonal law leads to relativism and undermines modernity's claims to have better knowledge than tradition (Giddens 1990).

Determinism/Choice

With the shift to a mechanistic worldview, the concept of causality changed. Previously events were explained in terms of beings, their intentions, and their actions. Now valid explanations had to be in terms of small, lifeless, elementary units in regularly changing relations governed by law. E. A. Burtt writes,

> The [medieval] scientist looked out upon the world of nature and it appeared to him a quite sociable and human world. It was finite in extent. It was made to serve his needs. It was clearly and fully intelligible, being immediately present to the rational powers of his mind; it was composed fundamentally of, and was intelligible through, those qualities which were most vivid and intense in his own immediate experience—colour, sound, beauty, joy, heat, cold, fragrance, and its plasticity to purpose and ideal. Now the world is an infinite and monotonous mathematical machine. Not only is his place in a cosmic teleology lost, but all these things which were the very substance of the physical world to the scholastic—things that made it alive and lovely and spiritual—are lumped together and crowded into the small fluctuating and temporary positions of extension which we call human nervous and circulatory systems. (1954, 123–24)

The gloriously romantic universe of Dante and Milton that set no bounds to the human imagination as it played over space and time had now been swept away. No longer was the world full of beings thinking and acting. Now space was identified with the realm of geometry, time with the continuity of number. The world in which people had thought themselves to be living—a world rich with color and sound, redolent with fragrance, filled with gladness, love, and beauty, speaking everywhere of purposive harmony and creative ideals—was crowded now into minute corners of the brains of scattered organic beings. The real, important world outside was a world hard, cold, colorless, silent, and dead; a world of quantity, a world of mathematically computable motions in mechanical regularity. The world of qualities as immediately perceived by humans was just a curious and minor effect of that infinite machine beyond. In Newton, Cartesian metaphysics, ambiguously interpreted and stripped of its distinctive claim for serious philosophical consideration, finally overthrew Aristotelianism and became the predominant worldview of modern times.

Now the world was seen as a perfect machine. Its parts act on one another in predetermined ways governed by impersonal, unchanging laws or principles that determine the one possible outcome for each event. It is these laws, not mere facts, that are universal. They state that *whenever* certain conditions are met (including those in the future), certain results will occur. For example, when scientists speak of "the laws of gravity," they are not referring to any particular event in the past, but what will surely happen, past or future, to everything that fulfills certain conditions. The result is a linear view of causality.

Medieval philosophy sought to answer the question of the *why* of events and saw God as the ultimate cause. In a mechanistic world, questions of purpose and choice are meaningless and eliminated as valid causal explanations. The question now concerns the immediate *how* of events.[13] The answer was found not in God but in the motion of physical atoms. God, if he was considered at all, was reduced to the first efficient cause. He ceased to be the supreme good. He was a huge mechanical inventor whose power was used to account for the first appearance of atoms. In time all causality was rooted in the atoms themselves, and the world was seen as a perfect, mathematically ordered machine. Burtt writes that "Just as it was thoroughly natural for medieval thinkers to view nature as subservient to man's knowledge, purpose and destiny; so now it has become natural to view her as existing and operating in her own self-contained independence, and . . . his destiny wholly dependent on her" (1954, 24).

Later the biological and human sciences took over these mathematical postulates after the triumph of mechanics in physics and chemistry.[14] The human being came to be seen as "human-the-machine." In this vast, self-contained, mathematical world, humans with their purposes, feelings, and other secondary qualities were shoved aside as unimportant products and spectators of the great mechanically determined drama outside. Bertrand Russell summarizes the new view of reality:

> Such, in outline, but even more purposeless, more void of meaning, is the world which Science presents to our belief. . . . That man is the product of causes which had no provision for the end they were achieving; that his origin, his growth, his hopes and fears, his loves and his beliefs, are but the outcome of accidental collocations of atoms; that no fire, no heroism, no intensity of thought and feeling, can preserve an individual life beyond the grave; that all

13. Galileo and Newton dropped final causes as valid explanations in science as a strategy for research. Later they were dropped as valid questions.

14. Newton's explanation of the heavens in the name of science in terms of gravity and centripetal movements of the celestial bodies radically transformed the world's understandings of the material universe. The poet Alexander Pope wrote, "Nature and Nature's laws lay hid in night; / God said, 'Let Newton be!'—and all was light." Newton developed calculus and wedded the experimental and mathematical methods that are the foundations of modern science.

the labours of the ages, all the devotion, all the inspirations, all the noonday brightness of human genius are destined to extinction in the vast death of the solar system, and that the whole temple of Man's achievement must inevitably be buried beneath the debris of a universe in ruins—all these things, if not quite beyond dispute, are yet so nearly certain, that no philosophy which rejects them can hope to stand. Only within the scaffolding of these truths, only on the firm foundation of unyielding despair, can the soul's habitation henceforth be safely built. . . . Omnipotent matter rolls on its relentless way. (2004, 46–47)

For medieval Europeans, life was meaningful, purposeful, and infinite. For modernists, humans are accidents, the chance and temporary product of a blind and purposeless nature. Parker Palmer notes, "We and our world become objects to be lined up, counted, organized and owned, rather than a community of beings and selves related to each other in a complex web of accountability called 'truth'" (1993, 39).

But a totally deterministic world rules out human choice and with it all sense of reason and meaning. The countertheme in modernity is the autonomy of the human mind, particularly that of the scientist and modern reason.[15] If the universe is a rational order, and the human mind, through precise reasoning, can understand that order, humans can engineer a better world. The modern project, therefore, was to develop objective science, universal law, and autonomous art according to inner logic.

Technique/Relationships

Central to a mechanistic view of reality is the focus on technique (Ellul 1964). Technique is a rational mechanical process designed to produce the maximum results with a minimum of input by focusing on efficiency and speed and reducing all that is spontaneous and irrational.

Technique requires routinization, breaking tasks down into parts that can be ordered logically and repeated routinely to produce a high degree of efficiency. In manufacturing this led to the automated assembly line. In bureaucracies, such as government, business, education, and even the church, it led to the division of labor with an increasing number of specialists who are experts in their field but know little of the overall processes involved.

Technique requires standardization of parts and processes to make them easily replaceable. Handcrafted goods are costly and unpredictable.

15. Descartes sought to restore humans to a central place in nature and did so with his famous metaphysical dualism. Hobbes pushed the mechanistic view to its logical conclusion and saw the soul simply as another body in motion. His pure mechanistic materialism was attacked from the start. Even the most materialist-minded modern scholars cannot accept the idea that humans and societies are nothing but engines moved by only two basic human emotions: desire for power and fear of death. But most social scientists have searched for laws of the mind and society similar to the laws of nature.

Standardization leads to the mass production of parts and products. Dealing with individuals in an organization as distinct persons is inefficient, so workers are reduced to standardized impersonal roles, such as secretaries, factory workers, and computer specialists, who can be moved to the same positions anywhere in the organization. People are reduced to impersonal units, and the organization relies more on methods and rules than on individuals.

Technique requires quantification. To be objective and reliable knowledge must be expressed in numbers. Languages are too imprecise, arbitrary, and subjective. It is hard to measure inputs, outputs, and efficiency without reducing them to numbers that can be compared and charted for the sake of rationally evaluating the effectiveness and efficiency of a technique. The scientist must have access to numbers.

Techniques are amoral. They focus on "how," not "why." Goals are assumed and peripheral, and the focal point is how to achieve them. Progress and innovation are assumed to be good and highly valued. Efficiency and profit are the supreme values. They are founded on utilitarianism and pragmatism, not on moral absolutes. The result is an engineering or "tinkering" mentality that reduces all life to mechanistic analysis. The result, as Max Weber notes, is that modernity has become "an iron cage."

Finally, technique turns everything into goods that can be produced and sold. The result is the commodification of public life—everything is valued in terms of its economic benefits.

As Peter Berger and his associates point out, the application of mechanical techniques has led to the factory, where people are reduced to efficient machines, and to bureaucracies, where people are reduced to impersonal parts in the organization (Berger, Berger, and Kellner 1973). Technique has come to dominate public life from business, politics, and government, to science, education, and even religion. As Ellul notes, it has taken over not just production and business but all human activities (1964, 4). As it enters into every area of modern life, people become less human and more captive to a worldview that controls most areas of their lives.

The expansion of technique to all areas of life can be seen in the clock, the first characteristically modern instrument. Ellul maintains that "the substitution of the *tempus mortuum* of the mechanical clock for the biological and psychological time of man is in itself sufficient to suppress all the traditional rhythms of human life in favor of the mechanical" (1964, xvi).

IMPACT ON CHRISTIANITY

It should not surprise us that the mechanistic root metaphor of modernity has shaped the church, although how deeply it has done so may be surprising. The church is in the world and always in danger of becoming captive to it, not when the world attacks, but when it lures us through its enticements. Here we will explore three such influences.

Emphasis on Law and Order

The first influence is the emphasis on mechanistic order over interpersonal relationships. We see this in the emphasis on clock time over relational time. In the former, people must be "on time" according to the clock, because punctuality is most efficient in coordinating the activities of many people doing different jobs. In much of the world people live by relational time, which means they do their best to meet at a given time, but other, human-related activities may intervene and delay them. Although they may set out for church in good time, on the way they may meet a relative or a friend they have not seen for a long time. They cannot simply say hello and good-bye in a few minutes. It takes time to rebuild the relationship, and they will eventually get to the service, which is held every week. Similarly, if unexpected relatives show up at a modern home just as the father is heading off for work, what should he do? Should he say how glad he is to see them, give them the key, and tell them he will be back at five, or should he invite them in for breakfast and call to tell his office he will be late? In much of the world, the answer to this question is obvious. Yet modern churches operate by clock time and regard arriving late as undisciplined and improper.

A second area in which we find an emphasis on order is in matters involving cleanliness. Cleanliness in modernity is defined primarily in terms of high order: of keeping categories uniform. Flowers in the grass are weeds, earth on the sidewalk is dirt, and spoons in the fork bin are out of place. Categories must also be clearly bounded. Pictures, windows, and doors should have frames setting them off, cracks in the wall should be fixed or covered by moldings, and floors should be differentiated from walls by baseboards. Wherever categories meet, the boundary must be marked to keep the distinctions clear. In modernity cleanliness is not only next to godliness but often above it. In the church, too, cleanliness is of high value. Sanctuaries, dress, and the order of rituals must be clean and proper. We see this emphasis in the tension between relationships and cleanliness. If long-unseen friends appear at church, do we invite them to our home for lunch, although our house is dirty because we left in a hurry, or do we greet them and invite them to our house on another day, after we have had time to clean it? In many cases we do the next best thing, in terms of relationships: we invite them out to a restaurant dinner!

A third area in which we see high order is in that of morality, which is defined not so much in relational terms as in terms of law and order. Morality is often seen as living by impersonal moral laws, sin as violation of these laws, and justice as punishment for breaking the laws. Breaking relationships is commonly viewed not as sin but as part of life. In much of the world, morality is defined more in terms of interpersonal relationships, sin as breaking relationships, and salvation as the restoration of relationships.

This emphasis on moral law and order is also seen in the debates of modern theologians. Reformed theologians stress the sovereignty of God: his power over and control of all things to bring his will to fruition. Ultimately this view comes close to seeing the impersonal moral law as unchanging and eternal, as coexistent with God himself. The countertheme stresses the love of God and his desire to relate personally with his human creations. Those holding the dominant theme are threatened by this view, because if taken too far, it means that humans have some freedom outside God's control. True love cannot force a "spontaneous" response. There is little room for the two to coexist as equals within the view of modern dualism, for that would open the door to paradox and threaten reason. The tension between these themes is really not between God's sovereignty and human freedom, but rather between God's sovereignty and God's love—it is in the very nature of God himself. Commensurate with the precepts of algorithmic rationality, our inclination is to make one or the other higher. Scripture does not do so.

The mechanistic metaphor of modernity has also profoundly shaped modern missions. The modern emphasis on order, time, and cleanliness has influenced the way Western missionaries work. They have tried to teach people to be on time; to construct straight walls; to paint without slopping on the window sills; to keep buildings clean; to plan for future activities; to keep accurate minutes and straight accounts; to stand in line; to maintain sharp borders on paths and roads; and to keep books, medicines, and other supplies in order on shelves. Their fear of chaos has often been a hindrance to turning work over to the nationals. They have been afraid that hospitals would become dirty, schools unorganized, churches disorderly, accounts irregular, and the order of the church chaotic if things are controlled by the local people. Moreover this distrust of the local people has undermined the missionaries' credibility among them.

In many traditional societies relationships take precedence over structural order. Work must wait when relatives and friends arrive unexpectedly. Caring for one another is an accepted part of community life, not an intrusion on one's personal plans. To live in peace with others is the greatest good; the greatest evil is to be alienated and alone. Because relationships are unpredictable, planning is always tentative. Decisions must be negotiated with others and are subject to unexpected change. To change an agreement because the situation changes is not only acceptable; it is wise. Agreements are not contracts that a person must carry out under any circumstances but rather desires people hope to fulfill. Notions of beauty in these societies are linked to relationships rather than to physical appearance. Beautiful people are generous people. They show hospitality to strangers and share their goods with others. Wise people are those who can untangle the knots in human relationships through impartial mediation.

Christians in other lands are often confused by the Western obsession with order and Westerners' lack of relational skills. Westerners rarely open their homes spontaneously to visitors. They are more interested in keeping possessions than in sharing them. They are often too busy doing things to take time just to sit and visit. For Christians in many non-Western societies, the central issue in Christianity is not right order but right relationships. The gospel to them is good news because it speaks of shalom—of a community in which harmonious relationships value human dignity, justice, love, peace, and concern for the lost and the marginalized.

Emphasis on Tasks and Techniques

Another way in which the church in the West has been shaped by modernity can be seen in its focus on tasks and techniques, rather than on community and relationships. Being the church and doing missions are tasks that we associate with our abilities to make things happen and to take control. The result is an engineering mentality. In churches business meetings focus on finding the right techniques to solve the problems of the church. In missions, church planting and growth can be done well if the right techniques are found through quantitative data, analysis, and testing of various methods.

Building Bureaucracies

The way to organize people in modernity is to create bureaucratic organizations that run according to constitutions and bylaws and use impersonal roles to order relationships. This results, too, in a focus on the importance of leaders and leadership defined in managerial styles.

Bureaucracies enable us to build far larger organizations than can be run based on personal relationships, the foundation for fellowship. Although fellowship groups can be added to introduce the personal dimension, the bureaucracy itself takes precedence over these.

Individual/Group

Central to the Enlightenment was the shift of the center of existence from God to humans and the self. Immanuel Kant wrote, "Enlightenment is man's release from his self-incurred tutelage. Tutelage is man's inability to make use of his understanding without direction from another. Self-incurred is this tutelage when its cause lies not in lack of reason but in lack of resolution and courage to use it without direction from another. . . . 'Have courage to use your own reason!'" (1959, 85). The Enlightenment stressed the importance of self-consciousness, not irrational emotions, as the basis of true reasoning and knowledge.

Alexis de Tocqueville, after his extended travels in the United States in 1831, noted this trend in his analysis of democracy in America.

Individualism is a novel expression, to which a novel idea has given birth. Our fathers were only acquainted with egoisme (selfishness). Selfishness is a passionate and exaggerated love of self, which leads a man to connect everything with himself, and to prefer himself to everything in the world. Individualism is a mature and calm feeling, which disposes each member of the community to sever himself from the mass of his fellows and to draw apart with his family and his friends; so that, after he has thus formed a little circle of his own, he willingly leaves society at large to itself. . . . New families are constantly springing up, others are constantly falling away. . . . Those who went before are soon forgotten; of those who will come after, no one has an idea: the interest of man is confined to those in close propinquity to himself. (1863, 119–21)

Peter Berger and his associates write that "Modernity has given birth to ideologies and ethical systems of intense individualism. Indeed, it has been suggested that the theme of individual autonomy is perhaps the most important theme in the worldview of modernity. . . . The conception of the naked self, beyond institutions and roles, as the *ens realissimum* of human beings, is the very heart of modernity" (Berger, Berger, and Kellner 1973, 196, 213).[16]

According to Anthony Hoekema, "The first moment of modernity was characterized by Descartes and Kant, who introduced the ideas of rationality and individual responsibility. From then on the individual became incredibly powerful, saying that 'nothing is either true faith or right morality which is not our own'; and that, in consequence, eternal authority is, in principle, an unsound basis, and the individual judgment not merely a right but a duty" (1986, 64). In modernity individuals insist on the right, individually and at any time, to do whatever they want or to do the same thing as others are doing. The sacred roots of traditional communities are contrary to the rights of individuals and liberal tolerance.

With God out of the picture, humans became the gods of the earth. During the Renaissance, Machiavelli took the next logical step and called for people to forget about salvation, which by his day had lost much of its clarity and urgency. Rather, they should focus on enjoying life here on earth, which is real and immediate. Personal health, comfort, and prosperity became the primary goals of modern culture, and science was seen as the means to achieve them.

Left alone, however, modern humans faced a crisis of meaning. Now they were gods, but what sort of gods were they? Mechanistic science has enabled humans to control nature, but it has also given them the power to destroy nature through violence, nuclear holocausts, chemical pollution, and deforestation. The same science sees humans themselves as animals ruled by needs and irrational drives, as stimulus-response machines, or as robots programmed by their societies and cultures. God is gone, but so is the human soul. There is no real meaning left in human life. Allan Bloom writes of Americans: "They are egotists, not in a vicious way, not in the way of those who know the good, just or noble, and selfishly reject them, but because the ego is all there is in present theory, in what they are taught" (1987, 256).

16. For further readings on individualism, see Bellah et al. 1985; Bloom 1987; Hsu 1963; and Todd 1987.

SELF/SOUL

To recover a sense of meaning, modern philosophers coined the term *self* to replace the concept of *soul* (Bloom 1987, 173). In the Middle Ages individuals were seen as spiritual beings in relationship to God and other humans. They were referred to as "souls," as in "twenty souls were lost at sea." Enlightenment thinkers rejected the term "soul," because it carried connotations of divine image and immortality; they introduced the term "self" to replace it. Bloom observes, "The domain now supervised by psychiatrists, as well as other specialists in the deeper understanding of man, is the *self*. It is another one of the discoveries made in the state of nature, perhaps the most important because it reveals what we really are. We are selves, and everything we do is to satisfy or fulfill ourselves. Locke was one of the early thinkers, if not the earliest, to use the word in its modern sense. . . . To sum up, the self is the modern substitute for the soul" (1987, 173).

The result of this shift is the emergence of the autonomous self as the new center of reality (fig. 7.3). Desire becomes an unquestioned good, and narcissism is its fruit. In the end, the self becomes the central project of moral interest, and self-enjoyment and self-development the central goals.

Figure 7.3
THE CONCEPTS OF SOUL AND SELF

Soul	Self
ontological	experiential
objective	subjective
nature given	nature developed
basic potentials	specific actualizations
universal	particular

The question now arose, however, concerning the essence of this *self*. Some philosophers, such as Locke and Descartes, believed it to be reason. Humans are different from animals because they think. Using reason, they can create a happy, peaceful, and meaningful world. Others, such as Rousseau and Nietzsche, disagreed. They believed that what makes humans different from other animals and what makes their lives meaningful is the ability to experience life—to envision better worlds and create them. Humans are culture builders. They are moral beings who find meaning in realizing their dreams about themselves. Both views, however, concur that meaning is to be found in self-fulfillment, in the good life here and now. The existential present, not eternity, is of primary importance.

Individualism led to an atomistic view of society. Just as the physical world was seen as an aggregate of realities made up of particles floating in an empty void, so societies were seen as aggregates of discrete, autonomous individuals.

Modern social systems are built on the notion of individualism. One result is the emergence of clubs and bureaucratic corporations where membership is voluntary and persons may leave.

SELF-ACTUALIZATION/SALVATION

The focus on the autonomous individual led to the belief that people must take the initiative for their own well-being. This position in its own turn led to an emphasis on freedom over control, rights over responsibilities, and the search for self-actualization and a good life defined in terms of comfort, consumerism, and entertainment.

The focus on the self and self-realization became the dominant theme in modern societies at the end of the nineteenth century. The traditional Protestant values of salvation, morality, hard work, saving and sacrifice, civic responsibility, and self-denial for the good of others were replaced by a new set of values: personal realization, health, material comfort, immediate gratification, and periodic leisure (Fox and Lears 1983, 4). These goals, it was believed, could be achieved through buying material goods (largely on credit) and accumulating wealth. The gospel of self-indulgence was preached by a host of advertisers and reinforced by therapists promising human dignity through the inner healing of the self. The result was an almost obsessive concern with psychic and physical health. Life owed us comfort, health, happiness, success, prosperity, and intense, ecstatic experiences. Failure, loss of self-worth, and boredom, rather than sin, became the implacable enemies. Therapy, consumption, and miraculous cures were the means of salvation. Modernity offered meaning based on self-realization, not forgiveness of sins and reconciliation with God and others. Self became god and self-fulfillment salvation. Personal biography replaced cosmic history as the framework in which human significance was found. The only story many modern people feel a part of is their own. Unrestrained individual freedom has become an unquestioned good. All social control is seen as oppression. Corporate accountability has been displaced by subjective self-expression.

Religious beliefs have played a key role in giving people a sense of ultimate and intrinsic significance. The decline of religious beliefs in the West, which gave purpose to life through self-denial, sacrifice, work, and corporate responsibility, led to a crisis of personal meaning. Individuals need a sense of significance in their lives—a sense that their lives are not mere accidents. They want to be taken seriously. Modernity offered a new transcendent framework based on self-realization. Salvation was tied no longer to the next world but to the good life in this one (Fox and Lears 1983, xiii). The new ideals were self-fulfillment and immediate gratification through periodic leisure, compulsive spending, and permissive morality; individual fulfillment replaced the earlier goal of transcendence. Individuals were encouraged to create themselves through human engineering.

Democracy/Socialism

The emphasis on the autonomous individual raises profound questions about the organization of social life. If the individual is more important than the group, how can groups be formed? As Stanley Hauerwas and William Willimon note, the underlying principle for organizing life is democracy, the notion that the group is made up of autonomous individuals linked together by contract: "The primary entity of democracy is the individual, the individual for whom society exists mainly to assist assertions of individuality. Society is formed to supply our needs, no matter what the content of those needs. Rather than helping us to judge our needs, to have the right needs which we exercise in right ways, our society becomes a vast supermarket of desire" (1989, 32).

The price of individualism and freedom is a lack of strong, permanent personal relationships and security. The autonomous person is a person alone, never in a community greater than he or she. Social groups are fluid and less important than the individual.

Clubs

W. Lloyd Warner notes that the most common way Americans organize themselves is by membership in associations or clubs: "Voluntary associations permeate every aspect of [North American] society. Whether for trivial and ludicrous or serious and important purposes, Americans use associations for almost every conceivable activity. . . . When 'something needs to be done' or 'a serious problem must be solved' in the United States, private citizens usually band together in a new association, or use one already available" (1953, 1991).

Clubs are voluntary associations of individuals for a specific purpose. For example there are associations to advance beekeeping, to play tennis, and to raise twins. In any city or town one finds myriad social, ethnic, recreational, educational, political, financial, patriotic, charitable, and religious clubs that appeal to many different constituencies.

In contrast to group-oriented societies, where the community deals with all dimensions of its members' lives, clubs are normally single-purpose gatherings. People gather in one club to meet a specific need and turn to other clubs to meet other needs. Attempts to make a club a strong group, such as a family, a clan, or a tribe, inevitably fail because the club, by its very purpose and nature, differs from strong groups.

The social glue holding clubs together is weak because group loyalties are based on personal interests. There is always the threat that relationships between members will founder because of arguments or loss of interest. Clubs are fragile, homogeneous groups governed by conformity to the majority. Idiosyncrasies and differences are not as well tolerated as they are in strong group societies.

Relationships in a club are based on contract. Members join because of what they hope to get, and they expect to receive essentially as much as they give. There is much talk of personal rights but little talk of sacrifice or giving one's life for others. In contractual relationships the individual is more important than the group.

Finally, decisions in such a group are based on consensus or vote. All members expect to have an equal say in actions that affect them.

Francis Hsu points out that clubs are a form of social organization particularly suitable for modern societies, which see the complete freedom of the autonomous individual as the highest value. He writes, "The lack of permanent human relations, the idea of complete equality among men, the contract principle, and the need for definite affiliation to achieve sociability, security and status combine and generate a situation in which club life is of the essence of existence" (1963, 208). The price of this freedom and autonomy, however, is a lack of permanent human relations and security. In the end, the autonomous person is a person alone, never in community, because he or she is not willing to sacrifice his or her interests for the interests of the group. The autonomous person is also a self-centered person who measures all things in terms of their benefits and costs to him or her.

Corporations

A second type of social organization thrives in modern society: the corporation. These are the "public" homes where most people spend their working days and earn a living. Peter Berger (1974) identifies the factory and the bureaucracy as the two main types of corporation in modern societies. Both are organized on the principles of a mechanical order in which people and tasks are broken down into standardized units and are structured to maximize quantitatively measured production and profit. Leadership is based on planning and management. Efficiency and technique become top priorities (Ellul 1964).

Corporations are formally organized, enduring associations with their own internal social organization and their own subcultures. The difference between companies and clubs is one of degree. Clubs are temporary, monofunctional associations. Companies are permanent, multifunctional, formally organized associations.

Corporations take a great many forms: business organizations such as factories, banks, supermarkets, insurance companies, professional organizations, and unions; political organizations such as parties and lobbies; legal organizations such as governments and armies; and entertainment organizations such as television networks, orchestras, and theatrical companies.

Relationships in corporations are based on formal contracts, and roles are defined on the basis of specialization. Professionalism becomes essential to doing complex jobs well. People join expecting to offer some service in exchange for some rewards. If they feel they are not receiving what they are worth, they are free to leave. On the other hand, management is free to dismiss those it feels do not fit the company's needs. The relationship is often tenuous at best. Roles inside a corporation are clearly defined on the basis of specialization.

Impact on Christianity

The impact of this individualism and self-centeredness on Christians and the church is far-reaching. The modern mission movement was based on the assumption that the gospel is addressed to individuals, calling them to an inner experience of personal conversion based on the cognitive affirmation that Jesus Christ is Lord. Lamin Sanneh notes, "The [modern] tendency to see the Church in terms of individual healthy mindedness, as a selfhood that is vulnerable to bouts of low self-esteem, is light-years removed from the Church as a fellowship of faithfulness to God's promises" (1993, 22). G. Stanley Hall, Harry Emerson Fosdick, Norman Vincent Peale, Bruce Barton, and others gave theological support to this gospel of the self, which promised vibrant health, prosperity, and self-realization here and now. For many the gospel has become one of health and wealth on earth and salvation in heaven.

This stress on individualism has also led to a weak understanding of the church as a family of families of faith. Because salvation has become a personal matter between the self and God, there is little emphasis on the formulation of a new community of shalom in Christ.

Modern Christians tend to organize their churches the same way they organize corporate action in other areas of their lives. Consequently, many churches are religious clubs. They focus on a single interest (religious life), have voluntary membership, follow democratic procedures in organization, and have their own symbols, property, and patterns of behavior. There are attempts at building deeper fellowship through small groups and church dinners, but few members are willing to pay the price of real community: involvement in members' daily lives and willingness to bear one another's burdens through sharing and financial assistance. When a church organizes itself using the social principles of a club, it soon becomes a club, no matter what it preaches about community.

Club-style congregations tend to be homogeneous groups, held together by the same theology, ethnicity, and social class. Members must constantly reaffirm their beliefs and the practices of the congregation to show that they are in good standing, and hide their disagreements for fear of being ostracized. Differences among members over the beliefs and practices of the group often lead to accusations of heresy and divisions in the church.

Relationships in these churches are contractual. People join by personal choice and are free to leave if the church no longer meets their needs. Their primary reason for joining is to get something personally out of participation, not because members have a lasting commitment to others in the congregation. They tend to overlook the fact that the center of the church is worship—what they bring to God, not what they get out of the service.

As churches grow and organize into denominations, they increasingly become corporations modeled after modern management structures. They are characterized by a professionalization of roles, paid staff, construction of large buildings with offices, establishment of bureaucratic rules and regulations, creation of budgets, organization of meetings, and long-range planning.

Relationships in such churches are based on contract. For those hired in the church, the contracts are formal and can be legally enforced. Promotions and rewards are based on performance and achievement. For the laity contracts are informal. Lay status is based on the level of participation and contribution to the organization. Voluntary service is encouraged, but it is generally seen as a lower level of ministry. Lay persons may attend services even if they are removed from formal membership in the congregation.

Corporate-style churches are characterized by a sharp division between leaders and laity. The former are thought to have specialized competencies, the latter to offer only general skills. The result is that such churches increasingly tend to opt for professional and paid leadership, whereas the laity become consumers who come to church for the services it offers them.

The processes described in the preceding paragraphs are essential to running a successful bureaucracy, but they make it difficult for members to feel that they are part of a single covenant community in which all are equal and Christ is the center of life. Some see the church in terms of social engineering: if subjected to the right formula of social and cultural laws, churches will grow. Others use an economic model and see the church as marketing the gospel. While these approaches may work in modern contexts, the question remains whether the gospel is transforming the culture, or whether it has become captive to modernity.

Individualism has fostered an entrepreneurial approach to missions in which individuals' and churches' mission outreach function not on behalf of the church as a whole but as autonomous bodies. This pressure to individualize missions also affects denominational mission agencies, which traditionally act on behalf of the church.

Finally, the focus on the individual has led to a neglect of the central message that Jesus preached during his ministry on earth, namely the kingdom of God. For many the focus of missions is evangelism—leading individuals to faith in Christ. Organizing them into churches is secondary, and kingdom ministries are what they should do while waiting for Christ's return. Even those who make church planting their goal see the kingdom largely as doing good deeds on earth, not as the commencement of God's reign on earth in our day.

Capitalism/Nation-State

Fundamental to the emergence of modernity is the rise of capitalism and the nation-state. John Rapley writes:

> What killed off the European Middle Ages was capitalism. The modern state system dates back from the Peace of Westphalia, in 1648, which recognized that governments were sovereign over their territories and that no institution within their borders was exempt from their rules. But medievalism was pushed aside for good only as national economies gradually developed and centralized governments supplanted the plethora of medieval authorities over the next couple of centuries. The growth of cities and the advent of overseas exploration boosted the tax revenues from trade and enriched the urban middle class. . . . At the same time, the rising business class began to eclipse the lords politically by filling the emergent states' bureaucracies, in which offices were often sold to the highest bidder. (2006, 98)

CAPITALISM

Modernity is tied to the rise of capitalism, the production and consumption of material goods and services to meet all basic human needs. Its goal is to do so most efficiently and profitably, which requires the rationalization of the processes of production and marketing. Earlier production was in the hands of human laborers, but as technology was developed, they were replaced. The introduction of the assembly line by Henry Ford further rationalized production. Parts were standardized, assembly was broken down into small steps, and workers were assigned to perform repetitive jobs as products moved by. The result was mass production that increased efficiency greatly and produced standardized products. In the early days of mass production, people had little or no choice of automobiles, for example, because there was virtually no variation in the number and quality of cars. In the post-Ford era choices have multiplied greatly, but cars are all made using standardized parts and assembly-line techniques. In later years the assembly-line technique spread to the manufacturing of other goods and to fast-food chains in a process some figuratively call McDonaldization.

Ironically, as George Ritzer points out, the attempt to rationalize different domains of life through emphasis on efficiency and profitability of production and consumption leads to the "irrationality of rationality" (2001, 144). The rationalization of production and distribution in the economic sphere has led to the dehumanization of workers and consumers. In factories, fast-food shops, and market chains, relationships among workers and between workers and consumers are increasingly depersonalized for the sake of efficiency and profit. Relationships between employees and customers are fleeting at best. Courtesies are exchanged, and attempts to personalize the relationships are made by using name tags and casual conversation, but both parties know that this is false friendliness. Employees are trained to interact in a staged, scripted, and limited manner with customers. Unlike small family stores in small communities where everyone knows everyone else, and shopping is often more a social than an economic event, in large department stores neither employees nor consumers can take the time to chat and get to know the other, and to build lasting relationships that extend outside the workplace.

The academy is influenced by the processes of rationalization as well. Ritzer writes:

> The modern university has, in various ways, become a highly irrational place. Many students and faculty members are put off by its huge, factory-like atmosphere. They may feel like automatons processed by the bureaucracy and computers, or even cattle run through a meat-processing plant. In other words, education in such settings can be a dehumanizing experience. The masses of students; large, impersonal dorms; and huge lecture classes make getting to know other students difficult. The large lectures, constrained tightly by the clock, make it virtually impossible to know professors personally. (2001, 41)

The same is true of health care. Control has shifted from the physician to rationalized structures and institutions run by managers who are not themselves physicians. The drive for efficiency often makes patients feel like products on a medical assembly line. In hospitals, instead of seeing the same nurse regularly, a patient may see many different nurses. The result is that nurses rarely come to know their patients as individuals.

Figure 7.4

ECONOMIC SYSTEMS

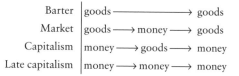

At the heart of capitalism is the accumulation and use of surplus wealth to accumulate more capital. William Greider writes, "Once set in motion, the surplus wealth . . . becomes one of capitalism's three classic factors of production, alongside human labor and nature (the land and resources consumed to make things). Capital puts up the money to build the factory, buys the machines, and pays the company's bills until its goods are produced and sold, thus yielding the new returns that pay back the lenders and investors with an expected increase. It is not simple, but that is the essence" (2003, 94).

In late capitalism, money is invested in money (as in the stock market and in speculation on the exchange rates between different world currencies) to make more money (fig. 7.4). The result of late capitalism is that everything can be reduced to a commodity to be bought and sold. This commodification extends far beyond the market to entertainment, politics and government, and, too often, the church.

In the end, as Max Weber observes, the secularization and rationalization of the market has led to its disenchantment. It no longer serves important social, psychological, or spiritual functions. The goal is to produce essential human goods at the cheapest prices. Left unchecked, capitalism encourages greed, creates ever greater wants to drive markets, destroys ecological balances, increases greatly the distance between rich and poor, dehumanizes work to meaningless mechanical routines, and defines everything in economic terms.

NATION-STATE

One of the characteristics of modernity is the emergence of the nation-state. Most traditional societies are built on ties of kinship, religion, or feudal bonds, which are seen as deeper than geography. Ethnic groups and castes are a community whose members share a common descent and therefore are of common "blood," real or fictive. Membership is controlled by marriage and descent. Generally the members of a group share the same language and culture, including gods and religious beliefs. They may also occupy a common territory. Religious states are communities of people who share the same gods and beliefs.

William Greider notes that the nation-state emerged as the countertheme to capitalism.

> The great accomplishment of the twentieth-century reform politics was to establish government as the counterforce to capitalism, the rival power center that confronted business and finance on behalf of the society, that could break the encroaching domination of private, economic power, curb the excesses and abuses, or clean up the social wreckage that business left in its wake. . . . Yet there is another discomforting reality to face: Government in the long run did not succeed in resolving the deeper collisions between society and capitalism. These conflicts wax and wane from one decade to the next, but no one can argue at this point that the enduring aspirations of people and society are fulfilled when so many of these public goals are in retreat and more insecure. (2003, 30–31)

The modern state came into existence in the sixteenth century, but national loyalties to the state may be no older than the eighteenth century. Before that time, aristocrats and administrators ruled over large populations of peasants who were forced to pay taxes but who professed little or no allegiance to the state. Ted Lewellen writes:

> The key idea underlying the nation-state is a myth, namely, that the state embraces a single people with a shared culture and that citizens are defined by their

residence within a given territory and owe allegiance and undivided loyalty to a common government. If this was a myth in the past, when migrants were expected to assimilate, it is even more so today, when migrants tend to be transnational, maintaining their ethnicities through constant economic and social connections with a home country, never truly assimilating. (2002, 196)

The shift to modernity is a shift to territory as the fundamental marker of personal and corporate identity. People are "Canadians," "Germans," or "Indians" because of the place where they were born, even though their parents are citizens of another country. Nation-states are more fundamental to the modern political scene than are tribes and other ethnic communities or cultures and religions. The emergence of the nation-state saw territorial frontiers transformed into well-defined borders demarcating the exclusive domain of centralized, sovereign power. Within those boundaries, the state exercised unchallenged authority, and ultimate allegiance was transferred to it. The state also claimed a monopoly on the legitimate means of violence. Politics in the nation-state became a matter of protecting, consolidating, and enlarging borders, endeavors that require the creation of large standing armies.

The nation-state is a nation because a nation is "an imagined political community, imagined because the members of even the smallest nation will never know most of their fellow-members, meet them, or even hear of them, yet in the mind's eye of each lives the image of their community . . . a deep, horizontal comradeship" (B. Anderson 1983, 6–7). It is a state because this national identification is wedded to the political ideology focused on the state defined in terms of a population, a territory, and a common, dominant culture that establishes the norms of nationality. "Even those who did not share the dominant culture were expected to make the state the primary loyalty, overriding local group identifications" (Lewellen 2002, 115). New immigrants were expected to assimilate in the national melting pot.

One consequence of this shift of primary identity to national citizenship has been the clash in many countries between ethnic and national identities. With the spread of modernity through colonial expansion, national boundaries were drawn by Western colonial governments without regard to ethnic boundaries. This practice often split ethnic communities between different countries, creating tensions between the ethnic and the national identities. It also lumped together different ethnic communities in a single nation, creating tensions in which ethnic loyalties subverted national governments. Vinoth Ramachandra writes, "Both religious and secular nationalisms provide an overarching moral framework, locating the individual in a larger collectivity. For secular nationalism, emotional identification with the geographic area of one's birth and the people of that locality is not only affirmed but is assumed to be a universal moral good" (1999, 151).

The emergence of the secular nation has led to a separation of state and church. In the Middle Ages, the state was seen as a religious kingdom that dealt primarily with matters of defense and trade. The church provided people their plausibility structure and took responsibility for their well-being. It established hospitals, schools, orphanages, and homes for the poor. The Enlightenment separated the church from civil society and made the modern welfare state responsible for maintaining the good life on earth. The state took such things as marriage and death out of the sacred sphere, where they were sacraments conducted before God, and put them into the civil sphere, where they were contracts, matters of public law that applied to everyone. In the nineteenth century, the state came to be the central institution ultimately responsible for the well-being of its citizens. It took control of education, medicine, and social welfare and set the limits of religion. It took the blame if people died from neglect caused by the state itself. When asked who in each society is in charge of taking care of the weak, powerless, poor, and marginal, people in traditional societies say the family or the community; modern people say it is the state. In return for primary allegiance, the state is ultimately considered responsible for the well-being of its citizens. The result is the welfare state.

The relationships between various religious communities and the emerging nation-state have been uneasy ones. In many parts of the world, religious leaders have sought to wed states to particular religions. The result has been the emergence of Islamic and Hindu nations. In these countries, however, tensions remain. Religious fundamentalists seek to make the state a servant of religion, and modern national leaders try to make the state the primary identity of the people.

The price of this shift in primary allegiances is that the state demands total allegiance, particularly in times of war. Unfortunately, the church has too often been an all-too-willing partner in this reorganization of loyalties and responsibilities. Increasingly it saw its primary responsibility to be in the private sphere concerned with eternal salvation, feelings, and values.

The modern nation-state claims an identity deeper than that of religion, becoming, in fact, a new religion with its own foundational beliefs and public practices. Ramachandra writes: "By claiming the ultimate loyalty of its citizens, the essentially religious character of the modern state is revealed. The state now becomes the sole sanction for violence. Martyrdom is redefined as laying down one's life for one's nation. Blasphemy, the worst sin in a religious milieu, has been transformed into treason. The nation-state offers protection from violence, both internal and external, in exchange for the willingness to kill other human beings on its behalf" (1999, 151). Ramachandra notes that, far from ending violence, the modern nation-state has been the greatest single cause of warfare over the past two hundred years.

Logical Positivism/ Traditional Wisdom

At the heart of modernity is a new way of viewing knowledge. Its roots are many. Auguste Comte argued that there are three stages in intellectual evolution. In the theological stage, people believed they were created by intelligent beings, invisible and resembling themselves. In the metaphysical stage, philosophers rejected the idea of gods and ancestors and sought to explain reality in terms of essences and faculties. Only in the positive stage do scientists give us certain knowledge by observing the mechanical action of bodies, by developing mathematics, and by offering verification by experience. Descartes, too, sought a new way of knowing, affirming three axioms: the supremacy of reason, a mechanical theory of the world, and the invariability of the laws of nature. The method he proposed was an analytical, algorithmic logic. His assumption was that the rigorous application of these methods would lead to an accumulation of objective, true knowledge—in other words, to progress, which replaced the older concept of providence. Like people in medieval cultures, Descartes affirmed a realist worldview, but unlike the earlier views his proposition separated the knower from the known and reason from aesthetics and morality. He rejected knowledge based on tradition and authority and called for people to think for themselves and for everything to be tested by reason. This detached the observer from the observed and led to an interest in knowledge for knowledge's sake.

Central to this Archimedean view of knowledge was the rise of a logical empiricism, or positivism. Positivism is based on the ontological assumption that there is a real world outside our minds—one that exists apart from our knowledge of it. Kathleen Nott writes, "For most of us there 'is' an 'external' world and however much we may affect it or interact with it by our explorations . . . we think of it not only as somehow existing in its own right but also that its 'real' description is somehow exhausted by the categories and calculations of physical science" (1971, 157–58). Positivism also believes that we can know through careful observation objective "facts" that correspond directly with external reality, and that these facts can be explained by objective, testable theories not linked to any culture or observer.

In philosophy, this assumption led to debates over the nature of *realis* and *realitas*. These words were coined by philosophers in the thirteenth century, and their meanings were assumed to be perfectly clear and obvious. Something is *real* if it has such and such characteristics, whether or not anyone thinks it has them. In other words, a "real" thing is anything not affected by human cognition *about it*.

The contrast between philosophical idealism and scientific realism is seen in scientists' response to the term "real." From the outset, scientists assumed a real world and began to explore it, systematically examining those primordial or brute sense experiences that cannot be reduced to anything else or shown to be illusions. They explored that which insists on forcing its way into human recognition as something other than the mind's creation. Upon this seemingly hard reality, they sought to build their knowledge.[17]

Comte argued for a new kind of knowledge that was certain. He called this *positivisme*. It would be based on the following principles: (1) introspection must be rejected, and the empirical methods of the sciences that seek simply to describe sensory experiences must be adopted as the only acceptable scientific methods; (2) the purpose of science is to formulate universal and immutable laws that must be verified by the facts of experience; (3) the function of science is simply to describe "how" things are and not why they are the way they are; and (4) empirical knowledge is the only valid source of knowledge (Rossi 1983, 2–3). Implicit in his method was a dichotomy between concept and reality and between subject and known object. Later the term "positivism" came to be used for what some call logical empiricism, a form of empiricism that views knowledge as a passive copy of reality. Today the term "positivism" is widely used as a label for the general epistemological foundations underlying much of modern scientific thought. This stance has seemed justified in view of the great strides made by science in the acquisition of knowledge, particularly when compared with the apparent wanderings of medieval philosophy.

KNOWN/KNOWER

Central to the modern philosophical debate is the dualism between knower and known. In a world that is increasingly seen as a giant machine, the place of humans as spiritual and intelligent beings has become problematic. Humans, too, have been reduced to mechanical parts in the self-regulating cosmic clock. Clearly humans are of this material world, but are they are more than that? Descartes tried to rescue humans as knowers by making a distinction between *rex extensa*, matter extended in space, and *rex cogitans*, the conscious mind; between soulless matter outside and immaterial soul within; and by restoring the knower to a prior position. His starting point was not God or the community, but "I"—the autonomous human individual, knower and arbiter of truth.[18] His "I" was a nonmaterial entity that inhabits a physical body. This radical separation between mind and brain, spirit and body lies at the heart of modernity.

Some scholars have tried to bridge this chasm with the doctrine of psychophysical parallelism in which physical and mental events run side by side but without mutual interference. But then physical events are fully determined by laws, and the mind is rendered unnecessary and unreal. Others have postulated an

17. Charles Peirce notes that philosophers, for the most part, saw reality as largely a creation of the human mind and sought by means of reason to explicate the meaning of *Ding an sich* (the thing in itself). But he argues that this task is doomed from the start because knowledge of the external world is based primarily on experience, not reason (1955, 299).

18. *Cogito ergo sum*: "I think, therefore I am." To this postmodernists will add, "Descartes thought he thought, therefore he thought he was."

interaction between the two, but this contradicts the very principles of physiology and physics, which argue that nonphysical realities cannot interact with physical processes. Moreover, there is no way to differentiate brain-physiological processes that are associated with conscious events and those that are not (Bertalanffy 1981, 90). In modernity, physical realities are taken to be real, while mental and spiritual realities are often rendered epiphenomenal.

In short, modernity has tried to reconnect the two, but with little success. Ludwig von Bertalanffy notes, "Do not say that the Cartesian dualism is a dead horse or a straw man erected to be knocked down, as nowadays we have 'unitary concepts' and conceive of man as a 'psycho physical wholeness.' These are nice ways of speaking, but as a matter of fact, the Cartesian dualism is still with us and is at the basis of our thinking in neurophysiology, psychology, psychiatry and related fields" (1981, 89).

OBJECTIVE KNOWLEDGE/SUBJECTIVE FEELINGS AND VALUES

Positivism was an attempt to acquire certain, objective knowledge about the material world. Immanuel Wallerstein observes, "The sciences were epistemologically very stable from about the sixteenth or seventeenth century to the 1970s, in the sense that Newtonian/Cartesian premises were fundamental to all scientific activity. Science was the search for the simplest laws. Science was objective. Science was neutral. Science dealt with equilibria. Science was cumulative" (1998, 5).

Positivists set out to construct science on fully objective, or "positive," knowledge—a new kind of objective, empirical knowledge not found previously. Key to their endeavor was the belief that the scientist can be the outside, dispassionate observer who can discover and understand the facts and universal laws of nature by means of totally objective observations. Such knowledge is allegedly true in the ultimate sense of the word. Traditional knowledge systems have little to contribute to our understanding of reality. David Harvey writes that the thinkers of the Enlightenment "took it as axiomatic that there was only one possible answer to any question. From this it followed that the world could be controlled and rationally ordered if we could only picture and represent it rightly. But this presumed that there existed a single correct mode of representation which, if we could uncover it (and this was what scientific and mathematical endeavors were all about) would provide the means to the Enlightenment ends" (1990, 27). Positivist knowledge is nonpersonal, noncommital, value-free, and objective in the sense that our subjectivity is mistrusted. "Intimacy, trust and desire for covenanted love, the capacity to endure for a dearly held belief, are all repressed" (Kavanaugh 1981, 42).

This emphasis on totally objective knowledge had three significant consequences. First, positivists made a sharp distinction between facts, on the one hand, and feelings and values, on the other.[19] They argued that scientists should not let their emotions or values affect their rational processes, for to do so would introduce subjectivity into their conclusions. The empirical sciences give us public, certain, clear, reliable, and verifiable truth—what John Locke called "dry truth and real knowledge," while the arts and religion are concerned with matters of entertainment and individual inner dispositions and have little or no bearing on the way things actually are. Hugh Montefiore writes,

> Logical positivism claimed that only statements which could be verified by sense-perception had meaning: these alone described facts. Value-judgments and religious judgments had no meaning and could properly be called nonsensical. Their function was purely emotive: to express feelings and to arouse the feelings of others. Science, by summing up the factual data derived from sense-perception, would then ideally codify all that could meaningfully be said. All discourse about anything else such as values or religious matters was not only rigidly excluded from this well-lit realm; it was also radically disconnected from it. There could (it was ruled) be no reasoning from facts to values. (1992, 45–46)

Only emotion-free and value-free statements that could be empirically proved were accepted as valid facts. As Harold Netland (1991) observes, such statements eliminated metaphysics, moral theory, emotions, and super realities as "cognitively meaningless"—as having no objective validity—because they could not be empirically verified or deduced from empirical propositions.

In time, the emphasis was no longer on knowing things that are of special value but simply on knowing things exactly, with absolute certainty. Montefiore notes that in the end modernity abandoned truth in favor of facts and reason. Knowledge became property, something that could be owned and controlled. The owner was detached from it, and it did not call the owner to participate in it. In the end, the knower is the master builder who constructs the edifice of knowledge from facts that are assumed to be identical with reality. In the process the knower is never up for examination. The self is the knower; the world is the known. The claim of the supremacy of science was self-evident and unchallengeable. What was venerated was the human scientific intellect.

Scientific knowledge was seen as value-neutral, that is, such knowledge might be used to promote a wide variety of causes, good or bad, but in and of itself was biased neither for nor against the realization of any one of them. Positivistic science is concerned with what is, not what ought to be. One consequence of this moral neutrality is that scientists have often failed to take the moral consequences of their findings into account in deciding whether to pursue a particular course of research. Lesslie Newbigin argues that this

---

19. Shaped by the Enlightenment worldview, Immanuel Kant made a clear distinction between knowledge, on the one hand, and aesthetics and morality, on the other, arguing that the latter concern inner experiences and do not add to our knowledge of the world.

separation of facts from values is the root of the malaise of contemporary Western society and Christianity.

A second consequence of this search for objectivity has been the reinforcement of the individualism that is one of the hallmarks of modernity. In the Middle Ages, authority was a central epistemological category located in tradition (the church, the Bible, the ancestors). Positivism relocated it in the individual as an autonomous and ontological being. It is the individual who has the epistemological authority to judge truth and error, because only individuals are "real." After Descartes it was important that the scientist withdraw from all social intercourse as preparation for asking fundamental questions about the nature of knowledge. To say that scientific knowledge is produced by social processes was thought to discredit it. In the end, the search for objective knowledge became an intensely individual search. Knowing was seen as the act of the solitary individual, a knower who uses senses and intellect to apprehend and interpret objects of knowledge "out there." Community hermeneutics was suspect.

A third consequence of this search for objectivity was the denial of mystery and the supernatural because they could not be known through objective empirical analysis, and the relegation of religion, the humanities, and the arts to matters of personal choice and conviction because they were particular and subjective, involving feelings and values and participation in the known. After the Renaissance, men and women were compelled to live either as emotional participants in the world or as outside objective observers of it. This led to the separation of intelligence and imagination and to a situation in which science served cognitive truth while the arts and religion satisfied emotional needs. The sciences came to dominate public life, and religions, the humanities, and the arts were assigned to the sphere of private truth—truth the individual could hold but could not assert as true for others. Rarely in history have past and other knowledge systems been so thoroughly rejected.

The human that emerged out of modern science was a cold, passionless, mechanical creature, devoid of feelings and values. In their public worlds, people were nameless and faceless numbers in large bureaucracies, where they were valued not as real persons but as part of a mechanical system. In modern cities, in particular, this often led to "nervous prostration," paralysis of the will, and the feeling that life had become somehow unreal.

As we will see, in the postmodern critique of modernity, this dehumanization of people led to a reaction, a yearning to experience intense "real life" in all its forms. Human emotions were difficult to analyze, but they were pervasive and important. This realization gave rise to a therapeutic ethos that valued feelings and experience rather than rational analysis. To people suffering from inner emptiness, therapists offered harmony, vitality, and the hope of self-realization and self-worth. "Abundance therapy" promised a new salvation by releasing people's deep reservoirs of emotions and energies and promising them richer, fuller lives (Fox and Lears 1983).

Detached Observer/Participant

To be objective, knowledge had to be true for all people at all times and unconditioned by history and culture. To achieve this Archimedean point, scientists had to be outside the reality they were observing. Science was seen as acultural and ahistorical. It was true for everyone in all the world and throughout all history. Huston Smith notes: "Science capitalizes on this freedom from context and tries to show us a contextless world, a view of things that is not affected by even the fact that it derives from our human angle of vision. And when it goes on to try to understand human beings (through the social sciences), this goal continues" (1982, 6). This claim of objective, context-free knowledge faced a problem internal to science itself. The theories scientists teach today are often superseded by new theories tomorrow. To preserve their faith in the objectivity of their knowledge systems, scientists periodically reinterpret their past views to fit present findings. Textbooks are written to present scientific knowledge as timeless, culture-free truth. Theories and data once accepted as fact are condemned as unscientific or are mercifully forgotten. But as science is constantly reinterpreted, the textbooks themselves must be rejected.

One consequence of the Archimedean point of view in which the scientist stands outside of history and culture was a separation of knowledge from action. The role of scientists was one of detached neutrality. They should not become deeply and personally involved in the problems, people, and societies they studied. The result was a separation of pure and applied science, and the denigration of the latter because of potential contamination. David Bosch points out that under the influence of the Greek spirit, ideas and principles were considered to be prior to and more important than their application. "Such an application was both a second and secondary step and served to confirm and legitimize the idea or principle, which was understood to be both suprahistorical and supra-cultural. . . . With the advent of the Enlightenment this approach received a new lease of life. In the Kantian paradigm, for instance, 'pure' or 'theoretical' reason was superior to 'practical reason'" (Bosch 1991, 421). The task of science then is to understand reality. It is the task of others to apply this knowledge in everyday life.[20]

In modernity, knowledge is grounded not in the relation in which we stand to that which we claim to know, but in treating it as a thing, a mechanical object from which we are inevitably distant. It is not to know, as in a relationship such as marriage, but to know "about." It is not relational and interpersonal, but objective and unaffected by and unaffecting the observed. Objective knowledge also avoids the tough methodological questions of hermeneutics, of getting into other people's minds since they cannot be observed directly.

20. In Christianity this led to the view that faith is believing the truth, not about transformed lives and covenant relationships. It was assumed that right knowledge leads to right personal living.

SKEPTICISM/AUTHORITY

The search for totally objective knowledge led to the question of its relationship to other systems of knowledge. By the standards of science, all systems of "traditional" knowledge were labeled superstitions. They were based on faith, not empirical verification. Other cultures have no "science" and can be ignored as "primitive." Western thought before the fifteenth century was prelogical and had nothing significant to offer to science. The result was a modern intellectual ethnocentrism that "assumes the intrinsic inferiority of all premodern thought and the consequent superiority of modern thought" (Oden 1992, 36).

This rejection of traditional religious authority in Europe led to a crisis that engulfed the intellectual scene during the sixteenth and seventeenth centuries. If religion no longer provided certain truth, what other foundation was there? Descartes responded to this crisis by arguing that certain knowledge could be gained only by beginning with skepticism, not faith, as medieval scholars had argued. All sources of truth, including revelation and authority, and all truth claims must be subject to fearless criticism, and only that which can be proved by evidence and arguments not open to doubt can be trusted. The starting point, for Descartes, is the seemingly self-evident fact that as a human he thought, therefore he must, in fact, exist.

The method par excellence by which scientists sought to examine the real world was to begin with skepticism regarding all knowledge and to apply reason to systematic empirical observations. Ernest Gellner writes that in positivism "there are no privileged or a priori *substantive* truths. (This, at one fell swoop, eliminates the sacred from the world.) All facts and all observers are equal. There are no privileged Sources or Affirmations, and all of them can be queried" (1992, 80).

In positivistic science the experimenter formulated a hypothesis about the nature of some realities based on earlier observations. The hypothesis in itself reflected a measure of sincere doubt, for if the scientists had no doubt, further experimentation was unnecessary. The next step was to conduct experiments or observations to test the hypothesis. The hypothesis was accepted or rejected on the basis of repeated empirical tests. If it was confirmed, it became a "fact" like other facts.

FORMAL, INTRINSIC, DIGITAL CATEGORIES/RELATIONAL, FUZZY CATEGORIES

At the heart of modernity is the search to discover the fundamental nature of reality. It does so by looking for the intrinsic nature and ultimate, unchanging structure of things.[21] Like the Greeks, modernists define this reality in terms of sharply defined, abstract, intrinsic, digital categories.

21. E. J. Dijksterhuis traces this search back to the Greeks (1986, see esp. chap. 2). In contrast, Hebrew logic draws us toward concrete relational knowing of others in the particularities of life. Parker Palmer notes, "We come to know the world not simply as an objectified system of

The sciences begin with the creation of abstract, digital taxonomies, in contrast to the folk taxonomies people use in everyday life. This fascination with taxonomies has come to dominate much of public modern life. Edward Hall writes, "The classification system is an excellent example of how the majority of Western peoples have been trained to think. Since the days of Linnaeus, the system has been highly respected and occupies a prestigious niche in the edifice of Western thought. . . . The result has been, however, that whichever way we Westerners turn, we find ourselves deeply preoccupied with [the] specific . . . to the exclusion of everything else. . . . Where do we go for the over-view? Who is putting things together" (1977, 123).

In this view, the fundamental components of reality are seen as self-contained intrinsic categories. The German mathematician Georg Cantor was the father of intrinsic, well-formed set theory, one of the greatest achievements of nineteenth-century mathematics. His essential point is that a collection of objects can be regarded as a single entity (a whole) if the objects share the properties that define a whole. Well-formed sets are those in which it is possible to determine whether an object is, or is not, a member of a set on the basis of what it *is*. Thus an apple is an apple because of the intrinsic characteristics it shares with other apples. Moreover, a category is "well formed"; it has a clear boundary. A fruit is either an apple or it is not. It cannot be 70 percent apple and 30 percent pear. There is no ambiguity, no multireferential or relational categories. We saw the significance of this shift in chapter 2, where we compared the relational sets most people use in traditional societies, and the intrinsic, scientific sets used in modernity. Relational sets speak of dynamic relationships between beings and objects. Intrinsic sets focus on the nature of impersonal things as autonomous units.

Objects in such bounded sets are seen as uniform in their essential characteristics. Their differences and uniqueness are of little importance. Thus, everything can be analyzed into constituent components, and everything can be reassembled and reassigned in terms of these components.

Furthermore, these sets are seen as essentially static. Reality is not viewed as an ongoing flux of unique entities. All apples are apples, and they remain so whether they are green, ripe, or rotten. In modernity, well-formed sets are regarded as ontological in nature. They involve the ultimate, changeless structure of reality, which is defined in terms of unchanging, universal, abstract, intrinsic categories.

The scientific approach orders categories into taxonomies of higher levels of generality and abstraction. Since Linnaeus, one of the first tasks in any

---

empirical objects in logical connection with each other, but as an organic body of personal relations and responses, a living and evolving community of creativity and compassion. Education of this sort means more than teaching the facts and learning the reasons so we can manipulate life toward our ends. It means being drawn into personal responsiveness and accountability to each other and the world of which we are a part" (1983, 14–15).

science has been to create taxonomies—of plants, animals, elementary particles, diseases, kinship systems, personality types, and so on, assuming that
these elements so grouped form universal types. Such classification systems
occupy a prestigious niche in the edifice of Western thought. As a result we find
ourselves deeply preoccupied with abstract classifications based on specifics
to the exclusion of everything else.[22]

Dividing all life into intrinsic categories was foundational to Greek philosophy. From this it was a small step to ranking them. The Greeks called
this graded hierarchy the "great chain of being." All things, from the least
kind that border on nonexistence to the most complex, were ranked on a
scale of complexity, with the most complex being highest. Within each category further hierarchies were created, each differing from that immediately
below and above it with the least possible degree of difference—angel is
over angel, beast over beast, bird over bird, fish over fish. Modern science
does much the same thing. Scientists classify plants and animals according
to their complexity, with the theory of evolution showing their progression
over time.

This graded hierarchy led to Darwin's theory of evolution. It also led to
social Darwinism and a hierarchical view of humans—for example, white
males viewed as higher than women, Jews, and people of color.[23] Degrees
of value are assigned to everything in the universe. Everything except God
has some superior; everything except unformed matter has some inferior.
In business, leaders rank workers on organizational charts and pay them

22. Edward Hall notes, "Science and taxonomy go hand in glove. In fact, implicit in every
taxonomy is a theory of nature of the events or organisms being classified. Yet a review of the
historical development of taxonomy of living things reveals that, paradoxically, the more Western
man classifies, the less useful are his classificatory systems" (1977, 122).

Peter Raven, Brent Berlin, and Dennis Breedlove note, "The taxonomic system we use *appears* to communicate a great deal about the organism being discussed, whereas in fact it communicates very little. Since, in the vast majority of instances, only the describer has seen the
named organism, no one with whom he is communicating shares his understanding of it. . . .
In dealing with the vast numbers of organisms that exist, we tend to overemphasize the process
of classification and the decisions it involves at the expense of the information *about* the organism" (cited in Hall 1977, 122).

23. Social Darwinism, even in its heyday, was not acceptable to all evolutionists. Today most
scholars would rather forget that it ever existed. But it should never be forgotten that this theory
was the foundation for the Superman ideology of Nazi Germany. H. L. Mencken unflinchingly
applied Darwinism to his social and political doctrine: "The superiorities already won—of men
over women, of whites over blacks, of gentiles over Jews, of the elite over the mob—must be
retained in the name of progress. Since men are stronger than women, women 'cultivate cun-
ning' in order to circumvent men, becoming shrewd, resourceful, and acute; but the very fact
that they are always concerned with imminent problems (because of their physical weakness)
and that, in consequence they are unaccustomed to dealing with the larger riddles of life, makes
their mental attitude essentially petty. . . . The net result is that feminine morality is a morality
of opportunism and imminent expediency, and that the normal woman has no respect for, and
scarcely any conception of, abstract truth" (2003, 104–5).

different wages based on some definition of their work. The government and the military enforce chains of command, universities rank professors, and hospitals classify staff and doctors. Class and ethnic hierarchies are accepted as normal elements of social organization and justify why some are richer and others poorer, some leaders and others followers. This concept of hierarchy has influenced the modern church.[24] This digital, abstract, analytical approach fits with the modern desire to have clear plans, high control, and everything run by the rules, but it leaves us with a problem of relevance.

Abstract, Algorithmic Logic/Faith

Modernity from Descartes through the Enlightenment championed autonomous reason, free from the constraints of authority, as the source of progress in knowledge and society, as well as the privileged locus of truth. Alister McGrath maintains that "the primary feature of [the Enlightenment] may be seen as its assertion of the omnicompetence of human reason. Reason, it was argued, was capable of telling us everything we needed to know about god and morality. The idea of some kind of supernatural revelation was dismissed as an irrelevance. Jesus Christ was just one of many religious teachers, who told us things that anyone with a degree of common sense could have told us anyway. Reason reigned supreme" (1996, 163–64).

The foundation for certain knowledge was no longer authority and tradition, but human reason. According to Immanuel Kant, "Enlightenment was man's emergence from his self-inflicted immaturity—his reliance upon external authorities and his reluctance to use his own understanding. No generation should be bound by the creeds and dogmas of bygone generations. To be so bound is an offence against human nature whose destiny lies in progress. . . . Mankind is in the process of coming of age, refusing to take external authorities and judging everything by its own understanding" (1959, 17). Kant personifies modern human confidence in the power of reason to deal with material things and its incompetence to deal with anything beyond. Only knowledge that stood up under careful scrutiny and could be independently verified could be trusted as "facts." Faith was a matter of personal conviction. Facts were proven to be universally true, involving no personal commitment. For the Enlightenment, the problem was not sin but ignorance.

24. Aquinas spoke of "a chain of being" beginning with God at the top and ranging down through angels, humans, and animals in the order of their intelligence, and then plants and nonliving things. He implies, without elaborating, that the hierarchy of the church—an ontological grading of persons—is modeled on that of heaven. Medieval cathedrals depict this chain of being in their carvings.

It is impossible not to suspect a correlation between a well-known Christian doctrine called the "chain of command" and the Greek and Darwinian philosophies. The question remains, however, whether the chain of command owes more to them than it does to Scripture.

The intellectual transition from authority based on faith in divine revelation to self-confidence in the power of human reason formed the philosophical foundation for the Enlightenment and prepared the way for the subsequent development of European thought.[25] To determine truth, modern scientists needed not only precise digital categories; they also needed an exact rationality that provided the one correct answer to any logical question. They found this in linear, abstract, analytical logic based on axiomatic rules.[26] These rules were based on some algorithm.[27] They were propositional in nature, mechanical in application, unambiguous in sense, and capable of producing the one correct answer. In this form of reasoning, given the same propositions, everyone will reach the same conclusions.

By means of facts and axiomatic, algorithmic reason, scientists sought to formulate precise, consistent, verifiable theories capable of predicting hitherto unknown phenomena, useful in reducing disparate phenomena to the same explanatory categories, and capable of solving more problems than did their predecessors and rivals.

Underlying this view of rationality is the assumption that there is one universal system of reason common to all humanity.[28] The rules of logical inquiry are the same in Africa and India as in the West. The fact that other cultures have other "logics" does not call this assumption into question. Rather, it shows that other people have yet to acquire positive knowledge. In other words, they are "prelogical" and "primitive." Modernity has sought to apply its definition of rationality to all areas of human life.

25. Locke saw the human mind as a blank slate on which what we now call culture wrote its messages. For him the human mind was not innately equipped with any preconceived notions or rules of reason. Baruch Spinoza (1632–77) noted that human passions generally acted more powerfully than human reason. Blaise Pascal (1632–62) observed that although humans are endowed with reason, they rarely act by its guidance.

26. The appeal to reason, which we take for granted, can be traced back to the Enlightenment, but this called for a clear definition of rationality. Modernity found this in Greek philosophy, which presupposed that abstract, analytical, algorithmic logic is the sole means of arriving at true knowledge.

27. An algorithm is a formal process that, if carried out correctly, produces the one right answer to the problem. It is precise and has no place for ambiguities. It is not a judgment call based on wisdom but a technique for arriving at the correct answer. Bertalanffy notes, "An algorithm is essentially a 'thinking' machine, a means of performing operations on symbols that give results difficult or impossible to attain otherwise. Calculating and thinking machines, mechanical or electronic, are the materialization of algorithms" (Bertalanffy 1981, 4).

28. Aristotle proclaimed that "all knowledge is of the universal" (Malik 1987, 4). Modern knowledge assumes this and seeks theories that are sufficiently abstract and universal to stand alone, free of embedding in a particular culture. The particularity of everyday life and of history are considered meaningless until they can be explained in terms of universal, abstract theories. Greek logic deals with abstract, universal, impersonal facts and theories.

This search for universals extends even to morality, which is normally assigned to the private domain. Democracy, human rights, individual human freedom, and equality are assumed to be "self evident" and therefore must command universal assent. In much of the world, they are not seen as such.

Components are then organized into systems that are understood in terms of physical causality. For example, in factories, tasks are broken down into subtasks and organized in sequence along an assembly line to achieve the desired outcomes. These subtasks must be reproducible by any properly trained worker. This "formula approach" produces the same results when the same inputs are introduced. Such an understanding enables humans to control the systems through engineering and technological advances. Ultimately this leads to the segmentation of culture into religion, politics, arts, and so on, and to the compartmentalization of the self.

The search for a comprehensive system of knowledge based on abstract, algorithmic logic assumes that humans can grasp the fullness of truth with clarity. It leaves little room for the ambiguities of life, the mysteries that transcend human comprehension, and the wisdom that can deal with the contradictions and paradoxes of a rapidly changing world. It is built on a linear logic acting on well-formed categories and cannot deal with the "fuzzy" sets and "fuzzy logic" of human experiences. It tends to be deterministic and reductionist in nature (Zadeh 1965).

Quantitative Data/Qualitative Data

At the heart of the modern mechanistic worldview is mathematics and quantification. Copernicus, using Pythagorean geometry, explained the movement of the planets. Galileo noted that this is the supreme example of the victory of mathematical reason over the senses, for the senses tell us that the sun goes around the earth, while reason shows us that the truth is the other way around. For Galileo and Descartes the whole world was fundamentally mathematical in structure. Because God played the mathematician in creating the world, mathematical principles, like the axioms of logic, were thought to be ultimate truths superior to God himself and independent of revelation (Burtt 1954, 173). Even humans were seen as "engines endowed with wills." Quantification separates "what is measurable from what is not. Whatever cannot be expressed numerically is to be eliminated from the ensemble, either because it eludes numeration or because it is quantitatively negligible" (Ellul 1964, 168). In the end statistics became the basis for determining objective truth, and truth was needed for planning and controlling society and the world.

This reduction of the real world to mathematically measurable motions in space and time raised a deeper question. Is the universe as a whole, including our earth, fundamentally mathematical in its structure? Increasingly, the answer was yes. The world was increasingly seen as a simple, beautiful, geometric harmony in which all things have their mathematical proportions, and "number is the first model of things in the mind of the Creator." Hence the important doctrine of scientific knowledge that all certain knowledge must be knowledge of quantitative characteristics. Perfect knowledge is always mathematical (Burtt 1954, 67).[29] In the end, if one cannot measure it, then it is not science.

If quantifiable characteristics of reality are the truly real, how do we deal with the many qualities we experience, such as pleasures, griefs, passionate loves, ambitions, and longings? These qualities were viewed as secondary and thus as unreal and dependent on the deceitfulness of the senses. They were worthy of study only in terms of primary qualities.

Quantification studied reality by breaking things down into uniform parts and counting them. This approach revolutionized military tactics (Crosby 1997, 12). It also led to a drive to measure not only collections of objects (balls, trees) but also things like weight, hardness, heat, color, light, and time, which are not immediately accessible to us as quantities of discrete entities. "The West's distinctive intellectual accomplishment was to bring mathematics and measurement together and to hold them to the task of making sense of a reality experienced through the senses, which Westerners, in a flying leap of faith, assumed was temporally and spatially uniform and therefore susceptible to such examination" (Crosby 1997, 17). Space and time were homogeneous and uniform and as such were the universal grid in which reality occurred. Between 1275 and 1325, clocks were invented and Arabic numerals adopted in Europe.[30] These developments led to the spread of quantification throughout Europe, beginning in business and manufacturing, and to the spread of a cash economy that reduced marketable items to a single standard of exchange. Every salable item became a measured item. The influence of these new means of quantification rapidly spread to cartography, music, technology, and science. In science especially, the truth was believed to be best discovered and expressed in numbers, formulas, and statistics. As Neil Postman notes, we can hardly imagine a modern economist presenting truth in the form of proverbs, poems, or parables (1985, 23). Numbers came to be seen as utterly neutral, in and of themselves morally and emotionally free of all value, as pure a tool as a shovel.

GRAND UNIFIED THEORY/MYSTERY, PARADOX, AMBIGUITY

Ultimately the goal of this search for truth was to understand the fundamental nature of reality in terms of a grand unified theory that is self-contained (requires no outside input and has no unexplained mysteries), exhaustive (explains

29. J. Kepler wrote, "Just as the eye was made to see colours, and the ear to hear sounds, so the human mind was made to understand, not whatever you please, but quantity" (Kepler *Opera* 1, 31).

30. The consequences of adopting the Hindu-Arabic numerals with their zeros and place values was profound. Imagine multiplying MCCCXXXXIIIJ (the *J* on the end signified the end of the number, ensuring that no one could attach anything more) by CCCXXVI, and dividing the product by MDLXXII. For centuries Europeans had trouble with 0. A sign for what was *not* was as conceptually discomfiting as the idea of a vacuum.

everything), and logically consistent (has no internal logical inconsistencies, ambiguities, or paradoxes).[31] This goal required higher and higher levels of standardization, abstraction, and generalization. For example, time and space traditionally were tied to local reference points—rivers, mountains, oceans. With the spread of modernity, a global grid was introduced using longitudes and latitudes. In the Middle Ages, each town reckoned its time according to the sun. With the spread of modernity, time was measured with reference to atomic clocks, Greenwich mean time, and global calendars. Time became a mysterious something independent of matter and motion, flowing on from everlasting to everlasting in its even, mathematical course (Burtt 1954, 161). Measurements, money, and many other areas of life were increasingly defined intrinsically and standardized.

Universalism/Particularism

The search for universal truth free of cultures and applicable to all people everywhere was tied to the modern agenda of universalism—for one homogeneous, civilized world based on modernity. It ignored the particularism of different peoples and cultures.

The universal claims of modernity were closely tied to the colonial expansion of European countries. Trade, colonial governments, and even Christian missions played a role in the introduction of the concepts of universal law, science, medicine, and education around the world. Ernest Gellner writes, "Positivism is a form of imperialism. . . . Lucidly presented and (putative) independent facts were the tool and expression of colonial domination: by contrast, subjectivism signifies intercultural equality and respect. . . . Objective facts and generalization are the expressions and tools of domination!" (1992, 26). The map of the world was laid out, not on the basis of local reference points, but on one world grid. Space became homogeneous, secular (no sacred space), uniform, abstract, and commodified (can be measured and sold).

Local cultures reacted to the introduction of modernity in different ways. In non-Western societies, modernity was a giant steel hammer distorting and destroying traditional communal institutions—clan, village, tribe, region. But people in these societies were never simply made over in the image of the West. Rather, they struggled in different ways with different degrees of success to deploy, reshape, and defuse imperial bureaucracies, expansive markets, mass media, and scientific theories. Some sought to become modern and make their societies modern. Others were not enamored of its manifestations and sought to preserve their cultures; such resistance often led to powerful countermodernity movements against secularizing forces. This was particularly

---

31. Kurt Gödel proved that explanation systems can have only two of the three qualities. Either a theory is not comprehensive, not powerful, or not logically consistent.

true as colonial rule ended and common local people gained a voice in their new governments.

SCHOOLING/APPRENTICESHIP

The most important legitimating agency of modernity is the school. Education, which had been the responsibility of the home and the church, was now vested in the school. New knowledge required new institutions to communicate it. Peter Berger and his associates write that the school's

> very presence serves to legitimate the new bodies of knowledge, and to bestow status upon those who have begun in whatever measure to acquire the new lore. Ivan Illich has very aptly called the school "the new universal church." The "religion" proclaimed by this new church is the mystique of modernity. As with the old church, the ritual representing the new mysteries need not be comprehensible to the people at large. Indeed, it may be argued that something is gained by incomprehensibility. . . . The children mumbling away in the schoolhouse are engaged in a ritual very similar to that of the priest and his helpers around the altar. The congregation watches and stands in awe. It is not at all necessary that it understand the Latin. (Berger, Berger, and Kellner 1973, 147)

SIGHT/SOUND

A mechanistic view led to a detached, observer-centered form of being and a shift from an oral to a visual society. Europe in the Middle Ages was based on oral communication. Written books were rare and had to be copied by hand. The theology of common Christians was expressed in rituals, songs, and stained glass windows. As Alfred Crosby notes, "The choice of the Renaissance West was to perceive as much of reality as possible visually and all at once, a trait then and for centuries after the most distinctive of its culture" (1997, 11).

Visual signs and photographs are detached from the immediate. Unlike spoken words, which are immediate and arise in specific contexts, printed words can be read far removed from the source and with no context to inform them. Sound is immediate and calls for a response. Sight is detached and calls for reflection. As Edward Hall notes, in a picture one never knows what is going on off camera (1977, 121).

IMPACT ON CHRISTIANITY

Christians live in particular historical and cultural contexts. It should not surprise us that they are deeply influenced by the modern worldview. One influential factor was the confidence that human reason could show the superiority of Christianity over other religions and persuade people to follow Christ. Brian Stanley writes, "The early missionary movement displays an immense confidence in the elevating and illuminating capacity of knowledge and rational argument—a confidence that is explicable only in terms of the philosophical environment of the eighteenth and early nineteenth centuries." This led them to establish modern schools as a means to convert and civilize the people they served. There was widespread skepticism about the capacity of "savages" to respond to the gospel without the preparatory leaven of Christian education (Stanley 2001, 18). It also led missionaries to engage in verbal and written polemics to prove the truthfulness of the Christian doctrine, confident that reason supported the claims of revelation.

In modernity the gospel increasingly was defined in terms of abstract doctrinal truths, not everyday living. The result was the development of systematic theology as a kind of science based on positivist presuppositions, a grand unified theory that explained everything (Hiebert 1999, 17–23).[32] Truth was to be determined by rational argument and encoded in propositional statements linked by reason. This work of experts assumed that human rationality is based on universal, transcultural, and transhistorical laws of thought. Moreover, to be objective, truth had to be separated from affectivity and morality.

The introduction of a mechanistic view of the world and the discovery of allegedly unchangeable laws in nature and morality played a key role in the emergence of deism. "The function of the Deity was virtually confined to originating the machine of nature, which, once regulated, was set beyond any further interference on His part, though His existence might be necessary for its conservation" (Bury 1932, 118). In conservative Christianity, this view led to an emphasis on "miracles" as evidence that God was present, for nature and natural laws are independent of his actions.

The focus on truth and the use of digital categories influenced evangelism and the mission of the church. The essential task was to bring people to salvation through conversion. Conversion was defined primarily in terms of affirming a particular set of doctrines (orthodoxy) or practices (orthopraxy). There were long arguments over what these essential doctrines were. If the list was too long, few could enter the kingdom; if too short, the danger of syncretism arose. Discipling of new converts was often haphazard and brief, often resulting in churches full of new, immature Christians.

This focus on truth, and the corresponding neglect of the affective and moral dimensions of the gospel, has led to divisions in the church. The holiness and revival movements have sought to bring morality back into the life of Christians, and the charismatic movements remind us of the importance of feelings in Christian life. Few churches, however, have reached a balance between truth, love, beauty, and holiness.

Another area of tension was the materialism of modern science. Rudolf Bultmann and others tried to make theology fit the sciences by explaining

---

32. W. O. Alexander, A. H. Strong, and, more recently, R. B. Griffiths have argued that theology is a science, indeed, the queen of the sciences.

"miracles" in terms of causes. Conservative Christians often resolved the tension through ontological dualism. Religion deals with spiritual realities and ultimate questions, which are beyond our immediate observation. Science describes our material world and makes humans the lords of nature. The only places spiritual realities impinge on the material world are in creation and in miracles that transcend or violate the laws of nature. As Newbigin (1989) points out, this led to the division between public truth, which concerns the "realities" of the world, and private truth, which concerns "super realities." All students must study mathematics, physics, chemistry, the social sciences, and history. No classes on Christianity, Islam, or Hinduism that seek to convert students to these religions are required in public schools. In fact they cannot be taught as truth in public schools.

What impact did this universalism have on Christian churches and missions? Abroad it led to the establishment of franchise churches that were extensions of Western churches. Missionaries sought to replicate their home churches abroad. A second consequence was that the church in the West was perceived as being Christian but as nonetheless lacking any prophetic voice that might challenge its own cultural enthrallment to modernity.

Affective Themes

The public focus of modernity is on the cognitive dimensions of culture. The affective dimensions have been relegated to the private sector—to music, the arts, movies, television, computer games, and religion. To study this situation, we need to examine the role of feelings in the everyday lives of modern people.

Emotional Control/Emotional Expression

In public life, modernity stresses emotional control. At work and in the university, schools, public buildings, and malls, people are expected to remain calm and self-controlled. In high-cultural performances such as concerts, operas, and theatrical presentations, the audience shows emotions with considerable restraint. The exceptions would be concerts by rock bands and popular singers, sports events, public parades, and political rallies, where emotions may be publicly expressed. Emotional constraint is particularly obvious at ritual occasions, such as funerals, weddings, high-church services, and national celebrations that are highly structured and public. Unrestrained emotional expression is largely confined to the private sphere of modern life, and even here it is generally more controlled than what one sees in cultures where emotional expressions, such as grief at the death of a relative, are publicly displayed by beating one's head on the ground or lashing oneself with whips.

Rational Discourse/Amusement

At the heart of the Enlightenment is the printed word. With the invention of print, it became self-evident that everyone should learn to read to understand the world, to carry on civil discourse, and to read Scripture for themselves. Private and public schools were established to educate the masses, not just the elite few. Literacy became an intellectual imperative and a moral duty. Lewis Mumford points out how "more than any other device, the printed book released people from the domination of the immediate and the local: . . . print made a greater impression than actual events. . . . To exist was to exist in print: the rest of the world tended gradually to become more shadowy. Learning became book-learning" (1934, 136). Neil Postman notes that in the United States from the seventeenth century to the late nineteenth century printed matter was virtually the only medium available to the public as a whole. "There were no movies to see, radios to hear, photographic displays to look at, records to play. There was no television. Public business was channeled into and expressed through print, which became the model, the metaphor and the measure of all discourse. The resonances of the lineal, analytical structure of print, and in particular of expository prose, could be felt everywhere" (1985, 41).

Print shaped the way people thought and spoke. According to Postman, "Print put forward a definition of intelligence that gave priority to the objective, rational use of the mind and at the same time encouraged forms of public discourse with serious, logically ordered content. It is no accident that the Age of Reason was coexistent with the growth of a print culture" (1985, 51).

In the mid-nineteenth century, several inventions changed the way modern people processed news. Prior to that time, public news was generally local. Discourse was based on an informed public and was debated in rational terms in village lecture halls by eloquent orators who often expounded for an hour or two. With the invention of electricity and the telegraph system, public discourse became national and eventually global. Now information could be transmitted instantaneously around the world. A shift toward information as entertainment occurred. Penny newspapers emerged that "turned away from the tradition of news as reasoned (if biased) political opinion and urgent commercial information and filled their pages with accounts of sensational events, mostly concerning crime and sex" (Postman 1985, 66).

Moral Themes

All societies need moral standards to define good and to judge and govern life. Modernity is no exception. Its moral foundations were laid in the French Revolution, which stressed life, liberty, and equality. In the Middle Ages, morality was built on sacred foundations—on the basis of an idea of a holy God who had preceded it and ordered its moral principles. In modernity, morality came to be understood in purely secular terms, based on rationalism and the will of citizens. The result was the emergence of the secular nation-state that excluded any divine legitimation for morality. God and his will ceased to be relevant in the public sphere or in the democratic formation of the public will. Morality came to be defined in terms of material progress, in which anything can become legitimate and even necessary; anything can become moral in the new sense of the term if it serves the common good. Moral laws were, for the most part, drawn from those of the Middle Ages, which were deeply shaped by Christian thought, but they were divorced from their original foundations.

Modernity argues that some values are "self-evident" because they are universal principles of moral justice recognized by all humans through their unaided reason. But modernity has precipitated an increasing separation between morality and reason. Reason cannot establish morality. The mechanistic worldview of modernity treats humans as objects of social technology and legislation. The absence of morality has been a consistent and problematic feature of modern societies. "The more the modern world is 'rationalized' the less the likelihood of living life in an ethically interpretable manner" (Smart 1993, 86). The loss of personal and ethical relationships is the central theme of Max Weber's analysis of the impact of modern reason on social and human experiences. Modern rationality has "disenchanted" the world and relegated religion and morality to the realm of the irrational. Some values, however, have persisted. For the most part these are memories of the Christian values of the Middle Ages tailored to fit the modern worldview.

Law/Relationships

The modern view of law is rooted in the Roman concept of the "rule of law." Law is defined as the impersonal rules necessary to maintain order and stop the spread of evil. The goal is to maintain justice, the symbol a blindfolded judge using a scale to measure someone's guilt or innocence. An impersonal code of laws provides the means for the impartial judge to weigh the case. Others are involved in or hurt by a violation of the law, but the central issue is the offender's relationship not to the others but to the impersonal law. The aim is to satisfy not the injured person but the abstract rules that define justice and injustice. A person is found innocent or guilty, just or unjust, depending on how he or she measures up against the abstract ideal or code.

This view has deeply affected the modern church's view of justification. Justification is now seen as a believer's personal experience of forgiveness and deliverance from a subjective sense of guilt. It is being free from the guilt of breaking an impersonal law. With this understanding of justice, we naturally think that for God to justify an individual is to pronounce him or her not guilty, that is, to view the person as if he or she had met the legal standard of justice.

Values/Morals

With the rise of secularism, the concept of "morality" became suspect because it assumes a divine author. In its place, modernity introduced the term "values," which are based on human choice, not divine mandate. Morals are assigned to the private sector and relativized by "values," which belong to the public sphere. Morals are personally enforced. Dominant values are encoded in laws and enforced by governments, often under a cloak of civil religion to give them validity and authority. But values are relative. They are cultural creations, not rational choices or divine mandates. Each community has its own, and none can claim its values are better or more moral than the values of the others. The result is moral relativism and utilitarianism.

Freedom and Rights/Responsibilities and Restraints

Among the all-important values of modernity are human freedom and rights. People want the right to choose and to be emancipated from all inhibiting traditions. In traditional societies, good people were those who cared for others. In the new world they know how to care for themselves.

The modern concept of freedom is closely tied to that of rights. Allan Bloom observes:

> The notion that man possesses inalienable rights, that they belong to him as an individual prior, both in time and in sanctity, to any civil society, and that civil societies exist for and acquire their legitimacy from ensuring those rights, is an invention of modern philosophy. Rights . . . are new in modernity, not a part of the common-sense language of politics or of classical political philosophy. . . . Right is not the opposite of wrong, but of duty. It is a part of, or the essence of freedom. It begins from man's cherished passion to live, and to live as painlessly as possible. (1987, 165–66)

We are quick to say, "I've got my rights," and assume that it is the duty of government to protect them. Morality is, to a considerable extent, defined in terms of respecting equal rights and enforcing fairness, by which we mean that the rights of all people should be respected. As Bloom notes, "Self-interest is hostile to the common good, but *enlightened* self-interest is not" (1987, 167). We assume that persons who care for themselves will really care for others.

It is here that theme and countertheme come into play. On the one hand, Locke argued that people are separate from and masters of nature. They will obey laws because these are created for the self-interest of everyone. For him, civilization is the peak of human development. Rousseau, on the other hand, argued that self-interest will not lead self-sufficient, solitary individuals to be good law-abiding citizens. They must choose between personal happiness and corporate security. Thus Rousseau sets nature over against society, which he sees as making impossible demands on humans.[33] Yet humans are different from nature because they create cultures. Here primitive societies are models of freedom from anxiety and cultural oppression. For Rousseau humans are born good. There is no original sin.

Equality/Hierarchy

Modernity is based on the assumption that all humans by their very nature are equal, and that they have rights to life, liberty, and the pursuit of property (Bloom 1987, 162). Its emphasis on the equal worth of all individuals is regarded as the essence of being human, and not given or modified by law or democratic vote. This assumption has led to emphasis on democracy in which people consent to be governed, and in which science and the humanities can conquer nature, providing prosperity and health. Equality was one of the central themes in the French and American revolutions.

There is, however, disagreement on what constitutes equality. Liberals see it as a leveling of social ranks and differences, which, they say, can only be achieved by government intervention. They see the need to limit freedom to achieve it. We see this in communism and socialism, which argue that equal opportunity for people with unequal talent or advantage leads only to hierarchy; consequently there is a need for strong governments. Conservatives define equality not as economic and social leveling but as equality of rights and opportunities. They are willing to live with hierarchy as long as everyone has an opportunity to rise in his or her social station. For them, freedom takes priority over equality. In conservatism the respect for private property is high, and government intervention in public and private life is viewed with suspicion.

Work/Leisure

In modernity, the identity of people is not primarily given by birth, by ascription, but by what they make of themselves, by achievement. For modern people it is obvious that hard work is required for prosperity and security. Moreover, the denial of leisure and personal gratification is essential to accumulating wealth and worth. Work no longer is a vocation, a calling from God, but a utilitarian activity to acquire a comfortable, prestigious life.

The work ethic dominated the rise of modernity. Through labor humans conquered nature, engineered a better world, and enjoyed the comforts of life. By the end of modernity, leisure had come to the fore. Allan Bloom points out, "As Western nations became more prosperous, leisure, which had been put off for several centuries in favor of the pursuit of property,

---

33. This dualism of nature/culture leads to other dualisms such as sciences/humanities, nature/nurture, and arts/sciences.

the means of leisure, finally began to be of primary concern. But, in the meantime, any notion of the serious life of leisure, as well as men's taste and capacity to live it, had disappeared. Leisure became entertainment. The end for which they had labored for so long has turned out to be amusement" (1987, 77).

Unlimited Good/Limited Good

Finally, a word must be said about the modern view of unlimited good. Because peasant societies view important goods as limited, jealousy arises when one person gains more because it is assumed that this gain is at the expense of others. In contrast, modernity widely believes that, particularly in the economic sphere, the amount of good, such as capital, production, and profits, can be increased through hard work and human ingenuity. Consequently one person's gain does not necessarily mean another's loss. In fact, stories of people who have worked hard and become famous, rich, and powerful are used as incentives to motivate people to work harder, and those who do not get ahead see mainly themselves to blame. The fact that some of the poor working class do make it in the modern world eases class tensions, because oppressive systems often lead the poor to believe that they are poor because of their own lack of effort.

Myths of Modernity

Worldviews define the deep stories of a culture, its root myths. Considering their importance in giving meaning and purpose to human lives, we should not be surprised that modern people have their myths as well.

Myth of Evolution and Progress

At the heart of modernity is the myth of evolution and progress. Seeking to answer the question, who are we? humans have commonly turned to origin myths that answer this question by telling us where we came from. This is true of the modern myth of evolution.

One of the roots of the theory of evolution is found in the Greek worldview. Dividing all of human life into digital categories was fundamental to Greek Neoplatonic philosophy. But once categories were established, it was but a small step to ranking them, and this is exactly what the Greeks did. They called it the "great chain of being," a hierarchy from the things that border on nonexistence to the most complex creatures, every one differing from the one immediately below and above with the least possible degree of difference. The categories were ranked from simplest to the most complex, with the latter judged highest (Lovejoy 1936).

A second root was the biblical view that meaning is found in history—a history that has a beginning, a long and often conflictual middle, and a perfect end. In modernity this view was secularized, and God's eschatological purpose for the world was transformed into the world-immanent goal of a better human society achievable through human effort. Most historians since the Enlightenment assume that God is not a factor in history. The universe is seen as a closed system that can be explained in terms of natural cause and effect.

The transition began with the rationalism of the eighteenth century and the romanticism of the nineteenth century.[34] In the eighteenth century, people in the West began to believe that investigations, primarily in the form of scientific research, would lead to an increase in knowledge and control of the world, which in turn would lead to human happiness and moral justice. Implicit in this belief was the notion of hierarchy. All of creation, life, and cultures were ranked on the basis of complexity, with humans at the top of the great chain of being and Western "civilization" at the top of cultures. Archaeology, history, and the technological marvels of the twentieth century were seen as proof for this interpretation of history.

Eloise Meneses notes that biological evolution holds that "humans were the species that was the wonderful result of an exceedingly long chain of accidental but adaptive changes, increasing in complexity and resultant ability. Our brains were the biggest and the best. Our hands were the most flexible. And hence our domination of the rest of the world was justified" (1997, 8). Humans were ranked in an evolutionary hierarchy based on body types and rationality.

Social scientists applied the evolutionary paradigm to sociocultural development, arguing that primitives are closer to an animal state, "promiscuous, superstitious, and less capable of rational thought than 'civilized' peoples, who [are] moral, scientific, and rational" (Meneses 1997, 9). This theory of social evolution accounted for both the inherent goodness of humans and the development and superiority of modernity. It led to the belief that whites are superior to blacks, men to women, and the elite to common people.

The theory of evolution is a secular substitute for the biblical metanarrative. It seeks to give meaning to human life by means of a broader story of which humans themselves are a part. It moves from a garden to a city, but it leaves out God, sin, and salvation. Jacques Ellul writes:

> The enormous technical progress of the modern world . . . restores to man the super world from which he had been severed, an incomprehensible world but one which he himself has made, a world full of promises that he knows can be realized and of which he is potentially the master. . . . He projects this . . . into the myth through which he can control, explain, direct, and justify his

---

34. Karl Marx took moral evil seriously and provided a grand counternarrative in which revolution, not development, leads to salvation.

actions. . . . The myth of destruction and the myth of action have their roots in this encounter of man with the promise of technique, and in his wonder and admiration. (1964, 192)

The myth of evolution has deeply shaped the Western worldview. First, it fosters a deep belief in progress,[35] which assumes that there will be growth; there is no competing hypothesis. It embraces faith in the inevitability of technological development and stresses the planning of large, unified technological and social systems to engineer progress by means of rationalization, standardization of knowledge, and progress. E. H. Carr writes, "I profess no belief in the perfectibility of man or in a future paradise on earth. . . . But I shall be content with the possibility of unlimited progress . . . towards goals which can be defined only as we advance towards them" (in Montefiore 1992, 27).

The theory of evolution gave rise to belief in "progress," which replaced the medieval concept of "salvation." It argued that social evils were attributable neither to sin or the innate disabilities of humans nor to the nature of things, but simply to ignorance and prejudice; therefore the improvement of the human condition and ultimate attainment of utopia (i.e., heaven) was only a matter of illuminating ignorance, removing errors, and increasing knowledge. Through progress, human societies would continue to improve. People were not sinners, they were unenlightened. What they needed was not salvation but enlightenment regarding how to live together in harmony and turn the earth into a paradise. Modern people are "civilized," and the belief was that being so is an unquestioned good. Others are "backward," but they can be civilized by programs of "development" that introduce modern technologies, formal education, and Western medicine. This perspective led to the Enlightenment agenda that it is the "white man's burden" to educate and civilize the "natives" and bring them into the melting pot of modernity. The result of this assimilation is the vision of a homogeneous, global modern culture. This belief was used to justify Western colonialism and the notion that Europeans had the responsibility to manage the native people's worlds for their own good. However, the West, which created modernity, will be the leader in progress and will remain so for a very long time.

35. Charles Malik points out that the word "progress" has many meanings, but in the modern university it is seen as the liberation of the mind from all Christian religious shackles. He writes, "The forces of this kind of progress have as their ultimate aim to obliterate from history the very mention of the name of Jesus and his cross. Inquire diligently what the word *progressive* means (progressive person, progressive doctrine, progressive law, progressive attitude, progressive system, progressive tendency, progressive movement, progressive society, progressive culture, progressive country) and you will find it for the most part directed, consciously or unconsciously, against Jesus Christ. There is always something else put forward to make us forget him: justice, science, culture, prosperity, pleasure, security, peace. The important thing is to replace him, to satisfy us without him, to crowd him out of existence altogether. Jesus radically disturbs, and the disturbance must once and for all be put to rest" (1987, 8).

Modernity is based on a linear view of history and sees itself as the end point of history. It assumes the intrinsic inferiority of all premodern knowledge and the superiority of modern knowledge. The old is seen as traditional, antiquated, animistic, and irrelevant. Scientific knowledge is self-evidently superior to all previous traditions. This rejection of the old is rooted in a culture of criticism and questioning of all dogma. Faith is ruled out as a valid foundation for knowledge. But modernity is uncritical of its own presuppositions. It focuses its attention on the future rather than the past. Development is seen as automatic and inevitable. Things can and will get better.

The myth of progress has been particularly strong in North America, where a dominant theme involves the concept of the "new land." The Renaissance gave Europe a new confidence in human capabilities, and the discovery of North America was seen as a sign of God's favor, giving humankind a new beginning in a New World. The Europeans who settled North America were chosen for a special mission in the world and especially blessed by God. Some saw the "New World" as a rebirth of humanity without poverty or injustice or persecution. This myth drove the Puritans and settlers to populate New England and build cities such as New York and New Haven. As the East Coast was settled, the new frontier became the West with its explorers, hunters, trappers, and frontiersmen, many of whom proudly lived lives of relative isolation. They were followed by cowboys and ranchers.

The basis of this myth was faith in a new beginning in which people could tame nature—the Wild West—and create a new utopia in which freedom reigned. The "rugged" individual (the Lone Ranger, the lonely cowboy) was the person to accomplish the task through self-reliance in battling both nature and the evils of Old World civilization. This battle required violence, which was justified if it achieved the right ends. Outlaws such as Jesse James and Calamity Jane became heroes because they stood against the oppressive institutions of the Old World and the East.

This vision of a New World pushed settlers west. It also gave the country an unquestioning faith in anything new: new brands of medicine, new technologies, new religions, new ways of life, and, more recently, the New Age. It also led to belief in the self-made person. New experiences and renewal of the self through therapies and "do-it-yourself" formulas are assumed to be good.

Change, too, was assumed to be good. The New World is better because it is new. So, too, are the New Deal and the New Frontier in politics. The result is unending progress as people compete and the fittest succeed, and as people re-create themselves in new possibilities. This faith in competition leading to progress underlies modern theories of evolution and capitalism. Combined with this notion of progress, individualism has led to an emphasis on self-fulfillment, self-indulgence (evidenced in TV ads associating comfort, cars, and beautiful people), and narcissism. Even love is defined as the fulfillment of a person's emotional needs, not as a commitment to and a relationship with others. As Tocqueville noted early on, Americans "never stop thinking of the good things they have not got" (1969, 536).

Closely related to the notion of progress is that of "development,"[36] which assumes change through incremental improvement, through competition and the success of the strongest, brightest, and best adapted. Competition gave rise to the Enlightenment assumptions of progress, autonomous individualism, faith in reason, and the innate goodness of humans. Jon Bonk writes, "The West continues to be the standard against which 'development' is measured; and Western aid and efforts have, until quite recently, been fueled by the certainty that given enough money, time and Western expertise, the rest of the world can become what the West now is—'developed'" (1991, 20).

Central to the myth of evolution and progress is the justification of violence if it is redemptive. Life creates diversity, and beings must compete to live. Darwin argued that the fittest survive, which results in progress. But such competition involves battle and violence. The result is biological, cultural, economic, and political Darwinism.

Myth of Redemptive Violence

Underlying the myth of evolution and progress is what Walter Wink (1992) calls the myth of redemptive violence, which was transmitted by peoples migrating from inner Asia to Europe, Mesopotamia, and South Asia, and became the basis for the religions of Babylon, Sumer, Canaan, Greece, India, and Nordic Europe, to name a few.

Fundamental to the Indo-European myth is the Manichaean worldview, in which good and evil are two independent, eternal entities in eternal conflict with each other. In this dualism, good and evil are represented by two opposing superhuman beings: a good god (e.g., Ninurta, Indra, Marduk, Mazda, Rama) and a bad god (e.g., Asag, Vritra, Tiamat, Ravanna). All reality is divided into two camps: good god and bad god, angels and demons, good nations and evil ones, good humans and wicked ones, noble governments and evil insurgents. Twofold judgments are the rule; something is either good or bad, moral or immoral, legal or illegal, right or wrong, sin or virtue, work or play, success or failure, clean or dirty, civilized or primitive, practical or impractical. The line of demarcation between the two sides is sharp. The good has no evil in it. Good beings may be deceived or forced into doing bad things to gain righteous ends, but, at heart, they are good. Similarly, evil beings, though at times they do good, are fundamentally wicked. Evil beings have no redeeming qualities and must be destroyed so that good may reign.

36. Peter Berger observes that the two myths for social change are that of development and that of revolution (1974). Both are modern in the sense that both seek the same goal—the betterment of human life through human effort. At present the former has won the battle and stands triumphant on the global stage.

Central to the myth is the cosmic battle to control the universe that takes place in the heavens between good and evil gods. The good gods seek to establish a kingdom of righteousness and order, and the evil gods seek to establish an evil empire. The goal of the conflict is to win the battle—to take control and establish order at any cost. The outcome of the battle is uncertain, because both sides are equally strong. And the battle is unending; when either good or evil is defeated, it simply rises from the rubble to fight again. It is hardly a coincidence that the game of chess was developed in Persia and reflects the fundamental Indo-European view of reality.

In the Indo-European myth, the battle between good and evil is fought on different levels. In the heavens, it is the battle between the gods and the demons, on earth, between righteous and evil kings, between good and bad, and humans themselves mirror what is happening in the heavenly realms. "When the elephants fight," goes the proverb, "the mice get trampled."

In the myth of redemptive violence, the center of the story is the battle, not the peace that follows. This fascination with battle is evident in modern sports: football, basketball, tennis, hockey, chess, and monopoly. People pay to see a football game and go home when it is over. The mystery ends when the detective unmasks the villain, the cowboys defeat the Indians, Luke Skywalker and Princess Leia thwart the Evil Empire, and Superman destroys the enemies of humankind.

Victory in the Indo-European myth is never final, however, nor is evil ever completely defeated. Because evil invariably rises again to challenge good, good must constantly be on guard. Today's Super Bowl does not make a team the unchallenged victor forever. It must defend itself next season.

The fight concerns power and violence, which are necessary to establish order, good or bad. Underlying this struggle is the belief that relationships in the cosmos are based on competition, that competition is good, and that the good (strong, successful, intelligent) will ultimately win. The results of this unceasing competition are progress (civilization), development (in the economic sense), evolution (in the biological sense), and prowess (in sports) as the stronger, better, and brighter defeat the weaker, less skilled, and duller. Eugene Peterson writes:

> War is dressed up in the Sunday best of "competition." We are trained from an early age to get what we want not in cooperation with others but in competition against them. The means are essentially violent, whether physical or psychological, weapon or propaganda. I want what my brother has, I covet what my sister owns, I envy who my neighbor is. I set out to satisfy myself by whatever means are present to my hand. Not for long does that person (or nation) retain a name or identity. Each is labeled as an obstacle, or an alien force to be overcome. (1988, 77)

Morality in power encounters is based not on a cosmic moral order of righteousness and sin but on the notion of "fairness" and "equal opportunity."

To be "fair" the conflict must be between those who are more or less equal in power. The outcome of the battle must be uncertain. It is "unfair" to pit a seasoned gunman against a novice, or the Chicago Bears against a high school football team. "Equal opportunity" means that both sides must be able to use the same means to gain victory. If the evil side uses illegal and wicked means, the good side is justified in using them too, but only after the evil side has acted. In westerns, the sheriff cannot draw first, but when the outlaw does, he can gun the outlaw down without trial—acting as judge, jury, and executioner in one moment. He is justified in doing evil in "self defense" and to win the battle so that he can establish the kingdom of good. In the end, both sides use violence, deceit, and intimidation to win, and the good become like their enemies, doing evil and justifying it because their goals are good. Success is the proof of right and enables the victor to establish order—the greatest good.

The Indo-European religions may have died in the West, but as Walter Wink observes, the myth of redemptive violence dominates modern thought. It is the basis for the theories of evolution and capitalism and is the dominant theme in Western entertainment. It is told and retold in detective stories, murder mysteries, science fiction, and American westerns. It is recounted in the adventures of superheroes such as Sherlock Holmes, Superman, Spider-Man, Underdog, and Luke Skywalker. It is a staple of most cartoons; witness the epic showdowns between Popeye and Bluto in which Bluto never learns to leave Olive Oyl alone, and Popeye never learns to take his spinach before he attacks Bluto in her defense. It is dramatized in video games and played out in sports, such as football, basketball, and tennis.

Myth of Romantic Love

"And they were married and lived happily ever after." So end stories of romantic love. But the real story is not about life after the wedding; it is about the chase and capture. After marriage there is no story worth telling. This myth is at the center of most modern romance stories.

At the heart of this myth of romantic love is the story of how two people "fall in love" and then, like Romeo and Juliet, must overcome great obstacles to marry. Either the families oppose the match, or the two belong to enemy camps, or the girl plays hard to get and the boy must "capture her heart."

One consequence of this view is that young people become disenchanted when their marriages don't work out as they anticipated. They decide that they "were not really in love" after all. This justifies divorce in order to find the "right person." There is little need to make the marriage work.

The biblical myth of love in the Old Testament is found in Hosea. God loves his people, but they keep pursuing other men. He keeps attempting to win them back to himself. His covenant cannot be broken, no matter what they do.

Impact on Christianity

The Enlightenment concept of progress deeply influenced American Christianity and missions. Although many Christians rejected the theory of evolution, the ideas that were part of the evolutionary zeitgeist were absorbed with the air they breathed. Charles Taber notes, "The superiority of Western civilization as the culmination of human development, the attribution of that superiority to the prolonged dominance of Christianity, the duty of Christians to share civilization and the gospel with the 'benighted heathens'—these were the chief intellectual currency of their lives" (1991, 71).

One fruit of this myth has been postmillennialism, which emerged fully in the eighteenth and nineteenth centuries. Postmillennialism is an eschatology that interpreted the kingdom of God as the progressive realization of good in the life of the world through human effort. God's Spirit, working through his people, will gradually subdue the world until God's rule is complete and perfect. The prayer "thy kingdom come" was interpreted as a prayer that God hasten this gradual process.

In America this vision led to the belief in Manifest Destiny. America was a providentially appointed nation established by God with the mission to bring the ideals of liberty and democracy to the world. One part of this mission was that America was to be a light to the nations in the task of global evangelism. But this mission faces an ongoing battle against those who oppose progress, freedom, and righteousness. The world can be divided into people and nations that are good and those that are evil. The result, as Robert Bellah notes in his classic essay, has been the emergence of American civil religion (1967).

This vision has influenced the modern mission movement. Wilbert Shenk writes, "The seventeenth-century New England Puritan missionaries largely set the course for modern missions. They defined their task as preaching the gospel so that Native Americans would be converted and receive personal salvation. The model by which they measured their converts was English Puritan civilization. . . . They gathered these new Christians into churches for nurture and discipline and set up programs to transform Christian Indians into English Puritans" (1980, 35).

In the past, missionaries, as people of their times, sought to both Christianize and civilize people around the world. They built schools and hospitals alongside churches and saw science, like the gospel, as an essential part of the curriculum.[37] Many missionaries believed themselves to be participating in a worldwide crusade of human advancement in which Christianity and science worked together to contribute to the betterment of the world morally and materially (Bosch 1991, 298–302). They often believed that the customs and beliefs of the people they served could be ignored, for it was clear that

---

37. This equation of the gospel with modern culture has made the gospel unnecessarily foreign in other cultures and hindered its spread.

in time these people would be enlightened by modern education and would reject their former ways.

The concept of "civilized" versus "primitive" had a deep impact on modern missions after the nineteenth century, bolstered by a deep belief in the manifest superiority and liberating potential of Western "civilization." Missionaries from Europe and North America sought to convert people to Christianity in the other parts of the world and, at the same time, to civilize them. In 1843 the *Baptist Missionary Magazine* reported, "The people are now dressed in British manufactures and make a very respectable appearance in the house of God. The children who formerly were naked and presented a most disgusting appearance are decently clothed. . . . Instead of a few wretched huts resembling pigsties we now have a regular village, the valley in which it stands which till lately was uncultivated is now laid out in gardens" (quoted in Ferguson 2002, 122).

David Livingstone, a preacher and a doctor, is an example of this double mission. In his application to the London Mission Society, he wrote that the missionary's "duties chiefly are . . . to endeavour by every means in his power to make known the gospel by preaching, exhortation, conversion, instruction of the young, improving so far as in his power the temporal condition of those among whom he labours by introducing the arts and sciences of civilization and doing everything in his power to commend Christianity to the ears and consciences" (quoted in Ferguson 2002, 123).

It is true that it was evangelical Christians who led the attack on slavery that finally led to its abolishment in England and elsewhere, and that most missionaries identified themselves more closely with the people to whom they ministered than did colonial rulers. They learned the local languages and translated the Bible into them. Nevertheless, most missionaries in the modern era saw their task as both Christianizing and civilizing the "natives." To these, Livingstone added the third C, "commercializing," because he believed that free trade would obviate slavery.

In recent years, the myth of redemptive violence has emerged in the emphasis on "spiritual warfare," which sees the world as a cosmic battle between God and Satan; the battle is fought in the heavens, but it ranges over sky and earth. The central issue is power: Can God defeat Satan? Can Christians cast out demons?

Impact of Modernity on Christianity

The impact of modernity on Christianity has been profound. As Os Guinness observes, "Modernity is a new kind of worldliness that has sneaked up on us without our realizing it. We have tried to use the forces of modernization to serve us, but unwittingly we ourselves have been shaped by them. We have set up endless patrols to detect the dangers of the world in our societies, but the devil has trundled this new worldliness right past our eyes and into the church" (1994a, 323). This is true of churches and of Christians in general. It is as true, or more so, of conservative Christians, who are often unaware of modernity's influences. It represents both a great opportunity and a great threat to the church. As Guinness reminds us, *"The Christian church contributed to the rise of the modern world; the modern world, in turn, has undermined the Christian church. Thus, to the degree that the church enters, engages and employs the modern world uncritically, the church becomes her own gravedigger"* (1994b, 324, italics in the original).

The effects of modernity on missions from the seventeenth to twentieth centuries have been equally great. On the positive side, transportation, trade, and colonialism opened the door for the global spread of the gospel. Today the majority of the world's Christians live in non-Western countries. On the one hand, with the gospel came the spread of education and medicine, which has helped countless millions to become participants in the increasingly global world systems. On the other hand, the translation of the Bible into local languages often was the catalyst that enabled local cultures to survive the onslaught of modernity.

On the negative side, Christianity often became equated with modernity in the minds of non-Western peoples. Missionaries often saw their task as Christianizing and civilizing the world. This led to churches modeled on those in the West and the stifling of any local expressions of Christianity. It also led to the introduction of the modern supernatural/natural dualism that denies the reality of spirit realities and led to the secularization of the worldviews of many people. Much more can be said on this subject, but we must now turn to the rise of postmodernity and its impact on the Christian church and mission.

8

The Worldview of Late Modernity
or Postmodernity

A sea change is taking place in the modern world. Peter Drucker writes:

> Every few hundred years in Western history there occurs a sharp transformation. We cross what . . . has been called a "divide." Within a few short decades, society rearranges itself—its worldview; its basic values; its social and political structure; its arts; its key institutions. Fifty years later, there is a new world. And the people born then cannot even imagine the world in which their grandparents lived and into which their own parents were born. . . . We are currently living through just such a transformation. (cited in Van Engen 1997, 437)

Postmodernity is the situation in which the world finds itself after the collapse of the Enlightenment project, which lasted from the latter part of the eighteenth century until well into the twentieth. That project, whose goal was for the world's diverse peoples to see things in the same rational way, is now questioned. What was secure, foundational, and established is now called into question. The assertion now is that our modern perception of "the way things are," rather than being knowledge based on reason and empirical evidence is instead merely a set of self-serving ideologies constructed by those in power, ideologies that marginalize those who disagree.

Such radical worldview shifts do not take place at a particular moment. Modernity has not run its course. Rather, such shifts often begin as countercultural movements within a dominant culture. The philosophical roots of postmodernism may be traced to Friedrich Nietzsche, Martin Heidegger, Jacques Derrida, Michel Foucault, Jean-François Lyotard, and other philosophers. Its roots in anthropology go back to the 1930s, when Bronislaw Malinowski and A. R. Radcliffe-Brown urged anthropologists to see the world through the eyes of the people they studied (emic views) rather than to import modern analytical theories (etic views). This approach introduced the notion of cultural relativism and, in time, the study of modernity from the viewpoints of different peoples around the world.

The term "postmodern" came into use in the 1940s to describe new forms of architecture and poetry. After the 1960s, books appeared using the term to designate a new era in history. Critics argue that it is a passing fad, the invention of intellectuals in search of a new discourse or a conservative reaction to modernity. Advocates argue that it represents a new era in Western thought, marking the end of the bourgeois worldview with its rationalism, capitalism, and efforts to control life. Others hold that it designates a late stage in modernity with a shift from manufacturing to information management and consumerism.

Modern and postmodern worldviews have coexisted in the West for the past several decades and are competing for general acceptance. The shift will occur if and when the new paradigm triumphs over the old. But such paradigm shifts rarely are total displacements of the old by the new. The new incorporates many elements from the old but gives them new meaning within a new configuration—a new way of looking at things overall. Richard Brown observes:

> More and more people recognize that late capitalism, post-industrial society or postmodern culture are qualitatively different from what has come before. Whether such changes are conceptualized in terms of a late consumer, global capitalism bearing a hyper-modern culture, or of a postindustrial information society embodying a postmodern sensibility, it seems clear that things are no longer as once they seemed and that these changes, though only bleakly understood, are of epochal proportions. (1994, 13–14)

Many factors have prompted the emergence of postmodernity as a rival paradigm. One is the loss of faith in the Enlightenment project after World War I. In the nineteenth century the central organizing concept in Europe and North America was "civilization." Western nations saw themselves as standard bearers of an expanding civilization that united them and set them apart from other nations, which were seen as primitive or uncivilized. World War I destroyed this illusion of Western unity and progress. As Richard John Neuhaus explains:

> With the Great War things began to go badly wrong. Until then, smart people, most Christian thinkers included, believed in the inevitability of progress. The

world and they in the world were getting better every day in every way. Then came the guns of August 1914, and it was announced that the lights were going out all over the world. . . . This presumably enlightened century has loosed more rivers of blood and piled up more mountains of corpses than any century in history. The victims of Stalin and Hitler—and of Mao, who killed more than both combined—are calculated to be somewhere around 200 million, give or take 10 or 20 million. We lost count along the way. And, of course, victors do not usually count at all the firestorms, both atomic and "conventional" of Hamburg and Dresden and Nagasaki and Hiroshima. (2000, 106–7)

The history of the world since World War I has added to this disillusionment and doubt about whether modernity leads to progress, or whether we have been led astray by the illusion of innovation, development, and progress. Two world wars, fought not by so-called primitive countries but by those that considered themselves civilized, shattered the notion of progress. The collapse of colonialism and the movement of people from around the world to so-called civilized countries also disrupted the status quo. Many believe that modernity has failed to live up to its promises of creating a human utopia. The construction of modernity has produced untold suffering through colonial domination and industrial oppression. The modern mind had confidence in the human intellect's ability to resolve the crises of human life; the postmodern mind has lost faith in any such claim. It argues that no human intellect can negotiate the labyrinth of life, so one should simply enjoy living for today.

But disillusionment with modernity runs deeper. Max Weber argued that the endless change and flux of modernity leads to meaninglessness: "The individual life of civilized man, placed into an infinite 'progress' . . . placed in the midst of continuous enrichment of culture by ideas, knowledge and problems . . . catches only the most minute part of what the life of the spirit brings forth ever anew, and . . . as such is meaningless" (1970, 139–40).

Barry Smart writes, "Specifically we might note the recurring difficulty which rational and methodological forms of life have had in satisfactorily answering questions about 'ultimate presupposition,' foundations, of grounds; the continuing problem of meaning in a 'disenchanted' modern world; and the accumulation of signs that the modern pursuit of mastery over all things through the continual refinement of calculating and purposive forms of rationality seems destined to remain unfinished, incomplete and frustrated" (1993, 87). Scientific rationality has given us artificial abstractions and material aplenty, but also psychological, social, and spiritual poverty. We have more and more knowledge, but less and less meaning in life.

A second reason for the current crisis emerges from the success of the modern era. Modernity spread around the world and conquered or colonized much of it. It organized cultures into a hierarchy, with the "civilized," modern Western people at the top, and other peoples labeled "primitive" and "aboriginal." Leaders in other countries, trained in modern schools, challenged this hierarchy as exploitive and exclusivist. They sought to overthrow Western colonialism and to develop their own cultures and nations. Moreover, modern people began to encounter other peoples and cultures at an increasingly deeper level. This deep encounter with others and otherness raised the question of how to categorize and relate to them. The first response was to see others as primitives—as backward and uncivilized, people whom modern nations could "civilize" and make into full humans by means of education and by introducing advanced technology, democracy, individual freedoms, and secular states. As the agents of modernity came to study and know other peoples and their cultures, it became increasingly clear that these had their own validity. Other peoples are not prelogical. They use other logics. Other cultures are not to be ignored and displaced. They must be seriously understood in terms of their own worldviews. This realization led to an anticolonial movement that affirmed other cultures and cultural differences and rejected ethnocentrism and its cultural arrogance. After 1930 the term "civilization" was increasingly rejected as arrogant and replaced with the word "culture." Colonialism and imperialism became pejorative terms. Modernity became one of many cultures and, for many, not necessarily the best of them. Postmodernity is anticolonial and antiauthoritarian.

The questions then arose: How should modern people view otherness? How should they deal with cultural and religious pluralism? Postmodernity rejects modernity's assumption of its own superiority and its rejection of other cultures as primitive. It affirms the worth of all cultures, and emphasizes tolerance and cognitive and moral relativism. No longer can modern Europeans and Americans speak for and define the world in terms of their own theories. The views of all peoples must be heard as told by themselves.

A third reason for the current crisis is a penetrating intellectual critique of the worldview of modernity known as the "hermeneutics of suspicion." Modernity is based on a suspicion of all traditional ideologies and the search for certain, universal truths based on positivism. This seemingly solid foundation for modern knowledge is itself now suspect. As Barry Smart observes, "Modernity produces turmoil, flux, and not certainty. . . . Nothing is sacred and nothing is spared, everything is potentially subject to its subversion, including the 'proletarian' science predicated upon the project of modernity, and more significantly, the claims of modern reason themselves. In short, modernity has become subject to its own critical imperative" (1993, 109).

Postmodern scholars criticize modernity for its search for a foundation of knowledge, for its universalizing and totalizing claims, for its hubris in claiming to supply apodictic truth, and for its allegedly fallacious rationalism. They advocate an antiscientific, antitechnological position, arguing that all knowledge is cognitively constructed by observers from particular perspectives and with personal agendas, and that all knowledge is power. Grand theories and metanarratives are particularly suspect. Defenders of modern theory, by contrast, attack postmodern relativism, irrationalism, and nihilism, and apply the hermeneutics of suspicion to postmodernity. Steven Best and Douglas Kellner write, "It is ironic that despite the war against totality by Lyotard and others, theorists identified as postmodern like Foucault and Baudrillard have produced extremely totalizing theories which are often abstract, overly general, and sometimes oversimplify complex historical situations" (1991, 280).

Postmodernity distrusts the universal totalizing nature of modern thought and seeks fragmentation, indeterminacy, and pragmatism as liberating forces against the tyranny of modernity. The roots of this critique are found in modernity itself. As scientists began to study not only the world around them but also scientists and science itself, they called into question the basic assumptions of positivist science. The psychology, sociology, anthropology, and philosophy of knowledge have shown that scientists, universities, and research centers are part of large sociocultural systems that shape their research and findings. Science itself came to be seen as a construct made by scientists in scholarly communities, influenced by the social and political agendas of their departments, schools, and nations. The privileged position of the scientist and the objective nature of knowledge became untenable, and positivism came under attack. As David Harvey notes, it is "no longer possible to accord Enlightenment reason a privileged status in the definition of the eternal and immutable essence of human nature" (1990, 18). No longer can science claim to present the truth. Moreover, the idea that all of reality can be grasped in one unified, scientific theory or from one Archimedean vantage point is rejected. Barry Smart writes that "intellectuals today encounter the impossibility of providing an 'authoritative solution to the questions of cognitive truth, moral judgment, and aesthetic taste . . .'; an erosion of their traditional legitimatory function by more economic and efficient mechanisms of 'seduction and repression'; and finally displacement from a (potential) position of influence and control in the expanding sphere of cultural production and consumption by 'capitalists' or 'bureaucrats'" (1993, 63). The result has been the loss of faith in a grand metanarrative—a comprehensive theory of the world—and in a confidence that we can know all truth, or even truth at all. Human history has no "story" or "plot" to it and is therefore meaningless. The histories of societies, groups, and even families are no more than the playing out of power struggles and are therefore also meaningless. Even one's own life has neither story line nor purpose nor goal. Only the present moment has any meaning, and it is gone before we have time to reflect on it.

A fourth reason for the current crisis is that modernity said little about ethics and the purposes for which knowledge, scientific or other, should and would be used. It had no empirical way to lay the foundations of morality and to assure that new knowledge would be used for the good of humanity. It did not provide an adequate guide for living or managing society (Rosenau 1992, 10). Critiques of postmodernity argue that it too has no vision and offers no path to a better world. Rather, postmodernists "promote nihilism and pessimism 'as the only possible basis of historical emancipation,' while having no conception of what could or should emerge from the detritus of modernity" (Best and Kellner 1991, 284–85).

A final reason is the changes taking place in modernity itself. Early modernity was characterized by an industrial society based on material progress. Late modernity is marked by the shift to a knowledge society in which information is central; physical and mechanical labor is replaced by machines and by knowledge and knowledge-related services. The result is an increasingly rapid rate of change leading to uncertainty and insecurity. Postmodernity is "a way of living with the doubts, uncertainties and anxieties which seem increasingly to be a corollary of modernity . . . from the remorseless spirals of flux, turmoil and perpetual transformation that seem to be intrinsic to modernity" (Smart 1993, 12). Postmodernity lives with fear, anxiety, and insecurity and calls for imagination and responsibility.

The nature and future of the worldview change we face is not clear. Some scholars, such as Lyotard, Foucault, and Derrida, argue that modernity is collapsing because it has failed to deliver on its promises, and its internal contradictions have surfaced. They argue that we are in a totally new era requiring new concepts and theories. A new and more humane postmodern era is emerging.[1]

Others, like Jacques Ellul and Dario Fo, say that postmodernity is a passing fad, the invention of intellectuals in search of a new discourse, and a luxury of the rich and the powerful who have food on their tables—a romantic reaction to their jaded experiences with modernity, which has failed to give them meaning in life and peace on earth. People and nations around the world are still seeking the fruits of modernity. Zygmunt Bauman argues that postmodernity is not a new era with new answers but a self-reflexive critique of modernity. Jürgen Habermas, David Harvey, and Anthony Giddens stress the continuities between modernity and postmodernity more than the discontinuities. They posit that we are entering the stage of late or high modernity—modernity carried to its logical conclusions—in which a higher stage of capitalism is emerging marked by a greater degree of capital penetration and homogenization across the globe, which generates counterthemes of cultural fundamentalism, different ways of experiencing time and space, and new ways of looking at experience. According to Bauman, it is "the modern mind taking a long, attentive and sober look at itself, at its conditions and its past works, not fully liking what it sees and sensing the urge to change. Postmodernity is

---

1. The term "postmodern" was used in 1870 by an English artist to designate post-Impressionist painting. In 1917 Rudolf Pannwitz used it to describe the nihilism and collapse of values in European culture. Arnold Toynbee used the term in the 1930s. By the 1960s it was used to note the decline of the modern movement and to characterize what was coming next. In the 1970s the term came to be used widely in many academic fields.

modernity coming of age. . . . Postmodernity is modernity coming to terms with its own impossibility; a self-monitoring modernity, one that consciously discards what it was once unconsciously doing" (1991, 272). Late capitalism extends commodification to virtually all of social and personal life, including the spheres of knowledge and information. However, this stage is allegedly not simply modernity intensified. It has distinct characteristics that emerge out of the internal contradictions inherent in modernity itself.

Arnold Toynbee, Huston Smith, and Larry Laudan see postmodernity as a radical challenge to modernity. In the modern worldview, reality is ordered according to laws that human intelligence can grasp on the basis of a positivist epistemology. Modernity promised order and fulfillment, but the fact is that today the world is full of chaos, dissatisfaction, and misery. The postmodern worldview sees reality as unordered and ultimately unknowable. Human knowledge is simply utilitarian, based on an instrumentalist epistemology. Smith and Laudan suggest that postmodern skepticism and uncertainty is a transition to a post-postmodern perspective that, one hopes, will be characterized by a more holistic and spiritual outlook and by a reaffirmation of truth on the basis of a critical-realist epistemology.

Cognitive Themes

There is no unified postmodern theory, or even a coherent set of positions. Rather, several diverse theories are lumped together as "postmodern" (Best and Kellner 1991, 2). Here we will examine some of the dominant themes and counterthemes found in major theories of postmodernity that are finding increasing expression in popular cultures where modernity is being challenged.

Crisis of Representation

In recent years there has been a far-reaching attack on empiricist foundationalism and modernity's conception of representing reality in words. Karl Popper, W. V. Quine, Thomas Kuhn, and others have challenged the traditional assumptions that scientific knowledge mirrors reality and gives us unmediated access to the external world, and that such knowledge is cumulative, value-free, unbiased, and verified by hypothesis testing. They argue that all theories provide only partial, biased, and perspectival understandings of their objects, and that all are historically and linguistically mediated. Knowledge is like a collage or a Rorschach. Nietzsche attacked Western philosophical assumptions of objective, acultural, and ahistorical truth and argued for a perspectivalist orientation in which there are no facts, only interpretations, and no objective truths, only the constructs of individuals and groups. Ultimately this line of thinking raises the question of the representation of truth. Pauline Rosenau observes:

Modern representation certainly stakes out its territory in the broadest terms. It is *delegation*; one individual represents another in parliament. It is *resemblance*; a painting represents on canvas what the painter observes. It is *replication*; the photograph (image) represents the person photographed (object). It is *repetition*; a writer puts on paper the words (language) that represents his/ her idea or thought (meaning). It is *substitution*; a lawyer represent a client in court. It is *duplication*; a photocopy represents the original. Representation in its diverse forms is central to every field in the social sciences, and perhaps for this reason the battle between modernism and post-modernism rages savagely on this terrain. (1992, 92)

IDEOLOGICAL CRITIQUE

One major postmodern attack is leveled against modern epistemological claims of rationality, objectivity, and cumulative value-free, true knowledge. It denies the possibility of detached, objective knowledge—all knowledge is constructed and self-serving. Kenneth Gergen notes, "Empiricist foundationalism and its associated practices may continue to be dominant, but for a substantial number of scholars they lie essentially dead" (1994, 58). The attack focuses on science. "If theoretical accounts cannot be rendered authoritative by virtue of empirical data, and if these accounts enter social life as catalysts or suppressants, then science is open to a form of evaluation scarcely voiced since the nineteenth century. Specifically, scientific theory can be evaluated in terms of its effects on the culture, the forms of social life which it facilitates and obliterates, or in short, its ideological impact" (Gergen 1994, 58–59).

Karl Marx and Friedrich Engels, in their critique of ideologies, deconstructed religions. Now the same critique is used to deconstruct Marxism and the sciences. Marx and Engels argued that religions and other ideologies of a society serve the interests of the powerful, and that the ideas of the ruling class are the ruling ideas in a society.[2] Postmodernists reject the privileged position science claims, and see it, too, as an ideology, shaped by academicians who have vested interests in their findings and who accept uncritically the very habits of thinking that themselves should be scrutinized. This skepticism is the reflexive application of scientific critique to scientists and science itself. Scientists have constructed a new sense of rationality—scientific rationality—that destroyed earlier rational systems. Max Weber writes that "science in the name of 'intellectual integrity' has come forward with the claim of representing the only possible form of a reasoned view of the world. The intellect, like all culture values, has created an aristocracy based on the possession of rational culture and independent of all personal ethical qualities of man" (1970, 355). But now science has become the dominant and dominating component of modernity and

2. Recent studies show that in place of a single dominant worldview, there are multiple and competing worldviews, and the hegemony of the ruling class is never complete (Simons and Billig 1994, 3).

serves the interests of those in power. Therefore, it can no longer be trusted to reveal the illusions of ideology. Weber argues that there are other rationalized worldviews, and that these have not disappeared but continue to shape history in significant ways. Modernity was built on skepticism toward traditional knowledge. Postmodernity is built on skepticism toward modernity.

REFLEXIVITY

If modernity moved the focus from the knower to the known, postmodernity moves it from the known back to the knower. It argues that scientific theories are reflexive, applying not only to the objects scientists study but to the scientists themselves, particularly when they study humans. Foucault points out this contradiction in modernity: humans are seen as beings shaped by heredity and environment and driven by subjective emotions and values, unable to transcend their world, yet scientists are seen as able to free themselves from this world and think deeply as human beings. But scientists cannot show that they are more rational than the people they study. Postmodernity seeks to restore the primacy and autonomy of the thinking subject. It is antiauthoritarian and antihierarchical.

DECONSTRUCTION

Postmodernists are deeply disillusioned with modernity. Two world wars, the threat of ecological collapse, the growing gap between rich and poor, and the dangers of nuclear and chemical destruction have led to cynicism and nihilism, undermining the optimism of the nineteenth century and the belief that the future will be better than the past.

Postmodernists question the Enlightenment project with its equation of reason, freedom, and faith in progress. Modern theories see knowledge as neutral, objective, universal, and fundamental to progress and emancipation. Postmodernists argue that all forms of knowledge are integral components of power and domination. Barry Smart notes, "Increased rationalization has not led to an increase in general awareness of the conditions under which we live our lives, or to an enhancement of personal autonomy. On the contrary, increasing differentiation of fields of knowledge and the associated growth of specialists and professionals have precipitated an increase in forms of dependence" (1993, 87).

Postmodernists reject totalizing theories as rationalist myths of the Enlightenment that are reductionistic, obscure the diversity of social realities, and suppress diversity. Moreover, as Max Weber observes, the constant change and flux created by "progress" driven by an endless pursuit of innovation and knowledge create restlessness and are unable to "teach us anything about the *meaning* of the world" (1970, 139–40). Barry Smart notes that the resurrection of the "sacred" as a sphere of experience and as a countertheme to the nihilism of the modern world constitutes part of the postmodern condition (1993, 89).

Postmodernists argue that all systems of knowledge, logic, and justice are culturally and historically created and have no ties to objective reality or any privileged claims to truth and morality. Because these systems are created by people on the basis of their own self-interest, all are suspect. Every claim to truth and authority falls under suspicion. Postmodernists, following Nietzsche, claim that power, not reason, determines the ruling ideas of a society, and that the powerful define these ideas. They challenge the modern conception of a grand unified theory of reality and replace it with collage, eclecticism, indeterminancy, chaos, play, irony, and cynicism. Differences and complexity are favored over unifying and simplifying theories. Postmodernists question the West's claim that its culture, science, and social organization have universal validity.

The crisis of representation has further undermined postmodernists' trust in the Enlightenment project, whose claims of discovering objective, value-free knowledge are under severe attack. No longer can positivism be defended as the foundational epistemology for discovering truth.

In the end, postmodernity deconstructs the autonomous, real person. Individuals are imploded into the masses, and become constructs—ultimately illusions or virtual realities.

Distrust of Reason

The failure of reason to build a better world and critical reflections on its processes have led to an increasing awareness of its limits and limitations. Increasing rationalization has led not to better, more meaningful lives and greater personal autonomy but to greater differentiation between fields of knowledge, to increasing specializations and fragmentation of knowledge.

In part the critique of reason is rooted in modernity itself, which subjected all other systems of belief to critical analysis and eroded their authority. Now that same critical reflection has been turned against reason and science and deconstructed their claims to truth and authority. Modernity has become the subject of the relativizing forces it initiated.

Rejection of Grand Narratives

The crisis of representation and the loss of faith in modernity have led to disillusionment with the grand unifying theory of progress underlying the Enlightenment. Postmodernists reject the philosophical effort to grasp systematically all of reality in one philosophical system, from one central, detached vantage point. They argue that our human perceptions of reality are determined, in part, by our particular situation and our worldviews. To comprehend the whole of reality, we need different approaches at different levels using different methods. Metanarratives, they say, are monocultural, imperialistic, and oppressive. According to Anthony Giddens, "post-modernity refers to a shift away from attempts to ground epistemology and from faith in humanly engineered progress. The condition of post-modernity is distinguished by an evaporating of the 'grand narrative'—the overarching 'story line' by means of which we are placed in history as beings having a definite past and a predictable future. The post-modern outlook sees a plurality of heterogeneous claims to knowledge, in which science does not have a privileged place" (1990, 2).

Postmodernists attack science and its belief in the unity of experience and its search for a unified theory of knowledge. Jean-François Lyotard writes, "We have paid a high enough price for the nostalgia of the whole and the one, for the reconciliation of the concept and the sensible, of the transparent and the communicable experience. . . . The answer is, Let us wage a war on totality; let us be witnesses to the unpresentable; let us activate the differences and save the honor of the name" (1984, 81–82). This critique extends to science and philosophy, which had replaced religion as the final authority on matters of truth. They must now renounce their metaphysical claims and view themselves as just another set of narratives (Harvey 1990, 6). No truth claims are privileged, not even those that expose the claims of the privileged. Robin Horton writes that the study of the rationality of sciences and religions "has cast doubt on most of the well-worn dichotomies used to conceptualize the difference between scientific and traditional religious thought. Intellectual versus emotional; rational versus mystical; reality-oriented versus fantasy-oriented; causally oriented versus supernaturally oriented; empirical versus non-empirical; abstract versus concrete; analytical versus non-analytical: all of these are shown to be more or less inappropriate" (1970, 152).

Postmodernity argues that there is no detached, outside vantage point from which scientists can view reality. They are very much part of the picture they are studying, and their very presence changes the realities they examine. This leads to a rejection of any grand or metanarrative. It also means that all we have is narratives from different perspectives, all of which are equally valid. Local and marginal narratives must be encouraged and heard. The result is cognitive relativism.

Postmodernity also holds that scientists and their theories are influenced by nonrational factors such as their culture, social positions, economic desires, and drive for fame, and by contingent historical factors such as where they study and teach. In the life of every individual, many more beliefs are taken to be true than those one acquires by personal verification. "Everyone, including scientists, relies on others for the overwhelming majority of information they accept about the way nature works" (Behe 2005, 18).

Ironically, postmodernity rejects the totalizing tyranny of modern metanarratives while simultaneously seeking to be the new totalizing metanarrative itself. As Kenneth Gergen (1994) points out, it vilifies males, heterosexuals, capitalists, communists, empiricists, moralists, and others for the dominating effects of their discourses and refuses to hear their points of view. Their voices are placed under attack and pushed to the margins for their hegemonic tendencies. Dissenters are labeled as "exclusivists," and dissent silenced in the name of political correctness. But in the end, in rejecting other overarching theories, postmodernity undermines its own claims to truth.

REJECTION OF GREEK DUALISM

The modern dualism of natural/supernatural, empirical realities/ideas, nature/life, natural order/miracles was challenged even earlier. Alfred North Whitehead writes, "The effect of this sharp distinction between nature and life has poisoned all subsequent philosophy. Even when the coordinate existence of the two types of actualities is abandoned, there is no proper fusion of the two in most modern schools of thought. For some nature is mere appearance and mind is the sole reality. For others, physical nature is the sole reality and the mind is an epiphenomenon" (1938, 150). The truth is that neither physical nature nor life can be understood unless we fuse them together as essential factors in the composition of the "really real."

ANTIREDUCTIONISM

Postmodernists argue that truth acquired by materialism and positivism leaves out realities that are as or more important than scientific knowledge, namely God, the absolute, the universe, morality, deep emotions, and the meaning in life, none of which can be reduced to language. Postmodernists seek to rehumanize a world that has reduced everything to machines.

Postmodernists also posit that knowledge of the external world can only be thought and communicated through language, and that all languages reduce the complexity of material realities to simple concepts so that the human mind can comprehend it. They deny the claim that representation can be objective and that the observer is separate from the thing or person being described. They, therefore, "abandon any attempt to represent the object of study 'as it really is,' independent of the process of inquiry. . . . [They claim that] modern representation is perverse, artificial, mechanical, deceptive, incomplete, misleading, insufficient, wholly inadequate for the postmodern age" (Rosenau 1992, 94, 98).

Particularism/Universalism

One cause of the emergence of postmodernity is the growing social pluralism in Western societies and their daily encounter with different peoples and cultures. Increasingly a myriad of other voices are clamoring for rights and power. But postmodernity is more than the fact of cultural and ethnic diversity. It is the acceptance of pluralism as the ideal way of organizing society. No longer do we speak of assimilating immigrant communities into the dominant culture. Rather we encourage them to affirm their distinct identities.

Barry Smart notes, "The aspiration now is not assimilation but 'integration through diversity' which means according legitimacy and value to ethnic and religious identities, communities and differences 'so long as they are ultimately subordinate to the overarching political community and its complex of myths, memories and symbols'" (1993, 40). Societies are now increasingly intrinsically pluralistic and lack a single overarching value system. Postmodern art is the eclectic mix of any tradition with the immediate past. Postmodernism rejects exclusive dogma or taste. It replaces the word "civilization" with "cultures," which it sees as positive and equal.

Linda Hutcheon views the affirmation of pluralism and contradiction as inherently good. "Willfully contradictory, then, post-modern culture uses and abuses the conventions of discourse. It knows it cannot escape the implications of the economic (late capitalist) and ideological (liberal humanism) domains of its time. There is no outside. All it can do is question from within" (1980, xiii).

FRAGMENTATION

Modernity sought a grand unified theory. Postmodernity rejects grand narratives as tyrannical and celebrates diversity. David Harvey writes, "I begin with what appears to be the most startling fact about post-modernism: its total acceptance of the ephemerality, fragmentation, discontinuity, and the chaotic. . . . But post-modernism does not try to transcend it, contradict it, or even to define the 'eternal and immutable' elements that might lie within it. Post-modernism swims, even wallows, in the fragmentary and the chaotic currents of change as if that is all there is" (1990, 44).

In its attempt to destroy the tyrannies of grand narratives, postmodernity seeks to dismantle our traditional ways of perceiving forms and space. It seeks fragmentation, disorder, and chaos, and little argument and counterargument. It affirms novelty, eclecticism, fiction, theater, and ephemerality. Postmodernity rejects as tyrannical the metaphor of knowledge as a photograph. It draws on the metaphors of bricolage, patchwork, and collage, which portray diversity and multiple stories. All human stories must be heard, and heard as told by those who live them. This fragmentation of life calls for tolerance and coexistence by the diverse groups that live together.

PERSPECTIVALISM

A major challenge postmodernity levels against modernity is modernity's claim to discover ahistorical, acultural truth. Postmodernists argue that science can no longer claim a privileged position above critique, a detached, objective Archimedean point from which to observe reality. Derrida argues that the binary opposition governing the Western worldview privileged some forms of knowledge, such as science and universal theories, and devalued or excluded other forms of knowing, such as religion and art. Knowledge systems must be located within human cultures and history and as such represent knowledge from particular perspectives.[3] This imperative radically alters how we must view science. It no longer holds a privileged position in defining knowledge and truth. Moreover, science must recognize that it, too, is made up of many different forms of knowledge. In postmodernity objectivity is replaced by subjectivity, context-free beliefs by context-bound beliefs, timeless truth by historically rooted truths, and pure propositional rationality by multiple rationalities.

Postmodern theories stress perspectivalism in their analysis of human societies and cultures. Discourse theorists, for example, argue that meaning is not simply given but is socially constructed by communities, institutions, and societies. Discourse itself is seen as a place in which different groups strive for hegemony and the production of meaning and ideology. In examining discourses we must analyze the social bases for the discourse, the viewpoints and positions from which people speak, and the power relationships these allow and presuppose. We must gather multiple interpretations of phenomena and reject the philosophical arrogance of trying to grasp systematically all of reality in one explanation system or point of view. Cultures and societies are not unchanging realities. They are constantly created and re-created in the many transactions of people in everyday life situations.

Postmodernity is self-referential, not world referential. It does not seek to look behind images to a master narrative or story. Rather it is content with images themselves—with a world of pure surface. It cannot go behind superficial appearances. In literature, texts do not point to authors or things or events. They point to other texts. This intertextuality becomes a ceaseless, playful process. Not only does this view argue against coherent plots and perspectives in art and distinctive styles in architecture; it also argues against any single system of objective truth. All truth, postmodernity holds, is perspectival, including science. Postmodernism stresses the local character of all truth. It is the disintegration of reality—a nonrelational vision of reality. The self, too, collapses. Individuals are no more than ephemeral variables in an eternally repeating machine of identification and rejection.

DEMOCRATIZATION

Postmodernity calls for an end to authority and replaces it with self-expression. All human voices must be heard as people themselves, not some outside authority, tell their stories. Postmodernity distrusts specialists and outside perspectives and denies that anyone can have a monopoly on truth.

3. In physics, Einstein's theory of general relativity put scientists into the world they were examining. What they see depends on their frame of reference. In sociology Karl Mannheim and Peter Berger demonstrate that scientists are part of social communities that influence their findings. Anthropologists show that science itself is a Western cultural system of beliefs shaped by Western history and worldview.

As Pauline Rosenau writes, "Post-modernists are anti-elitist, in the sense of doing away with the expert role in judging art, music, and literature" (1992, 100). They celebrate the popular culture, not elite culture, and demand popular control.

Postmodernists argue that political representation distorts political discourse and action because people are so easily manipulated through the mass media, the "consciousness industry," which encourages candidates for public office to give only superficial considerations to political issues. "Politics has become popular theater and media image, rather than public discussion of political policies" (Rosenau 1992, 99). Surveys and polls influence politicians, but they do not encourage deep discussions of political policies between the representatives and the people.

Instrumentalism

Postmodern philosophers challenge the modern worldview assumption that modernity has a solid foundation on which to build knowledge, an absolute bedrock of truth that can guarantee the truthfulness of its scientific explanations. Postmodernists "emphasize that the world is cognitively constructed differently by different people at different times. Culture may be interpreted as a process of negotiating meaning. This calls into question any claims of objectivity, even within the physical sciences" (Lewellen 2002, 41). Burtt argues that although the sciences seek to proceed on a firm foundation of facts, with no metaphysics, the only way to avoid becoming a metaphysician is to say nothing. "There is an exceedingly subtle and insidious danger in positivism. If you cannot avoid metaphysics, what kind of metaphysics are you likely to cherish when you sturdily suppose yourself to be free from the abomination? Of course, it goes without saying that in this case your metaphysics will be held uncritically because it is unconscious; moreover it will be passed on to others far more readily than your other notions inasmuch as it will be propagated by insinuation rather than by direct argument" (1954, 229).

As we will see, the attack on positivism came from philosophers, sociologists, psychologists, and anthropologists of knowledge. The epistemological foundations for postmodernism that emerged are instrumentalism or idealism (Hiebert 1999).[4]

SOCIAL CONSTRUCTION OF KNOWLEDGE

Sociologists of knowledge, such as Karl Mannheim and Peter Berger, have shown that human knowledge systems, including the sciences, are socially

---

4. The impact of postmodern subjectivism is widely felt in the church, where increasingly "experience" is the arbiter of truth, and individual beliefs take priority over church confessions. This is a corrective to the modern emphasis on truth as cognitive affirmation, but it leaves us with theological and religious relativism.

constructed. What scientists observe depends on their culture, history, and place in society. Moreover, they have their own personal interests in mind. In the end, as Larry Laudan (1996) points out, science is no different from religions or other ideologies.

Jacques Derrida, Michel Foucault, and Roland Barthes attacked structuralists who explained humans in terms of underlying systems, whether social or cultural. They stressed the importance of history and the unpredictable nature of everyday life, which were suppressed by the abstractions of the structuralist project. Postmodernists focus not on the structure of language and culture (lingua) but on what people say and do (parole).

Saussurian Signs

Following the lead of Wilhelm von Humboldt, Ferdinand de Saussure (1916) argued that signs are made up of forms and meanings. The forms (the signifier) are the external signs created by humans. The meanings (the signified) are the ideas in the mind. Given this semiotics, knowledge is actively constructed by the mind, not passively received from the external world. Language has no direct relationship to the real world. It is only symbolic, and because symbols are human creations, it is culturally arbitrary. Since all statements are mediated by language, ideas can never be exchanged between people with any degree of certainty. This has become the semiotic foundation for postmodern thought.

Saussurian semiotics differentiates sharply between what the author says and writes and what the listener hears and the reader reads. Communication is no longer what the author means; it is measured by how the listener interprets the text. This semiotics undermines the presumption that human statements and texts carry truth or profundity; they contain only as much as interpretive communities are willing to grant them. "Not only does the object of the text disappear as a serious matter, but so does the mind of the author as its original source. . . . Under these conditions, all attempts by authorities to establish knowledge, convey wisdom or establish values are placed under suspicion. . . . There is virtually no hypothesis, body of evidence, ideological stance, literary canon, value commitment or logical edifice that cannot be dismantled, demolished or derided with the implements at hand" (Gergen 1994, 59). In the end, all forms of truth are ultimately fictions or myths.

Subjectivism

One consequence of constructionism is subjectivism: the belief that the realities we know are created by our minds, not by external verities. Walter Anderson observes:

> In recent decades we have passed, like Alice slipping through the looking glass, into a new world. This post-modern world looks and feels in many ways like the

modern world that preceded it; we still have the belief systems that gave form to the modern world, and indeed we also have remnants of many of the belief systems of premodern societies. If there is anything we have plenty of, it is belief systems. But we also have something else, a growing suspicion that all belief systems—all ideas about human reality—are social constructions. (1990, 3)

For postmodernity all reality is subjective. It sees history not as a series of real events that make up a coherent story but as a set of cultural constructs used to interpret the present and the past. That construct is created and controlled by the powerful. It is a facade. It is told in staged events and so becomes theater.

Power

Foucault traced the intimate connection between power and knowledge, concluding that the search for systems of meaning to explain the world is meaningless and futile. The real force driving world history is power. He writes:

Here I believe one's point of reference should not be to the great model of language (*langue*) and signs, but to that of war and battle. The history which bears and determines us has the form of a war rather than that of a language: relations of power, not relations of meaning. History has no "meaning," though this is not to say that it is absurd or incoherent. On the contrary, it is intelligible and should be susceptible of analysis down to the smallest detail—but this in accordance with the intelligibility of struggles, of strategies and tactics. (1980, 114)

He noted that the production of knowledge itself is a means of power and domination through schools, newspapers, television, and other information brokers.

Foucault's stress on power led to the hermeneutics of suspicion. In every human encounter, we must ask what is the personal gain for the information broker in his or her creation and dissemination of information. The postmodern critique notes that science itself is an ideology that shapes social and cultural systems and thus must be evaluated on whether it enhances or oppresses different groups of people. If all knowledge is constructed by groups motivated by self-interest, then, as Paul Ricoeur notes in his hermeneutics of suspicion, we must ask of every ideology what privileges the supporting community gains by insisting on it. Every claim to truth is immediately placed under suspicion. Knowledge becomes no longer an issue of truth but one of power and control. In this sense, postmodernity is a code name for the crisis of confidence in Western conceptual systems, their certainty, and their metanarratives. It is an attempt to demolish the grand structures of modernity.

J. Baudrillard (1992) argues that modernity is the era of production controlled by the industrial bourgeoisie, and that postmodernity is the era in which power lies in information governed by media, computerization, information processing, and cybernetic control systems. This is the age of information, and the information experts are the elite.

Not only is knowledge based on power; so too is politics. The talk about a common public discourse involving all parties on how to live together is increasingly rejected in favor of power politics. Richard Neuhaus writes:

> Abandoning the idea of moral truth, politics is no longer the deliberation of how we ought to order our life together but is now, in the phrase of Alastair MacIntyre, warfare carried on by other means. All politics is combat politics. There is no longer, some say, a common American culture, and we should stop pretending that there is. There are only subcultures. Choose your subculture, take up its grievances, contentions and slogans, and prepare to do battle against the enemy. . . . We are urged to recognize the futility of being locked in civil argument and accept the fact that there is no substitute for partisan victory. (2005, 28)

Hyperreality

In postmodernity the boundaries between information and entertainment, between images and reality, are blurred. TV news and documentation assume more and more the form of entertainment, and entertainment is turned into advertising. Reality is now virtual, created by media artists who can make anything appear real. The boundaries between politics and entertainment are also blurred. In political campaigns, image is more important than substance, and political campaigners depend on media and public relations experts and pollsters to shape the image of the candidate and to test the popularity of issues. In this world the distinction between real and simulation or virtual reality disappears. We should thus not be surprised that an actor who played a doctor on TV received thousands of letters asking for medical advice. "Hyperreality points to a blurring of distinction between the real and the unreal in which the prefix 'hyper' is more real than the real whereby the real is produced according to a model. When the real is no longer simply given (for example as a landscape or the sea), but is artificially (re)produced as 'real' (for example as a simulated environment), it becomes not unreal, or surreal, but more real than real, a real retouched and refurbished in 'a hallucinatory resemblance' with itself" (Best and Kellner 1991, 119).

Relativism

Many postmodernists deny the possibility of knowing truth (Lyotard 1984). They say it is impossible to distinguish between truth, rhetoric, and propaganda. They see truth claims merely as power plays by those whose interests they serve. They argue, "It is impossible to separate truth from power, and so there is no real possibility of any absolute uncorrupted truth" (Rosenau 1992, 78). Truth claims are seen as a form of terrorism that justify the powerful and silence those who disagree.

Some postmodernists reject universal truth of "what is out there" but accept the possibility of personal and community forms of truth. People and communities can have their own versions of truth, and conflicting claims are not a problem because those making them each live in a different world. These postmodernists emphasize the importance of personal and community-based narratives rather than grand narratives, because they are presented as one interpretation among many. Common stories unify people and are social bonds that give meaning to individuals in their everyday lives.

Egocentrism

Postmodernity has moved the central focus from human centeredness to egocentrism. This is captured in the bumper sticker that reads, "It's all about me." As we noted earlier, the word "soul" in the medieval sense has been replaced by the word "self." The former connotes relationship to God, eternal existence, and moral nature, the latter an autonomous individual with intrinsic characteristics and rights. Relationships are secondary.

SELF-DIVINIZATION

Postmodernity is the worship of the self. Self is the center of reality, self-determination the supreme value, freedom an inalienable right, and self-fulfillment the goal. The rise of the autonomous self has led to belief in the construction of self as a reflexive project, in the right to seek self-fulfillment, self-achievement, and self-realization, and in the moral prerogative to act for self-preservation and to kill in self-defense if necessary. We are the center of existence, so we owe it to ourselves to live for ourselves today. The postmodern person has no higher interest than himself or herself.

This search for the "self" is a reaction to modernity with its depersonalization of human beings. Lamin Sanneh notes, "Our new orthodoxies are now constructed and validated as psychological uplift, self-esteem, and other versions of emotional quick-fix, in the name of all of which we would make sacrifices that we would begrudge Church and fellowship" (1993, 221).

What starts with the collapse of grand narratives ends in the collapse of self. From the beginning science has found it difficult to define "self." Some psychologists argue that there is no abiding individual self with a universal human nature but only a series of many selves constructed and constantly changing. The person is not an immortal soul but only a cluster of functions.

The price of self-determination is living with increasing contingency. Self-determination requires an awareness of options and that one can make choices, and introduces indeterminacy, ambivalence, and "a seemingly inexhaustible capacity to transform seductive prospects for satisfaction into frustrating experiences of dissatisfaction" (Smart 1993, 99). But this challenges modernity's promises of certainty, and the modern idea that life can be predicted and controlled, and it raises existential anxiety. The modern answer to this tension between self-determination and corporate order is greater application of modern social engineering and the offer of more promises of a good life. The postmodern response is to learn to live with contingency, ambiguity, paradox, and dilemmas.

EXISTENTIALISM

The emergence of instrumentalism as the underlying epistemology leads to existentialism. The only reality is now, the present. We focus on news, not history; on health, not the meaning of life; on the pursuit of self-centered happiness with little thought to the happiness of those around the world we see on television or the Web. As a result people lead frenzied lives, seeking but finding no meaning in life.

Late Capitalism/Nation-State

We are witnessing the spread of late capitalism. We are also seeing "the rolling back of what we have come to know as the welfare state; the increasing commodification of health, welfare and educational provision and concomitant promotion of the alleged virtues of the untrammeled market, business culture and entrepreneurship; the growth of conspicuous and not-so-conspicuous consumption on the back of a rising tide of debt; and the radical transformation of [socialist societies] . . . towards those 'Western' forms of economic political organization formerly regarded as anathema" (Smart 1993, 24–25).

CONSUMERISM

One focus of late capitalism is consumerism. Increasingly consumers and consumption have replaced laborers and production as the focus of life and the integrating bond of society, and seduction rather than repression is now the predominant mechanism of social control. The pursuit of pleasure through consumption of commodities and services has become the dominant cultural value of postmodernity, replacing the deferral of gratification and self-denial. Consumerism offers people meaning through buying and living the good life in a world in which they feel increasingly meaningless, insignificant, and unreal. Eugene Peterson observes that people "live in a vast shopping mall where they go from shop to shop, expending enormous sums of energy and making endless trips to meet first this need and that appetite, this whim and that fancy. Life lurches from one particular satisfaction to another, interrupted by ditches of disappointment. Motion is fueled by the successive illusions that purchasing this wardrobe, driving that car, eating this meal, drinking that beverage will center life and give it coherence" (1988, 60).

Consumerism is nourished by human dissatisfaction and craving. Once existing needs are adequately met, new needs must be created to keep the market going. People who are relatively happy with their lives, enjoy spending time with their children, enjoy walks and times of prayer, meditation, and silence, and have a peaceful sense of who they are, are not good for the market. But those who are unhappy and dissatisfied with their lives, live in anxiety, and are unsure of their identity and their relationships to others, want more, and the market promises to fulfill these ever-expanding needs and wants (Kavanaugh 1981, 46–47).

Postmodernity encompasses more than the commodification of everything and the spread of hyperconsumerism. It has reenchanted buying commodities by giving them meanings that far transcend economic utilitarianism. For many it offers a form of entertainment, of having fun. "Malls are designed to be fantasy worlds, theatrical settings for what Kowinski calls 'the Retail Drama.' Both consumers and mall employees play important roles in this drama. After all, many Americans' favorite form of entertainment is shopping. The mall is loaded with props, with a backdrop of ever-present Muzak to sooth the savage shopper. . . . There are the restaurants, bars, movie theaters, and exercise centers to add to the fun. On weekends, clowns, balloons, magicians, bands, and the like further entertain those on their way from one shop to another" (Ritzer 2001, 28).

For others, reenchantment has led to therapeutic consumption, which offers new paths to healing and wholeness, with marketing and entertainment as the new preachers selling this new salvation. Advertising associates pleasure with buying products and fear with failure to buy them. Dirt, bad breath, yellow teeth, excess weight, headaches, body odors, and shabby furnishings are ills to be overcome through consumption. Spotless bathrooms, dazzling smiles, and comfortable cars are supreme evidence of what is good. Even religion is packaged and marketed (using uncritically all the techniques of modern advertising) as a product offering peace of mind, health and prosperity, heaven, and the answer to all problems. The therapeutic society, rather than turning good into evil, instead eliminates the differences between them. Everything is reduced to needs, satisfactions, and self-fulfillment. Everyone is encouraged to "do your own thing."

For still others, reenchantment has led to a new religion in which shopping malls become "cathedrals of consumption" (Ritzer 2001, 4). Buying leads to new forms of salvation. Buying a new computer gives meaning to life for a few months, a new car for a year or two, especially if it is one symbolizing high status, and a new house for a few years. When this meaning begins to fade, new purchases restore the feeling of well-being and self-fulfillment.

However, consumerism cannot answer the deeper longings of human hearts because the satisfaction it offers is illusory. We deceive ourselves into thinking that we are truly having fun. We create the illusion of intimacy. We settle for temporary, transient feelings to give meaning to our lives.

COMMODIFICATION

In late capitalism, production, profit, and money reign as supreme values, and consumerism, competition, hoarding, planned obsolescence, and unnecessary waste are its manifestations. Central to this is the commodification of everything so that it can be bought and sold in the marketplace. Information, cultural events, politics, government, even churches are driven by business models. Modern, standardized, mass-produced houses cease to be "homes" with their distinct personalities, stories, and memories, and become "machines for living," bought and sold as investments. Foreign cultures become esoteric places marketed to tourists.

People, too, are reduced to commodities to be bought and sold. Secretaries, mechanics, athletes, movie stars, academicians, administrators, and many others can be bought and sold. They are dispensable and can be replaced by others who bring more value to the organization. As James Kavanaugh notes, "Money, Moloch, the 'Tyranny of Production' strip us of our humanity. Living only to labor and to cling to the products of our labor, we re-create ourselves in the image and likeness of our products. We alienate ourselves from each other in competition and in the struggle for possession and profit. We become alienated from our own humanness. . . . We can no longer speak of our being or perceive our personhood. Human relationships, activities, qualities, become thing-like relationships, actions and qualities" (1981, 110). Even the value of people is reduced to their marketability.

The driving forces behind capitalism are marketability and consumption. "They have profoundly affected not only our self-understanding but also our modeling of human behavior (into manipulation and aggressions), human knowledge (into quantification, observation, and measurement), and human affectivity (into noncommittalness and mechanized sexuality)" (Kavanaugh 1981, 21). People buy sprays, clothes, cars, and houses to find meaning in life, and to find friendship, intimacy, love, and happiness. Their self-worth is measured in terms of production, consumption, and competition. They relate to one another as things. They are disposable and can be replaced by others who have greater economic value. They find meaning in having and happiness in having more.

Human bodies, too, are reduced to commodities to be shaped, colored, and sold. In their natural state they are inadequate, marred by lumps, acne, balding, and old-age wrinkles. The study of sexuality is a science clinically described by outside observers who have no personal involvement, no commitment, and no recognition of the participants as personal beings. In the end, people are produced or aborted, marketed and consumed.

NATION-STATE

With the triumph of market capitalism and the reaffirmation of religion and ethnicity as the most fundamental identities of people, the nation-state has been weakened. It is losing its effectiveness to integrate its people into a single society. Barry Smart notes:

> First, there is evidence of increasing opposition to the intervention of the state in social life and to its extension beyond the domains of "public entrepreneur and participant in international relations." . . . Second, global diffusion of economic activity and trade, and communications media and cultural production, coupled with higher levels of international travel, and a significant increase in supranational political and economic organizations and forums, has precipitated an erosion of the political sovereignty and cultural specificity ascribed to the "national state." (1993, 57)

We live less and less in national frameworks because of the growing internationalization of economy and culture and the growing divisions in our countries.

Affective Themes

In reaction to the rationalism of modernity, postmodernity reaffirms the affective dimension of cultures. It replaces Descartes' famous maxim, "I think therefore I exist," with "I feel therefore I exist." The exploration of the affective dimensions of life began in the eighteenth century. It has found its fulfillment in postmodernity.

Neil Postman traces the shift from the rational discourses that characterized modern speeches, publications, and advertisements to entertainment as the dominant mode of communication. This development spread from films and radio to television and now the Internet. "Entertainment is the supra-ideology of all discourse on television. No matter what is depicted or from what point of view, the overarching presumption is that it is there for our amusement and pleasure" (Postman 1985, 87). People turn to television for soap operas, presidential addresses, baseball games, rock concerts, world news, and religious services linked together by advertising, none of which assume rationality on the part of the viewers. "Television [and we must now add the Internet] is our culture's principle mode of knowing about itself. Therefore—and this is the critical point—how television stages the world becomes the model for how the world is to be staged. It is not merely that on the television screen entertainment is the metaphor for all discourse. It is that off the screen the same metaphor prevails" (Postman 1985, 92).

Even news has lost its historical moorings and become disconnected events to be viewed with detachment. After seeing a report on the hundreds killed in battle, we see an advertisement for toothpaste and then the scores of recent football games. All are on the same level because all are selected to entice and entertain us. Novelty, action, variety, and movement are used to keep our attention. There are few serious arguments and counterarguments, and no single narrative, no significance. As Vinoth Ramachandra observes:

> All over the modern world, we are bombarded by a barrage of "information," in the press and on the TV screen, images of fleeing refugees in Rwanda and Bosnia jostling with images of the rich and the famous, vying for our attention with the latest sexual gossip involving the American president or the British monarchy. Football and politics, soap operas and religion, beauty contests and ecological calamity, they are all more or less of equal import. . . . The most awesome beauty and the most unspeakable horror, along with the crass and banal, are all shredded at the end of the day. (1996, 17)

Eugene Peterson notes that "the one virtually foolproof way for getting noticed in our culture is to do something bad—the worse the act, the higher the profile. In the wake of whatever has gone wrong or whatever wrong has been done, commentators gossip, reporters interview, editors pontificate, Pharisees moralize; then psychological analyses are conducted, political reforms initiated, and academic studies funded. *But there's not one line of lament*" (1997, 116, italics added). There is no lament because truth is not taken seriously; love is not taken seriously. The news is reduced to virtual realities outside our experience. Tragedies, mass starvation, killings are called "incidents" and trivialized. Background music tells us what emotions to feel and assures us that there is no reason to be greatly alarmed. Knowledge of the news shows others we are up to date and gives us something to talk about, but little leads to meaningful action. Human life doesn't matter as *life*: God-given, Christ-redeemed, Spirit-blessed life. It counts only as "news." There is no dignity to any of it. Human experiences are trivialized.

One social manifestation of entertainment is theater, temporary gatherings for specific purposes. There is a major social division within gatherings such as a rock concert or a football game between leaders, performers, and hired personnel, on the one hand, and the crowd made up of people who join simply to participate to be entertained, on the other. Performances must be carefully staged to draw the crowd, and after the gathering, people go their own ways until the next game or concert.

The postmodern church is pulled toward becoming entertainment. "On television, religion, like everything else, is presented, quite simply and without apology, as entertainment. Everything that makes religion an historical, profound, and sacred activity is stripped away: there is no ritual, no dogma, no tradition, no theology, and above all, no sense of spiritual transcendence. On these shows, the preacher is tops. God comes out as second" (Postman 1985, 116–17).

Some modern churches see themselves as multimedia performances staged by a skilled few for a mass audience. They may seek to communicate the gospel, but the underlying worldview message is that this is really religious entertainment, and that to live a religious life all people really need to do is to participate regularly in the services. There is little call for live-in covenant communities or for radical discipleship that challenges the dominant culture in which most of the members participate.

The great evil in postmodernity is boredom. Entertainment provides us meaning in an otherwise meaningless world. It gives us temporary, often intense, experience that alleviates anxious boredom, our implacable enemy. Entertainment has become our new religion.

Moral Themes

Postmodernity critiques the amoral nature of modernity and the sciences. It offers a morality rooted primarily in the self and in feelings.

Therapy/Salvation

One postmodern theme is the emphasis on health and therapy. R. Fox and T. J. Lears note there has been

> a shift from a Protestant ethos of salvation through self-denial toward a therapeutic ethos stressing self-realization in this world—an ethos characterized by an almost obsessive concern with psychic and physical health defined in sweeping terms. . . . In earlier times and other places the quest for health had occurred within large communal, ethical or religious frameworks of meaning. By the late nineteenth century those frameworks were eroding. The quest for health has become an entirely secular and self-referential project, rooted in particular modern emotional needs—above all the need to renew a sense of selfhood that had grown fragmented, diffuse, and somehow "unreal." (1983, 4)

The medieval emphasis on eternal salvation has given way to the modern and postmodern focus on earthly health—a shift from sin to sickness, from repentance to therapy. In postmodernity, the human problem is no longer sin but sickness. Health not only offers freedom from disease but exuberant life full of tremendous vitality. Salvation is to be achieved not by self-control but by experiencing everything one can get out of life. This abundant life can be achieved through therapy, which offers the fulfillment of emotional longings, vitality, liberation, and self-fulfillment. The doctors of the body, the mind, and society have become the new professional elite dispensing salvation, giving hope when there is despair, healing and health when there is illness, and meaning to life. Religious ministers, too, often use medical models in making judgments and giving advice.

In the therapeutic society people read reality through the prism of their personal subjectivities. Everything is reduced to the psychological state of the individual. The goal of life is self-actualization and the pursuit of one's own needs, satisfactions, and self-interest. It is the world of radical subjectivism. People are seen no longer as rebels against God and sinners but as victims of society or low self-esteem. They need health, defined primarily in terms of feelings of self-worth, not an objective reconciliation with God and with one another. They must seek self-realization, not justice and peace. The problem, in other words, is not morality but morale. Feel-good religion and spiritual pills are used to elevate our consciousness and put us in touch with our "real" selves. H. Richard Niebuhr noted that, even in Christianity, many preach a gospel in which a "God without wrath brought men without sin into a kingdom without judgment through the ministrations of a Christ without a cross" (quoted in Neuhaus 2000, 117).

The modern garden of salvation is no longer the garden of Eden restored but the morally uncomplicated garden of earthly delights. In this shift from "sin" and "redemption" to "sickness" and "cure," therapy becomes a new theology of evil and power that has shifted from church and community to the state. The prolonging of life at any cost is justified. Death is the great enemy to be denied. Therapeutic religion is indeed the Valium that provides people with a sense of security and well-being for themselves and their families, institutions, and nations.

Spiritualism/Materialism

Modernity says we live in a disenchanted world in which God and the gods are no longer present, if they ever were here. Postmodernity allows us again to speak of spiritual realities, including gods and even God. The door is open to new spiritualities, but many of these are not the great religious traditions that trace their doctrinal histories down through the centuries. For some these are the struggles for social justice and equality, for others the battle to preserve the environment. Some, as Richard Rorty observes, want a utopian America with its divine destiny and national mission to change the world to replace God as the unconditional object of desire (Neuhaus 2005, 26). Surya Das, a popular American Buddhist writer and lecturer, notes that each spiritual seeker should make his or her own religion from scratch (1999). He advocates Buddhism as the ideal answer to the postmodern mind. This, however, is not classical Buddhism, but Westernized, sanitized, and commercialized Buddhism. And as Neuhaus has observed, "The children of postmodernity know that they are making it up. Whether it is the ironic liberalism of tenured professors cleverly 'constructing' reality or whether it is the popular peddling of New Age 'spiritualities,' it is a matter of telling fairy tales. And no matter how many fairy tales we tell, when we know that they are fairy tales, they cannot re-enchant the world" (2000, 104).

A sense of abandonment, loneliness, and alienation is widespread in the postmodern world. Our cultural icons in literature, music, and philosophy take up the themes of fragmentation, alienation, forsakenness, and abandonment. Even orthodox Christians find it difficult to bring God back into their daily lives. Something has been lost. Postmodern religions seek to fill the void by saying that, indeed, we are like God and can be so by nature and on our own terms.

Dominant Myths

Today the notion of progress is under attack. World War II marked the end of the grand narratives that have shaped Western civilization for the past two hundred years. The vision of utopia provided by modernity has been lost. The same science and technology that brought skyscrapers, space shuttles, comfortable homes, cars, computers, jets, economic abundance, and doubled life spans has also brought the threat of atomic annihilation, germ warfare, and genetic engineering gone awry. Rejecting the belief that violence can be redemptive and lead to progress, Foucault asserts that "humanity does not gradually progress from combat to combat until it arrives at universal reciprocity, where the rule of law finally replaces warfare: humanity installs each of its violences in a system of rules and thus proceeds from domination to domination" (1980, 151).

Technical progress does not answer spiritual questions. "We have conquered the world, but somewhere on the way, we seem to have lost our soul" (Bertalanffy 1981, 13). The price paid for "progress" is constant and increasingly rapid change. Max Weber argued that the endless flux and turmoil associated with modernity, the constant transformation of culture and knowledge, and the possibilities and problems generated by these changes is the source of the meaninglessness that increasingly characterizes modern existence. There are fleeting experiences of satisfaction, but modernity "is driven by an endless pursuit of innovation or change which creates restlessness, discontent, and dissatisfaction, and in consequence diminishes the experience and meaning of existence" (Smart 1993, 88).

Myth of Apocalypse

The myth of unending progress has increasingly been displaced by the myth of a coming apocalypse. The specter of terrorist attacks, global warming and other ecological catastrophes, poverty and homelessness, population explosion and mass starvation, global pandemics such as AIDS and avian flu, military conflicts, thermonuclear annihilation, and even invading aliens undermines confidence that the world will be a better place in the future.

The myth of apocalypse has emerged particularly in the fields of philosophy and literature (Dellamora 1995). The apocalyptic theme is also prominent in popular books, such as Hal Lindsey's *Late Great Planet Earth*, and movies, such as *Terminator* and *Terminator 2: Judgment Day*. As K. Wolff notes, "For the first time in history there exists the possibility, if not probability, of the *man-made* end of all human beings, of life, of the planet itself" (1989, 321).

Apocalyptic themes have been a major stream in Christian thought, particularly since Augustine turned Revelation's elliptical plot into a linear, progressive, and universal narrative of human destiny. One branch of this stream is premillennialism, which views history as quickly winding down to an imminent showdown between God and Satan and regards contemporary political events as fulfillment of the prophecies recorded in the book of Revelation. Premillennialists interpret the war on terror as part of a historical design to bring about the battle of Armageddon and the inevitable second coming of Jesus.

In recent years, the apocalypse has surfaced in the Left Behind novels written by Tim F. LaHaye and Jerry B. Jenkins. On the back cover of the first novel in the series, *Left Behind*, these words appear: "In one cataclysmic moment, millions around the world disappear. Vehicles, suddenly unmanned, careen out of control. People are terror stricken as loved ones vanish before their eyes," and as "devastating as the disappearances have been, the darkest days may lie ahead" (Koester 2005, 274). The novels, which first appeared in 1995, have sold tens of millions of copies and shaped the thought of many Western Christians.[5] The authors anticipate the sudden rapture of the saints followed by seven years of tribulation that climax in the battle of Armageddon in which the Antichrist is defeated by Christ, who returns to battle God's enemies and bring in the millennial kingdom. Craig Koester notes that these novels tap

> into a deep sense that the present age is sliding inexorably into violence and moral decay . . . [and] offer help in coping with a world in which weapons of mass destruction can annihilate civilizations, while advances in communications and computer science aid networks of global terror and make surveillance and manipulation of public opinion more feasible for those in power. . . . The novels also provide for personal salvation. God may have determined that the world must undergo devastating events, but individuals can change their own futures by coming to faith. Those who accept the Christian message now will be raptured up to heaven and escape the horrors of the end times. (2005, 278)

The battle between modernity, with its view of progress, and postmodernity, with its view of apocalypse, is being fought in Christian debates over eschatology.

5. The novels are based on the theological system known as premillennial dispensationalism developed by John Darby (1800–1882) and popularized by Cyrus Scofield in the *Scofield Reference Bible*, first published in 1909.

End of History

Many postmodernists criticize conventional historical analysis as reasoned analysis claiming to be the truth about the past (Derrida 1984; Foucault 1980). They argue that history was created by the modern Western world to justify colonialism and the oppression of the rest of the world. It is important to study history only as an ideology that has an impact on the contemporary scene because the contemporary is the time frame that counts most. The future is only an anticipated present, and the past a former present (Rosenau 1992, 64). This perspective has led to the "end of history" philosophy (Fukuyama 1989).

Postmodernity has challenged the dominant worldview of modernity and the latter's arrogance, exclusion of affective and moral dimensions of reality, and denial of transcendent realities. However, it offers no answers in a world that is increasingly caught up in crises of many types. Moreover, postmodernity is largely the luxury of those who have resources to live and time to reflect. In much of the world, people continue to struggle for the basic necessities of life with little thought to the philosophical clashes taking place largely in the academy. What lies beyond postmodernity? The answer is not clear, but there has been growing discussion over the impact of global forces and the reaction of local cultures to them.

9

The Post-Postmodern or Glocal Worldview

The postmodern critique of modernity has led to a reconceptualization of the nature of sciences, political agendas, ethnicities, nationalisms, and religions as constructed ideologies that exercise power, for good and for evil, over societies and individuals. But postmodernity does not offer answers to the growing human needs around the world. What lies beyond this postmodern critique? Ian Barbour (1974), Huston Smith (1982), Larry Laudan (1996), and other scholars are seeking new epistemological, semiotic, and worldview foundations to serve an increasingly globalized world. Smith calls this emerging paradigm the "post-postmodern" era. Parallel discussions have centered on the nature of globalization as the new paradigm for our understanding of our world.

In recent years there has been much discussion about the rapid globalization of the world. Globalization, however, already has a long history. Christianity and Islam have both claimed universal truth and sought to convert peoples on a global scale. Modernity began to spread with the conquest and settlement of the Americas and, later, the establishment of colonial empires. But the pace of globalization has increased markedly in the past few decades. How are we to understand this phenomenon, and where does it take us?

Anthony Giddens defines globalization as "the intensification of worldwide social relations which link distant localities in such a way that local happenings are shaped by events occurring many miles away and vice versa" (1990, 64). Hsin-Huang Michael Hsiao argues that "globalization refers to all the processes by which the people of the world are incorporated into a single world society. . . . Globalization means an increase in global interdependence along with the awareness of that interdependence" (2002, 49). Many scholars define globalization in purely economic terms as the spread of neocapitalism. Ted Lewellen is more comprehensive: "Globalization is the increasing flow of trade, finance, culture, ideas, and people brought about by sophisticated technology of communications and travel and by the worldwide spread of neoliberal capitalism, and it is the local and regional adaptations to and resistances against these flows" (2002, 7–8).

According to many scholars, globalization is modernity spreading around the world. For others it is a new, postindustrial, post-Western era. Still others see it as the beginning of a new era after postmodernity's deconstruction of modernity. It is important to keep in mind that globalization is an ongoing process of change, not a static state, and that every region and country experiences and responds to it differently. Moreover, theories of globalization are generated by the academic elite. We must examine these theories at the ground level, in the lives of ordinary people, most of whom are poor and marginalized. It is also important to distinguish between globalization as sets of data about market forces, transnational flows of people, and global institutions, and globalization as theories that seek to explain these data.[1]

Finally, we must be exceedingly cautious in using globalization theories to predict the future. As Lewellen notes, scholars at the beginning of the twentieth century made predictions, but they missed the most significant changes of that century—two world wars; the collapse of colonialism; the development of atomic energy, computers, and the Internet; and the discovery of the structure of DNA (2002, 27).

Cognitive Themes

Several cognitive themes have emerged out of the discussions about the nature and direction of post-postmodernity.

Globalization/Localization

The move from horticulture to agriculture gave rise to peasant-based empires, which spread their cultural ways to people on their margins. In Asia, Chinese, Japanese, Korean, and Indian empires covered wide regions. In Africa, Egyptian and Ghanaian empires had long histories of flourishing civilizations. In Europe, Greece, Rome, Italy, Spain, Germany, Holland, and other countries built empires that ruled expansive territories. In the Americas the

---

1. Three early theories of globalization were Adam Smith's self-adjusting market, Immanuel Wallerstein's world systems, and Eric Wolf's proposition that many people ceased to be indigenous long ago.

Maya and the Aztec built extensive empires. All of these empires, however, were regional in nature.

The first truly global systems emerged with the Age of Exploration and the ensuing European conquest and colonization of many parts of the world. During this era, worldwide trade, political institutions, and religious missions spread largely from Europe to the rest of the world. Globalization meant the extension of Western cultural and social systems around the world. The first signs of this development in many areas were pens and watches, hallmarks of the value of literacy and clock time. They were followed by Western clothes, foods, entertainment, and motor vehicles, and now by jets, computers, cell phones, and the World Wide Web.

With the collapse of colonialism and Western dominance, and the reemergence of old civilizations, such as those in China, India, and the Middle East, a new form of polycentered globalism has emerged, one in which there is no one dominant culture and in which different globalisms are emerging.

A key element of the new globalization is the emergence of large-scale systems: large cities, global governing agencies, and global corporations. A second element is the movement of people and information around the world at an ever-increasing speed.

GLOBALIZATIONS

Peter Berger and Samuel Huntington (2002) argue that there are many globalizations, which can be understood in two ways. First, a number of carriers are spreading modernity in its different forms around the world.[2] Underlying this spread is the English language in its American rather than British form, which is the *koine* of the emerging global culture. Second, different globalizations are emerging as people around the world interact with and re-create new modernities in their own cultures. Early on, Japan reshaped modernity to fit its worldview. Today China and India, in particular, are interacting with modernity in different ways and spreading their versions of it in their regions.

Peter Berger identifies several carriers of globalism. The most obvious is business and finance, which spread the Protestant work ethic; the sense of clock time; mechanistic-based factories and bureaucracies emphasizing management, engineering, and efficiency; and the focus on material comforts in life. Large-scale corporations, global banking, transcultural financial flows, sharing of technology and innovation, and outsourcing have deterritorialized production and finance and shifted industrial modernity into a postindustrial

---

2. Peter Berger discusses several streams of globalization: the international culture of business and political leaders (which Samuel Huntington calls the "Davos culture" after the World Economic Summit meeting in that Swiss mountain resort); the global academic community, which Berger calls the "faculty club culture"; the popular culture of food, clothing, and entertainment; and the popular religious and social movements such as Christianity, environmentalism, and feminism. I use these distinctions with some modification and additions.

phase where the focus is no longer on production but on consumption. Management has moved away from the hierarchical models of early modernity to the management of synergy, which cuts across hierarchical levels to develop teams that foster entrepreneurship through cross-fertilization of ideas, rapid innovation, engineering, and production of new goods. Marketing has become the important dimension of the global business culture. People identify and are identified by the products they buy, because these products have brand images. BMW, Gucci, Chanel, McDonald's, and Disneyland are markers of different values and cultures, and managers now seek to create markets rather than to serve them.

The dominant ideology of the global market is economic neoliberalism or expansionist capitalism characterized by private ownership of property and the means of production, and free markets driven by the profit motive and laws of supply and demand, free from government regulation. Ted Lewellen captures the underlying assumptions of this view well:

> Neoliberalism is the semi-official philosophy of the United States government, of the World Bank, and the International Monetary Fund, as well as most university departments of economics and myriad political and financial organizations, such as the Trilateral Commission. It is the view that a certain form of global capitalism is good: if Third World countries carry out a few specific prescriptions, standards of living will be raised. Greater economic integration will ensure greater cooperation among peoples and countries, leading to world peace. (2002, 9)

A second factor contributing to the spread of globalism is the emergence of global governing bodies, such as the United Nations, and regional bodies such as the European Common Market, the Association of Southeast Asian Nations, and the North Atlantic Treaty Organization. Arnold Toynbee writes:

> There is among us a profound and heartfelt aspiration for the establishment, not of a universal state, but of some form of world order . . . which will secure the blessings of a universal state without its deadly curse. The curse of a universal state is that it is the result of a successful knock-out blow delivered by one sole surviving member of a group of contending military Powers. It is a product of that "salvation of the sword," which we have seen to be no salvation at all. What we are looking for is a free consent of free peoples to dwell together in unity, and to make, uncoerced, the far-reaching adjustments and concessions without which this ideal cannot be realized in practice. (1947, 552)

A third carrier of globalism is the academy. Western-style schools, colleges, and universities have been introduced in many parts of the world by Christian missionaries. Now most nations give high priority to establishing government schools based on the same assumptions about education, and first-class universities exist around the world. Nevertheless, many students from non-Western nations often try to get their degrees from Western schools because they are held in high esteem. When they return to their countries, often to prestigious positions, they become the carriers of global values. On another level, the academy has shaped the world through research and publishing. The world academic elite conduct global research for governments and the United Nations and now also for transcultural corporations.

A fourth factor in the spread of globalism is the rapid movement of people around the world. Immigrants, transnational migrants, refugees, and diasporic peoples flock to other countries in search of jobs, freedom, and a better life. The result is an explosion of multiculturalism in cities and even rural areas in many countries. For example, Los Angeles, Chicago, and New York each have more then eighty distinct ethnic communities, and Paris has many North African communities. The result is growing intercommunity tensions, raising questions of how to deal with interethnic relationships. Guest laborers, transient populations, and illegal immigrants further complicate the social picture. Tourists travel the world for short-term adventures in exotic places and bring back an awareness of other locales. Families around the world have relatives living in the West who send money home and periodically return to visit it, adding to the home people's awareness of the outside world.

Migration raises questions of personal and corporate identity. It is no longer possible to fit many people into neat social and cultural categories, as anthropologists tended to do in the past. Identity now has many faces. As Ted Lewellen observes, "It is the Palestinian businessman who routinely flies to New York from his home in Jordan, where he was born. It is the Rwandan Hutu refugee living on the edge of starvation in a camp in Burundi, terrified to return home as long as the Tutsis hold power. It is the thoroughly Americanized woman from Calcutta getting her graduate degree in biology at Princeton. . . . The very concept of local has become ambiguous" (2002, 35–36).

Migration also raises the issue of worldviews. As individuals and groups move into new contexts, they encounter different worldviews. They must learn to mediate between their own worldview and those among which they live. Consequently, the concept of worldview itself becomes fluid. Hybrids and various forms of assimilation emerge. In many cases it is more useful to speak of "mazeways," A. F. C. Wallace's term for personal worldviews. Spouses in intercultural marriages, individual migrants, transcultural corporation employees, and students studying abroad are a few examples of persons who formulate their own hybrid worldviews.

A fifth carrier of globalism is popular culture, which has penetrated masses of people around the world and includes music (pop, jazz, and rock), movies (Hollywood and Bollywood), fast foods (Coca-Cola, McDonald's, Starbucks), clothes (jeans, T-shirts, Nike, Adidas), sports (NBA, NHL, Michael Jordan), and television programs (Disney, MTV, TV sitcoms, *Bay Watch*), as well as many other examples of Western culture, including Italian clothes and accessories (Gucci), vanity products (Chanel), cars (BMW, Mercedes), and classical music and literature. For many people around the world, participation in Western culture has become a part of normal life. For some, however, such participation constitutes a conscious identification with the West and its worldview, which affirms personal freedom and a strong sense of entitlement to enjoy better lives here on earth. One advertising director has noted, "We . . . have noticed that places and countries don't matter to consumers anymore. The media is the glue that binds world society together and the media is selling brands. . . . Brands in turn represent a cluster of values—the BMW man, the Nike man—which define people, not places" (Bernstein 2002, 216). The spread of a global popular culture is most evident among the emerging urban middle-class composed of young professionals.

Global cultural movements also link regions and the world together. Religious movements in Christianity, Islam, Buddhism, and Hinduism are spreading around the world. Cultural movements focused on gender equality, environmental issues, and human rights are becoming important issues in many countries. Finally, the rapid growth of information technology such as cell phones, computers, and the World Wide Web are networking people around the world and providing access to knowledge on an increasingly global scale.

While the West, particularly America, was the center for recent globalization, today many centers have emerged, each with its own adaptations. Early on Chinese restaurants spread around the world. Today China is rapidly becoming a global power. Japan, India, and Korea are becoming regional and global centers of their own versions of globalization.

Globalization has produced a transcultural elite made up of business, government, academic, mission, and other personnel abroad. These people move easily from country to country, living in protective "bubbles" that shield them from serious contact with the indigenous cultures around them. The bubble also shields them from doubts about what they are doing. The exception to this is Christian missionaries who identify with the people they serve.

LOCALIZATIONS

Even as globalization spreads, however, life for most people around the world continues in local sociocultural contexts, affected in varying degrees by their encounters with the outside world. Relatively isolated societies in Amazonia, New Guinea, and India maintain kinship as the primary form of social organization, and the local community provides the resources and relationships that maintain life from generation to generation. These societies are increasingly threatened as multinational corporations seek to exploit lumber and minerals in their lands. In many parts of the world, pastoralists and peasants are increasingly tied to regional and global markets but maintain their social and cultural identities despite external pressures. Others are integrated into national and global systems through cash cropping, trade, specialized production, and circular migration, thereby losing their local sociocultural identities. "Yet for them, the integration is incomplete; they remain trapped on the margins, maintaining numerous elements of nonmodern culture, in shanty-towns, inner city slums, and migrant labor camps" (Lewellen 2002, 94). Although we relate in varying ways and degrees to global forces, we in fact live our everyday lives in local contexts—in our neighborhood churches, schools, shops, and associations and in the ordinary events of everyday life.

On the global scale, although neoliberal capitalism may be hegemonic, regional and local communities respond to it very differently. The assimilation model of the "melting pot" is no longer appropriate. People adopt, protest, adapt, and reinterpret the various forces of globalization depending on their contexts. Ethnic, cultural, and religious conflicts have brought about a resurgence in local and regional identities. Jonathan Friedman writes, "It should not again be necessary to emphasize that global process includes by definition and is ever constituted by the articulation between local and global structures. The former is never a deduction from the latter" (1994, 232). For example, the boom in international brand-name foods in India has also led to a boom in indigenous foods. Peter Berger and Samuel Huntington note, "McDonald's has a product that poses certain market problems in a country like India, and the idea of a beef patty on a bun is not one that appeals to the majority of Hindu Indians, even among the very westernized. . . . It is significant that after four years in India, McDonald's had sold only 7 million burgers. In comparison, over 7 million *dosas* are made in India every day and 75 million movie tickets are sold every week" (2002, 95). Most movies are now made in Bombay, which has surpassed Hollywood in the number of movies produced each year, and Bollywood has its own plots, styles, and staging.

The affirmation of local cultures is not always a reaction to modernity. Cultural differences are often marketed as tourist attractions offering esoteric experiences and thus are absorbed into the global market. Chinese, Indian, Thai, and other ethnic restaurants are found in cities around the world. Shops market art, music, and handcrafted goods from remote regions.

While most studies of globalization examine the world as a whole, anthropologists stress the need to study its impact on people in the narrower sense as well, who live out their everyday lives in their local worlds. If top-down analyses, which are stratospheric, are to incorporate information about everyday realities, they need to be tied to bottom-up studies that show how people and groups react defensively or adaptively to global threats. Anthropologists do, however, need to add another level of analysis to demonstrate how the people they study belong to a much larger world.

REGIONALIZATIONS

The model of global versus local forces overlooks an important third variable, namely, the growth of regional cultures. The same forces that spread globalization also draw local communities into regional bodies seeking to sustain their particular cultural forms of life.

Samuel Huntington argues that the system of nation-states has already been replaced around the world by eight ideological and political "civilizations" based on patterns of culture, usually religious, which ignore national boundaries (1996). These include Western, Latin American, African, Islamic, Hindu, Sinic (Chinese), Japanese, and Orthodox. The modernizing influence of the West is provoking other civilizations to turn inward and counterpose themselves over against other civilizations. Huntington argues that future wars will be fought on the "fault-lines" of these civilizations as they rub against one another.

It is clear that nation-states, which in modern history have served as the basis for the world order, are increasingly threatened by regional powers. States rely for their legitimacy on their meaningful presence in a bounded territory, but such boundaries are being eroded by migrations; transnational communities; borderless media such as movies, television, radio, and the Internet; transcultural business, banking, and trade; and the formation of regional governments. Moreover, border wars, revolutions, inflation, serious flights of capital, and dependency on foreign labor and arms threaten the stability of nation-states. Localization in the form of grassroots movements and heightened sociopolitical ethnicity has weakened state control over citizenry (Lewellen 2002, 195, 197).

Of particular importance is the emergence of religion as a foundational cultural identity. In India, the coming of modernity has given rise to a nationwide Hindu fundamentalist movement seeking to gain power and make India a Hindu nation. Islam is increasingly the major identity for nation-states in the Middle East and is also the rallying cry for regional bodies that seek to counter the forces of modernity. Israel has also emerged as a religious state.

In seeking to understand "glocalization," it is important to take into account regional national alliances, transnational corporations, and their responses to globalizing forces.

GLOBAL/LOCAL CONFRONTATIONS

The rapid move of the world toward a global community raises the question of the nature of that emerging community. On the one hand, there are forces toward global homogenization, and on the other, forces toward resurgent local and regional diversity. The result is a clash of worldviews. Ted Lewellen notes, "There is no such thing as a passive response to globalization. People protest, adapt, invent, accommodate, assimilate, make alliances, whatever. Specific responses will be constrained—not determined!—by the global

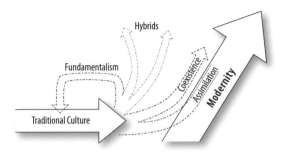

Figure 9.1
REVITALIZATION MOVEMENTS

system, but only in conjunction with local history, culture, the physical and social environment, leadership, and individual decision making. Underlying this is the question of how different cultures respond to these forces" (2002, 26). One thing is increasingly clear: the world is not moving toward a greater homogenization. On the one hand, ethnographies reveal increasing growth of ethnic, national, and tribal identities in many parts of the world. On the other hand, locals are increasingly participating in global agendas. Michael Herzfeld writes, "If anthropologists still want to be 'participant observers,' hiding in the villages while the villagers are themselves busily commuting, tracking old friends through the communications superhighway, or refusing to engage with the myriad national and international agencies that assist and confound people's everyday lives, will not suffice" (2001, 6).

A. F. C. Wallace's model of culture collision can help us understand the tensions between globalization and localization (1956). He notes that when cultures are overtaken by modernity and globalization, they and the individuals within them react in different ways (fig. 9.1). Some individuals and even segments of traditional societies are more open, join the flow of modernity, and assimilate into its systems. These people are willing to replace the local culture with the global culture. They are often those who learn English, seek modern education, gain jobs in modern businesses or institutions, adopt modern dress and food, drive cars, and use computers connected to the World Wide Web. In a few generations their descendants are fully modern.

A second group of individuals and cultures is more closed. They draw on elements of modernity but seek to preserve their own sociocultural identity. Their core identity remains traditional, but they adapt modernity in ways that enable them to live as distinct communities alongside the flood of modernity. They learn English, adjust to modern ways at work, and know how to negotiate the modern world, but they highly value their core cultural values, religious beliefs, dress, food, and identity apart from modernity. They develop many different hybrids that draw on both their traditional culture and modernity. They may be Middle Eastern royalty and business tycoons

who have mansions in the United States, where they speak English, visit the
United Nations, have modern wives dressed in the latest European fashions,
and eat Western food; at home they live in traditional palaces where they
speak Arabic, have traditional wives clothed in burkas, and eat traditional
foods. They learn to shift from one worldview to another depending on their
context. Regarding such glocalization in Taiwan, Peter Berger and Samuel
Huntington write, "Side by side with the Americanization, Europeaniza-
tion, and Japanization of lifestyles and popular culture here, there has also
been a rise in 'repackaged' cultural localization and indigenization, in which
many local cultures and traditional lifestyle elements, including traditional
Taiwanese cuisine, opera, puppet shows, antique collecting, tea houses, and
tea drinking, as well as Taiwanese rock music and modern art have been
revitalized and reinvented" (2002, 57).

Hybrid groups differ in the degree to which they accept and reinterpret
modern ways. Some seek a synthesis of their traditional culture and the global
culture. Others compartmentalize the two: maintaining one at home and the
other at work—global and local cultures coexist without significantly merging.
The question they face is how to respect the rich traditional heritage, while at
the same time incorporating aspects of modernity. Lewellen notes:

> In Africa, Asia and Latin America, tradition is not something that only existed
> in the past; it is every bit as contemporary as jet planes or computers; people
> live it every day. Nor is it the same traditionalism that existed in the past, since
> all communities are constantly changing and adapting. It is quite legitimate to
> speak of . . . contemporary traditionalism in which people drive motorcycles
> rather than ride ox carts and get their weather reports from the Internet, but
> still gain status through a religious cargo system and recognize kinship as their
> primary social structure. (2002, 101)

In much of the world societies are emerging in which some newcomers
assimilate into the dominant culture while others fashion lifestyle enclaves
in which they maintain some allegiance to a small group identity in order to
maintain a healthy community and individual identity and yet simultaneously
draw on broader cultural beliefs and values external to the enclaves that provide
the common ground that makes a nation possible. In some cases members of
immigrant communities outnumber the local society's population and become
the dominant group in a city or region, but they must adapt to the broader
cultural practices at the level of the nation.

A third response is to reject modernity outright. These people give birth to
revitalization movements that seek to revive the old culture and expel the forces
of modernity that overwhelm them. These movements may be fundamentalist
religious or ethnic and cultural isolationist movements.

Increasingly globalization has become a two-way street as immigrants bring
new cultures to the west, and Japanese cartoons, pop music from Hong Kong,

karaoke bars, Bollywood movies, and World Cup soccer matches compete for attention with American sports, Starbucks, and Hollywood movies.

Today the central question is how unity and diversity can coexist. On the one hand, assimilation models lead to stability at the price of the loss of the rich diversity of cultures around the world. On the other, cultural fundamentalist movements shatter global harmony in their attempt to preserve distinct cultural identities. In between, attempts to maintain diversity in the midst of an underlying unity face the tension of instability. Barry Smart observes, "The growing social problems and conflicts threatening community life in America demonstrate that if integration through diversity is the aspiration, fragmentation, aggression and disintegration is the more familiar reality" (1993, 40, 41).

Berger and Huntington point out that globalization has led to the breakdown of traditions previously taken for granted and raised the challenge of pluralism and of multiple options of beliefs, values, and lifestyles. However, they argue, "if one values freedom, one will be very reluctant to deplore this development, despite its costs. One will then be most interested in the search of middle positions between endless relativization and reactive fanaticism. In the face of the emerging global culture, this means middle positions between acceptance and militant resistance, between global homogeneity and parochial isolation" (2002, 16).

While economists, sociologists, and political scientists generally examine macro, high-level systems, studying the city, the nation, or the world from the vantage point high above the land, anthropologists, for the most part, identify with the ordinary people in the particularities of their everyday lives, studying them at street level. Ted Lewellen argues, "To understand globalization we must study it at the level of real people who imagine new lives, make plans, travel, form networks, assume identities, and socialize their children" (2002, 26). We must link our theories to the minutiae of everyday living, a task that is both uncertain and often contested.

At the level of intercultural contacts, old theories spoke in terms of diffusion, acculturation, and syncretism. Today scholars use terms such as "hybrid," "creole," "intermixing," and "transcultural" to refer to the many ways individuals and communities absorb bits and pieces of different cultures and reinterpret and use them selectively in different settings.

Diversity and Flux / Unity and Stability

All cultures change constantly, and people have always moved from one place to another. The Greek and Roman policies of colonization, the spread of Islam, the migratory conquests of Genghis Khan, the forced deportation of African slaves, and the mass migrations to the United States are but a few examples of mass human displacements.

The problem is not change as such, but the increasing lack of core cultures with a measure of unity and stability. Local, small-scale tribal and peasant communities continued for centuries with only occasional encounters with the outside world. Cities were more connected by trade and migrations than were the smaller communities, but they remained stable for long periods of time. Today societies and cultures are changing with ever-increasing speed. The result is that people have little time to adapt to new changes before they are overwhelmed by even newer changes.

TRAVEL AND MIGRATION

One area of change involves communication, travel, and migration. The demand for high-tech workers, doctors, academicians, and other professionals has led to global migrations of specialists. "The huge growth in multinational corporations has created the need for a new breed of deterritorialized transient executive or highly specialized labor migration that travels from country to country, from Singapore to New York or from Johannesburg to Moscow, as a routine part of the business week" (Lewellen 2002, 126). These transnationals move freely from their home countries to their adopted lands. The result of this brain drain often has a devastating effect on the development of their countries of origin, even though they often send remittances home to relatives.

At the level of common folk, peasants seeking better lives are moving to cities, migrants willing to work for minimum wages are moving to areas where work is available, refugees fleeing for their lives are settling in areas foreign to them, transient labor forces follow seasonal markets, and undocumented aliens seeking their fortunes move to new countries. Many of these people suffer high levels of poverty, exploitation, maltreatment, and insecurity.

In terms of the impact of migrations on worldviews, it is helpful to differentiate between short-term migration and permanent international immigration. Temporary migrants tend to keep their home identities and seek to preserve these by living in cultural enclaves. They raise their children with the expectations of "going home" and plan to return home for their retirements. Long-term immigrants face crises of assimilating into a new culture and the tensions that arise between generations. Migrating adults have a sense of their identity shaped in the country of their origin and then add surface changes that enable them to live in their new context. They generally seek to pass on their traditional culture and worldview to their children. The children, during their early formative years, grow up between two worlds and experience an identity crisis. At home they are raised with their parents' traditional worldview. At school and in the outside world, they are shaped by the local worldview. Many only hear about the culture of their parents and have not actually been "home" for any length of time. Their home is where they live. The result is often a generational conflict as the parents seek to preserve their old culture whereas the children want to assimilate into the new one.

Children respond to this bicultural identity crisis in several ways. Some, often those who come to the new country as older children, reject assimilation into the new culture and identify with the old. Others, often those born in the new country, identify with the new and do not want to be labeled by the old. Others learn to move freely from one context to the other but lack a clear sense of their identity. Still others become transculturals who enter vocations enabling them to move from culture to culture while never finding a home in any one of them.

Global migrations also deeply affect the migrants' home communities. With rapid transportation and instant communication, migrants expose their families and friends to the outside world and its forces. Ideas of liberation, human dignity, individualism, and women's rights come to these communities, along with capitalist ideas of commodification, consumption, and cost accounting.

IDENTITIES AND MAZEWAYS

The increasing flow and mixing of peoples, technologies, ideas, and cultures are eroding the notion of worldviews as coherent wholes characteristic of stable bodies of people. Relatively isolated tribes still exist with their worldviews largely intact, but rural peasant societies are rapidly being overrun by external forces and worldviews. The result is a social and cultural fragmentation of these communities. Although urban people may participate in many unconnected communities, such as work, neighborhoods, churches, clubs, and shops, each of which has its own people, social organization, and worldviews, they may find their primary identity in none of these. Whereas in small, stable, traditional societies, people acquire their identities largely from their communities, in the flux of modern life they are increasingly forced to construct their own identities out of the otherwise unconnected bits and pieces of their lives.

Identity is a person's sense of self and of self in relation to others. On the local level, in the course of a week, glocal people participate in a number of social contexts: workplace, church, neighborhood, clubs, and other associations. In each they gain status and with it an identity. In each they encounter a different culture and worldview. As persons, they are forced to negotiate among these different cultures, prioritize them, and deal with the contradictions inherent between them. A. F. C. Wallace calls these personal worldviews "mazeways" (1956).

People also participate in larger societal groupings. Prominent among these are gender, ethnicity, class, nationality, culture, and religion. Ethnicity is a vague and much-debated term.[3] Lewellen defines it as "a self-conscious or

3. Often the term "ethnicity" is used to replace "tribe," which has acquired negative associations in many parts of the world. In some places, such as India, the term "tribe" has a positive connotation because it means that people are not members of "castes" embedded in a caste system. The definition of ethnicity is much debated, and it takes different forms such as tribe,

projected group identity that emphasizes and naturalizes one or, usually, a number of specific attributes, such as skin color, language, religion, place of origin, ancestry, descent, or territory. . . . [It] can refer to a self-defined group with some sort of collective identity, or it can be an ascription of the larger society" (2002, 105). It is the degree to which people have a sense of common identity, and the degree to which surrounding people perceive them to be different. In other words, it is not an analytical category created by anthropologists, but one created by people on the basis of their perceptions of themselves and others.

Ethnicity has come to refer to groups of people who live in mutual contact, rather than in isolation, but who are clearly different from other groups. Ethnic groups are often created by dominant societies that have the power to define who is ethnic, or by subordinate groups for their own self-interest. While ethnic identities are constantly being constructed and modified, they are often based on common histories, cultures, and lands. Lewellen notes, "The simple recognition that most ethnic groups really do have depth in time, that no matter what their present invented, mythologized, or selective histories, there is really a 'there' there, does not diminish their present day creativity and agency. For the people themselves, primordialism is not a problem, it is a validation" (2002, 109). Ethnic groups need shared worldviews to define and validate their identities.

Lewellen points out that nationalism is one of the most powerful motivating forces in the world. "People will kill for money or power, but they will only enthusiastically die for ideology. The processes of globalization seem to have unleashed a plethora of such nationalisms, each, by definition, claiming its homeland as a natural right" (2002, 113). Although the modern nation-state emerged in Europe in the sixteenth century, nationalism as we know it today did not develop until the late eighteenth century as a product of the Enlightenment. Benedict Anderson defines the nation as "an imagined political community . . . imagined because the members of even the smallest nation will never know most of their fellow-members, meet them, or even hear of them, yet in the mind's eye of each lives the image of their common nation . . . a deep, horizontal comradeship" (1983, 6–7). In the West, nationalism was equated with the nation-state, which is a population inhabiting a political territory coterminous with a dominant culture, including a language and a shared political worldview. Even those who do not share in the dominant culture are expected to make the state their primary loyalty. The result is the notion of a secular nation-state.

The idea of the nation-state spread around the world with colonialism, often in the form of anticolonial movements demanding "home rule." The

---

caste, and macroethnic communities in cities and nations (Lewellen 2002, 103–20). To some extent it has become largely meaningless as an analytical term.

nations that emerged often are made up of diverse and divided groups, so the critical question concerns the nature of the underlying unity holding them together. To answer this question, common histories, bordering on myths, are created to show that the people are, indeed, one. Moreover, nationalism is often wedded to religious or ethnic identities to strengthen its claims. But ethnic and religious identities often run deeper than national identities, leading to internal violence and civil wars.

In recent years, cultural and religious identities have emerged as powerful forces on the global scene (Huntington 1996). In India, the Middle East, North Korea, and elsewhere such forces have sought to co-opt national identities to gain control of states.

Glocalization raises the critical issue of multiple identities. In traditional societies, the self is situated in and defined by a person's culture in a set of rules and totalistic cosmology of meaning. In modernity, with its shift to a human-centered worldview, people chose their identities from the repertoire of roles in the society. In postmodernity and post-postmodernity, the shift is to the self, which must construct itself. This requires separating the self from the fixed and concrete structures of traditional forms—family and society, culture and religion—and participating in the global systems that offer new worlds and encourage such separation.

Neoliberal Expansionist Capitalism/Mercantilism

Globalization has been occurring for millennia as empires have expanded their control over greater areas. Modern globalization is more the expansion of markets than of nation-states and political rule. Under mercantilism, the state controls the economy. Under neoliberal capitalism, markets are free from government control, and the state seeks to protect private property, open new territories to business, and use its military power to promote and protect the private interests of its people (Lewellen 2002, 14). The current rapid spread of globalism began after the end of the Cold War, the adoption of market economies by many non-Western countries, and the explosion of global travel and communication made possible by jet travel and computers.

On the global scale, the conflict is between global capitalist markets and traditional economies. In the world market, size, high technology, and cheap labor give companies an advantage. In local economies, cheap imports and the export of consumer goods to rich countries undermine traditional economic systems such as subsistence farming and patron-client relationships. It was originally thought that capitalist markets would come to dominate, but it is becoming increasingly clear that most people, while participating in the world market, never leave the base of family, household, community, and local culture (Lewellen 2002, 135). Local forces articulate with global markets in many different ways. This tension has led to various national and regional responses, such as socialism, restricting imports, and controlling foreign investments.

From a macro perspective, although proponents of globalization can show how globalization has helped countries such as Brazil, India, and China, neoliberalism favors the rich. From the ground level, many of the poor have benefited little if any from the spread of the world market.

The manufacturing of goods by means of assembly lines and automation gave rise to the commodification of mass culture. In recent years a marked change has taken place in the modern world as it has moved from asceticism and thrift to self-gratification and conspicuous consumption. "Consumer culture is more than the 'leisure ethic,' or the 'American standard of living.' It is an ethic, a standard of living and a power structure" (Fox and Lears 1983, xii). Borrowing has replaced saving as the way to fund lifestyles. Affluence and material comfort are highly valued.

Consumerism reduces life to commodities. Everything can be bought and sold at a price. Education, medical care, entertainment, and religion are marketed as commodities to be bought and sold. The movement of production around the world has led to an explosion of different commodities tailored for individual tastes. "Three or four television channels have given way to literally hundreds. The world of the Internet . . . is one in which every individual can indulge his own taste in choosing interest groups, chat rooms, or mail-order sellers. With more and more work being done at the home computer, on the car phone, or on the laptop computer on the plane, the cubicle environment is giving way for many to a deterritorialized workplace where the office clock no longer determines linear time" (Lewellen 2002, 22). Even rituals are reduced to displays of wealth. The August 1961 issue of the National Funeral Service Journal noted, "A funeral is not an occasion for a display of cheapness. It is, in fact, an opportunity for the display of a status symbol which, by bolstering family pride, does much to assuage grief. A funeral is also an occasion when feelings of guilt and remorse are satisfied to a large extent by the purchase of a fine funeral" (cited in Mitford 1963, 18).

Increasingly, people derive their identities from the things they purchase, the kind of homes in which they live, and the vehicles they drive. However, this is true mainly in the elite and emerging middle classes around the world, who have the money to participate in the global economy. "Those economically marginalized by global processes or prevented from participating in such processes by deep-rooted religious values will more likely increase their sense of cultural autonomy and differentiation, perceiving global culture as a threat or simply as irrelevant to their lives" (Lewellen 2002, 54).

For many people shopping has become a religious experience, providing meaning to life. But filling their emptiness with food, clothes, and possessions leaves many people feeling more empty than ever. Because often both husband

and wife must work to purchase goods, parental attention to children declines, with a corresponding loss of a sense of family and community.

Commodification is not a one-way street. Local people are not controlled by the global market. Locally and regionally they assimilate, modify, and invent new commodities and markets. Regional Indian foods have gone national and even global as people migrate around the country and abroad. Latin American music has been welcomed and hybridized in North America.

Religions/Secularism

With the spread of late modernity around the world, subglobalizations have emerged as regional communities seek to maintain their own cultural identities in light of their traditional civilizations. The result is tension between global processes of rationalization and secularization, and regional forms of cultural specificity, often centered on religions. Secularism, one of the hallmarks of modernity, has been particularly strong among the educated elite of the West. The academy has been at the forefront of the movement. In recent years there has been the resurgence of religions as a key element in the identities of the people. This is true in the great civilizations of Islam and Hinduism, in China, and is increasingly the case in the United States.

One example of this is the response of Muslims to modernity. Zeyno Baran writes:

> Islam and the West are not engaged in a clash of civilizations—at least not yet. But the West is being drawn into the clash of two competing ideologies within the Islamic world. Proponents of the first believe that Islam is compatible with secular democracy and basic civil liberties. Proponents of the second are committed to replacing the current world order with a new caliphate—that is, a global Islamic state. They are the ones who seek to trigger a new clash of civilization, partly in order to force the more moderate Muslims to choose their interpretation of Islam. . . . The target population is well aware of the basic Western alternative and is largely rejecting it. More and more Muslims—and not just terrorists—believe that they will always be looked down on in a U.S.-led world order. (2005, 68, 75)

A growing response on the part of Muslims is to establish theocratic states that draw on modernity but whose primary identity is based on Islam. Similar battles are being fought in India with the revival of Hindu fundamentalism and its efforts to establish a Hindu state.

In the West, too, secularism is under attack, particularly in the United States. There religion has always played an important role in the society, to the consternation of the European intelligentsia who see it as an anomaly in contrast to secularized European nations. As Thomas Howard observes, "Hegel championed liberalized directions in Christianity, which he regarded as the ascendancy of *conceptual* Christianity (meaning ethics, freedom, and modern rationality) over *representational* Christianity (meaning the biblical narrative and confessional doctrines). To his mind America was deficient because it lacked a state church, a European-style ministry of culture and receptivity to the rationalized Protestantism he sought to advance. . . . 'This explains the proliferation of sects, to the point of sheer madness'" (2006, 13). European scholars have criticized the United States for its lack of a sense of history, its shallow culture, and its holding to irrational sectarianism and fragmentation of the church.

Religion in America has been largely confined to the private sector of life. In recent years, however, it has begun to assert itself in the public sector through alliances with political parties and public movements.

Electronic Information/Print

It is clear that the world is going through one of the great revolutions in the storage and dissemination of information. The first such revolution was the invention of the phonetic alphabet, with its ability to store and communicate information on leaves, parchment, and paper. The second phase of this revolution was the invention of the printing press, which replaced thousands of scribes in scriptoriums copying manuscripts using decorative calligraphy and pictures to impress the literate elite who could afford books. Print reduced writing from an art to a business and gave information to the populace. This revolution radically changed the way societies were organized. The emergence of kingdoms, empires, and great civilizations was based on writing.

The invention of the telegraph, telephone, radio, movies, television, and now the Internet mark a second major revolution, with an impact on cultures and societies that is still only vaguely understood. Electronic media open the door for the information age in which knowledge and ways of knowing become dominant worldview themes. They blur the line between real and virtual and break down time and space. They give rise to short attention spans and multitasking. They lead to branching logics that seek broader patterns rather than precise linear progressions. They open the door to universal, instantaneous access to more information and people but with less depth of understanding and fewer relationships. As the electronic generation takes over the dominant society, we can expect to see major changes in cultures and worldviews and the social organization of the glocal world.

Critical Realism/Positivism and Instrumentalism

Although the great differences in the world and the rapidity of change make it fallacious to speak of an emerging global epistemology, changes can be seen in the academy. The modern positivism that stresses objective empirical knowledge and often equates theories with facts has come under increasing attack in the academy. Postmodern instrumentalism reduces everything to theory—there are no uninterpreted "facts." But this reduction provides no answers to a world caught increasingly in crisis. In some circles critical realism is seen as a humble, more nuanced form of realism (Barbour 1974; Laudan 1996; Hiebert 1999). This realism distinguishes between facts and theories and examines the link between them. It is "realist" because it affirms that there are entities existing independently of our perceptions or theories. It is "critical" because it recognizes that our understanding of those realities is always subjectively interpreted by humans in their social, cultural, and historical contexts.

The question for critical realism is to determine the nature of the relationship between the world outside and the worlds we construct inside. Critical realism holds that there must be a great measure of correspondence between the two for us to survive in the world. Although knowledge is approximate and partial, its essential claims can be true. This correspondence between external and internal worlds is supported by Peircean semiotics, which holds that signs are not diadic, as in formal linguistics, where signs point to objective realities, or as in Saussurian linguistics, where signs are linked to subjective images in the mind, but instead are triadic. Charles Peirce argues that signs point to objective, external realities and link these to subjective images in the mind (1958). They have forms, realities, and meanings. This linkage makes it possible for humans to gauge whether what they mean corresponds to what others mean by examining the external realities in question.

Once we accept that reality places constraints on our interpretations, it becomes possible to test various interpretations with regard to their "fit" with reality. In other words, human knowledge, including the sciences, does not consist of photographs of reality (as positivism affirms) or of collages (as instrumentalism affirms), but of montages and maps that can give us accurate information about certain aspects of reality—maps that can be tested to determine their truthfulness (Hiebert 1999).

Critical realism recognizes the inadequacy of language to fully capture reality, but it is only through language and other sign systems that we can create our images of reality. It recognizes that all knowledge is from a particular perspective and that all knowledge is power, but this does not mean knowledge is necessarily untrue. Critical realism also links the cognitive dimension with the affective and evaluative dimensions of belief systems and worldviews. If detached objectivity is unattainable, then the distinction between description and prescription breaks down. Feelings and values must be included in all discussions of key issues.

The breakdown of the radical separation between observer and observed does not lead to less empirically based forms of knowledge, but calls for a hermeneutical community in which scholars share different perspectives of reality and test which is closer to the truth. It also calls for reflexivity on the part of the observer regarding the assumptions he or she brings into the setting.

For critical realism, human knowledge is based on critical engagement with the world rather than a distant magisterial, management explanation of it (positivism) or personal knowledge limited to particular situations (instrumentalism). It stands between the disembodied abstractions of general theory and the ingrown self-absorption of local interests; between self-satisfied rationalism and equally self-gratifying nihilism. It calls for a greater humility regarding what we know and can know about others, ourselves, and the world. It is ready to raise questions and does not provide quick prescriptive answers.

Affective Themes

Although little has been written on the affective impact of glocalization, a couple of themes do appear.

Yearning for Home

Among migrants, refugees, and diasporic people, one often finds a nostalgic "yearning for home," which frequently takes the form of a sense of common history and of a common former homeland. In their new contexts, these people are often successful economically but marginalized within the dominant society. They find their identity by maintaining ties to the cultures from which they came, often through foods, clothes, language, rituals, religion, and other symbols that reinforce their identification with the lands of their origins. An example of this is the Jewish Diaspora. Most Jews identify with Israel as their cultural homeland, even though few are willing to return. Similarly, "African Americans, descendants of slaves, may feel that they have never been assimilated, that even after many generations the immigrant ideal never really worked for them. In such cases, a certain diaspora consciousness may emerge among long-time citizens who construct themselves in diasporic terms, perhaps by taking on the religion, dress, and culture of North African Islam" (Lewellen 2002, 161). Many Algerian and Moroccan immigrants to France "have never felt 'at home' in France, and dream of returning to their villages of birth as they slowly lay aside savings to build homes there for comfortable retirement" (Gross, McMurray, and Swedenburg 2002, 205). The same nostalgia can be found among many immigrant and refugee communities around the world.

Hybrid Entertainment

The spread of modern entertainment, such as rap, rock, and pop music, has given rise to many hybrid forms of music, art, drama, and movies. One example is Algerian *rai*, which emerged in the 1920s "when rural migrants brought their native musical styles into the growing urban centers of north-western Algeria. . . . *Rai* developed as a hybrid blend of rural and cabaret musical genres, played by and for distillery workers, peasants dispossessed by European settlers, shepherds, prostitutes, and other members of the poor classes" (Gross, McMurray, and Swedenburg 2002, 200). This and many other cases of hybrid entertainment forms make it clear that affective responses to globalization are very diverse and depend on the interaction of local cultures with the spread of global forms of entertainment. Much more research is needed on how affectivity influences the interaction between local and global worldviews.

Moral Themes

Modernity focused on knowledge; postmodernity focuses on feelings. Glocalism raises profound moral questions. What are the responsibilities of people in one part of the world for those in another part? How should we respond to poverty, oppression, and violence around the world? In recent years such questions have become part of the public and academic discourse on living in one world.

Development

Development became a key term after the 1950s. Massive programs were set up to help "underdeveloped countries" join the so-called developed world. Development as modernization "held that development would take place in linear stages and come about through the West supplying the capital and technology that traditional nations lacked. This was to be accomplished on the large scale, through massive foreign aid to build hydroelectric plants and to improve export agriculture, and through multinational corporate investment" (Lewellen 2002, 69).

In recent years the modern agenda of fostering global development has come under serious postmodern critique. Some postmodernists see it as a great failure because of its top-down, techno-economic approach and its use of modern bureaucratic institutions that consume much of the funds designated for field distribution. Others see development as the West's new way to retain its control of the world now that colonialism has collapsed. James Ferguson writes:

> The modernization narrative was always a myth, an illusion, often even a lie. We should learn to do without it. If the academic rejection of modernization and development is not simply to reproduce at another level the global disconnects of capital, migration and information flows, we must replace them with

other ways of building relationships of historical connectedness and ethical and political responsibilities that link Africa and the rest of the world. . . . It will be necessary to find new ways of thinking about both progress and responsibility in the aftermath of modernism. (2002, 149)

The development project has been a mixed blessing. It has benefited many, resulting in increased life expectancy, higher literacy rates, and democratic freedoms. It has also wiped out cultures, destroyed ecosystems, disempowered marginal peoples, and created military dictatorships.

In recent years the moral responsibilities of scholars have become matters of academic debate. Anthropologists traditionally study a non-Western community, earn their degrees, and acquire tenured faculty positions in universities, but give little back to the community in exchange for what it has given them. There is a growing awareness that anthropologists have moral obligations to help the people who help them.

Today applied anthropologists have begun to make significant contributions to development projects. Old theories of development have been deconstructed and new ones introduced that stress development from the bottom-up, such as locally initiated projects, microloans, and small-scale, locally tailored programs. These empower the local people by increasing their options to decide their own futures, use local knowledge and social systems adapted to local settings, and develop partnerships of mutual respect and trust between outsiders and the local people. The last of these requires new attitudes and relational skill on the part of the development personnel, who too often come with attitudes of arrogance and control.

Of particular importance in recent years has been the empowerment of women whose lives have often been devastated by modern development projects. These women have led the way in dealing with local, everyday problems, "such as domestic abuse, food prices, health care, schools and environmental conditions" (Lewellen 2002, 84).

It is clear, in a global world, that humans have moral responsibilities to help one another. What is needed are new models of development that truly benefit the poor and oppressed. In this endeavor, anthropologists, with their ground-level research and interest in the world as a whole, can play a significant role.

Migration and Assimilation

Globalization has led to diverse and extremely complex migration patterns around the world. The moral issues raised by migrations of elites, legal and illegal workers, and refugees vary greatly. How should legal immigrants relate to local dominant cultures? How should the host culture respond to immigrants? What should be done with undocumented people who cross borders illegally?

Modern theories of migration assumed that immigrants would accept modern values such as individualism and entrepreneurship and assimilate into their host culture over a period of generations. On visits to their homelands, they would bring this set of values back to their countries, breaking down the old beliefs that kept the locals from progressing. It became clear, however, that this was not happening.

In recent years, new theories have emerged that seek to explain the current world situation. Among these is transnationalism. As Lewellen observes, this is less a theory than a set of conceptual tools for analyzing what is happening in local settings. This set includes concepts such as "border theory, transculturation, transnationalization, creolization, hybridity, diaspora and diasporic communities, to name a few" (2002, 136). The diversity and complexity of contemporary migrations raise innumerable moral questions that must be answered at the ground level by people in the host culture and by the immigrants.

Root Myths

Globalization has its own myths. Ted Lewellen describes the leading one:

> Globalization is impacting people everywhere by erasing local boundaries and transforming identities. Restrictive categories like tribal, peasant, community, local and even culture are giving way to terms that emphasize blending, plasticity, and ongoing identity-construction: ethnic, hybrid, creole, national and transnational. . . . In this amorphous and deterritorialized world, people are increasingly seeking identity in the imagined communities of nationalism and ethnicity. Meanwhile the nation-state is weakening . . . [through the] loss of control of the economy to transnational markets, subordination to global institutions such as the UN and WHO, and the loss of control of ideology to the communications media that cross national borders at the speed of light. Internally, the nation-state is challenged by the rise of ethnicities, nationalisms, and multiple grassroots organizations that have taken over state functions. (2002, 234)

Those who see globalization as positive argue that it creates jobs, gives rise to a growing middle class, increases trade, brings development, and fosters global partnerships that benefit everyone concerned. Others see capitalist globalization as a disaster, leading to greater inequalities; to a marginalization of the poorest people, especially women, and countries; to labor/management conflicts; and to the destruction of the global environment. Communities are disrupted by migration, and farms are consolidated. At the level of the poor working people, neocapitalist adjustments "undercut domestic production prices, cause unemployment, create sweatshops that utilize underpaid child and female labor, disrupt families, disempower peasants, and encourage environmental despoliation" (Lewellen 2002, 19).

One must maintain a healthy skepticism toward broad theories of glocalization, since the encounter between global forces and local cultures differs greatly from local community to local community and even within local communities themselves. No theory can account for such diversity. It is clear, however, that we are entering a new era in human history, that worldview clashes underlie many of the developments we see today, and that we need to understand these clashes if we are to help guide a world to peace and justice in so diverse and yet so interlinked a world.

10

Toward a Biblical Worldview

In one sense, it is arrogant to claim that there is a biblical worldview. Many point out that in Scripture there are many worldviews. There are marked differences in the way the early and the late Israelites and the early Christians viewed their worlds. The history of the church is full of debates over the essentials of the gospel.

This is true, but this approach defines "biblical worldview" as the human understandings of the underlying givens in Scripture, rather than as the creation as God sees it. All our attempts to understand what God has revealed in Scripture are partial and biased by our historical and cultural perspectives. Just as we do not understand the material world fully, even at the level of particle physics, so we do not understand the full scope of the gospel. This does not mean that we should give up seeking to understand the substructure of truth revealed in Scripture. It does mean that we need to be more humble in our claims and more open to listening to our sisters and brothers in faith.

This view also overlooks the fact that worldviews are profound themes that have persisted for millennia despite variations in their interpretations. Moreover, as part of living systems, they grow over time while maintaining an underlying continuity, just as a baby is very different from the adult she or he becomes but is the same person throughout.

To say that there is no biblical worldview is to deny that there is an underlying unity to the biblical story, to say that the God of Abraham, Moses, David, and Jesus are different gods, that the New Testament is discontinuous with the Old, and that Scripture is simply the record of individuals and ever-shifting

265

beliefs shaped by history and sociocultural contexts. It is to say that there is no single story running from creation to Christ's return, no underlying unity and dignity of humanity, and no universal morals. The danger is that we see worldviews as static forms, rather than as dynamic growing entities that are more akin to living systems than mechanical ones. The other danger is that we equate a biblical worldview with our conscious theological formulations rather than with the categories, logics, and assumptions we unconsciously use in creating these formulations.

To understand Scripture, we must seek to understand the worldview themes that underlie the whole. The unity of Scripture lies first in its insistence that all the biblical events are part of one great story—in other words, a central diachronic worldview theme. On a synchronic level, it affirms that the God who spoke to Abraham and David is the same God who revealed himself in the person of Jesus, that all have sinned and come short of the glory of God, and that there is no salvation apart from God's divine plan.

We must keep in mind that the Bible itself is the history of God's progressive revelation of himself to humans. The Old Testament is a record of the unfolding of a single cosmic story. In it, after the fall, God chose a people and prepared them to be recipients and messengers of his revelation. In their history he shaped a worldview that could adequately understand the content of that revelation. When he called Abram, Abram knew God as El, but this was the word for God used by the pagans of his community. God then began the process of teaching Abram that he was not like the *els* of the surrounding peoples, that he was El Shaddai, El Elion, and El Olam. In other words, God started the process of creating in the Jewish worldview a concept of God that was adequate to communicate the gospel, a process that continued through Moses when God revealed himself as YHWH. This was the word used in God's community, not a word it could use to declare him before the nations. Through the prophets, God revealed himself as righteous.

Similarly, throughout the Old Testament God shapes and refines the Jewish understanding of sin, sacrifice, salvation, Messiah, and other concepts essential to an understanding of the gospel. It was in this context of a worldview shaped over two millennia that God made his final revelation.

This progressive unfolding of God's self-revelation culminates in the person of Jesus, God become incarnate among us so that we see and hear him. Christ Jesus shows us who God is as far as we can comprehend him. He also shows us what it means to be truly human. Had Christ come at the time of Abraham, the people would not have had the fundamental categories and worldview to understand his self-revelation. Even for the disciples, deeply trained in the Jewish worldview of their time, his revelation was hard to grasp. But their understanding of Jesus grew from the point when they first followed him to the time when they gathered to see him rise into heaven. Even that knowledge was human and finite and will be overshadowed when they meet God face to face in eternity.

To say that there is no biblical worldview is also to say that conversion to Christ is essentially a change in behavior and rituals or of beliefs and attitudes. The history of missions shows us that conversion on these levels is not enough. If worldviews are not also converted, in time they distort the explicit message of the gospel and turn Christianity into Christo-paganism. The behavior and beliefs are Christian, but the underlying assumptions, categories, and logic are pagan.[1]

On another level, it is arrogant to claim that we fully understand the biblical worldview. The church, for two millennia, has argued over different worldview issues with vehement disagreements. It is important to remember that here we are seeking to understand some elements of a biblical worldview, and that this understanding is a human endeavor. Our understandings of a biblical worldview should never be equated with ultimate realities. Rather, they are our partial models or maps seeking to comprehend the underlying unity of divine revelation. But without these tentative models, we have no way to understand the whole of Scripture. Through careful study of the Bible and discussions in the church as a hermeneutical community, we can at least become aware of the reality that our own understandings of Scripture are deeply shaped by our own worldviews and therefore learn to read the Bible with fresh eyes. This process can help us raise deep questions that we often do not address because our theological debates usually take place at the level of conscious beliefs rather than at that of the fundamental assumptions underlying these beliefs. What is presented here is more a set of tentative issues to be examined than a set of final definitive statements.

In a world of competing worldviews, what, as Christians, do we have to offer? Following the postmodern awareness of the importance of power in shaping worldviews and its destructive criticism of modernity, we still face the question of finding foundations for establishing truth and morality. Without these we live in a meaningless and unjust world.

In seeking to understand the biblical worldview we must begin with the person of Christ (fig. 10.1) and the Scripture that points to him, which is our definitive authority on his nature and life.[2] We also must see Christ in the context of the Old Testament prophecies and the New Testament teachings of the early church leaders. We must study the early church fathers. Although their works are not as authoritative as the biblical texts, they wrestled with the paradigm shift created by the coming, death, and resurrection of Christ. We also must study the history of church theology and of our own denominational

---

1. We see this in Acts 8 when Simon accepted the gospel Peter preached, but reinterpreted it in terms of his old magical worldview. An incomplete conversion of worldviews leads to split-level Christians who worship Christ on Sunday for eternal salvation but revert to their old religious practices during the week for healing and guidance (Hiebert, Shaw, and Tiénou 1999).

2. This diagram and the theoretical framework behind it is the work of one of my doctoral students at Trinity Evangelical Divinity School, School of Intercultural Mission.

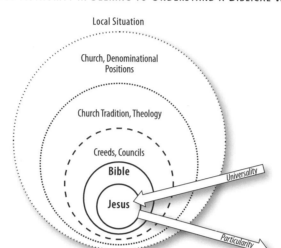

Figure 10.1

LEVELS OF AUTHORITY IN SEEKING TO UNDERSTAND A BIBLICAL WORLDVIEW

theologies as these have sought to understand the gospel in its context. Finally, the dialogue must include our sisters and brothers in young churches around the world today, who read the Scripture in very different ways.

What are some of the underlying themes in a biblical worldview? Although the answer to this will require considerable discussion among Bible scholars, a few tentative suggestions can be made. To avoid the modern divorce of beliefs from feelings and value, it is important to look at affective and moral as well as cognitive themes.

Cognitive Themes

Several key themes and counterthemes emerge in the Old Testament that are then fleshed out in the New Testament.

Creator/Creation

The fundamental dualism in Scripture is not supernatural and natural, which is foundational to modern thought. This understanding of dualism has led to the false dualisms between this world and other worlds, religion and science, natural order and divine acts, facts and faith, and evangelism and social concern. It also has prompted us to deny spiritual realities on earth and limited God's involvement primarily to "miracles" in which he breaks the natural order.

There is a fundamental dualism in Scripture, that of Creator and creation. The Bible is clear—in the beginning there is God. All else is creation. This is not an ontological but a contingent dualism. God alone is one and eternal. All creation—angels, humans, animals, plants, matter, and energy—is dependent at every moment on God's ongoing creation for its very existence.

The implications of this worldview shift are profound. In the modern worldview the natural world is autonomous, and God must intervene through miracles that violate the laws of nature. The biblical view calls us to reject the dualisms of natural and supernatural, natural and miracle, body and soul, sacred and secular, evangelism and social concern. It calls us to see everything as God's activity. For God everything is natural; for us, everything is marvelous. The more we explore the far reaches of space, the more awesome it becomes. The more we probe the microcosmic world, the more mysterious it becomes. What we call "natural laws" are not independent, impersonal, unchanging laws, but the commands of God (Job 38). When he commands, they change in obedience to his orders. This shift also calls us to take seriously the spiritual dimensions of creation. In the Indo-European worldview, angels, demons, and other spirits are in heaven with God. In Scripture, angels—good and fallen—and humans are part of this creation, and we must take them and their work seriously in our everyday lives.

This worldview also calls us to take this material world seriously as a part of God's eternal purposes. It is not a temporary stage on which human history is played out. It too will be redeemed when God creates a new heaven and a new earth.

CREATOR

Our understanding of the cosmos must begin with our understanding of God as Creator and sovereign over all creation. He is the Lord of the universe and its history, and his reign is never questioned. There is no power that can challenge him, for he is the source of all power.

God is also the God of love. In Genesis 3, when creation, including humans, rebelled, God manifest his redemptive love. He did not destroy fallen creation and create a new universe. He reached out in unconditional love to redeem and restore the lost. In this lies a great mystery. The old debates between Calvinists and Arminians are misplaced. The question is not God's sovereignty versus human freedom. The mystery runs much deeper. It is within the nature of God himself. At the heart of this paradox is the fact that God is not only powerful, but *is* love (1 John 4:8, 16).[3] As sovereign, God reigns over all things. As lover,

---

3. The contradiction we feel between these two aspects—God is sovereign and controls everything, and God is love and gives us freedom to love him in return—rests in our Enlightenment worldview, which seeks to develop a grand unified theory that is comprehensive, powerful, and logically consistent. This has been the goal of the sciences and of systematic theology. But as we saw earlier, Gödel showed that any grand theory can have only two of these elements. Either

he seeks to restore a relationship with humans whom he created in his own image, but he cannot predetermine their response. Love is a spontaneous, mutual relationship between persons. We can show unconditional love to another person, but we cannot force a spontaneous response on his or her part. In his unconditional love, God foreknows those who will love him, but he does not predetermine that response. The question then is how humans respond to God and his unconditional love. Those who repent and turn to him in love he makes new creatures. Those who are truly his followers love their brothers and sisters (1 John 4:19) and their enemies (Matt. 5:43–48).

CREATION

Three events in history mark its stages: creation, incarnation, and the return of Christ. In each of these God acts in direct and extraordinary ways, ways that have no parallel in history.

The first divine act was creation. God created all things, and that creation was perfect. That creation is the standard against which we must measure good and evil. Too often we start with Genesis 3 and the fall, but then there is no standard against which to understand where we have fallen from or what the end will be when good is restored for eternity. The Bible starts and focuses on good, not evil, as the central theme of the cosmic drama. Evil is contingent, the distortion of good, not ontologically eternal.

God created the material world as a bearer of meaning. He became flesh and blood and treats the material world, even though it is affected by the fall, as a meaningful environment for us to enjoy, explore, and develop. We need to reject the ancient suspicion of the goodness of physical matter. It is God's gift to us, and we are given the stewardship of this creation (Gen. 2) to participate in his purposes for creation. Nature, as manifest in our awareness of the natural order, is also a witness to the beauty of God's creation. Creation itself is already praising God.

God created the material world. Out of it he shaped life and ordered it into a bewildering array of plants and animals. He then shaped humans in his image as distinct creatures and gave them the responsibility of caring for creation. Humans are part of creation, but set apart as God's special creation. We are the center of God's love.

This perfect world was damaged by the fall, by rebellion against God on the part of some of his angels, and this sedition spread to humans, who became corebels. Sin, therefore, is not ontologically eternal. It is not equal and coexistent with righteousness. It entered into creation through rebellion against the Creator. Ultimately, it is a break in relationships—an attempt to

---

there are outside variables (for science this would be God), the theory is limited in scope (science explains only certain things), or there are internal logical contradictions. In theology we must remember that any attempt to reduce God to finite human terms is a great error. There will always be mysteries about God that transcend our rational understandings of him.

reject God as Lord and make ourselves gods. The fall led to hate rather than love, to pride rather than humility, and to fear rather than trust.

The second extraordinary divine act in human history is the coming of Christ, God himself, incarnate as a human to bring redemption and restore God's reign on earth. He is the center of history—the culmination of the previous age, the center of the present age, and the promise of the age to come. Lesslie Newbigin writes, "Everything in the Bible is to be understood by its reference to Him; He is the turning point of the story. The purpose of everything in it is to lead us to Him. We do not understand any of it rightly if it does not lead us to Him; but equally we do not understand Him rightly except by seeing Him where He is, at the center and turning point of actual history. That is why we need the whole Bible" (1954, 76).

At the center of human history is God incarnate. At the center of Christ's incarnation is the cross, the supreme victory of God over evil. It is hard for us to understand that the cross, not the resurrection, is where God defeated Satan, the principalities, and the powers. On the cross he bore the consequences of our sin. It is harder for us as Christians in the West to realize that the cross is also central to our existence and witness on earth. As G. K. Chesterton once wrote, the problem with Christianity is not that it has "been tried and found wanting," but that "it has been found difficult; and left untried" (1994, 37).

The great news is that God has taken the initiative to restore his creation to perfection and to restore his relationship with us. He has reached out in love. He has died our deaths and given us new lives that are pure and perfect in Christ. The sins we committed are no more. We are pure and perfect in God's eyes, and we seek to live holy lives not for our salvation but because that is our new character. Holiness reflects who we really are in Christ.

The third and final extraordinary entry of God into the history of the present age is the telos, the return of Christ and the end of the world as we now know it. This is not the straight line of development from our present world to a future utopia. It is God breaking into human history to definitively establish his kingdom of righteousness and peace on earth as it is in heaven. As we will see later, there is a story to history, and because we know the end, so also do we know its meaning. The end is in God's hand and is good, very good.

Revelation/Human Knowledge

Central to the Creator/creation contingent dualism is the question of the relationship between divine revelation and human knowledge.

DIVINE REVELATION

Traditionally, a distinction has been made between general and special revelation. In the former, God revealed himself through his creation. We see his power and reign in the greatness and orderliness of the universe. We see his love in his continuing to create a world in which sinners and sin exist so that he may redeem them and make them his bride.

In the context of this general revelation, God revealed himself in specific settings in special ways. He spoke to Abraham, Moses, David, and many others. He gave prophetic words to Isaiah, Jeremiah, Hosea, and others. He revealed his word through visions and dreams and through extraordinary events such as the parting of the Red Sea. Above all, he himself came as Jesus Christ to reveal himself to us in the limits of our finite human capacities. It is in Christ that we have the definitive revelation by which we must test all other revelations.

These special revelations are recorded in Scripture. It points us to the realities about which it speaks. The books of the Bible are human documents, recorded in human languages by human authors. But they are ultimately divine documents whose recordings are true because they were superintended by the Holy Spirit in the recording process.

Human Knowledge

It is important to differentiate between divine revelation and human understandings of that revelation. Revelation is what God makes known to us. Human knowledge is how we interpret that revelation in our specific contexts. There are two dangers we must avoid. We must not equate our theologies with revelation. Our understandings are always partial and context shaped. The other danger is to think that we are all free to interpret revelation as we will without reference to the universal objective truth revealed in Scripture. We may see only through a glass darkly, but we do see.

The first danger was prominent during the Enlightenment, with its focus on the epistemological foundations of positivism. Scientific knowledge was seen as an objective, accurate photograph of reality, a one-to-one correspondence allegedly obtained between knowledge and reality. Positivists set out to construct science on fully objective, empirical knowledge, believing that the human mind can discover fully the facts and universal laws of nature by means of totally objective observations.[4] Their goal was to construct a grand unified theory explaining everything in terms of theories that were internally, logically consistent, and needed no external factor.

The Christian academy was shaped by this epistemology and came to see theology as objective accurate statements of truth, unaffected by the theologian, his or her context, and the issues confronting the church at the time. Right theology corresponded directly with Scripture and was universal, timeless truth unaffected by the mind of the theologian. This view of human knowledge as full, not approximate, truth led to debates and divisions over

4. For a fuller analysis of the impact of epistemological and semiotic theories on how we view science and theology, see Hiebert 1999.

different theological interpretations of the biblical text. Sharp lines were drawn, according to which people were classified as orthodox or heretical. Ultimate authority was reason using digital, intrinsic categories and Greek abstract, algorithmic logic. In this epistemology, we claim to understand with certainty the biblical worldview—the world as God sees it—and we claim to understand that worldview accurately and fully.

The second danger emerged with postmodernity, which makes this view of knowledge untenable. As scientists studied scientists, it became clear that scientists are not external, objective observers. They are very much a part of what they describe. Moreover, although the knowledge they formulate is based, in part, on external facts, it is also deeply shaped and interpreted in light of their own theories, personalities, and sociocultural and historical contexts. Knowledge here is in the minds of humans living in the world. It is not an abstraction on a printed page. Moreover, scientific knowledge is not morally neutral. It has great power, and power plays are very much a part of the scientific process.

The postmodern epistemological response was instrumentalism. Knowledge is what we as individuals and communities construct. Ultimately, it is totally subjective and relative. There may be correspondence to some external realities, but we cannot prove this. There are also different systems of logic and category formation, all of which make sense. Moreover, we cannot use reason to justify reason as our final arbiter of truth. Finally, when we discuss alternative theories we need to recognize that knowledge is also power. In short, knowledge is like a collage—everyone, seeing the same thing, can nonetheless construct his or her own image of it. There is no public truth, only many subjective personal truths.

As a consequence of this concept of worldview theory, there are no worldview universals, nor are there community worldviews. There are only personal "mazeways." Even people in the same culture do not see and interpret the world in the same way, nor is there any way to build cognitive bridges whereby they can understand one another. The result is total relativism and a denial that there is truth, or a denial that even if there were such truth that it can be known. There are only personal "truths."

In the Christian academy, instrumentalism has given rise to postmodern theologies and to religious relativism, which affirms that there are different roads to salvation and God. The search for the truth—universal and suprahistorical truth—has given way to an emphasis on the creation of personal theologies tailored to the specific needs of each individual, theologies based as much on feelings and values as on reasoning. In missions this development has led to calls for radical contextualization in which the gospel is severed from its objective-specific, historical foundations, and evangelism and cultural transformation are seen as forms of imperialism and oppression.

Epistemologies are our human creations, our reflections on what is reality and our hermeneutics on how we can know that reality. Although we cannot equate any of them with divine revelation itself, some are more compatible with revelation than others. One of these is critical realism (Hiebert 1999), which avoids the two dangers we have noted. It does not equate revelation and theology, as positivism does, nor does it totally divorce the two, as instrumentalism does. It is also compatible with the ways in which the leaders in the early church and, indeed, throughout Scripture seem to have understood the gospel and truth.

The semiotic foundation for critical realism is Charles Peirce's theory of signs. In positivism, signs pointed to objective realities and therefore were seen as objectively true. In instrumentalism, signs, as Saussure argues, evoke images in human minds. They are subjective personal and cultural constructs with no demonstrative correspondence to external realities. Peirce argues that signs are triadic. A sign does point to some external reality, and it evokes an image or thought in the mind. In other words, signs liken the objective world outside to our subjectively constructed worlds inside. While different cultures construct different internal maps of reality, all of them must correspond in significant ways to that external world or humans cannot exist. Thus all our knowledge is partial and approximate—reality is much greater than we can grasp. It also means that we can check to see whether our mental maps or models correspond to reality in essential ways. A road map does not give us total information about a place—every tree, house, cloud, stone, animal, and bird, but the information it seeks to convey—the roads and the relationships between them—must be accurate for the map to be of any value. Similarly, human knowledge is made up of many different "maps" seeking to answer different questions, but each map is limited and approximate. Knowledge in critical realism is not one or a series of photographs, nor is it individual Rorschachs. It is many complementary maps or blueprints.

Critical realism affirms a real, objective world and historical facts that transcend cultural constructs of it. It also affirms that knowledge has a subjective dimension to it. It is constructed by individuals and societies and encoded in their cultures. Systems of signs are the linkage between objective external realities and internal subjective perceptions of those realities.

Central to critical realism is the hermeneutical community. Within a research tradition, if each individual sees reality only in part and in terms of his or her own subjective constructs, how can a community of scholars know the truth? It is through dialogue with one another that they check one another's biases and come to a closer approximation of the truth. In critical realism, human knowledge is never exact and complete, but it can be true in the essentials with regard to the questions being asked.

Critical realism has several implications for our search for a biblical worldview. First, it is important to note that our understandings are culturally constructed by communities of people. Worldviews are encoded in the languages, products, rituals, practices, and beliefs of the people. It is the underlying patterns, the gestalt, that links all of these together in a way that seeks to make sense of the world in which people live. It is important, therefore, not to equate any attempt to describe a biblical worldview as complete and fully accurate. It is our attempt to understand the deeper underlying order in Scripture and in cosmic history. We can and do speak of truth but recognize that our understanding of it is partial and finite.

Second, our understandings of worldviews must be extracted from the many historically particular experiences of our lives. In Scripture, we are told many stories of Abraham, Moses, David, and Jesus, whose inner character we begin to discern from these historical facts. The big picture, the worldview, is a montage we construct by discerning the pattern behind many particularities. In other words, human knowledge is like a collage—in the faces of thousands of Christians the face of Christ emerges, for they reflect his likeness. A worldview is not the sum of the many cultural parts. It is the configuration by which we seek to interpret those parts.

Third, in a critical-realist approach the church is the hermeneutical community in which all members participate in seeking to understand the truth and to apply it to its setting. Various theological understandings of the truth must be tested in the community of faith. Experts in different areas add insights and corrections, but the decision on how to live as Christians in everyday life is made by the church led by its elders. The church must seek the guidance of the Holy Spirit seriously in reaching its decisions.

Fourth, as we have seen, worldviews are constantly changing. Abraham's worldview was not the same as that of Moses, David, and Jesus, but it was the basis on which the others were built. The final revelation of God's view of reality was given to us by Jesus Christ, God himself.

Finally, cognitive realism rejects the elimination of feelings and morals from knowledge in attempts to render truth totally objective. It recognizes that observers are part of the scenes they are observing and bring with them not only their minds but also their feelings and moral judgments. Moreover, because knowledge is power, observers have a moral responsibility for the people they study and for the consequences of what they make known. In Scripture the focus is not only on truth but also on beauty and holiness. The three cannot be divorced.

How is a Christian approach to critical realism different from that of secular scholars? First, we affirm that Scripture, the foundation of knowledge, is not human searching for God, but God's revelation to us. In other words, Scripture is not only the record of human history, it also gives us God's understanding of that history. We are never to equate our human knowledge with revelation itself.

Second, we affirm that not only is truth given to us in Scripture, but that God as the Holy Spirit works in the minds of his people to help them interpret the

Scriptures rightly. Christians have traditionally recognized that human reason has been affected by the fall; but they also recognize that, purified and assisted by the Holy Spirit and illuminated by revelation, human reason can grasp the shape of reality, albeit looking at the world through a glass darkly.

Third, we believe that Scripture is the unfolding of God's self-revelation, that the Old Testament is critical to the foundations of our understanding of all Scripture, and that Christ is the final and definitive revelation of God and his purposes.

Fourth, we recognize that our knowledge as humans is always finite and imperfect, and we are never to equate it with truth as God sees it. We are surrounded by a divine mystery and can never fully understand. Our knowledge is partial and, at best, an approximation of reality. This does not mean that we cannot know truth in part. We can use the minds God has given us, but we must recognize their limits and our fallenness. It is not a matter of dealing with an opposition between reason and revelation as sources and criteria of truth, but of subordinating human reason to God's self-revelation.

Fifth, we affirm that interpretation of the Scriptures belongs to the church as a community of faith that seeks to understand and live the truth, beauty, and holiness of our Lord. Parker Palmer writes, "Knowing is a profoundly communal act. In order to know something we depend on the consensus of the community in which we are rooted—a consensus so deep that we often draw upon it unconsciously. For example, the scientific community agrees that reality consists of that which is available to our senses. It does not matter that all of us, including scientists, depend on realities that our senses cannot detect" (1993, xv).

Kingdom of God/Kingdoms of This World

What is the central message of the gospel? Some people emphasize the priority of evangelism. Without this, they argue, there will be no visible church or manifestation of the kingdom in lands where the gospel has never been preached. This conviction has motivated missionaries to go to the "unevangelized" or "least reached" people groups, and to give their lives so that all might hear the good news of salvation. The church around the world is largely a testimony to their labors.

This approach, however, is limited and weak. It often leads to shallow Christianity because there is little follow-up with new converts as missionaries move on to new areas. It also has a flawed ecclesiology. Little attention is given to building churches into mature communities of faith and witness. Developing worship, fellowship, ministry, leadership, and outreach is left to others. This approach also defines salvation in modern individualistic terms. Success is measured in the number of converts, not in transformed lives or mature congregations.

A second approach stresses the planting of churches as the agent and goal of missions. Our task in missions is to build churches. To do so we must organize congregations, train leaders, and disciple converts to maturity. It is the church that preserves the gospel from generation to generation.

The strength of this view is its concern for worship, spiritual growth, and the planting of churches. It sees the church as God's light in this world. A danger is that the church becomes ingrown and self-serving and loses its passion for evangelism. Institutionalization leads to more energy and resources being focused on maintaining and developing the church than on outreach. Another danger is that this approach focuses on human efforts. We come to believe that we build the church by planning, programs, and activities. Prayer and God can be pushed to the margins of our ministries.

A third group focuses on the kingdom of God as the central theme of the gospel. Conversion and church are not ends in themselves but means to proclaim the kingdom already come. Jesus came preaching the kingdom and referred to it more than a hundred times. Our central task, these people argue, is to proclaim justice and peace in a world full of oppression and wars.

The strength of this view is its concern for righteousness on earth and its comprehensive view of the mission of the church. Mission is not finished until the kingdom has fully come and God's will is done on earth as it is in heaven. A weakness of this view is that it loses sight of how lost human beings are without Christ and the urgency of evangelism. Another is that the church becomes a political player in the arena of world politics. It is no longer a countercultural community on earth, a prophetic voice of the reign of God in the lives of his people. Christianity becomes a civil religion, used to justify democracy, capitalism, individual rights, and Western cultures. If we start with the kingdom, however, we make it whatever we want it to be—capitalist, socialist, or cultic communist.

THE KING

We must begin with the King, for it is the King who defines the kingdom. The central message of the gospels is the coming of Jesus Christ as King and Lord over all creation. Matthew makes it clear that Christ's coming was a threat to the established kingdoms of the earth. He was heralded as king at birth (Matt. 2:2), he made the kingdom of God his message (4:17; 5:1–7:28), and called it the good news—the gospel (Matt. 4:23; Luke 4:43). He made it the first petition of the Lord's Prayer (Matt. 6:10)—"Thy kingdom come"— and defined it in the second—"Thy will be done." When we preach Christ as Savior and Lord, we speak of his rule in the lives of his people (fig. 10.2).

In the end Jesus was tried for treason by the Jewish and Roman courts and executed as all insurrectionists were—on a cross. The high court in heaven found Jesus innocent, and Satan and humans wicked. Jesus rose from the dead and ascended to his lawful throne, and cast out the principalities and

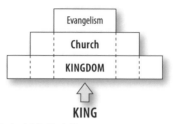

Figure 10.2
THE KING AND HIS KINGDOM

- The kingdom is defined by the King.
- The church is a sign and witness to the kingdom.
- Evangelism is inviting people into the kingdom.
- The mission is the restoration of the kingdom on earth as it is in heaven.

powers that had opposed him. Ironically, his death, which looked like defeat to humans, was the means by which God wrought salvation for those who turn to him in repentance. In the end, every knee, in heaven and on earth, will bend before the King (Phil. 2:9–11).

THE KINGDOM

With the King comes the kingdom. The kingdom is quite simply the reign of God. The two are inseparably linked. E. Stanley Jones writes, "A rediscovery of the Kingdom without the rediscovery of the King would . . . be a half-discovery, for it would be a kingdom without a king. . . . Jesus shows us what God is like and also shows us what the kingdom of God is like in operation. The kingdom of God is Christ-likeness universalized" (1972, 34). The kingdom of God affirms God's present rule and points to Christ's final rule on earth in the future.

With Christ came the kingdom of God to earth, not in its fullness but in its presence. The kingdom is present and active in Christ. The new age is come. The reign of God has broken into this world. Whoever receives Christ experiences the power of the kingdom and tastes the power of the age to come. Lesslie Newbigin writes:

> The central proclamation of the New Testament is that in Christ the new age has already dawned. . . . In Christ the powers of the new age are at work. The domain of Heaven has touched that of earth and God's rule is actually being exercised in the world through Jesus. Those who accept Him come within the sphere of operations of the powers of the Kingdom: they may in fact be said to have been translated out of the present age into the new age which is to come. The new age is no longer something in the distant future. It is already present proleptically. . . . Or, using the metaphor of space instead of that of time—they

are said to be a colony of heaven, an outpost of the transcendent Kingdom of Heaven within the ordinary world of men. (1942, 27)[5]

The kingdom of God has already come with Christ as King and manifests itself in the church, his body, while we await its final and full establishment when Christ himself returns. "The pattern of cross and resurrection precludes any purely this-worldly eschatology. But this does not authorize or excuse what has been common in contemporary Christian thinking, namely the alliance of a (proper) otherworldliness with an (improper) privatization of hope. The Christian hope is not merely hope for the soul, but hope for the world" (Newbigin 1993, 11).

We must be careful not to equate the history of the kingdom with the secular notion of "progress" underlying the modern myth of redemptive violence, which holds that variation, combat, and natural selection lead to development. This belief underlies the capitalist philosophy of progress, the Nazi philosophy of race and blood, and the Marxist materialist interpretation of history. It also underlies the liberal theology that emerged between the world wars with its belief that ignorance and sin can be gradually eliminated from human life, and that the time will come when humans live in harmony.

That humans cannot build the kingdom of God does not mean we passively await the realization of that kingdom. As Albert Schweitzer noted, "Christian action is a prayer for the coming of the Kingdom . . . such action is a kind of prayer offered to God that He may hasten His Kingdom" (quoted in Newbigin 2003, 51). Now we must long and pray for the coming of God's kingdom with the certainty that perfect love and righteousness will then be realized. In Christ the new age has already dawned. Those who follow him are in the sphere of the kingdom; they are a colony of resident aliens on earth. They are a pilgrim people, people on the way, exiles from their true home.

Emphasis on the King and the kingdom gives us a sense of urgency. The King is returning in person to set up his kingdom on earth, and we are preparing for his return. The eschatological home keeps us from becoming too institutionalized in the church and too at home in this world. As Christians we must always have a temporary spirit about our lives on earth.

The adequacy of our models of the kingdom can be tested by three questions. First, does Jesus remain the ultimate reference point in our understanding of the kingdom? For he is the King who defines the kingdom, and he emerges more clearly from Scripture than the profile of the kingdom. Second, does our understanding of the kingdom generate and maintain a living Christian community of worship, witness, and mutual interdependence of a given model?

5. For an excellent analysis of Lesslie Newbigin's theology of the kingdom of God, see Jürgen Schuster 2006.

Third, does our understanding of the kingdom inspire and nurture redemptive Christian witness and living in the world?

The church has always been in danger of equating the kingdom of God with kingdoms of the earth—of equating it with nations where Christianity is dominant. This leads to divided allegiances, with the public declaration that our primary loyalties are to Christ countered by our de facto worship of our nation in the way we live our lives. The second and greater danger is that of equating the kingdom with our nation. Then the Christ the world sees is the Christ they see in our national actions. We see these dangers in the colonial expansion of the so-called Christian Western nations. We see it today in the equation of Christianity with America and America's belief in its divine destiny.

The Church

At the heart of God's kingdom is the church. As Lesslie Newbigin repeatedly notes, "It is a sign, an instrument and a foretaste of the kingdom. It represents the reign of God in the life of the world, not in a triumphalist sense, and not in a moralistic sense, but in the sense that it is the place where the mystery of the kingdom represented in the dying and rising of Jesus is made present here and now" (Newbigin 1995, 54). The church is God's new order, living in the world as a community that not only preaches but lives holiness and reconciliation, even though it is made up of humans who are involved in the sin and blindness of this age. It is present in the kingdoms of this world but is not of them. When the church equates the kingdom of God with the earthly kingdom in which it lives, it has lost its divine and prophetic voice.

The church is not a gathering of individuals engaged in their own privatized religion and beliefs. Nor is it a human organization with clear boundaries defined in terms of orthodoxy or orthopraxy, in terms of who Christians are intrinsically. It is made up of those who follow Jesus Christ as their Lord and Savior. Newbigin observes, "An entity can be defined either in terms of its boundaries or in terms of its centre. The Church is an entity which is properly described by its centre. It is impossible to define exactly the boundaries of the Church, and the attempt to do so always ends up in an unevangelical legalism. But it is always possible and necessary to define the centre. The Church is its proper self, and is a sign of the Kingdom, only insofar as it continually points men and women beyond itself to Jesus and invites them to personal conversion and commitment to him" (1980, 68). In other words, the church is defined not in terms of intrinsic but relational categories, not in terms of what it is or has but in terms of its relationship to its Lord. Moreover, from a human perspective it is a "fuzzy" category, because we cannot see into the hearts of people. We should not judge them, but bear witness to them, and seek to draw them to Christ. God, who sees the heart, knows who are his, and for him there is a clear boundary between those who are saved and those who are lost.

In Scripture the church is a covenant community of faith, a single body with many members. What would the church be like if it were a community? Clearly it would not act as a club, a corporation, or a crowd. Rather, it would be a radical alternative—a covenant community in which the desires of the individual are second to the vision and well-being of the group.

To follow Christ means to relate to one another with the mind of Christ, that is, to relate to one another as Christ did to us—in servanthood and humility. "Discipleship is walking together on the same path. While still living wholly *in* this world, we have discovered each other as companions on the same path and have formed a new community. While still subject to the power of the world and still deeply involved in the human struggle, we have become a new people with a new mind, a new way of seeing and hearing, a new hope because of our common relationship with Christ" (McNeill, Morrison, and Nouwen 1982, 49).

In one sense the church is a community like other human communities, a living reality fleshed out in the concrete human relationships and experiences of life. In another sense, it is a unique community because it is a community of the Spirit—a gathering in which God is at work (Phil. 1:1–11). Membership in the church is based not on relationships between members but on their relationship to the same Lord. The center of the church is Christ, its Lord. It is he whom they gather to worship. It is he who makes them one body drawn from every tongue, tribe, and nation. It is he who, as the coming King, is the center of their proclamation to the world.

Because they follow the same Lord, members of the church are committed to one another. The inner bond and essence of life that holds them together is love—the commitment of each member to "be there for" the other in self-giving service. This love transcends all social, economic, sexual, and racial distinctions that divide human societies (Gal. 3:26–28; Col. 3:10–11). The result is a new family, a new race, a gathering of those who share the same Lord and Spirit and who devote themselves to one another's well-being (Acts 2:42). In such a community, members must learn to live together in harmony—when necessary to sacrifice their personal interests for the sake of the unity of the body and its good. They are not free to reject one another.

This indeed is what the early church was. There were numerous associations, clubs, and corporations in Greco-Roman society that the first Christians could have emulated. But the believers used the term *ekklesia* to describe the church. Members of the church are children of the same family (Acts 11:29; Eph. 5:23); they are parts of the same body (Rom. 12:4–5; 1 Cor. 12:12); they are citizens of the same colony (Phil. 3:20). In all these metaphors the church as a community is greater than its individual members. It is life in a community of the Spirit characterized by *agape* (love) and *koinonia* (selfless caring).

Life in the community church is multidimensional. There is no division between spiritual, social, and economic needs. Members minister to one another as whole persons. Moreover, this reciprocity is not based on a quid pro quo. Members contribute according to their gifts and receive according to their needs. There is no calculation of equality of exchange.

The unity of the church is its essence, not a goal to be sought. There is but one Lord Jesus Christ so there can be only one church. Christ is not divided. There is one Spirit and so there is one Body. The same Spirit that makes us one body sends us out to be ministers of reconciliation, beseeching people to be reconciled to God.

CITIZENS OF THE KINGDOM

The church is made up of believers, but who are they? Modernity defines identity fundamentally in intrinsic categories. A Christian is a person who *is* a Christian. Who *is* a Christian? It is a person who believes certain things (orthodoxy) or lives a certain lifestyle (orthopraxy). There is endless debate on what beliefs and practices are essential to becoming a Christian. Modern categories are also digital. The world is divided by a sharp line into Christians and non-Christians. Conversion is to cross the line. The important thing is to be sure that people are saved and become Christians.

In the Bible the fundamental categories are relational. A person is a person because she is a mother, sister, wife, and friend. A Christian is a person who is a follower of Jesus Christ as her Lord and Savior. Being female or male, Jew or Gentile, and beautiful or plain are of this world and are temporary, not eternal, identities.

Conversion is to turn away (*shub*) from idols and to make Christ the central relationship in our lives. Salvation is by faith alone. It is the gift of God. But faith means first dying to ourselves, then taking up our cross and following Jesus. It is to be pilgrims on the way, sinners in need of grace. After death we are resurrected to a new life of growing intimacy and allegiance to God.

What about boundaries between saved and lost? For God, who sees into our hearts, the category "Christian" is digital. He knows who are truly his followers and who are worshiping other gods. For us humans, the boundary is often fuzzy. We see the outside, not the heart. Some whom we believe to be Christians may not be so, and some we believe to be lost may, indeed, be followers of Christ. The test is not what they believe or do but who is the Lord of their lives. New believers often know little about Christ, but they are seeking him. So-called old believers may make Christ a part of their lives but live mostly for themselves. Our task in evangelism, then, is not to determine who is in and who is out, but to encourage everyone, nonbeliever and believer alike, to become a totally committed follower of Christ and to grow in relationship with him.

To become a Christian is not simply a personal matter. All Christians are members of a new family. They are "newborn babes," "brothers" and "sisters," and "spiritual mothers and fathers." These identities are not added to their other identities in the world. They are the essence of their identity. Moreover, all followers of Jesus become our brothers and sisters, whether or not we admit or like it. The church is not a gathering of individuals seeking to build community. By its very nature it is a family with Christ as the head.

KINGDOM, CHURCH, AND MISSION

At the heart of the kingdom is mission. The church is a community called by God to invite people to enter the kingdom of God.

> [We] must recognize that obedience, as an attentive listening to God, is very much a communal vocation. It is precisely by constant prayer and meditation that the community remains alert and open to the needs of the world. Left to ourselves, we might easily begin to idolize our particular form or style of ministry and so turn our service into a personal hobby. But when we come together regularly to listen to the word of God and the presence of God in our midst, we stay alert to the guiding voice and move away from the comfortable places to unknown territories. (McNeill, Morrison, and Nouwen 1982, 56)

When we meet God, who is a missionary God, we cannot ignore the plight of our fellow humans, nor can we be content to simply sit and commiserate with them. We must share the good news of salvation and hope that was given to us as we live in a world lost in evil and despair.

How does the church live in a fallen world? Ultimately the church does not exist for the well-being of its members. C. Norman Kraus argues that the goal of Christianity is not "the self-sufficient individual secure in his victory through Christ enjoying his own private experience of spiritual gifts and emotional satisfaction" (1974, 56). The church does not even exist for itself as a community of fellowship. Kraus notes that the early Christians "did not announce the formation of a new religious society gathered out of the larger social order to nourish and sustain itself as a community of faith" (1974, 27). The church exists because of and for Jesus Christ. It is the body, his family, his colony. Its mission is to announce the coming of the kingdom to all peoples on earth. Hauerwas and Willimon write, "Christian community . . . is not primarily about togetherness. It is about the way of Jesus Christ with those whom he calls to himself. It is about discipling our wants and needs in congruence with a true story, which gives us the resources to lead truthful lives. In living out the story together, togetherness happens, but only as a by-product of the main project of trying to be faithful to Jesus" (1989, 78).

What then is the church's mission to the world? Newbigin writes poignantly:

> The task of the Church in relation to the events of world history is not to be the governor and controller of them, but to be the suffering servant and witness of the Lord, manifesting in its witness the true meaning of these events.

The Church is not the instrument of God's governance of the world, but the witness of his governance both by speaking and by suffering. The closeness of our missionary thinking to the New Testament may perhaps be in part judged by the place which we accord to suffering in our understanding of the calling of the Church. . . . The New Testament makes it plain that Christ's followers must expect suffering as the normal badge of their discipleship, and also as one of the characteristic forms of their witness. (1963, 41–42)

Like Christ, the church bears witness through speaking, acting, and suffering. Suffering is an integral part of the church's mission because it is placed in the middle of the conflict of the powers that are exposed in light of Christ's lordship and his victory on the cross. As individual Christians we hear about terrorism, armed conflicts, famines, epidemics, droughts, and countless other forms of human suffering close to home and far away, and we suffer a sense of helplessness. But we are part of the church, and its presence in these situations reassures us that God is at work, and we are present as a witness of love and redemption.

The church and believers are called to worship God, to have fellowship with one another, and to bear witness to the gospel in a lost world. Of these three—worship, fellowship, and mission—the church and believers will do the first two better in heaven. It is only the last that they can do best here on earth. Worship and fellowship that do not lead us to mission are not true worship and fellowship. God has left the church and his children on earth to be his witnesses and representatives in a fallen world.

The Church in Mission

Living in the world but not being of it is at the heart of the mission of the church. Hendrikus Berkhof writes that "The church can be missionary only if its being-in-the-world is, at the same time, a being-different-from-the-world" (translated and quoted by Bosch 1991, 386). The church is the beachhead of God's kingdom on earth. By being something the world is not and can never be, it is a sign to the world of God's presence and rule on earth, and it participates in the Spirit's ministry of witnessing the lordship of Christ to the world and of inviting people to follow him and join his body. Hauerwas and Willimon write, "The confessing church seeks the *visible* church, a place, clearly visible to the world, in which people are faithful to their promises, love their enemies, tell the truth, honor the poor, suffer for righteousness, and thereby testify to the amazing community-creating power of God" (1989, 46).

The church's witness is to individuals, to the lost, the poor, the hungry, and the oppressed. Evangelism is central to the life of the church, not only for those who are saved, but also for the vitality of the church. The church's witness is also corporate. Newbigin notes that "A salvation whose very essence is that it is corporate and cosmic, the restoration of the broken harmony between all men and between man and God and man and nature . . . must be communicated in and by the actual development of a community which embodies—if only in foretaste—the restored harmony of which it speaks. A gospel of reconciliation can only be communicated by a reconciled fellowship" (1998, 190–91).

The church's witness is also cosmic. A whole new creation, an eternal story, does not end with the return of Christ. Unfortunately, a distinction between church and mission has emerged. "In the thinking of the vast majority of Christians, the words 'Church' and 'Mission' connote two different kinds of society. The one is conceived to be a society devoted to worship, and the spiritual care and nurture of its members. . . . The other is conceived to be a society devoted to the propagation of the Gospel, passing on its converts to the safe keeping of 'the Church.'" (Newbigin 1998, 194). This division removes mission from the core of the church and leads to an institutionalized view of the church. It reduces mission to the rescue of individuals out of this present age and does not attach importance to discipling them in Christian maturity and to planting churches that have a vision of their mission to the world.

One great danger the church faces is equating itself with an ethnic community or culture. The result is cultural Christianity. This leads to a loss of the universal nature of the gospel and of a mission passion to reach the ends of the world. A second danger is that of wedding itself to nation-states and thereby becoming a civil religion. It is the danger of believing that one country is more blessed by God than others, that one nation is at the forefront of advancing his kingdom on earth. This has been one of the great failures of the church throughout history.

The mission of the church is to bear witness to what it knows and believes. It is to point to, report, and affirm a new reality that stands over against other realities. It is not God's lawyer seeking to prove the gospel using the methods of the world to convert others, but it is simply telling others the message it has received. It is the Holy Spirit, who can touch the hearts of seekers of the truth.

Organic/Mechanistic

The root metaphor in Scripture is organic. In the beginning was God, a living being, not energy, matter, karma, or any other impersonal foundation of being. In the beginning was God, not matter and laws, natural or moral. It is God, a living being, who created a material world that operates according to the order he placed in it, and he created humans as beings who can shape and use the world because they understand the intrinsic order in it.

God's supreme creation is human beings, made in his image. They are at the center of his work of redemption. A Christian worldview rejects the reductionism that sees people as epiphenomenal, as the accidental end product of a long chain of events. They are the center of creation. It also rejects a naturalistic

Figure 10.3
Views of Human Beings

Impersonal Commodities	Living Beings
• known as a thing: impersonal, observed, detached, measured, controlling	• known as a person: intimate, relational, involved, loving, mutually giving
• worth: valued by marketability, production, consumption	• worth: of intrinsic value as a being, for who one is
• relationships: self-centered, controlling, manipulating, competing, retaliating, hating, exclusive, violent	• relationships: other-centered, respecting, forgiving, restoring, self-giving, serving, caring, loving, inclusive, life-giving
• stance: invulnerability, self-gratification, coolness, hardness, doubt, fear	• stance: vulnerability, generosity, tenderness, compassion, love, hope

Source: Adapted from Kavanaugh 1981, 96–97.

view that reduces them to sociocultural and psychological beings that have no eternal existence. As John Stott notes, they are body-spirit-community (1979). Without all three, they are not fully human. The fall shattered this wholeness. Suffering and death entered the material world. Sin and rebellion alienated us from God. Our common humanity was fragmented into warring communities and isolated selves.

The mechanistic worldview of modernity sees humans as objects of study and exploitation. They are depersonalized and objectivized and are regarded as dispensable commodities that can be used for personal gain. The organic worldview of Scripture focuses on humans as living beings, each with his or her own personal story, and on the relationships among humans. It is hard in our modern world to mentally and behaviorally regard others not as external objects but as living persons who belong to our story and are members of our human family. It is even harder to learn to love them—to be interested in them as individuals, not as people we can use in fulfilling our tasks, and to be unconditionally committed to them, not because of what they can bring into our lives, but because they are beings created in the image of God and are our sisters and brothers (fig. 10.3).

The central message of Scripture concerns relationships between God and humans—shalom, love, and peace. To be human is to be in relationships. Humans are created for true community. Without it there is no fullness of life. In a perfect world, relationships of love lead to mutual service and to peace and growth. In a fallen world relationships are potentially chaotic insofar as each person seeks to control the other for his or her own advantage.

At the heart of deep relationships is love—the unconditional commitment to be there for the other. Such love is at the very being of God: God is love. He is interested not in punitive justice but in restorative justice. He loves us when we are rebels and totally undeserving. But, as Eve MacMaster writes:

The central paradox of the Christian life is that just when we begin to believe God loves us, something inside us wants to think this is not because God is love, but because we are lovable. The more religious we are, the better our outward behavior, the nicer we become and we easily come to believe that what God wants from us is our niceness, our goodness. Then being such nice people, content in our niceness, we have no need to go further with God. . . . But it's dangerous to identify ourselves and our faith community with those who bring peace—the danger of identifying ourselves with goodness and our enemies with evil. (2006, 12)

God's love for us was present even when we were rebels and deserved no mercy. His love continues when we, his followers, wander off after other gods and worship ourselves. His love is not conditioned on our response to him or our lovableness.

Group/Individual

In contrast to the modern, postmodern, and post-postmodern emphasis on the autonomous and self-fulfilled individual involved in impersonal relationships, the biblical worldview focuses on deep interpersonal relationships and on the priority of the community. In the Old Testament, God chose to work with Israel as a people. He used Abraham, Moses, David, and others, but their ultimate significance lies in their contributions to God's people. In the New Testament, Christ came to seek and save the lost, but he formed them into a new body, his one bride.

What is a biblical view of humans and individuals? The idea of the Cartesian-Kantian autonomous individual is absent in Hebrew thought and biblical teachings. The family, the tribe, the people of Israel were the center not only of the social interaction of its members but also of the spiritual story that gave meaning to their lives. Biblically, relatedness and community are at the heart of the gospel because they are of the essence of God himself. "Interpersonal relatedness belongs to the very being of God. Therefore there can be no salvation for human beings except in relatedness. No one can be made whole except by being restored to the wholeness of that being-in-relatedness for which God made us and the world, and which is the image of that being-in-which is the being of God himself" (Newbigin 1995, 70). As humans we are created for community and must be seen not as autonomous, free individuals but as persons in relationship in which community is more important than the individuals that constitute it. As individuals we find our true being only in relationships, supremely in relations of self-giving love. It is only in our existence for and with others that our particularity and distinctiveness are preserved. Jeremy Begbie notes, "Genuine freedom is not constituted by independent self-determination, nor by the absence of limits, nor by multiplying the number of possibilities open to us; it is realized only in *relation* to real possibilities, by acting in accordance with the way things are" (1992, 71).

Sin broke this corporate bond, leading to the alienated individual. The modern assertion that it is the right of each individual to pursue happiness and freedom is self-destructive and runs counter to the biblical theme of community, which maintains that we are to seek the good of the group over the individual, to empower rather than to grasp power.

If our being in community is the essence of our identity, we must regard relational sets as of greater importance than intrinsic sets. It also calls for thinking in terms of relational rather than abstract analytical logic.

If relationships are at the heart of our created nature, then we must view conversion not as knowing and affirming certain doctrines or living according to certain rules. Rather, conversion is turning from our old idols of self and world and becoming followers of Jesus Christ. Relational knowledge breaks down the barrier between cognitive knowing and affective and moral knowing. Faith involves truth, love, and obedience. Conversion means changing our fundamental allegiance—making Christ the Lord of everything in our lives. This may seem simple, but it is very costly given the temptation to worship ourselves.

Relational thinking also means that the "individual gospel" is not true to the biblical concept of salvation, since it focuses only on individual redemption and being saved from the world. "According to this view, the significance of life in this world is exhaustively defined as the training of individual souls for heaven. Thus there can be no connected purpose running through history as a whole, but only a series of disconnected purposes for each individual life. History, on this view, would have no goal, no *telos*" (Newbigin 2003, 24). Salvation in the Bible is individual, but it is also corporate and cosmic, focusing on God's preparation of the church as his bride and on his creation of a new heaven and earth. In a fallen world, I must die to the fallen self and find a new life that is the real me. "Only when I give up on the search for myself in abandonment to another—to the Other—is my 'I' reconstituted by the 'I' to whom I surrender. The endless rummaging through memories, the poking about in the cluttered attic of self-consciousness, the removing of layer after layer of worn-out 'identities'—none of this can produce the authentic self. The truth of the self is in the *telos* of the self" (Neuhaus 2000, 134).

If we exist in communities, how should we relate to people in other communities? As fallen humans we naturally distinguish between "us," made up of those who are the same "kind" of people as ourselves, and "others," who are not "our kind of people." We naturally see ourselves as the quintessential humans, civilized and superior. Others are semihumans, savages, and beasts. For example, at the end of the fifteenth century, Europeans exploring the world discovered unknown lands and strange people. This experience raised profound questions. Who were these others? Were they humans? Did they have souls that needed to be saved? Could they be enslaved and killed, or was this murder? They became "barbarians" and "savages" and later "primitives" and "aborigines"—human beings but uncivilized, childlike, and like our ancestors (Hiebert 2006). As Westerners came to know these others more deeply, they began to see them as equal but different, and others then became "natives." Their cultures were seen as good, and changing cultures was considered evil.

What is a biblical worldview of others and otherness? First, it affirms the common humanity of all people. The Scriptures lead us to a startling conclusion: *at the deepest level of identity as humans, there are no others—there is only us.* On the surface humans are males and females, blacks, browns, and whites, rich and poor, old and young; beneath these features, however, we are one humanity. This oneness of humanity is declared in the creation account (Gen. 1:26) and affirmed by the universalism implicit in the Old Testament (Gen. 12:3; Ps. 67; 72:17; Isa. 11:10; 19:23–25; Jer. 4:2; 31:1; Mic. 4:1–2). David Bosch observes, "The entire history of Israel unveils the continuation of God's involvement with the nations. The God of Israel is the Creator and Lord of the whole world. For this reason Israel can comprehend its own history only in continuity with the history of the nations, not as a separate history" (1991, 18). The nations are waiting for Yahweh (Isa. 51:5). His glory will be revealed to all of them (Isa. 40:5). His servant is a light to the Gentiles (Isa. 49:6), and they will worship in God's temple in Jerusalem (Ps. 96:9).

The New Testament and Christ develop the implications of this common humanity more fully. We see this in Christ's teachings about the other. When a Pharisee asked him, "Who is my neighbor?"—in other words, who is one of us—Jesus turned the question on its head and asked, "If your other, a Samaritan, is a neighbor to your brother, a suffering Jew, who are you to the Samaritan?" The Pharisee was forced to admit either that he was indeed a neighbor to the Samaritan, or that he had cut himself off from his fellow Jew. Jesus taught, "You have heard that it was said, 'You shall love your neighbor and hate your enemy.' But I say to you, Love your enemies and pray for those who persecute you" (Matt. 5:43–44 NRSV). As long as we see humans as others, they are potential enemies, and we will have wars. War demands that we hate our enemies and brand them as others. When we see others and enemies as *us*, the walls between us can be torn down.

In affirming the oneness of humanity, Christians must not deny the great difficulty in understanding people in other ethnic communities and cultures. It is easy to say that we love them when we have few deep relationships with them. The more we relate to other people, the more we realize how difficult it is for us as fallen creatures to see them as us and to build deep relationships of mutuality and love.

A biblical worldview leads us to a second conclusion: *in the church all are members of one new people.* In Christ God's kingdom has come to earth (Matt. 4:17–25). A new age has begun. The church is the sign and manifestation of the kingdom, and all who follow Jesus as their Lord become members of one new people. John Stott writes, "For the sake of the glory of God and the evangelization of the world, nothing is more important than that the church should be, and should be seen to be, God's new society" (1979, 10).

The importance of the unity of and fellowship within the church is seen in Christ's high priestly prayer. Peter learned this lesson when he went to the house of Cornelius. Amazed at what was taking place, he said, "Truly I perceive that God shows no partiality" (Acts 10:34 RSV). Paul wrote that Christ "tore down the wall we used to keep each other at a distance" (Eph. 2:14 Message). Then he started over. Instead of continuing with two groups of people separated by centuries of animosity and suspicion, he created a new kind of human being, a fresh start for everyone. For Paul, unity and living with fellow citizens is the way the church demonstrates being God's work in the world. He describes the hostilities that divide humans (Eph. 2:11–12), shows how Christ brought those hostilities to an end (2:13–18), and says that Christian unity is God's object lesson to the world, breaking down the hostilities brought about by sin (2:19–22). "Ephesians sees the church as the community in which the deepest hostility between men was healed. . . . When the church views herself in the light of Eph. 2:11–12 then it is impossible for her to conform to the divisions which exist in society. It is her nature to be the place where divisions are healed" (Rader 1978, 253, 255). During this age when the kingdom of God has come, but not in its fullness, Christians continue to live in the kingdoms of this world with all their divisions and hostilities, but their identities in the world are relativized because they are passing away. The Christian's new identity is as a member in the family of Christ, an eternal identity that takes precedence over all earthly identities.

Scripture leads us to another startling conclusion: *in the church there are no others, there is only us—members of one body, brothers and sisters in faith.* The unity of the church is not a product of the good news; it is an essential part of the gospel.

In missions we must identify with people in our common humanity. We are all humans, part of creation over against the Creator and formed in the image of God, fallen but redeemable. Just as Christ identified with us in our humanity, so we are called to be one with those who need salvation. Only then will we model an incarnational mission in our identification with the poor, the oppressed, and the lost. Only then will we avoid the arrogance and colonialism that too often have characterized our outreach. Bosch notes, "We are not the 'haves,' the *beati possidentes*, standing over against the spiritual 'have nots,' the *massa damnata*. We are all recipients of the same mercy, sharing in the same mystery" (1991, 484). We must go with an attitude of humility because Christian faith is about grace, which is freely received, and it finds its center in the cross, which judges us all.

Affective Themes

In our modern worldview with its emphasis on cognitive truth and its divorce of truth from feelings and morals for the sake of objectivity, it is important to remember that in Scripture these three dimensions—the cognitive, the affective, and the moral—are not separated. They are all present in every human experience. They are all central to the gospel message.

Affective knowledge is a different kind of knowledge and cannot be reduced to cognitive knowledge. Stephen Neill writes, "It is possible mathematically to analyze in detail a fugue of Bach—a highly useful exercise for the student of music, but one which will not bring us much nearer to apprehending that which it was the intuition of the musician to convey. To hear the music played involves an entirely different approach. It is only when the last note has been reached that the experience has reached its fullness; it is unlikely that we shall find words that can in any way express the nature of the reality into contact with which we have been brought" (1960, 11). In the Christian worldview, feelings are as important as truth in our understanding of God, ourselves, and our relationships to one another. Comparatively little theological reflection has been accorded to the affective dimension. Much more is needed.

Mysterium Tremendum

The most profound human experience is not joy, or peace, or excitement. It is the *mysterium tremendum*, the holy awe we will face when we enter into the presence of God. The Greek church father Chrysostom wrote, "He whom we call God is the unutterable, the inconceivable, the invisible, the inapprehensible; the One who surpasses the power of human utterance and transcends the grasp of human intellect; the One whom the angels cannot trace out, whom the Seraphim cannot see, whom the Cherubim cannot conceive, the One whom authorities and principalities and powers, in a word every created existence, cannot behold" (quoted in Neill 1960, 10). In his presence, we will fall flat on our faces, shielding ourselves from his glory and majesty. Our modern worldview engages in an extremely dangerous venture when it seeks on the basis of reason to analyze, define, and, in a sense, master God. We must submit our whole selves to the totality of someone remote, majestic, and mighty, beyond all experience and comprehension, someone who cannot be reduced to logical consistency, but transcends human reasoning. Our only possible attitude is one of submission—the recognition that this reality goes far beyond us in its sovereign majesty (Job 11:8).

Fruits of the Spirit

The fruits of the Spirit are affective signs of Christlikeness—love, joy, peace, patience, kindness, and gentleness (Gal. 5:22). The fruitless deeds of darkness are pride, hate, bellicosity, envy, and lust.

LOVE

As Christians we love because God *is* love. Within the Godhead there is perfect love between Father, Son, and Holy Spirit. God shows perfect love in his relationship to his creation, and that love is central to the gospel of forgiveness and reconciliation of the lost.

What is the nature of God's love? The Christian concept of love (*agape*) is radically different from the modern view (*eros*). Love, in the modern view, is a feeling of deep affection, devotion, usually accompanied by yearnings or desire for affection between persons of the opposite sex, founded in the combination of compassion and desire. E. Stanley Jones contrasts these two kinds of love:

> [The] Eros approach is self-salvation, trying to reach god by its own efforts and its own merits. Its key word is struggle. Agape is God-salvation—God comes to us and offers us salvation by grace. Its key is surrender.
>
> The Eros approach is always wistful and uncertain, an attitude which it mistakes for humility. It never has a sense of arriving—it is always on the way. Agape is joyous and certain, with a deep sense of real humility, based on a gratitude of grace. It knows it has arrived, for the arrival is God's reaching us on the lowest rung of the ladder. . . .
>
> The Eros approach is a guilt-conscious piety based on self-condemnation with a sense of half failure. Agape knows that condemnation has been lifted by grace, so it is free, abounding and joyous.
>
> The Eros approach makes religion a demand upon the will, a constant whipping up of the will. Agape means the surrender of the will to God; hence the will is given back, purified and released. (1957, 141)

Eros loves for what it can get. It turns everything—even God—into means to our ends. We love people for what they can give us in return. They meet a need in us. We love God because we expect something in return. Jones writes, "We go to church, we pray, we pay to church and charitable causes, we are faithful in our duties; therefore, we feel that God is under obligation to us—to shield us from harm and danger, ward off our sicknesses, provide us with plenty of material goods, and give us a home in heaven" (1957, 130). We expect God to love us when we are good and to hate us when we are sinners. And we ourselves love our friends and hate our enemies.

Agape love is radically different. It involves a revolution in outlook without parallel in history, a complete transvaluation of all human understandings of love. It is to be unconditionally committed to the well-being of another. It is sacrificial, seeks not its own, is gracious and forgiving, spontaneous and joyful. It is empowering, not controlling. It is directed to both the good and the evil—it is love for one's enemies and one's friends. It is redemptive, not punitive. It seeks to win one's enemies, not destroy them. It seeks peace, not violence, in the name of redeeming the situation.

Agape is the very nature of God, who reaches out to the worst of sinners to forgive and redeem them. It is this kind of love that lies at the heart of Christian fellowship in the church and of the sacrificial mission of the church in the world. It is one of the most revolutionary messages that we can share with the lost world.

The outworking of agape is compassion—"suffering with." But it is more than general kindness and tenderheartedness. It is a radical call to identify ourselves fully with the poor, hungry, oppressed, and lost, just as Christ identified himself fully with us in taking on our human nature. Twelve times the Gospels use the expression "moved with compassion" and only with reference to Jesus or the Father. When Jesus saw the crowd like sheep without a shepherd, he felt compassion for them (Matt. 9:36). When the blind, paralyzed, and deaf were brought to him, he experienced their pain in his own heart. "The great mystery revealed to us in this is that Jesus, who is the sinless Son of God, chose in total freedom to suffer fully our pains and thus to let us discover the true nature of our own passions . . . Jesus who is divine lives our broken humanity not as a curse (Gn 3:14–19), but as a blessing" (McNeill, Morrison, and Nouwen 1982, 15). Out of compassion Jesus healed. The great mystery is not the cures but the infinite compassion which was their source. The compassionate life is the antidote to the competition and rivalries of modern life rooted in the myth of redemptive violence.

Compassion is more than passing feelings of sorrow and sympathy. It is costly identification with those who suffer in their suffering and oppression. This goes against the grain of our natural instincts. We do not want to suffer, and the less we are confronted with it the better. But compassion calls us to identify with the suffering of others and experience their brokenness. This requires a total conversion of heart and mind.

As fallen humans we cannot begin to comprehend, let alone express, agape love. Our natural response is to love in order to be loved, and to hate and defeat our enemies. It is only as we experience God's love for us through Christ that we can begin to understand and reflect in our lives true agape love (1 John 4:19). Only then can we learn to love our enemies and seek their salvation (Matt. 5:43–46; Luke 6:27–35). Only then are we willing to suffer and die rather than to inflict suffering and kill. As humans we cannot live without love. Without it our lives are meaningless. If we do not love others as Christ loved us, they cannot experience it and make it their own.

Joy and Peace

Joy and peace are fruits of the Spirit. They manifest the characteristics of God himself. It is important to differentiate between joy and the satisfaction of desire. The latter is self-centered, focuses on fulfilling desires, and treats others as objects for personal pleasure. Such satisfaction is never fulfilled, for as old desires are satisfied, new ones arise. There is no lasting contentment.

Joy is the fruit of good relationships with God and with humans. It often surprises us unexpectedly. It is other-centered, the deep contentment of seeing others joyful and happy together. It is complete.

God is the God of peace. Peace is not the avoidance of conflict. Nor is peace established through the conquest of enemies by means of violence. As long as we have enemies, we will have war. Peace is a proactive process. It is to love our enemies and to go to them to seek justice, forgiveness, and reconciliation. It seeks not punitive but restorative justice. God did not sit on his throne and send his angels to punish humankind. He took the initiative and came in human form to invite us into a relationship with him. He loved us when we hated and rejected him. He bore the punishment for the sins of the whole world, which had rejected him. He forgave those who crucified him. He rose from the dead and invited everyone, including those who had crucified him, to become his disciples in a community of love and mutual respect.

We as Christians are to walk in the ways of Christ. We love when we are hated, forgive unconditionally when sinned against, and seek reconciliation. We pray "forgive us our sins, as we forgive those who sin against us" and give God the right not to forgive us if we do not forgive others. We are willing to be killed rather than to kill, because we seek to win those who oppose us. God's goal is not just simple justice, but justice that leads to reconciliation, which breaks the cycle of violence. Christopher Marshall writes:

> Without diminishing the reality of evil, without denying the culpability of those who commit crime or minimizing the pain of those who suffer at their hands, and without dispensing with punishment as a mechanism for constraining evil and promoting the change, the New Testament looks beyond *retribution* to a vision of justice that is finally satisfied only by the defeat of evil and the healing of its victims, by the repentance of sinners and the forgiveness of their sins, by the restoration of peace and the renewal of hope—a justice that manifests God's redemptive work in making all things new. (2001, 284; italics in original)

PATIENCE AND LONG SUFFERING

One of the most difficult fruits of the Spirit that we as modern people need to cultivate is patience. We live our lives with constant hurry and stress. As children we associate patience with having to wait until our parents come home, the bus arrives, or the rain stops. We associate it with powerlessness, the inability to act, and a general state of passivity and dependence. As adults we associate it with waiting passively until someone in power decides to move on: we regard patience "as an oppressive word used by the powerful to keep the powerless under control" (McNeill, Morrison, and Nouwen 1982, 90).

This is not what patience means in Scripture. Donald McNeill and his associates observe:

True patience is the opposite of a passive waiting in which we let things happen and allow others to make the decisions. Patience means to enter actively into the thick of life and to fully bear the suffering within and around us. Patience is the capacity to see, hear, touch, taste, and smell as fully as possible the inner and outer events of our lives. It is to enter our lives with open eyes, ears and hands so that we can really know what is happening. Patience is an extremely difficult discipline precisely because it counteracts our unreflexive impulse to flee or to fight. (1982, 20–21)

Patience is a difficult virtue to incorporate into our way of living not only because it goes against our impulses but also because it radically challenges the fast pace of modern life and its concern for staying in control of one's life. Patience involves learning to listen to and live under the guidance of the Holy Spirit. It requires stopping and listening when someone in pain needs immediate attention. It requires searching for forgiveness without having to forget shameful memories. It is "a willingness to be influenced even when this requires giving up control and entering into unknown territory" (McNeill, Morrison, and Nouwen 1982, 91).

Patience concerns time. When we are impatient, we want things to change. Impatience betrays an inner restlessness. It is living by external time ruled by the clocks, watches, and calendars that dominate our lives. Patience and contemplation are time lived from within and experienced to the full. They are the antidote to the hurried, harried lives we too often live in our contemporary world.

Evaluative Themes

Biblical moral themes derive from the character of God. He is holy, righteous, pure, and just. God created us for such a perfect world, and in our fallen hearts we still long for it.

Good/Evil

Scripture affirms that God is holy (Ps. 71:22; Isa. 6:3; Rev. 4:8), and his creation is to be holy too. Christians are called saints (Eph. 1:1; Phil. 1:1; Col. 1:2). But who are saints?[6] They are Christians known for their holiness, regarded as perfect (Matt. 5:48; 19:21; 1 Cor. 13:10; Col. 1:28; 2 Tim. 3:17). But how can we be perfect in a fallen world? What are the foundations for holiness?

6. In Protestantism, the Christian model is the scholar. Little is written about "saints" or "holy people." This reflects the Enlightenment emphasis on reason and truth and its relegation of feelings and morals to the private sector because they subjectivize truth. The Catholic Church, with its roots in a premodern world, finds its model in the saint, stressing the moral dimension of Christian life. The New Testament refers to Christians as saints some fifty times. As Protestants we need to rediscover the importance of saintliness and models of holy living.

In modernity we think of holiness as living in obedience to the moral laws of the universe, which parallel its natural laws. God is holy because he keeps these moral laws perfectly. But this view is Hindu. According to Hindu belief, karma, the moral laws, are above the gods, who often sin and must be reborn in the endless cycle of life. God is holy not because he keeps the moral laws but because holiness is his very nature and way of being.

The biblical view is that sin is a rupture in relationships with God and with one another, not the violation of an impersonal code of laws. Judgment is based on one's faithfulness to agreements, obligations, or covenants with God and with other people. To act justly is to be faithful to the people one is committed to by agreement or covenant. Relationships, not impersonal law, are central. "In the Old Testament God gave Israel the laws not as a standard to use in rewarding and punishing individuals, but as an expression of God's intention for relationships in his redeemed community. Law presupposed a covenant relationship in which there were provisions for forgiveness and repentance and in which God was gracious. Israel was considered by God to be just/righteous, not because Israel met some perfect standard, but because of God's resolute faithfulness to Israel—people he had a covenant with" (Baker 1999, 100–101). God gave the law to teach the people about righteousness and sin, and to provide a moral fence to keep them from egregious sins that would destroy society. But the law could never make them perfect (Heb. 7:19).

The law is inadequate because its locus of control is external, not internal. People obey the law out of duty, not because it reflects their inner character. It is inadequate because it keeps people from sinning but does not foster the positive fruits of the Spirit: love, joy, peace, gentleness, goodness, meekness, and patience. The law is inadequate because it cannot make anyone perfect, and heaven has no place for anything that is not perfect.

Restitution and reconciliation are not central to the biblical view of righteousness. Biblical righteousness is God's declaring that we belong to the covenant community. It is being placed in right relationship to God and made a full participant in the community of God's people. Righteousness seeks inclusion, not exclusion.

If the law makes nothing perfect, then what are the foundations of holiness? Holiness is the very being of God. The laws are not impersonal moral laws that order the moral universe. They are God's commands given to his people, laws that he can change as they grow and mature. Moral laws are like the commands the general issues to his troops. He orders them to march, and they do. He orders them to bear right, and they do. In the Old Testament, God gave Israel fundamental moral commandments to keep them from sinning. In the New Testament he gave a new commandment, that they love one another (John 13:34). This was rooted in a new covenant that superseded the old (Heb. 8:13). Metaphorically speaking, the new wine was put in new vessels because the old could not contain it (Matt. 9:17; Mark 2:22; Luke 5:38).

The old moral commands are not abrogated; rather, they are superseded by our becoming new persons who no longer live under the law but are righteous because we are new creatures in Christ. Stephen Neill writes, "Christian perfection is not the observance of a code of moral rules, or the avoidance of transgression, or an inner state of devotion. It is a manifestation of the conquering power of Christ in every situation and in every relationship of human life. . . . Judging by this standard, the word 'perfection' dies on our lips. We are conscious only of the infinite distance that, even when we desire to follow Him most closely, still separates us from our Lord" (1960, 42). Christians become holy not by keeping the law but by living out the new life that God has given them through the power of the Holy Spirit within them. Holiness is not rooted in their behavior. It is rooted in their very being—to live holy lives is to live naturally as children of God. To sin is relapse into the old self.

Neill notes that Christian holiness must be considered in three aspects:

> Primarily, it is a change of status in relation to God, and under this aspect it is wholly His work; it was He who delivered us from the power of darkness, and translated us into the kingdom of His beloved Son (Col. 1:13). Secondly, it has a quality of permanence, and this is best expressed in the word "abiding" so constantly used in the Fourth Gospel; a relationship of total dependence on Christ, continually maintained through daily and hourly turning to Him. There is, thirdly, the aspect of crisis and conflict. The right choice has to be identified and firmly accepted. The possible wrong choice has to be firmly rejected. This is the situation in which the Christian finds himself a hundred times a day. This is the situation in which he needs grace to help him in time of need. (1960, 124–25)

How do we make these daily decisions? Christ has promised us his wisdom and the guidance of the Holy Spirit. We need to see God's guidance through Scripture and the Spirit, but in doing so we must first commit ourselves to doing his will when he makes it known to us. God does not make known his will as one option among others. The deeper question is not whether our decisions are right or wrong, but whether in making them we are seeking to be obedient to Christ as Lord of our lives. God has also given us the church and elders to help guide us in our lives. We are accountable to one another as well as to Christ.

What are some of the manifestations of holiness in people's lives? Neill suggests several. One is an "unfailing spring of joy, not for themselves only, but for the enrichment of all those with whom they have to do" (1960, 128). Another is equanimity, believing that all things work together for good for those that love God. A third is a sense of humor that is compatible with a deep seriousness: to recognize to the full the tragedies and follies of life, and yet to see God's underlying goodness in all things, and to not take themselves too seriously. A fourth is to see themselves as the chief of sinners. "It is paradoxical,

298   Transforming Worldviews

but true, that progress in saintliness always means at the same time progress in penitence" (Neill 1960, 128). Peter writes that we are made perfect through suffering (1 Pet. 5:10).

Scripture speaks much of goodness and holiness. It also says much about sin. But what is sin? Our modern worldview defines sin as breaking the universal moral laws. It calls for restitution and punishment to pay the penalty of sin. As modern Christians, we often think of morality in legalistic terms. To sin is to break the moral laws that God established at creation and revealed to us in the Old Testament. Here we face a deep contradiction. Is God righteous because he lives in conformity with the moral laws? If so, the moral law is higher than he.[7] If God is God, then what he decrees are moral laws, but they are reflections of his character, and he can change them as he wills.

In Scripture, sin is fundamentally not the breaking of universal moral laws but the breaking of relationships with God and with other people. It calls for repentance, forgiveness, and reconciliation. Morality is the outworking of God's holiness in his relationship to his creation. Righteousness is living a holy life (Lev. 11:44–45). The moral laws of the Old Testament were "put in charge of us until Christ came that we might be justified by faith. Now that this faith has come, we are no longer under the supervision of the law" (Gal. 3:24–25 TNIV). When we are in Christ, we no longer keep the law out of obedience. It was a poor shadow of God's holiness. Now we seek to live righteous lives because of our new nature given us by Christ.

As humans we often rank sins: some are great and others are small. And we count sins and feel righteous when we have fewer than our neighbors. This enables us to live with ourselves, for we know we are sinners, but, so our reasoning, at least we are not sinners like those murderers, rapists, and terrorists. In God's sight sin is sin and deserves death. There is no place for sin in God's new creation. But God's response to sin was to bear its consequences and to seek our reconciliation with him. We are like adulteresses who constantly go after other gods, but God is seeking to win us back and to restore us to our position with him (Amos).

In God's holiness as seen in Christ, we realize the awfulness of sin. As Christians we can no longer rank sins as great and small or keep track of their number. We no longer compare ourselves favorably with others and become smug in our self-righteousness. We realize that we, not they, are the worst of sinners and deserve only to die, that the ultimate sin is to deny our sinfulness (1 John 1:8–10). We are not saints leading sinners to salvation; we are great sinners inviting fellow sinners to follow Christ. Therefore we rejoice in God's salvation offered to us and to our enemies and seek it for all people.

---

7. This is the view of Hinduism, which holds that even the gods are subject to the moral law of karma and must suffer the consequences of their sins by being born at lower levels in the hierarchy of life as punishment.

Justification and Restoration

Central to a biblical worldview is God's deliverance of fallen humans from the consequences and presence of sin. Not only are our old sins wiped away; the very sin nature in us also is taken away, and we become new creatures in the image of Christ. Holiness is not something we strive for. It is of the essence of our new nature, our natural, God-given way of being in the world.

Sin in a mechanistic worldview is seen as breaking the impersonal moral laws of the universe. This calls for punitive justice, which demands that the offenders receive the punishment "they deserve." The Western legal system, based in part on Emperor Justinian's code from the late Roman Empire, introduced punishment into the Christian way of dealing with offenses. In an organic worldview, sin is breaking relationships. In Scripture, it begins with our breaking our allegiance to God and leads to broken relationships with one another and with nature. The focus here is not punitive justice but restorative justice. God's central concern is that we suffer punishment for our sins. He bore that punishment in full on the cross. He desires forgiveness and the restoration of the fallen into fellowship in the church, reincorporated as full members in the life of the community. Restorative justice focuses on the harms done, the needs unmet, the obligation to put right the wrongs, and restores all parties into the fellowship of the community (Zehr 1990). We are no longer under the judgment of the law, because Christ bore the judgment of our sins. God has opened the door for reconciliation and restoration to a personal relationship with him and with one another throughout eternity.

Salvation in the New Testament is both corporate and personal. It is personal because it invites everyone to follow Christ regardless of his or her sinfulness. It is corporate because it is the creation of a new community in communion with God and other people. This community is not a loose gathering of autonomous individuals, like a club or a crowd. Nor is it an impersonal bureaucracy. It is a new body, one and whole, made up of many parts all serving one another and the whole.

Salvation is also comprehensive. Lesslie Newbigin writes that salvation is the "restoration to the whole creation of the perfect unity whose creative source and pattern is the unity of perfect love within the being of the triune God. It is in its very sense universal and cosmic" (1998, 188). This universal character of salvation is rooted in God's love, which reaches out to all humans, "goes to all lengths to recover one lost sheep, and cares and must ever care for the rebel and the traitor with all the passion of Calvary" (Newbigin 1998, 189). This leads us to reject the reduction of Christian ministry to the private spheres of life. We must bear prophetic witness in the public sphere of politics, economics, and culture as well as in the private world of intimate personal relationships. The Christian is to be one whole person at home and at work.

Diachronic Themes

Central to a biblical worldview are its views of God's cosmic story and human history. The Bible is not a set of theological treatises or devotional meditations, although both are found in it. It is basically the story of God and his relationship to humans. Several key diachronic themes emerge.

Cosmic Story/Human History

The gospel is in essence a history embedded in a cosmic story. The doctrine of creation states that we are not timeless but rooted in time as well as space. Sin and evil too are historical in character. It is not surprising that our redemption pivots on real events in history. Ramachandra writes, "It is precisely this biblical stress on the historical 'particularity' (or situatedness) of human life, a particularity that God takes seriously in his dealings with his creatures, that challenges both the ancient Indian and the post-Enlightenment Western worldviews" (1999, 97). Hinduism denies the ontological reality of this world and its history. The Enlightenment tried to give meaning to human history without embedding it in a cosmic story. The postmodernist denies that history is in any sense story-shaped. To the world, the biblical scandal of particularity is its insistence on a once-for-all Christ, who died that all may live—its claim that there are no other ways to God and eternal life. Christ did not simply bring us insights into the state of human affairs; he actually brought a new state of affairs. Paradoxically, it is this once-for-all incarnation of Christ that guarantees the value and significance of our common humanity and ourselves as individuals.

The Bible is primarily a story of God's acts in creation, not a list of religious doctrines or devotional writings. It provides a unique, comprehensive interpretation of universal history and a unique understanding of humans as responsible actors in history. Newbigin writes, "The Bible is unique among the sacred scriptures of the religions in that it offers an interpretation of history as a whole, human history and cosmic history, and not just of the life of man apart from this history. Its centre of attention is not, if one may put it so, the possibility of man's escaping out of this world into another; it is the promise of God coming to this world to redeem it and to complete what he has begun" (1976, 8). A biblical worldview asserts the existence of a real world and real events that form a common history. It also claims there is a story of the whole. Without a story or plot, we are left with merely a vast array of events that cannot be brought together as a whole.

At the center of a biblical view is the affirmation that God is the central agent. Eloise Meneses writes:

> The whole of the Old Testament is primarily a chronicle of God's activities.
> Human ones are recorded mostly insofar as they relate to our deviation from

or following of God's path for us. Our anthropocentrism is so great that even as Christians we are inclined to read the Old Testament stories as accounts of Abraham's life, rather than God's call; Israel's journey out of Egypt, rather than God's emancipation; or David's exploits, rather than God's concession to his people by giving them a king and then blessing the king for his heart-felt devotion. But the emphasis is clear in the text; the bible is a record of God's activities for his people. (1997, 20–21)

The same can be said of the New Testament. It is the revelation of how God views history as revealed to those who followed Christ.

The biblical story is not cyclical, unlike the metanarratives found in most small-scale societies and in formal religions such as Hinduism and Buddhism, in which the natural world moves through repeated cycles of birth, growth, maturity, decay, and death, and religion offers release from this cycle. The biblical story is also not linear, unlike the modern view of evolution and progress, the onward march of human mastery over nature. The biblical story also differs from the postmodernist perspective, which rejects any overarching metanarrative as oppressive and denies the possibility of any true, universal history or ethic.

In contrast to these interpretations of history, Newbigin argues that biblical history is U-shaped (1992, 1). It starts with a perfect creation, but then sin enters the scene and mars that creation. The story then is God's working out his purposes to restore all creation, not a few individuals or a small body of saints, to a perfect new creation. All creation must follow this pattern. As individuals we begin with the sheer gift of being, but we are sinners destined to death and hell. Through Christ, however, we are offered the foretaste of becoming new, perfect beings. Biblical history is the story of the fall and of the re-creation of a new world. Charles Taber writes, "I suggest, in fact, that the gospel of the kingdom of God is the only valid universal meta-narrative, the only one which is not ruthlessly homogenizing and totalitarian, because it is the only one based on self-sacrificing love instead of worldly power, the only one offered by a king on a cross, the only one offered by a conquering lion who turns out to be a slaughtered lamb (Rev. 5:1–10)" (2002, 189).

As humans our lives take on meaning because they have "plots" or story lines connecting the seemingly disconnected events of our lives into one whole story. In one sense, our lives are detective stories, in another sense, divine romances, and in another, comedies and tragedies. Our stories take on meaning because they are part of a larger story, the story of the church, which continues down through the centuries. For example, in Scripture, the stories of Moses, Rahab, David, and Esther are told because they are significant parts in the story of Israel.

Community stories, in turn, take on meaning because they are part of human history, and history takes on meaning because it is part of a cosmic

Figure 10.4
MEANING IN HISTORY
World history is part of God's big story.

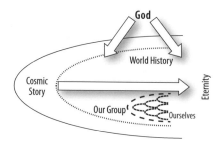

Figure 10.4
MEANING IN HISTORY
World history is part of God's big story.

story (fig. 10.4). This cosmic story has meaning because it has a telos, an end, and that end determines its meaning. The problem is that we live in the middle of the story and don't know its end. We can formulate our own hypotheses of the outcome of history, or we can listen to the one who is in charge of the cosmic story. God affirms through Scripture that there is a telos and that it is good—the restoration of a perfect creation. That eschatological future has become present as a foretaste in Christ, and those who follow him enter the sphere of the kingdom—in a sense they live in the old age but also in the new age that is fully yet to come.

The affirmation that human history is connected to God's cosmic story creates the tension between the "already" and the "not yet," between the history in which we live and the cosmic telos to which we look forward. This tension between missionary obligation and eschatological hope is at the heart of the church's witness to the world. Newbigin writes, "Between the Church militant here on earth, longing for the full possession of that which she has in foretaste, and consummation for which she longs, the marriage supper of the Lamb, there lies the unfinished missionary task. The first answer to her prayer, 'Come Lord Jesus,' is his commission—'Go ye into all the world—and lo I am with you'" (1998, 193).

The church affirms that the biblical story it tells, embodies, and enacts is the true story, and that other stories are to be evaluated by reference to it. Newbigin continues, "The story the church tells is a competitor in the field where secular historians tell the story of a society, a nation, a civilization, or the story of the world. The church's story is not a different kind of story from the one these historians tell; its difference is with respect to the interpretation of the records, which are the raw material common to them all. It is not a special kind of history isolated from the work of secular historians. It is, if you like, a counter history, interpreting the same evidence in different ways" (1995, 76–77).

In a biblical worldview, there is no division between secular and sacred history. Newbigin notes:

The Church is indeed the agent of God's mission and a clue to his dealing with mankind, but this does not mean that the work of God in the world is to be simply identified with the progress of the Church in mission and unity. It does not mean that the events of secular history are mere background for the story of the Church, or merely scenery for the drama of salvation.... The Gospel of God, with which both Testaments are concerned, does not refer merely to one of the strands of man's cultural history. It refers to the beginning and end of all things and therefore to the real meaning of all that happens. It follows that there cannot be an absolute separation between the history of our redemption, and the sacred story of the Old and New Testaments, the story of the Church and the whole story of mankind. (1963, 24)

A biblical worldview restores the diachronic story to central stage and thereby gives meaning to life and history.

Shalom/Warfare

The biblical images of spiritual realities are radically different from their Indo-European counterparts that underlie modernity, and they give us a very different view of the cosmic spiritual warfare in which we are engaged.

According to the biblical testimony, good is eternal and evil is contingent. The Bible is clear: God and Satan, good and evil are not two independent realities in coexistence from eternity. In the beginning was God, and God was good. Sin appeared later in the biblical account. Satan and his hosts are fallen angels, and humans, created in the image of God, are sinful rebels. Moreover, God's creation depends on him for continued existence. God did not create a universe that exists independent of him. Satan and sinners, like all creation, are dependent on God's sustaining creation. Their very existence in rebellion is testimony to God's mercy and love.

The central issue in spiritual warfare, therefore, is not one of brute power. God's omnipotence is never questioned in Scripture. Even Satan and his hosts acknowledge it. God does not need to destroy Satan—he needs only to stop sustaining his existence. The issue is holiness and evil, righteousness and sin. God is holiness, light, love, and truth. Evil does not exist independently. It is the perversion of good. It is darkness, deceitfulness, and the source of death. It is broken relationships, idolatry and rebellion against God, alienation, and worship of the self.

At the heart of the gospel is shalom. Shalom begins with a right relationship with God, involving worship, holiness, and obedience. Prayer in the Indo-European myth is a means to control or manipulate the gods. In biblical thought, it is submission to God. In prayer we begin with worship and adoration. In this we renew our commitment to Jesus Christ as the Lord of our lives. We give God permission to do his will, not our will, in our lives. We give him permission to use us and our resources to answer our prayers. When we pray for the lost, we are willing to be sent. When we pray for the poor, we are ready to give our possessions. When we pray for justice, we are willing to take a stand with the people. Prayer is costly.

Shalom also involves right relationships with humans. Right relationships are not characterized by hierarchy and exploitation, as in the Indo-European worldview, in which the strong lord it over the weak. Right relationships are expressed in loving and caring for one another as people created in the image of God, however broken or flawed we are. Shalom means to be unconditionally for the other, rather than for oneself, and to commit oneself to the other, regardless of his or her response. Shalom gives priority to building community over completing tasks. This priority requires that we give up our modern need to control people and situations around us, and accept the chaos that comes with negotiated relationships. It means we accept corporate decision making and accountability to the community.

If the central message of the Bible is not a cosmic struggle between God and Satan to determine who will rule, what is it about? The battle between God and Satan rages on; that is clear. But the battle is for and in human hearts and societies; it is not a showdown to see who is stronger, God or Satan. In this battle for human hearts, people are not passive victims of combat on a cosmic plane. We are the central actors and the locus of the action. We are the rebels, and since the temptation of Adam, self-worship has been the basis of our idolatry.

God's goal is to win the enemy over and bring peace, reconciliation, and shalom. Jesus instructed us to love our enemies, because then they are no longer enemies (Matt. 5:44; Luke 6:27–35). As long as we have enemies, there can be no peace. Satan's goal is to keep people from turning to God. We must learn to see all fallen humans as us, not as other. At the deepest level we are one humanity, called to worship God and love one another. God's methods are the power of love, truth, peace, life, and light. Satan's methods are deceit, fear, violence, darkness, and death. We are called to love our enemies, not hate them, because they are us, and because they are redeemable. We cannot use unrighteous methods in our struggle in the name of fairness, for then we fail and become one with our enemies.

Power encounters, in the biblical view, can lead to great opposition and persecution. The supreme power encounter is the cross on which Jesus defeated Satan. That the cross is the ultimate victory makes no sense in Indo-European terms. Christ should have taken up the challenge of his tormentors and come down from the cross with his angelic hosts. One word would have been enough, and his enemies would have been destroyed. He should have defeated Satan when he met him in the desert (1 Cor. 1:18–25). And yet the cross is not, in biblical terms, an apparent loss saved at the last moment by the resurrection. It is God's way of unmasking Satan's evil power and intent, and of demonstrating God's own unconditional and unending love, even to the death, if need be. If our understanding of spiritual warfare does not make sense of the cross, then it is wrong.

As we develop a biblical approach to the question of spiritual realities, we must avoid two extremes: (1) denial of the reality of Satan and the spiritual battle in which we are engaged, and (2) undue fascination with and fear of Satan and his hosts. Our central focus is on Christ. In our immediate peripheral vision are the angelic hosts. In our outer peripheral vision are the forces of evil.[8] Our message is one of victory, hope, joy, and freedom, for we have the power of the Holy Spirit to overcome evil. The cosmic battle is over. We are messengers to declare to the world that Christ is indeed the Lord of everything in the heavens and on earth. For all authority has already been given to Jesus, the risen Lord (Matt. 28:18).

Marriage

The Bible is a love story (Hosea; Luke 5:34; Rev. 19:7), but not like that of the Indo-European myth in which the suitor woos a pure virgin. Rather, it is the story of a loving suitor seeking to win a wayward woman to be his bride. She rejects him and follows others who profess to love her but do not. Even those in the church who accept his hand spend little time with him, and are caught up flirting with other gods: idols, demons, money, honor, luxury, and self. Yet he persists and shows her unconditional love, forgiving her every time she turns her attentions to other suitors but repents and turns back to him. For God, love is not a sentiment that strikes and goes. It is an unconditional commitment to his bride, no matter her waywardness. It puts her well-being above his own. It is not the excitement of chase and capture—it is the beginning of an eternal marriage, to use a biblical but very human metaphor, that is characterized by perfect harmony, shalom, and joy.

It is impossible in a few pages to outline a biblical worldview. At best, we can begin a dialogue and suggest areas that must be addressed, particularly in a modern, postmodern, and glocal world. Christians in each culture will need to examine its worldview, to define the gospel in their sociocultural contexts, to be transformed as a church, and to be prophetic to their people. This process continues as cultures, societies, and individuals constantly change.

---

8. There are four times as many references in Scripture to angels as to demons, yet we often make no mention of them.

11

Transforming Worldviews

Spiritual transformation is the work of God in the life of a sinner, making him or her a child of God and a citizen of the kingdom of God. It is also the work of God in the church, the community of those who follow Christ. Because it is the work of God, we cannot fully comprehend it. Only in heaven will we begin to understand its magnitude and its cost. Yet we must seek to understand, even though as through a glass darkly, the divine nature of transformation. Because transformation involves sinners, it also has a human dimension. People are called to respond to God's invitation, and when they do, they are transformed in their lives. Spiritual changes have earthly consequences. Humans cannot be divided, with their spirits functioning independently of their bodies.

In spiritual transformation people are called to leave their false gods and their self-idolatry with its obsession with wealth, power, pride, sex, and race, and to return to God as their Creator and Lord. Biblical conversion involves real people in their real everyday lives. Consequently it always takes place within the particularities of history. Furthermore, it is both individual and corporate, for people do not exist outside societies and cultures. It is our purpose here to examine the human side of transformation and the sociocultural and historical processes involved.

We must keep in mind that our analysis is from a human point of view. God sees the human heart and knows what is ultimately real. We, however, must base our knowledge on what people say and do. Even our understanding of Scripture is affected by our cultures and societies. Consequently, we must approach our study with humility and with a willingness to learn from Scripture, experience, and one another.

Nature of Transformation

In analyzing transformation from a human perspective, we must examine the worldviews we bring to the study. Here we will examine a few of them as they shape our understanding of transformation.

Transformation and Cognitive Categories

Concepts and definitions are at the core of every worldview. They are attempts to make sense of and give coherence to our experiences. As we saw earlier, they differ not only in the categories they create but also in the ways these categories are created. This raises questions: how do we define "transformation," and to what extent is our definition influenced by our own cultural ways of creating categories?

INTRINSIC AND RELATIONAL SETS

As noted earlier, humans create both intrinsic and relational categories. The categories we are most familiar with in modernity are intrinsic sets, which are formed by placing the "same kind" of things together to form discrete categories. Thus we put together people who share one set of beliefs and practices and call them "Christians" and differentiate them from "Hindus," "Buddhists," and "Muslims."

In this mode of thought, it becomes important to define exactly what we mean by "Christian," and we must do so in intrinsic terms (what a person is in himself or herself), because the definition must draw the boundary between those who are Christian and those who are not. What is it that makes Christians "one kind" of people in contrast to people who are of "other kinds"?

If we define conversion in intrinsic terms, we must define the characteristics a person must have to be a part of the set. We define a Christian in terms of beliefs. A Christian is one who believes certain things: the deity of Christ, the virgin birth, Scripture as divine revelation, and so on. We ask people if they "believe this to be true," assuming that if they believe this, they are saved. We debate what must be included—should these essentials be few (this leads to cheap grace) or many (who then can enter?)? We spend much time making certain that people's beliefs are set right by preaching and teaching.

Some of us are not content with creedal orthodoxy. Christians must also live godly lives. Abstinence from smoking, drinking alcohol, using drugs, dancing, and other vices, or spending hours in prayer and Bible study, or the presence of glossolalia and prophecy become signs that a person is a "true" Christian.

If we define conversion in relational terms, we observe whether people make Jesus the Lord of their lives—the one they follow, worship, and serve. Conversion is turning from following one god to following another.[1]

Two relational stages are at work in conversion. First, we must reject our old gods, turn around, and follow Jesus. Second, having turned, we must move closer to him by learning to know and serve him more fully. In this view, making Christ the Lord of our lives is not a single decision. It is an initial decision followed by decisions to obey him. In theological terms, justification and sanctification are parts of the same conversion and cannot be divorced.

One can also speak of the closeness of the relationship. A person may be far from Christ in understanding and life, yet turn and move earnestly toward him, as in the case of Mary Magdalene. Or people may know much about Christ and be close to him, yet be moving away, as in the case of the Pharisees.

In relational categories sin is fundamentally idolatry (the deification of self, or of something other than God) and a broken relationship with God leading to broken relationships among humans. Transformation is repentance (turning from other gods) and turning to God, who forgives us and opens the door for reconciliation and a new relationship with him. The biblical metaphors that communicate this unfathomable truth speak of God as "father," "Lord," "bridegroom," "King," and "friend."

Digital and Ratio Sets

If we use ratio ("fuzzy") sets to think about conversion, the picture looks different. Conversion from Hinduism to Christianity becomes a process in which the change may take place suddenly or gradually. In the transition the person can be seen as three-quarters Hindu and one-quarter Christian, half and half, one-quarter and three-quarters, and finally 100 percent Christian. The steps may be defined either in terms of a growing knowledge and acceptance of Christian beliefs (orthodoxy) or changes in life (orthopraxy).

A fuzzy set approach to conversion raises difficult theological questions. It is true that many people seem to move through a series of stages in their conversion to Christ, and that conversion must be seen, at least to some extent, as a process. But is there no moment of salvation? Can a person serve Hindu gods and Christ at the same time? We who look from the outside may not see a point of conversion, but what about God, who looks at the heart? May it be that what appears fuzzy to us, because we cannot see into the heart, is clear to God? In missions should we work more on drawing people to Christ

---

1. A pastor has remarked, "Jesus never said, 'Believe in me as your savior.' He said, 'Follow me as your Lord and I will save you.'" There is a big difference in these two perspectives. The first focuses on salvation and often leaves discipling new believers to others. The result is weak Christians and weak churches. The latter sees salvation and discipleship as parts of a full conversion.

and focus less on seeing salvation as a single decision and discipling as a less critical process that will somehow take care of itself?

BIBLICAL VIEW OF TRANSFORMATION

How should we define transformation? Given the great influence of Greek thought on modernity since the Renaissance, those of us who are modern or postmodern think primarily in terms of intrinsic, digital sets, and emphasize precise definitions with clear boundaries. In doing so we define conversion in terms of what people are in and of themselves. In doing so, however, we risk thinking of conversion as something people believe or do. While verbally denying salvation by works, we are in danger of ignoring the fact that it is first and foremost the work of God.

What about the biblical approach to transformation? Extrinsic or relational sets are fundamental to Hebrew thought. The emphasis is not on what things are in themselves but on what things are in relationship to other things and to history. For example, the Hebrew term *shuv* (used 1,056 times in the Old Testament) means to turn in the opposite direction and conveys the idea of turning, turning away, and turning back. A person leaves the way he has been walking and changes to a new, opposite direction. *Shuv* may also mean a return to a former place or state.

These meanings are clearly illustrated in Jeremiah 8:4b–6: "If one turns away (*shuv*) does he not return (*shuv*)? Why then has this people turned away (*shuv*) in perpetual backsliding (*shuv*)? They hold fast to deceit, they refuse to return (*shuv*) in perpetual backsliding (*shuv*). I have given heed and listened, but they have not spoken aright; no man repents of his wickedness, saying, 'What have I done?' Every one turns (*shuv*)" (translated by Kasdorf 1980, 42–43; note the implications of the term referring to turning away–turning toward). The prophets continually called Israel to turn from its worship of idols and return to Yahweh, the true and living God.

Similarly the New Testament words for conversion, *metanoein* and *epistrephein*, mean "to turn around," "to proceed in a new direction." Although he was writing in Greek with its emphasis on intrinsic, static categories, Luke used dynamic terms such as *epistrephein* nearly twenty times to denote physical movement. Paul used terms such as *apostrephein* and *anastrephein* (Eph. 4:22; 1 Tim. 4:12), which convey the idea of turning and then walking.

We need to return to a biblical view of transformation, which is both a point and a process; this transformation has simple beginnings (a person can turn wherever he or she is) but radical, lifelong consequences. It is not simply mental assent to a set of metaphysical beliefs, nor is it solely a positive feeling toward God. Rather it involves entering a life of discipleship and obedience in every area of our being and throughout the whole story of our lives.

TRANSFORMATION AND MISSIONS

How we define transformation determines how we go about evangelism and missions. If in digital, bounded-set terms becoming Christian means a mental ascent to certain truths, acquiring a certain amount of knowledge, or changing certain behaviors, how much of each is needed? In the case of Papayya, whom we examined earlier, we can hardly say, "Yes, he can become a Christian."[2] He has only a minimal knowledge of Christ, certainly not enough to be considered orthodox. Moreover, he expresses concepts such as God, sin, and salvation in Hindu terms, which have radically different meanings from their parallel Christian concepts. Nor is there much change in his behavior. On the one hand, if we say, "Yes, he can become a Christian," are we not in danger of preaching a cheap gospel that leads to Christian nominalism? On the other hand, if we say, "No, he cannot become a Christian until he understands the gospel more deeply," are we not making it nearly impossible for people without a Christian upbringing to be saved? And are we not likely to divorce justification from sanctification, and evangelize the lost while leaving the raising of newborns to others?

A ratio or fuzzy intrinsic-set approach to missions solves some of these problems by allowing transformation to be a process. A person may make many decisions, no one of which is decisive, but all of which, taken cumulatively, make the person a Christian. This fits our human view of things. There are people who are clearly Christians, and others who are clearly not. But many seem to be in between. Moreover, many Christians report no one decision marking their conversion. But as we have seen, a fuzzy, intrinsic-set approach raises difficult theological questions concerning the Christian claims that Christ alone is the only way to salvation and that we either follow him or reject him.

These problems disappear, in part, if we turn to a Hebraic approach to category formation. Conversion then is a point—a turning around. This turning may involve a minimal amount of information regarding Christ, but it does involve a change in relationship to him—a commitment to follow him, however little we know of him, to learn more and to obey him as we understand his voice. But conversion is also a process—a series of decisions that grow out of this initial turning. Viewed in this way, Papayya can become a Christian after hearing the gospel once, but those who lead him to Christ have a great responsibility to disciple him, to root him solidly in his new faith. Without discipleship he may be a stillborn Christian, as it were. Throughout his life he may grow in faith. He may also "backslide." But he remains a Christian as

---

2. In at least one case this situation led missionaries to conclude that older adults would never learn enough to become Christians. They focused their attention on founding Christian schools to teach children Christian doctrines and hoped to start the church with the younger generation.

long as he seeks to follow Christ. In this view, we cannot divorce evangelism from nurture or conversion from the church.

Transformation and Cultural Dimensions

A second question regarding transformation concerns its dimensions. Earlier we examined the three dimensions of culture: cognitive (beliefs), affective (feelings), and evaluative (norms). Conversion involves all three.

COGNITIVE TRANSFORMATION

The Protestant reformers (influenced by the Enlightenment) and more recently evangelicals have stressed the importance of cognitive transformation. They emphasize the importance of defending the truth against heresy. Certainly truth plays an important part in spiritual transformation. As Christians we are concerned not with conversion in general but with conversion to Jesus, and not to Jesus as a good man but to the Jesus of the Bible—the Christ, the Son of God, who became flesh, died, and rose to save people from their sins.

A person with minimal knowledge of Christ may seek more and eventually have enough to make a deep decision regarding him. Knowledge alone, however, is not enough. Satan knows much better than we that Jesus is Lord, yet he is not saved because he is not willing to worship and follow him.

AFFECTIVE TRANSFORMATION

In recent years the Pentecostal and charismatic movements have reminded us of the importance of the affective dimension in conversion. It is not enough to have a full head; one must also have a full heart. This is not to say that evangelicals and other Protestants have neglected the affective side completely. The sense of awe and mystery in the face of an infinite, transcendent God as father has been the classical feeling associated with the "high church" and its cathedrals, liturgy, gestures of kneeling and bowing, organs, chants, and classical music. Evangelical churches, influenced by Pietism, have tended to stress the presence of Christ among his people, and to feel the peace and inner joy a person gets from intimate fellowship with God and other people. This is manifested in their emphasis on meditation and silence, order, congregational hymns, restoration of personal relationships to Christ, and admission into the fellowship of a local congregation. The Pentecostals and charismatics have focused on ecstasy that manifests itself in freedom of expression, raised hands, dance, glossolalia, and the presence of God the Holy Spirit within us.

Feelings often provide the initial impulse for conversion. People come to a church and "feel at home." They enjoy the warm fellowship of Christians and are attracted to the gospel. We need to remember that we are not God's lawyers proving the gospel. We are witnesses to a new life, and the affective dimensions are often what first attracts people to the gospel. In discipling it is hard to convert feelings, partly because our discipling processes focus on cognition. Feelings are caught, not taught, and in discipling we need to include them more in times of informal fellowship and in personal sharing. Feelings, like knowledge, are parts, not the whole, in the process of spiritual transformation.

Evaluative Transformation

There is a growing awareness that although transformation may begin with cognitive and affective conversions, it must also include the moral dimension of cultures and their worldviews. Christians are called not only to know the truth and experience beauty and joy but also to be holy people. Before God in our new being in Christ, we are saints. Although the old person continues to tempt us to sin, we must learn to live our daily lives as we truly are, as eternal beings. Holiness is the most neglected area in Christian transformation, but it is the most important, for it manifests the very nature of God.

At the heart of moral transformation is decision making. We think about things, have feelings about them, and then evaluate them, decide, and take action. Some decisions we make are based on rational thinking, with little emotional and moral input, such as solving math questions or buying the cheapest clothes we can find. Others spring from high emotions with little cognitive or moral input, such as buying costly but stylish clothes, cheering at football games, and buying flowers for a fiancée. Still other decisions focus on moral issues, such as fighting racism, deciding on abortion, and killing another person. We vary from one type of decision to another, from person to person, and from culture to culture. For example, people educated in schools are taught to place great importance on knowledge and reason, while people involved in mentoring relationships, like the disciples and Christ, are involved in all three dimensions of knowing.

Recent studies reveal that an initial conversion is generally followed by a period of evaluation during which the new way of life is critically reexamined. If the new is no better than the old, or the cost of adopting it is too high, the person or group turns back to traditional ways. But those who choose a new way and reevaluate it are open to knowing and experiencing it more fully. Enduring transformations are the result of many decisions to adopt and develop a new worldview. We must remember, too, that people who initially reject a new way often reevaluate their decision and may be open to conversion. Their "no" may not be a final "no" but a "not yet."

The implications of this reevaluation process for missions are far reaching. Follow-up becomes critical in nurturing faith, not only to disciple individuals but to transform whole communities into churches capable of testing the faithfulness to the gospel, and transmitting it from generation to generation. We must also not be discouraged by initial rejection. People often take time to think and process our witness, both personally and corporately, before making a long-term decision. Great turnings to Christ often occur after many years of faithful witness.

Evaluative transformation involves making decisions, but decisions are not only acts of the will. To be more than abstract and theoretical, they must transform human lives and behavior. Public affirmations, warm feelings, and verbal decisions are not enough. There must be evidences of repentance, discipleship, and turning to God. Jim Wallis writes:

> Current intellectual belief was a major concern of the Greeks. The early Christians, in contrast, were more concerned with transformation. The first evangelists did not simply ask people what they believed about Jesus; they called upon their listeners to forsake all and follow him. To embrace his kingdom meant a radical change not only in outlook but in posture, not only in mind but in heart, not only in worldview but in behavior, not only in thoughts but in actions. Conversion for them was more than a changed intellectual position. It was a whole new beginning. (1981, 4)

Conversion is far more than an emotional release and far more than an intellectual adherence to correct doctrine. It is a basic change in life direction.

Levels of Cultural Transformation

We started the book by asking whether a nonliterate peasant can become a Christian after hearing the gospel only once. Our answer can only be yes. If a person must be educated, have an extensive knowledge of the Bible, or live a good life, the good news is only for a few. But what essential change must take place when Papayya responds to the gospel message in simple faith? Certainly he has acquired some new information. He has heard of Christ and his redemptive work on the cross and a story or two about Christ's life on earth. But his knowledge is minimal. Papayya cannot pass even the simplest tests of Bible knowledge or theology. If we accept him as a brother are we not opening the door to "cheap grace," syncretism, and a nominal church? What must take place for a conversion to be genuine? What must take place for Papayya to grow into Christian maturity? And what changes must take place in the local church that emerges in his community?

When we win people to Christ, we look for some evidence of conversion. Our first tendency is to look for changes in behavior, use of Christian signs, and participation in Christian rituals.[3] We search for evidence that people are

---

3. Change in behavior was central to Catholic missions after the sixteenth century. Francis Xavier baptized converts who could recite the Lord's Prayer, the twelve articles of the short Catholic creed, and the Ten Commandments. Catholic theology does not make the sharp distinction between beliefs and behavior, between forms and meanings in symbols, that Protestant theology does. Consequently behavioral transformation is seen as evidence of transformed beliefs.

truly converted, such as putting on clothes; giving up alcohol, tobacco and gambling; putting away all but one wife; attending church regularly; and participating in baptism and communion. Such changes are important as evidence of conversion, but it has become clear that they do not necessarily mean that the underlying beliefs have changed. People can adapt their behavior to get jobs, win status, and gain power without abandoning their old faith. They can give Christian names to their pagan gods and spirits and so "Christianize" their traditional religions.

Protestant missionaries have stressed the need for transformations in people's beliefs. People must believe in the deity of Christ, virgin birth, and death and resurrection of Christ to be saved. They must repent inwardly of their sins and seek Christ's salvation offered to those who believe. Right beliefs are essential to conversion, and missions have set up Bible schools and seminaries to teach orthodox doctrine. It has become increasingly clear, however, that transforming explicit beliefs is not enough to establish biblically based churches that are faithful to the gospel. People often say what others want to hear, and they use the same words but mean different things.

As we have seen, underlying explicit beliefs is a deeper level of culture that shapes the categories and logic with which people think and the way they view reality. An example of worldview misunderstandings can be found in Jacob Loewen's experience as a missionary to the Waunana in Panama, discussed in the introduction. Such reinterpretation of Christianity into non-Christian understandings of reality is not uncommon. In fact, it is one of the most common and serious dangers in the church, including the churches in the West.

Conversion to Christ must encompass all three levels of culture: behavior and rituals, beliefs, and worldview. Christians should live differently because they are Christians. However, if their behavior is based primarily on their culture, it becomes dead tradition. Conversion must involve a transformation in beliefs, but if it is only a change of beliefs, it is false faith (James 2). Although conversion must include a change in behavior and beliefs, if the worldview is not transformed, in the long run the gospel is subverted and becomes captive to the local culture (fig. 11.1). The result is syncretistic Christo-paganism, which has the form but not the essence of Christianity. Christianity becomes a new magic and a new, more subtle form of idolatry. If behavioral change was the focus of early Protestantism, and changed beliefs the focus of the twentieth century, transforming worldviews must be central to church and mission in the twenty-first century.

At the core of worldview transformations is the human search for coherence between the world as we see it and the world as we experience it. Humans seek meaning by looking for order, pattern, symmetry, coherence, unity, and noncontradiction. Learning is "meaning-making"—a process of making sense or giving coherence to our experiences (Mezirow 1991). On the surface, we do so by compartmentalizing our belief systems into religion, science, medicine,

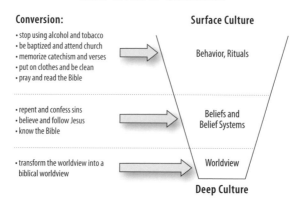

Figure 11.1

THREE LEVELS OF CONVERSION

yoga, cooking, car repairing, and the like. At a deeper, worldview level, we seek, often unconsciously, on the one hand to integrate these into a coherent structure and story that makes sense of reality. On the other hand, the deep patterns or orders that emerge shape our surface cultural domains.

As missionaries and ministers, we should remember that transformation must begin in us. We must first experience transformation in ourselves and our churches. Only then can we bear authentic witness to the gospel and exemplify the transformation to which everyone is called.

Types of Worldview Transformation

Cultures are constantly changing, and these changes often lead to changes in worldviews, which tend to change more slowly because they are at the subconscious level. When worldviews change, the world itself does not change, but after the transformation people live in a perceptually different world. Within a worldview there are themes and counterthemes with advocates for each. Moreover, in larger societies there is not one worldview but rather many competing worldviews, generally with one dominant worldview that determines public discourse and action.

Worldviews change in two ways: through growth and through radical shifts. Normal transformations in worldviews are precipitated by surface contradictions, life's dilemmas, and new experiences that cannot be resolved by simply acquiring more information, enhancing problem-solving skills, or adding to one's competencies. Resolution of these dilemmas requires a change in our worldviews.

NORMAL WORLDVIEW TRANSFORMATIONS

In a constantly changing culture, tensions between surface ideologies and between these ideologies themselves and the underlying worldview lead to incremental changes in ideologies and worldviews. The development of new understandings of pharmacology leads to new medicines and medical procedures that change the way people deal with diseases. The introduction of television alters the way people view reality by opening up worlds not seen before.

Worldviews are constantly changing in response to changes at the levels of surface culture. To use a metaphor, normal worldview changes are like remodeling and adding to an existing house.

Paradigm Shifts

Worldview changes may be radical reorganizations of underlying components. Thomas Kuhn calls these "paradigm shifts" (1970). Jack Mezirow writes, "When a meaning perspective can no longer comfortably deal with anomalies in a new situation, a transformation can occur. Adding knowledge, skills, or increasing competencies within the present perspective is no longer functional; creative integration of new experience into one's frame of reference no longer resolves the conflict. One not only is made to react to one's own reactions, but to do so critically" (1978, 104). Paradigm shifts are like rebuilding a house using parts and pieces of the old, but with a radically new way of ordering the fundamental configuration. Examples of such radical shifts are the introduction of writing, which changed the way people stored information and communicated with one another. On the one hand, writing broke down the old barriers of time and space and allowed one generation to read the thoughts of previous generations, and people in one part of the world could communicate with those in other parts of the world. Moreover, it allowed for the storage of vast amounts of information in libraries. On the other hand, writing was impersonal, detached from specific contexts, and linear in its logic. The result was a profound reorganization of the way societies could be built.

Thomas Kuhn shows how the Copernican revolution changed the way first scientists and later the populace viewed the place of earth in the universe (1970). No longer was it the center. Now it was a minor planet circling one of millions of stars forming one of billions of galaxies that are flying apart at speeds approaching that of light. It had lost its cosmic significance, and humans had become transient beings in a cosmos that stretched back billions of years to a big bang, and ending in billions of years with cosmic burn-out. Similarly, Einstein's theory of general relativity and Maxwell's theory of quantum mechanics have radically changed the ways in which we think of time, space, matter, and energy.

To help us understand the nature of paradigm or worldview shifts, it is helpful to go back to the illustration of the configurational nature of worldviews used in chapter 2. There we saw that different configurations can be imposed on the raw data of our experiences. Looking at a set of dots, some people see

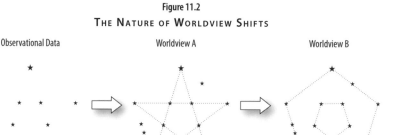

a star. But new experiences add new points of information, and many of these lie outside the star model of reality. At one point someone suggests a totally new way of interpreting the data, namely, as a pentagon (fig. 11.2). But which paradigm is closer to reality? Additional new experiences add more points of information, and it becomes clear that the pentagon "connects" more of the dots than does the star. The result is a paradigm shift in the way we fundamentally view reality. In time, however, growing amounts of data do not all fully fit the pentagon interpretation of reality. Someone breaks the implicit worldview rule that patterns emerge by connecting the dots using straight lines and proposes that we see the world as two concentric circles (fig. 11.3). This radical proposal integrates more fully the many bits of data we have, and in time we undergo another worldview shift and think in terms of connecting dots by curved as well as straight lines. In all of these there remains a constant worldview assumption that order is seen through connecting dots. At some point it might make sense to draw curved lines circling the dots rather than connecting them, but this calls for an even greater paradigm shift.

A configurational understanding of the nature of worldviews helps missionaries and Christian leaders understand the nature of Christian conversion. Some people argue that conversion requires a rejection of all the elements of the old religion, for it is made up of the sum of its parts. To include elements from the old in the new is to contaminate the new. If meaning is found more in the configuration that orders elements than in the elements themselves, old elements may be kept if they fit into the configuration of the new paradigm because they take on new meaning in it. Furthermore, not every fact must be present, or even totally complete, to see the larger pattern. Partial and approximate data are often adequate to understand what is happening. It is possible, therefore, to use traditional elements in creating Christian responses in specific cultural contexts, but they must explicitly be given new meanings.

Figure 11.3
Further Worldview Shifts

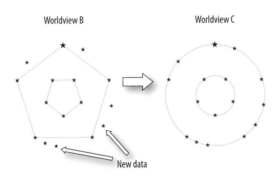

Worldview B   Worldview C

New data

Finally, it is important that Christians provide a credible alternative to the existing paradigms of the world. It is not only the message we preach, but the lives we live that will draw people to the gospel.

Transforming Worldviews

How then can we transform worldviews? As we have seen, there are two basic ways worldviews are transformed. Normal change occurs when changes on the level of conscious beliefs and practices over time infiltrate and bring about change at the worldview level. Paradigm or worldview shifts take place when there is a radical reorganization in the internal configurations of the worldview itself to reduce the tensions between surface culture and the worldview. In their own turn, these paradigm shifts reshape the surface culture. The relationship is two-way: conscious beliefs reshape worldviews, and worldviews mold conscious beliefs.

Normally when we think of conversion, we think of radical paradigm shifts. Conversion replaces an old set of beliefs and practices with new ones. It involves turning from an old path and beginning on a new one. At the worldview level it changes the fundamental ways in which we configure our view of reality. But most worldview transformations are an ongoing process in all individuals and societies. As new technology is developed, new experiences are encountered, and new ideas are raised, these affect underlying worldviews. We must see worldview transformation as a point, conversion, and as a process, ongoing deep discipling.

Examining Worldviews

One way to transform worldviews is to "surface them"—to consciously examine the deep, unexamined assumptions we have and thereby make explicit what is implicit. Dean Arnold writes:

> Cultural assumptions are insidious, not necessarily because they are wrong, but because they are hidden and affect the way members of a culture see and interpret the world. Cultural assumptions affect what we see and what we believe is true, right, and proper without question. They are so obvious to us that they seem to be universal and are seldom questioned unless they come in conflict with a set of assumptions from another culture. More frequently than not, we fail to recognize that the values and assumptions that drive our culture are not in the Bible. (2005, viii)

The problem with worldviews is that they are largely unnamed, unexamined, and unassailable. It is particularly difficult to examine our own worldview because it is hard to think about what we are thinking with.

Examining our worldviews in schools and churches, particularly when we are part of the dominant culture, often leads to denial, then anger and hostility. Minority groups are aware of their own worldviews because they stand in contrast to the dominant worldview. Dominant communities deny that they have a constructed worldview. They accept without question the established ways in which they live. They reason well in their worldview but cannot reason outside or against it because they have no other worldview in which to express their thoughts. Worldviews invest people with a compelling sense that things really are the way they seem. Lack of awareness of alternatives also means that any challenge to their worldview is a threat of chaos, of the cosmic abyss, and therefore evokes intense anxiety. By presenting dominant communities with conscious alternatives that "make sense," the validity of the establishment worldview comes to be seen as less absolute and loses something of its hold. At the same time, a challenge to it is no longer a horrific threat of chaos.

In seminaries we need to begin by examining the worldview of the culture in which we ourselves live and how it shapes the way we think. We need to compare this against a biblical worldview in order to transform ours in light of the gospel. Only then will we guard against civil religion[4] and against becoming captive to our culture.

Christian transformation calls for a paradigm shift in which God is known to us through Christ and replaces our selves or any other god as the center of our lives. This is a radical shift, the consequences of which take a lifetime to be completed. But we can start by making Christ the Lord and center of our lives. Many dissonances between this and our old worldview must be worked out: for the rich, give all and follow Christ; for the poor, turn from old feelings of being a victim and be proactive in living in a Christlike way.

---

4. The term "civil religion" was coined by Robert Bellah (Bellah and Hammond 1980). For a good discussion of the implications of this for evangelical churches, see Linder and Pierard 1978.

Exposure to Other Worldviews

A second way to transform worldviews is to step outside our culture and look at it from the outside, and to have outsiders tell us what they perceive as our worldview. Mezirow writes, "Transformation in meaning perspective can happen only through taking the perspectives of others who have a more critical awareness of the psychological assumptions which shape our histories and experience. Cultures vary greatly in the opportunity for perspective taking" (1978, 109). Learning to see our own worldview is a long and difficult process. When we enter another culture, our first response is to examine it using our own cultural assumptions. We begin to study the culture and become aware, as outsiders, of aspects of the people's worldview of which they themselves are unaware, aspects they simply take for granted as the way things really are. As we learn to see the world through the eyes of others and then return to our own culture, we come back as "outsiders" and begin to see it through new eyes. This is why the Christian critique of Western cultures has been led by missionaries and missionary kids returning from long stays abroad, where they identified deeply with the local cultures.

In conversion and discipling at the worldview level in mission settings, we should examine not only the worldviews of the new converts but also of ourselves as missionaries, for in the past we have often been shaped more by modernity than by the gospel. In a sense, missionaries experience a double conversion—we learn to see the world through the eyes of others, and we learn to see the way in which we have learned to see reality. Both worldviews are brought under the scrutiny of the gospel, and both must be transformed by it. Seeing the world through two sets of eyes relativizes both and makes it easier for us to see the deep changes that are needed in our own worldview as well as in those of the people we serve.

On another level, it is important that the church globally seek to articulate a biblical worldview. Christians in any one culture find it almost impossible to do so because they see the world through one set of eyes. It is important that missionaries, theologians, and church leaders meet and dialogue with one another, both to learn to see their own worldviews and also to recognize alternative Christian responses and, in the process, to read the Scriptures in a new light as transforming all worldviews we bring with us. In this dialogue we need to listen carefully to non-Western Christians who tell us how they see us. Although our initial tendency is to say that they don't understand us, on further reflection we find that their views help us see ourselves more clearly and help us examine our own worldview in light of Scripture. We need to share in love our concerns about their worldview assumptions and invite them to reexamine these in light of Scripture. Together we need to develop credible biblical alternatives to the specific worldviews in which we find ourselves. In the process we become a transcultural community made up of transcultural people—people who can live in different cultures but whose real identity is

increasingly that of an outsider-insider in all of them. We must act to be salt
in the land, subverting human systems when they oppose the kingdom of God.
Lesslie Newbigin puts it well:

> If I understand the teaching of the New Testament on this matter, I understand
> the role of the Christian as that of being neither a conservative nor an anarchist,
> but a subversive agent. When Paul says that Christ has disarmed the powers
> (not destroyed them), and when he speaks of the powers as being created in
> Christ and for Christ, and when he says that the Church is to make known the
> wisdom of God to the powers, I take it that this means that a Christian neither
> accepts them as some sort of eternal order which cannot be changed, nor seeks
> to destroy them because of the evil they do, but seeks to subvert them from
> within and thereby to bring them back under the allegiance of their true Lord.
> (1991, 157)

Creating Living Rituals

A third way to facilitate transformation is through the creation of living
rituals. Western Protestants tend to be antiritual. For us the term carries negative connotations—of dead meaningless forms or of idolatry and magic. But
we are in danger of divorcing realities, forms, and meanings from signs and
of reducing these elements to simple verbal communication.

Living rituals are nondiscursive. They speak of the transcendent—of our
deepest beliefs, feelings, and values—which cannot be reduced to words. They
point to mystery, root myths and metaphors, and fundamental allegiances,
and express our deepest emotions and moral order.

In rituals we bracket ordinary signs in a ritual format to show that we are
speaking of extraordinary realities. By singing or chanting ordinary words,
we raise the level of their significance and enable them to integrate beliefs,
feelings, and moral commitments. We put on special clothes and go to special
places at special times. We bow our heads, kneel, or raise our hands and say,
"Our Father . . ." and "Amen" to show that we are talking to God, not to one
another about him. Even the most informal worship services embody hidden
rituals to speak to God and to worship together as a community. To mark
important events in our lives, such as conversions, we need living rituals that
point to the sacred and highlight the significance of the occasion. Without
them we reduce these events to ordinary everyday experiences.

Many living rituals are also performances—in doing them, we are transformed. When the judge pronounces, "You are guilty," he is not simply communicating a message. He is transforming the defendant into a criminal. When
the minister says, "I now declare you husband and wife," he changes the social,
legal, and, for us, religious status of the persons from single to married.

The extent to which the importance of ritual has been diminished in
modern culture can be seen in marriage. In high-church rituals, the marriage

pronouncement does not merely reflect a covenant between two persons; it is a covenant before God that changes their ontological status in the order of heaven itself. They are now "married in the sight of God"—the marriage is recorded in the books of heaven. This is why divorce is so serious. In low churches marriages are often covenants made before the church as a community of believers. In our secular society, the vows have largely become contracts between two individuals before a justice of the peace, with little ontological or social significance. Such covenants can be broken when either party fails to live up to the agreement.

Our Western antiritual stance is reflected by our attitude to Sunday morning services. We say, "I go to church in order to worship." Worship is what we get out of the service. If we do not "feel" like we have worshiped, we call the service a dead ritual. People with a high view of ritual, as is true in many cultures around the world, say, "In going to church I am worshiping." Worship is something they offer to God, not what he and the congregation give them. The fact that they get up, put on special clothes to appear before God, go to church, and participate—all are acts of worship that express their beliefs, feelings, and allegiances and proclaim these publicly to the world around them.

Given our antiritual bias, we in the modern world often overlook the importance of rituals in worldview transformation. In the past, conversions often occurred at evangelistic meetings in which converts made a public declaration of their transformation. These were rites of transformation marking radical paradigm shifts in their thinking. In New Testament times, they were followed by public baptisms in which the converts confirmed their decision before the world. Now baptisms often occur much later and in church and mark admission into church membership. Conversion has become a private, individual matter—a change in heart in which there are few outward social and public symbols.

We must ask, has our modern view and practice of conversion become truncated and weak in part because we have no real rituals by which we can express the realities of life meaningfully to ourselves and to the world around us? With no clear living ritual, religious conversion becomes simply another ordinary decision, like the many other decisions we make every day. There is nothing to mark its life-transforming nature. Furthermore, the fact that we find it difficult to determine when conversion takes place reflects, in part, the extent to which we have internalized and privatized it.

In much of the world, decisions, especially religious conversions, are public affairs and must be marked by signs that both perform and communicate. That is why baptism, not an inner personal affirmation of faith, is often the crucial issue in mission churches. People may express a personal faith in Christ and remain in the community, but when they are baptized, they are excommunicated from their old group. In such cases we face the difficult question: Is conversion a private, inner affirmation, or is it public testimony and obedience to the call to follow Christ?

Some rituals of transformation mark major changes in a person, a community, or a nation. Rituals of transformation are like remodeling houses. We must tear down parts of the old to give rise to the new. We must move through chaos to reach a better order. These rites include baptism, evangelistic crusades, retreats, and pilgrimages.

There are also rituals of intensification, which are like cleaning the house. Normal living creates chaos—dirt on the rugs, clothes lying around, unwashed dishes. Periodically we set aside a time to restore order to the home. In rites of intensification, such as Sunday morning services, Christmas, and Easter, we recall and reaffirm our worldviews.

We need to rediscover the importance of appropriate rituals to help structure and express our worldviews. We need to overcome our fear of rituals. The answer to dead traditions and idolatrous rituals is not to do away with rituals. It is to constantly consciously examine and re-create our rituals to keep them vibrant and to transform us through participation in them. Without living rituals, we have no appropriate ways to affirm our deepest beliefs, feelings, and morals, which lead to new lives in a new community and in the world.

Worldview Transformation and Other Human Systems

We have examined some of the cultural, particularly worldview, dynamics involved in transformation. But as we noted at the outset, cultural systems are only one type of system in our understanding of humans. How do cultural transformations relate to social, personal, biological, and even physical systems? Above all, how do they relate to spiritual realities?

In discussing worldview transformation we need to remember, as we saw earlier, that a systems approach must avoid foundationalism. Worldviews are not the engines that drive culture. Rather, they are repositories of deep corporate assumptions and ways of looking at reality. As surface culture changes, the worldview, often over a long period of time, is reshaped to fit the customs and beliefs of the people. This is probably the most common reason for worldview changes. Worldviews, however, also deeply shape cultures and the ways in which cultures change. In other words, deep culture and surface culture are in constant interaction, and either can be the source of change.

It is important to remember that worldviews, like the cultures in which they are embedded, are in constant conflict and change. As Morris Opler notes, there are themes and counterthemes with different social groups contesting for one or the other (1945). In larger societies there are the dominant worldviews held by those who form the dominant culture, and the subordinate worldviews of ethnic groups, immigrants, religious minorities, and others who have less power and say in the society.

In a system-of-systems analysis of humans, change in cultural systems will shape and be shaped by the other systems that make up human realities. Cultural transformations deeply affect the social system—the way people relate to their families, friends, and community, and to other Christians, and the ways they organize their societies. They affect psychological systems—the ways individuals see, feel, and evaluate reality. They affect biophysical systems—the churches people build and the signs they use to show their new identity.

Changes in the other systems also affect the cultures and worldviews of those involved. The introduction of agriculture changed much of the world. The introduction of railroads and roads contributed to the urban explosion. Similarly, biological changes affect people in all areas of their lives. The introduction of modern medicine and drugs, the spread of AIDS, and the effects of global warming all have profoundly shaped societies and cultures. Social changes, too, affect the whole system of systems in which humans live. Migrations, social revolutions, and wars often change the lives of people, even those who want to return to the past. Above all, Christian transformations speak of spiritual realities—the relationships of communities of faith and individuals to God, to one another, and to the world in which they live.

As modern people, we emphasize individualism and personal choice. We stress individual conversions, inviting people to make Jesus their personal Lord and Savior, without considering the consequences their decision has for their families and communities, even though they may be living in societies where the group, not the individual, is most important. Decisions are personal, but most of them have broader social consequences. Conversion often involves a break with our old community and entry into a new covenant community. We are not individuals before God. We are individuals-in-community before God. We need to examine the nature of transformation in the cultural, social, and psychological systems, and the ways in which these three systems interact.

Personal and Group Conversions

One example of the interaction between systems is the relationship between personal and corporate decisions. It is important to differentiate between conversion as personal transformation, and conversion as corporate transformation. Leading individuals to faith in Jesus Christ is the evangelistic dimension of mission. People come as they are, with their histories and cultures. We cannot expect an instant transformation of their behavior, beliefs, and worldviews. It is important, therefore, to disciple them into Christian maturity. This includes a transformation not only in the way people think and behave but also in their mazeways. They must learn to think biblically.

Transformation must also be corporate. This is the faithfulness side of the church and mission, the side that seeks to understand and live the gospel in specific human contexts. The church in each locale, as a community of faith, must define what it means to be Christian in its particular sociocultural and historical setting. It must take responsibility for defining and keeping biblical orthodoxy, and it must do so by defining how Christianity is different from its cultural surroundings. The apostle Paul is clear in his assertion that we as individuals and the church are to live in this world, but not to be of the world. He uses the terms *sarx*, *archeon*, and *eon* to refer to the contexts in which we live. Too often we see these terms as referring to a fallen world from which we must flee. But when we withdraw into Christian colonies, we take the "world" with us. We cannot simply outlaw sin and thereby live in holy communities. The flesh and the world are what we are now. They are good because humans are created in the image of God and can create cultures and societies that have much good in them. But the flesh and the world are also fallen and sinful, and humans create structures that do evil. The fundamental characteristic of the flesh, the world, and the age is not that they are good or evil—they are both—it is that they are temporary. They stand in contrast to the kingdom of God, which is eternal, totally righteous, and good. The process of maintaining true faith in this world and age is ongoing, for each generation must learn anew to think biblically about being Christian in its particular context.

So far we have focused on conversion. In so doing we have divorced it from discipling. We speak of justification and sanctification as two separate things. We must reject this divorce, for if we divide the two, we excessively emphasize the role conversion plays in making a person a Christian, and in so doing we make it inappropriately difficult for many to be included. On the other hand, if we reduce the level of the essential transformation, we introduce cheap grace and a church open to syncretism and heresy. Only if we reconnect justification and sanctification as a single process can we avoid these two problems and the prioritization of one over the other. Combining the two, we realize that people can enter the kingdom with a minimum of understanding, but also that this is only the beginning of a lifelong process of growth in understanding and godly living. Both are part of the same process—turning around and following Christ as the Lord of our lives.

People Movements

In strong group-oriented societies, such as small-scale, peasant societies and sociocultural enclaves, decision making is a corporate matter. Young people do not choose their spouses, places to live, vocations, or friends. Their parents and clan heads make these choices. Decisions involving the group as a whole, such as moving to new camps, conducting religious festivals, and going to war, are made by the elders and chiefs after hearing discussions in the community. Only unimportant decisions are left to the individual.

In such communities, choosing one's religion is not a personal right. It is a most serious decision because it involves not only the individual but also his or her family and community, and not only the living but also the ancestors, the unborn, and community gods as well. If individuals are allowed to convert, the very existence of the group is threatened.

In these societies important decisions are made by a corporate process involving the whole group. People talk about matters, and eventually the elders become involved. Finally, the group as a whole, led by the chief and elders, makes a decision based on these discussions, often after consulting with the ancestors and the unborn. Even if not everyone agrees with the decision, everyone is expected to go along with it to affirm the identity and unity of the group. Later, individuals may be permitted to disagree personally but still remain members of the group.

Not surprisingly, converting to Christianity in these societies often involves groups or the whole community. Although a few individuals, marginal to the society, may well be willing to convert, real transformation begins only when respected leaders in the community begin to convert. In many cases this involves whole families. In other cases it extends to clans, tribes, and castes and whole communities.

Conversion in group-oriented societies often takes the form of "mass" or "multi-individual" movements. Entire extended families and communities decide to become Christian as groups. Other families and related communities hear that their relatives and friends have done so and begin to discuss converting themselves. The gospel is "gossiped" down mountain trails and along flatland roads long before the missionary arrives.

How should we respond to such movements? Often in the past missionaries, with their emphasis on individual decisions, rejected them and required that people come one by one. This often killed the movements. To immediately baptize the whole group, however, opens the door to syncretism and neopaganism. Many in the group will not agree with the decision, and few, if any, will have more than a superficial understanding of Christianity. Furthermore, there is the danger of Christianity becoming equated with a particular ethnic group, and baptism with initiation into that group.

Group decisions, however, open the door for further teaching. In a sense, in their first decision, the people are saying, "Tell us more about your gospel." Follow-up, therefore, is most crucial in group movements. The greatest hindrance to the spread of the gospel in such circumstances is the shortage of trained workers to teach new converts what it means to be Christian.

The initial group decision is followed by times of reassessment. Those who disagree are often permitted to leave Christianity without fear of ostracism, because in the initial decision they affirmed their unity with the group. After

Figure 11.4
THE MULTISTEP NATURE OF GROUP DECISION MAKING

a period of several months of teaching, the group divides naturally into those who wish to remain Christians and those who wish to return to their old ways. If possible, baptisms should be delayed until this second decision and division takes places (fig. 11.4).

Are group conversion movements genuine? Although the group acts as a corporate body, individuals in it make their own decisions, particularly in the second stage of the movement. Consequently, we should speak of "multi-individual decisions." Orlando Costas notes, "The concept of multi-individual decisions gives a sociological orientation to the experience of conversion because it affirms that conversions, which depend on a personal act of faith in Christ, can take place in a group setting, where all the members of a given group (family, clan, tribe, or mutual interest groups) participate in a similar experience with Christ after considering it together and deciding to turn to Christ at the same time" (1974, 128). Such movements remind us that conversion is not just a personal response. It is affected by and in turn affects our social relationships with others.

Do such movements have lasting results? In a classic study, Waskom Pickett examined the consequences of corporate movements in South India (1933). He found that not only were people's lives transformed, but also their decisions were reinforced by their new Christian community. Individuals were not torn out of their social networks. Rather, whole communities were changed. There are problems unique to group transformations, but the overall evaluation has been positive. We must keep in mind that individual conversions do not lead to the passing on of the gospel from generation to generation if they are not incorporated into communities of faith. Christ came to save the church, which is made up of individuals but is more than the sum of them.

If this is the case, are there ways to encourage group decisions? More study is needed, but a few examples can help us think about the matter. In the late nineteenth century, Baptist missionaries in South India sought to baptize whole families. Husbands or wives who converted were not immediately baptized. Rather, they were encouraged to win their spouses and children. In recent years, evangelists in Asia sought to use group dynamics to get villagers to discuss

the gospel. Each night, at the end of the evangelistic meeting, instead of inviting interested individuals to come forward, they announced that everyone
would have to make a decision for or against Christ on the last night of the
street meetings. The people began to discuss their decisions in their families
and with neighbors all week, so their decisions were socially processed and
carefully made. On the last night the invitation was given, and whole families
and groups came together to become followers of Jesus.

Yet another example comes from the Baptists in South India. The missionaries preached in villages for years with little success. When a famine came,
the missionaries were deeply involved in distributing food and medicines and
creating work for the people. Afraid that the people might become "Christians" to get food and work, they placed a moratorium on baptisms. Only
after life returned to normal for a couple years did they resume baptizing
converts. By now the people had had time to talk about the gospel, and the
Dalits responded in great numbers. In three days, 3,536 adults were baptized,
and before the end of the year the total reached 9,606.

Churches that emerge out of group movements are often indigenous in
social organization. They have a strong corporate identity and tend to have a
polity based on their traditional ways of organizing their social systems.[5] In
South India, the leadership of many of these churches is patterned after the
panchayat (council of elders) rather than on elected offices.

Stages in People Movements

Group or multi-individual conversions belong to what A. F. C. Wallace calls
"revitalization movements" (1956). These are movements in which a radical
change takes place in the thinking of a group of people whose old beliefs
no longer provide them with meaningful lives. Some of these movements are
"nativist"—they seek to revive the old faith. Others are "conversionist"—they
call for conversion to a new system of beliefs. Many lead to what Harold
Turner calls new emerging religious movements (1981). History is full of such
revitalization movements. More than six thousand have been reported in Africa alone (Barrett 1968). Thousands of cargo cults and prophetic movements
have arisen in New Guinea and Oceania, and since World War II, hundreds
of new religions have appeared in Japan and the Philippines (Worsley 1968;
McFarland 1967). Turner points out that many of these movements are
messianic or millenarian, the intended or unintended offspring of Christian
missions. For example, the African-, Indian-, and Chinese-initiated churches

---

5. Ironically, even more than technology, modernity today is exporting leadership styles
based on modern management principles. In the church we are increasingly aware of the need
to contextualize the gospel in other cultures, but we are often more willing to contextualize the
gospel than our forms of leadership and church organization. The danger is that we turn planting
churches into a science in which we can engineer growth if we follow the right formula.

range from thoroughly biblical movements indigenous to the local cultures to neopagan syncretistic movements with some Christian meanings and symbols.

Wallace defines five stages through which revitalization movements pass. While each movement is colored by local differences, the basic structure of such movements is often the same. The first stage is *steady state* in which culture and religion provide people with more or less meaningful lives. There are normal personal stresses, but individuals are able to cope with these in culturally accepted ways. The people do not question their belief systems, for these are what they were taught and these meet their needs.

The second stage is *increased individual stress*, often brought about by ecological changes, epidemics, military defeats, political subordination, or the introduction of new ideas from without that cannot be assimilated into the old worldview. Although a culture remains relatively stable and integrated, many of the individuals in it experience high levels of stress to the point of becoming neurotic. The old ways no longer adequately meet people's needs. At this point some people begin to look for alternative solutions to their problems, but doing so only increases their personal stress. They are afraid the new ways will be no better than the old, and that the new will destroy their existing lives. There is anxiety about leaving the security of the old and familiar way of life, however imperfect it is, and striking out on a new and uncertain course.

The third stage is *cultural distortion*. As personal stress mounts, social tensions increase. Conflicts arise between various groups in the society, particularly between those who want change and those who do not. In the end, the sociocultural order itself is threatened. If this process of deterioration is not stopped, the society dies out or is defeated and absorbed by another society.

The fourth step is *revitalization*. During times of high corporate stress, revitalization movements may emerge, many of them religious in nature. They offer new beliefs and ways of coping with life in more satisfactory ways, thus restoring meaning to the people's existence and renewing the culture. Revitalization often begins with a dynamic person, prophet, or leader, who has heard of a new way or who has a vision or insight providing a new explanation of life and its possibilities. Others are converted and join the movement. Opposition and conflict arise between supporters of the old and the new ways, further increasing the social stress. When the movement attracts a significant portion of the population, the final step, *a revitalization of faith and life*, takes place. Personal, social, and cultural stresses are reduced for those in the movement, enabling them to cope with their problems and find meaning in their existence.

Wallace's theory sheds light on the multi-individual conversions that account for much of the expansion of Christianity throughout history. Christians have been most effective in winning people from small, strong communities when they first come into contact with the outside world. These contacts bring about changes in their cultures. The result is high cultural stress and a search for new answers to the people's felt needs. Often these felt needs involve "cargo"—prosperity and well-being. The gospel does speak to matters of health, prosperity, and power, but there is a danger in focusing on these felt needs and not moving on to the heart of the gospel, which deals with deep spiritual needs, such as sin and reconciliation with God, and with holiness, love, and witness. Many revitalization movements, however, end up as political movements or prosperity gospels. We must not forget that although God does care for the well-being of people here and now, these are not the eternal transformations that we need as humans. The other danger is that such movements become millenarian and have little concern for the quality of this life.

Studying people movements helps us understand and assist transformation movements in societies with a strong group orientation. But what about transformation in those that focus on the individual, and have weak group ties, such as in modern cities? So far they have been largely immune to multi-individual conversions. Here the social dynamics of friendships, networks, and the building of small, intimate groups have been more effective. Much study is needed to understand how individuals and communities are transformed in such societies.

Wallace's theory also reminds us that conversion itself is a stressful process. It is easier to stay with old familiar ways, no matter how inadequate they are, than to change. Inviting people to become followers of Jesus is to promise them that the future of their lives will be more joyful and meaningful. For the moment, it is a call to decision, and such major decisions create great anxiety. In our follow-up to conversion experiences, we must be particularly sensitive to the anxieties of those converting to Christ and stand with them in their inner struggles.

We must also realize that new converts often experience "conversion shock." Their initial reaction is often one of euphoria and joy. When this wears off, they begin the difficult task of learning to think and live as Christians. They must learn a new language, behave in new ways, and form new relationships. In short, they must be enculturated into a new culture and socialized into a new community. During this period new converts often face periods of doubt and depression. They question their decision, and some return to their old beliefs. During this time of reevaluation, the support of the Christian community is extraordinarily important. In people movements, converts often form intense, inward-looking groups in which they find most of their fulfillment. These groups often appear to be sects. When individuals convert one by one, however, they often lack strong group support. Only the most committed sustain their new faith outside a supporting community of faith.

It is not enough to seek the conversion of people to Christ. We must emphasize the fact that each following generation in the church must also be converted into a deep living faith. Socially, we bring our children to church and act as if they are Christian. We must be reminded that they need to be transformed by the gospel. We must also reexamine and reaffirm our own conversions, for transformation is not a once-for-all event. We turn to Christ, and we renew our commitment to follow him in every decision we make in our lives. Only when conversion becomes an ongoing process in our lives will there be lasting transformation.

Over time even the conversion process itself runs the risk of becoming routinized. It becomes socially acceptable for young people to make a decision at evangelistic services or to respond around a campfire. Moreover, when some convert out of genuine conviction, their friends may join them. It is important to keep conversions meaningful through careful teaching and discipling.

Finally, Wallace's analysis reminds us that the church itself needs to undergo constant revitalization. Over time religious movements become institutionalized. Even though second-generation converts do not pay the high price their parents paid to become Christians, they are often still deeply influenced by the vitality of their parents' faith. By the third and fourth generations, however, nominalism begins to creep into the church. New Christians often continue traditional religious practices without critically evaluating their validity, and old Christians do not consciously examine the meanings of their religious practices.

It is important that the church itself periodically undergo revitalization movements in which it reexamines its response to the gospel in its particular context and renews its commitment to living in the light of a biblical worldview. Those who have grown up in a Christian tradition and have experienced a conversion in their past need to learn the wonder and cost of conversion from their brothers and sisters in many parts of the world, where those who become Christian pay high prices, even their lives. Only then will we experience the freshness of new life and genuine revival in our churches.

Concluding Comments

The gospel is about transformed lives. When we bear witness to Christ, we invite people to a whole new life, not simply some modifications of their old lives. This transformation is radical and total. It involves changes at all levels of their culture, including their worldviews. It also changes them physically, biologically, psychologically, socially, and spiritually. This is the transformation that God works in them if they follow him.

The gospel is also about us transforming our lives. Paul writes, "Therefore, I urge you, brothers and sisters, in view of God's mercy, to offer your bodies as living sacrifices, holy and pleasing to God—this is your proper worship as rational beings. Do not conform to the pattern of this world, but be transformed by the renewing of your mind. Then you will be able to test and approve what God's will is—his good, pleasing and perfect will" (Rom. 12:1–2 TNIV).

As Christians we live in the world, but we are not to be of the world. We are those transformed by the power of the gospel to show to the world a new worldview, one that brings about eternal salvation and manifests itself in love, joy, peace, gentleness, and witness. We are not called to fight the world or to flee from it. We are to be like salt and yeast, bringing about transformation in the world. One danger is to withdraw and form Christian communities that have no impact on the world. Another is to become so captive to our culture that we lose the gospel. We are to live as a countercultural community and as individuals in the world, exemplifying Christlikeness in our lives as individuals and as communities of Christ's disciples.

We can close our reflections with no better challenge than that given us by George Ladd. "We are a disobedient people. We argue about the definition of worldwide evangelization and we debate the details of eschatology, while we neglect the command of the Word of God to evangelize the world" (1999, 75).

Appendix 1

A Model for Worldview Analysis

SYNCHRONIC	*DIACHRONIC*
WORLD MAPS	**WORLD MYTHS**
• worldview, ethos, cosmology, root metaphors	• metanarrative, cosmogony, root myths
• synchronic: looks at the structure of reality	• diachronic: looks at the cosmic story

1. Cognitive Themes and Counterthemes:
   - *time/space*
   - *person/other*
   - *categories of realities*
   - *causality*
2. Affective Themes and Counterthemes:
   - *mystery/awe, peace/shalom, ecstasy/thrill*
   - *joy, sorrow*
   - *fatalistic, optimistic, pessimistic*
3. Evaluative Themes and Counterthemes:
   - *universalist versus particularist*
   - *ascription versus achievement*
   - *equality versus hierarchy*
   - *individual versus group*
   - *high emotional expression versus emotional control*
   - *other themes and counterthemes*
4. Root Metaphors:
   - *organic, mechanical, abstract*
5. Epistemological Foundations:
   - *naive realism, instrumentalism, critical realism, idealism, etc.*

1. Stories:
   - *cosmic, human, group, personal*
2. Dramatic Themes:
   - *tragedy, comedy, romance*
   - *other themes and counterthemes*
3. Progression:
   - *progression, regression, cyclical*

Appendix 2

A Comparison of American and Indian Worldviews

AMERICAN WORLDVIEW

1. Empiricism Most Americans believe that the physical or natural world around them is real and orderly and that they can experience it with a measure of accuracy by means of their senses. They therefore take the material world seriously. This natural life is seen as important, and comfort and material possessions are regarded as worthy goals for human striving. To a great extent, material goods provide a measure of a person's status and success.

1.1 Absolutes In a real world, there are absolutes. There is a categorical difference between the reality of the natural world and the fantasies created by our minds and between history and myth, fact and fiction, truth and error, right and wrong. People experience reality most accurately when they are awake. Dreams and inner visions are illusions, and those who lose touch with the realities of the external world are considered mentally ill.

INDIAN WORLDVIEW

1. Maya To many Indians, the natural world has no ultimate reality. It is a world of subjective experiences—a transitory, ever-changing creation of our minds. In a chaotic, unpredictable world of experiences, order, meaning, and truth can be found only within oneself. The Ultimate Reality, or Brahman, cannot be perceived by the finite person, confined as one is to the prison of one's mind. A person can gain a glimpse of it only through meditation, introspection, and the deep, innermost experiences of the self.

1.1 Relativism In the world of maya, there are no absolutes—no sharp distinctions between "real" or objective experiences and illusions, between fact and fantasy, between absolute truth and error. Myths of the past merge imperceptibly into histories, which are subjective interpretations of events. Dreams and visions are as much a part of people's experiential world as their "awake" life. Even right and wrong are personal interpretations of moralities that are relative to one's station in life.

AMERICAN WORLDVIEW	INDIAN WORLDVIEW
1.2 Naturalism There is a sharp distinction between the natural and the supernatural world. The natural world is experienced directly through the senses and can be studied by means of the sciences and humanities. Supernatural experiences, on the other hand, are, for all practical purposes, confined to inner feelings, which cannot be empirically tested, or to miracles and visions, which are not seen as common, ordinary experiences and are, therefore, somewhat suspect. Few people, even those who are religious, live with a constant awareness that the world around them is inhabited by spirits that directly influence their everyday experiences. This living in a "natural" world is the basis of Western secularism.	**1.2 Supernaturalism** There is no sharp distinction between natural and supernatural. Gods and spirits are as real in everyday experiences as natural objects. Natural and supernatural explanations are freely interchanged in rationalizing daily occurrences. This blending of the supernatural and natural realms into a single framework lies at the heart of what is sometimes referred to as India's supernatural orientation.
1.3 Linear Time Time, like other dimensions of the world, is linear. It extends along a uniform scale into the future and past without repeating itself. Since people have only one life to live, they must make the most of it: the religious ones by preparing for heaven, the secular ones by enjoying themselves. There is a sense of finality about this life, which must be lived without the benefit of a dress rehearsal, without a practice run.	**1.3 Cyclic Time** Time is a continual rerun of persons and events. The universe repeats itself in an almost unending series of epochs of prosperity and decay, of existence and nonexistence. Individuals are reborn a hundred thousand times on a thousand different levels of life. This transmigration of all things from one life to the next further blurs any distinctions that may appear to be real in this life.
1.4 Order and Immutability The world is seen as consistent and orderly—as operating according to natural laws that apply uniformly over time and space. Changes take place according to predictable processes and then only within certain limits. People do not suddenly and without explanation become demons, nor do lions become humans.	**1.4 Mutability and Unpredictability** Things are not always what they first appear to be. The passing beggar may be a king or a demon; the lion may be a god. In folk tales, animals live and talk in a world that mirrors that of humans. In scriptures, gods and demons frequently enter the world of humans in various forms. Unexplainable changes are constantly taking place on earth. It is the world to which Americans are exposed on TV, in which Clark Kents become Supermen and Shoeshine Boys become Underdogs.

AMERICAN WORLDVIEW	INDIAN WORLDVIEW
1.5 Knowledge There exists a deep faith that the human mind, by its rational processes, can discover knowledge of the order that underlies the universe and that with this knowledge humans can eventually control it for their own benefit. Moreover, knowledge in itself has high value. A person is often judged by his knowledge and intellectual commitment to the right ideological creeds, more than by his behavior in everyday experiences.	**1.5 Wisdom** Humanity's goal is to gain wisdom (*jnana*)—an intuitive understanding of the true nature of reality. Unlike knowledge, which comes by rational analysis and often has little effect on a person's behavior, wisdom comes as an inner light, as a flash of insight, which completely transforms a person's life and relationships to the world. No longer bound by ignorance or attached to this world by desire, he or she is freed to live out this life in deep inner peace and, after death, to be released from the futility of future rebirths. Like a drop of water that falls back into the ocean, so the fragment of reality in humans, the spirit, is reabsorbed and lost in the cosmic Brahman. Release, not self-realization, is the supreme end. The wise realize that in a world of maya, a person's best course of action is nonattachment and noninvolvement.
2. A Particularistic and Categorized World Americans commonly use distinct categories and dichotomies to organize experiences. They classify the world into types of objects, people, and ideas and differentiate between good and bad guys in westerns, success and failure in business, and passing and failing in school. The sciences are elaborate systems for categorizing and relating experiences. For example, many Americans tend to divide living beings into different types of life: supernatural beings, people, animals, and plants. And the distinctions among them are sharp. To worship people as gods is sacrilegious. However, people cannot be killed for food, nor harnessed to a plow, as can the lower animals.	**2. The Unity of All Things** Human experiences are endlessly varied and fragmented, but beneath the diversity of this phenomenal world lies a single essential unity. All things are manifestations of one spirit. The result is that Indians often organize their varied experiences along continuums. Like ladders, these have many rungs but form a single whole. Life is segmented into an infinite variety of beings: gods, demigods, spirits, demons, people, animals, plants, and material objects. But life itself is one. It is easy, therefore, to understand why Hindus refuse to kill animals, such as cows. It also explains why they feel it proper to worship saints, since these, like the gods, are above them in the continuum of life. Characteristically, in music, the total spectrum of sounds is divided into notes, and these into quarter notes and sixteenth notes, until the glide becomes the hallmark of Indian music.

AMERICAN WORLDVIEW

2.1 Equality There are fundamental differences among categories within a single taxonomy or domain, but within each category things are more or less the same and equal: they are of the same kind. In the hierarchy of life, all people belong to the same category, "homo sapiens"; therefore, they are equals. The ideal society is one in which all people have equal opportunities. Every person should have the right to contract and to break relationships and the right to be respected as an autonomous person. Ideally, all people should be converted to the same religious and political point of view and observe the same customs. Integration in the universe is based on homogeneity, not on diversity.

2.2 Individualism The individuality and worth of each person is taken for granted. It is assumed that all people have inalienable rights to "life, liberty, and the pursuit of happiness." Applied to society, the stress on individualism leads to an idealization of freedom. Communism, socialism, and other economic systems that are thought to restrict the individual are rejected in favor of free enterprise and capitalism. Democracy, in which people have the right to choose their rulers, is the ideal form of government. With regard to the individual, the emphasis is on self-realization. On earth, this is expressed in a search for identity and praise for the self-made person, in heaven, in the ultimate self-fulfillment of the individual.

INDIAN WORLDVIEW

2.1 Hierarchy Segments in any continuum are organized on the principle of hierarchy, and hierarchy is both necessary and good. The caste system is only part of a larger social order that extends up through the spirits and down through the worlds of animals and plants. Each person has a unique place in this order. All religions lead to the truth, but some are higher than others. The highest are the paths of wisdom in which the devotee gains insight into the true nature of the universe by means of meditation and asceticism. Below these are the many paths of mental devotion to the god of one's choice, and at the bottom are the paths of ritual duty—of bringing offerings to an image. Values, too, are ranked. The highest are spiritual values of release from transmigration, then the metaphysical ones of wisdom and insight, then the biological ones of health and offspring, and at the bottom, material possessions and power.

2.2 Specialization and Interdependence Segments of a whole are also integrated on the principle of interdependence. Each caste has certain unique skills and specialized functions that are essential for the operation of the society as a whole. Each individual has certain tasks to fulfill within the family. Diversity and cooperation, not uniformity and competition, are the ideals.

AMERICAN WORLDVIEW	INDIAN WORLDVIEW
2.3 Competition In an individualistic world, all forms of life compete for resources and dominance. Therefore, people must be aggressive in their relationship to nature. Humanity "conquers space" and "beats the heat." The allopathic system of medicine is aimed at *killing* germs and *overcoming* disease. In the social order, individuals must compete for status. Their station in life should be determined not by birth but by ability and effort.	**2.3 Patron-Client Relationships** Some people are clearly born to greater rights and responsibilities, others to service. The ideal social relationships are those that combine both the principles of hierarchy and interdependence into hereditary patron-client bonds.
3. Natural and Moral Management By their knowledge of natural and moral laws, people are increasingly able to control their destiny. They and not fate are primarily responsible for the engineering of the future.	**3. Karma or Cosmic Law** In an organic universe, in which each part contributes to the harmonious operation of the whole, all processes are governed by the law of karma. Just as there is no distinction between natural and supernatural worlds, so there is no sharp difference between natural and moral laws. All actions are governed by karma and have both natural and moral consequences.
3.1 Science and Technology If one wants to understand the culture of the United States, one must look at its universal education in the natural sciences, its universities, technological institutes, and research laboratories, and its industrial complexes. Americans' commitment to science and technology goes beyond mere gadgeteering. They know that science grows even though individuals may have no personal knowledge of any of its fundamental principles, and they have faith that it can provide the grounds on which can be built a secure way of life for people.	**3.1 Samsara or Pilgrimage** The condition of each life in people's spiritual pilgrimages is determined by the actions, good or bad, of their previous lives. The fruits of one's actions are not always seen in this life. Transmigration is not fatalistic. People's present positions and the things that happen to them are determined by past deeds. But by their response to life now, they are shaping their future destinies.

AMERICAN WORLDVIEW	INDIAN WORLDVIEW

3.2 Uniform Morality and Justice People are responsible for building a society based on "self-evident" principles, such as love, equality, freedom, respect for the rights of others, and on a general humanitarian compassion for one's fellow humans. These principles apply equally to all and are the basis for legal systems. Thus, for example, war criminals are held accountable not only for the orders of their superiors or the laws of their countries, but also to universal principles of humane conduct during a conflict. The primary concern of law and morality is to mete out justice. Good must be rewarded and evil punished in this lifetime. Beyond this life, the consequence of one's actions are expressed in terms of heaven and hell.

3.2 Relative Morality Right and wrong depend for people on their place in the universal and social orders. Consequently, there is no absolute morality. More is expected of those higher in the spiritual and caste hierarchy in terms of orthodoxy and ritual practice. "Right" lies in conformity to the cosmic order. People who live according to their social position and in harmony with the universe acquire the spiritual force of truth, which is moral and nonviolent. This force (*satyagraha*) is ultimately superior to physical force in the establishment of a harmonious society. In a system of relative ethics, the aim of law is not justice defined in some absolute terms but the restoration of harmony in society. Actions cannot be divided into the good and the evil, and there is no sharp difference between offender and offended. Nor is it the task of people to punish actions whose causes they can never fully understand. Final justice is meted out by the cosmic law of karma.

3.3 Missionary Those who have knowledge and the truth, whether this is scientific or religious, have a moral obligation to share it with the rest of the world. All over the world, American experts are helping people of other nations to improve their educational systems, their agricultural production, their military forces, their industrial growth, and their religious destinies.

3.3 Inclusivism and Tolerance Cultural pluralism and ethnic relativism are inclusive—they accept a diversity of thought and action in the same world without demanding conformity to a single standard. People pride themselves on their own unique cultures. Individuals can simultaneously follow several apparently contradictory courses of action without inconsistency. Closely tied to inclusivism is a spirit of tolerance, in which each must respect the cultural differences of others and not seek to convert them to his or her own way of life.

AMERICAN WORLDVIEW	INDIAN WORLDVIEW
4. Self-reliance As Francis Hsu has pointed out (1961, 217), the dominant value directing everyday American behavior is self-reliance. There are few fears as great as those of dependence on others and running out of money. This value has its roots in the stress of individualism, freedom, and management.	**4. Dharma or Functional Responsibility** The universe and human society are organic wholes in which each part has a unique function to fill. Only as each caste and each individual fulfills their responsibility or duty (dharma) can the whole operate smoothly. It is wrong to abandon one's prescribed role and seek another. People should live on the level at which they were born, and by fitting themselves dispassionately into the cosmic order, fulfill the task to which they were destined.
4.1 Expanding Good There has been, until recently, a belief that the world of all that is good is expanding, that there are new frontiers for people to conquer. As the geographic limits of the earth were explored, people turned their attention to the expansion of knowledge, technology, and gross national products in order to create their utopia of self-realization. People compete for what is good, but one person's advance need not come at the expense of another's fall. New opportunities are there for those who seek them.	**4.1 Limited Good** There exists only a limited amount of all the desired things of life, such as wealth, land, power, status, friendship, and love, and there is no direct way to increase the quantities available for all to use (Foster 1965). Therefore, one individual's gain or advancement can come only at the expense of others. Since it is not always clear who is losing, any significant attempt by some people to improve their social or economic situation is seen as a threat to all individuals, to the community as a whole.
4.2 Achievement Orientation Personal achievement, not illustrious background, is the measure of an individual's worth and social position. Hard work, careful planning, efficiency, and saving of time and effort are intrinsically good. In a predictable world, the individual is ultimately responsible for failure. For example, people may not be able to prevent all disasters, such as accidents, illness, or death, but they can minimize their harm by means of insurance and a will. It is important, therefore, to fix blame when anything goes wrong, and the consequence of blame is guilt. Achievement is closely tied to social mobility. People should be allowed to rise to their levels of ability and not be tied down by their kinsmen or their past. The results, in part, are shallow social and geographical roots and insecurity.	**4.2 Ascription Orientation** Security and meaning are found in the groups to which one belongs and in the relationships one has with others, rather than in the material possessions one acquires. The building of relationships, particularly those to which one is born, is of greatest importance, for they are a measure of an individual's status and power. Because the world is not fully predictable, failure leads not so much to blame and self-accusation as to a sense of frustration. This tension is often reduced by dropping out of the situation and turning inward or by anger at the situation and turning to violence.

AMERICAN WORLDVIEW	INDIAN WORLDVIEW
4.3 Associational Groups Social groups above the level of the family are based primarily on voluntary association or contractual relationships. Status in the middle-class rests primarily in the groups a person can join. Participation in a group, however, demands involved commitment to a program and conformity to its practices. Groups must guard themselves by ostracizing the nonconformists and by segregating themselves from those inferior fellow humans who might encroach upon them from below.	**4.3 Jatis and Castes** People's primary ties are to their *jati*, or caste, to those who are the same kind of people. Because membership is by birth, a great deal of individual variation can be permitted by the members. However, if one defies the dictates of the caste, the ultimate sanction is ostracism—to be cut off from the group.
4.4 Success and Progress Success and progress are unquestionably good. They are measured by the ability to produce results, such as expanding programs or growing institutions, and making a profit. The practical test for any course of action is pragmatism: Does it get results? Security for the individual comes largely through personal success. Failure leads to loneliness and a shameful dependence on others. Progress is tied to the American dream, a basic optimism, an orientation toward the future, and a stress on youth. Success is equated with superiority and right, and since Western cultures have obviously succeeded, they are superior. This sense of cultural superiority is particularly obvious in American relationships with other cultures.	**4.4 Moksha** The goal of life is not self-realization but release from the hardships of life (*moksha*). The cultural hero is the person of wisdom and insight who can rise above the troubles of this passing life and understand the significance of all things.

Appendix 3

Modern/Postmodern Shift

Modernity	Postmodernity	Globalism
Positivism • critical detachment	Instrumentalism/Idealism • critical detachment	Critical Realism • begin with faith and foundations
Reason and algorithmic logic • reason divorced from feelings and values • rejects intuition • detached, disinterested, no power play	Intuition and affectivity affirmed • vested interest, power based • hermeneutics of suspicion	Rational + affective = evaluative • reason linked to feelings, morals • algorithmic logic embedded in wisdom
Individual scholar • detached lone scholar • group dynamics contaminates the findings	Corporate hermeneutics oppressive • corporate captivity • corporate oppression	Corporate hermeneutics a strength • corrects for personal and cultural biases
Grand unified theory and grand narrative • photographic view of knowledge	No grand narrative: • collage view of knowledge	Many narratives make a metanarrative • montage view of knowledge
Formal symbols • discursive, diadic $F=O$	Metaphorical symbols • diadic $F=S$	Tropes and referential symbols • discursive and non-discursive triadic symbols, $O=F=S$
Science is well-founded knowledge • positivism, objectivism	Science is undetermined • subjectivism	Science is approximate but true • subjective–objectivism

Modernity	Postmodernity	Globalism
Stresses truth • objective, ahistorical, and acultural	Stresses experience and love • truths are personal and relative	Stresses truth in love • truths are approximations of Truth
Other is primitive, aboriginal, traditional • science is in a privileged position • all will become like us	Other is equal to us • there is no privileged position • all preserve their distinctiveness	Other is us at a deeper level • all share a common humanity • all celebrate differences but have an underlying unity

A COMPARISON OF MODERN AND GLOBAL WORLDVIEWS

Modern	Global
Materialistic Naturalism • mechanistic, deterministic • bottom up • algorithmic logic, machine logic, computer calculators • order, bounded sets • general revelation	Spiritual/Material Intertwined • live in harmony with nature • wisdom
Segmented • supernatural/natural dualism • specialized and segmented lives	Holism • spirits and humans interact
Grand Unified Theory • reductionist • uniformity • arrogance, acultural, ahistorical	Complementarity • nonreductionist • metasystemic framework • hermeneutics of suspicion, in culture, historical context
Detached, Individual Human Centered • divorced from emotions and values • human centered • skepticism • reason based	Group Hermeneutics • community check on biases • theocentric • combine cognition, affectivity, valuations
Hierarchy • control, line and staff organization • evolution	Equality • networking, partnership, mutuality • divine history

References Cited

Anderson, Benedict. 1983. *Imagined Communities: Reflections on the Origin and Spread of Nationalism*. Rev. ed. London: Verso.

Anderson, Walter. 1990. *Reality Isn't What It Used to Be: Theatrical Politics, Read-to-Wear Religion, Global Myths, Primitive Chic, and Other Wonders of the Postmodern World*. San Francisco: HarperSanFrancisco.

Antoine, Robert. 1975. *Rama and the Bards: Epic Memory in the Ramayana*. Calcutta: Thompson.

Arnold, Dean. 2005. Foreword to *The Fall of Patriarchy: Its Broken Legacy Judged by Jesus and the Apostolic House Church Communities*. Ed. Dell Birkey. Tucson: Fenestra Books.

Baker, Mark B. 1999. *Religious No More: Building Communities of Grace and Freedom*. Downers Grove, IL: InterVarsity.

Baran, Zeyno. 2005. "Fighting the War of Ideas." *Foreign Affairs* 84 (November–December): 68–78.

Barbour, Ian G. 1974. *Myths, Models and Paradigms: A Comparative Study in Science and Religion*. San Francisco: Harper.

Barnard, Alan. 2000. *History and Theory in Anthropology*. Cambridge: Cambridge University Press.

Barrett, David. 1968. *Schism and Renewal in Africa: An Analysis of Six Thousand Contemporary Religious Movements*. Nairobi: Oxford University Press.

Baudrillard, J. 1992. "The Anorexic Ruins?" In *Looking Back on the End of the World*, ed. D. Kamper and C. Wulf, 29–45. New York: Semiotext.

Bauman, Zygmunt. 1991. *Modernity and Ambivalence*. Cambridge: Polity Press.

Becker, Ernst. 1973. *The Denial of Death*. New York: Free Press.

Begbie, Jeremy. 1992. "The Gospel, the Arts and Our Culture." In *The Gospel and Contemporary Culture*, ed. Hugh Montefiore, 58–83. New York: Mowbray.

Behe, Michael. 2005. "Scientific Orthodoxies." *First Things* 154 (December): 15–20.

Bellah, Robert. 1967. "Civil Religion in America." *Journal of the American Academy of Arts and Sciences* 96: 1–21.

Bellah, Robert, and Phillip Hammond. 1980. *Varieties of Civil Religion*. San Francisco: Harper and Row.

Bellah, Robert, et al. 1985. *Habits of the Heart: Individualism and Commitment in America*. Berkeley: University of California Press.

Benedict, Ruth. 1934. *Patterns of Culture*. New York: Houghton Mifflin.

Berger, Peter L. 1967. *The Sacred Canopy: Elements of a Sociological Theory of Religion*. Garden City, NY: Doubleday.

———. 1974. *Pyramids of Sacrifice: Political Ethics and Social Change*. New York: Basic Books.

Berger, Peter L., Brigitte Berger, and Hansfried Kellner. 1973. *The Homeless Mind: Modernization and Consciousness*. New York: Random House.

Berger, Peter L., and Samuel P. Huntington, eds. 2002. *Many Globalizations: Cultural Diversity in the Contemporary World*. New York: Oxford University Press.

Berger, Peter L., and Thomas Luckmann. 1967. *The Social Construction of Reality*. Garden City, NY: Anchor Books.

Berlin, Brent, and Paul Kay. 1969. *Basic Color Terms: Their Universality and Evolution*. Berkeley: University of California Press.

Bernstein, Ann. 2002. "Globalization, Culture, and Development: Can South Africa Be More than an Offshoot of the West?" In *Many Globalizations: Cultural Diversity in the Contemporary World*, ed. Peter L. Berger and Samuel P. Huntington, 185–249. New York: Oxford University Press.

Bertalanffy, Ludwig von. 1968. *General Systems Theory: Foundations, Development, Applications*. New York: Braziller.

———. 1981. *A Systems View of Man*. Ed. Paul A. LaViolette. Boulder, CO: Westview Press.

Best, Steven, and Douglas Kellner. 1991. *Postmodern Theory: Critical Interrogations*. New York: Guilford Press.

Bloom, Allan. 1987. *The Closing of the American Mind*. New York: Simon & Schuster.

Bonk, Jonathan. 1991. *Missions and Money: Affluence as a Western Missionary Problem*. Maryknoll, NY: Orbis Books.

Bosch, David J. 1991. *Transforming Mission: Paradigm Shifts in Theology of Mission*. Maryknoll, NY: Orbis Books.

Brody, Howard, and David S. Sobel. 1979. "A Systems View of Health and Disease." In *Ways of Health*, ed. David S. Sobel, 1–14. New York: Harcourt, Brace, Jovanovich.

Brown, Richard H. 1994. "Reconstructing Social Theory after the Postmodern Critique." In *After Postmodernism: Reconstructing Ideology Critique*, ed. Herbert W. Simons and Michael Billig, 12–37. London: Sage.

Burtt, E. A. 1954. *The Metaphysical Foundations of Modern Science*. Garden City, NY: Doubleday Anchor Books.

Bury, J. B. 1932. *The Idea of Progress: An Inquiry into Its Growth and Origin*. New York: Dover.

Camery-Hoggatt, Jerry. 2006. "God in the Plot: Storytelling and the Many-Sided Truth of the Christian Faith." *Christian Scholar's Review* 35 (4): 451–69.

Chesterton, G. K. 1994. *What's Wrong With the World*. San Francisco: Ignatius. (Orig. pub. 1910.)

Chomsky, Noam. 1986. *Knowledge of Language: Its Nature, Origin, and Use*. New York: Praeger.

Costas, Orlando. 1974. *The Church and Its Mission: A Shattering Critique from the Third World*. Wheaton: Tyndale.

Cox, Harvey. 1966. *The Secular City: A Celebration of Its Liberties and an Invitation to Its Discipline*. New York: Macmillan.

Crick, Francis. 1994. *The Astonishing Hypothesis: The Scientific Search for the Soul*. New York: Scribners.

Crosby, Alfred W. 1997. *The Measure of Reality: Quantification and Western Society, 1250–1600*. Cambridge: Cambridge University Press.

Danquah, J. B. 1965. *The Akan Doctrine of God*. London: Frank Case.

Das, Surya. 1999. *Awakening to the Sacred: Creating a Spiritual Life from Scratch*. New York: Broadway Books.

De Bary, William Theodore, et al., eds. 1958. *Sources of Indian Tradition*. New York: Columbia University Press.

Dellamora, Richard, ed. 1995. *Postmodern Apocalypse: Theory and Cultural Practice at the End*. Philadelphia: University of Pennsylvania Press.

Derrida, Jacques. 1984. "Of an Apocalyptic Tone Recently Adopted in Philosophy." Trans. John Leavey Jr. *Oxford Literary Review* 6 (2): 3–37.

Descartes, René. 1991. *The Philosophical Writings of Descartes*. Ed. John Cottingham, Robert Stoothoff, and Dugald Murdoch. Vol. 3: *The Correspondence*. Cambridge: Cambridge University Press.

Dijksterhuis, E. J. 1986. *The Mechanization of the World Picture: Pythagoras to Newton*. Trans. C. Dikshoorn. Princeton, NJ: Princeton University Press.

Douglas, Mary. 1954. "The Lele of Kasai." In *African Worlds: Studies in the Cosmological Ideas and Social Values of African Peoples*, ed. Daryll Forde, 1–26. London: Oxford University Press.

———. 1966. *Purity and Danger: An Analysis of the Concepts of Pollution and Taboo*. London: Routledge and Kegan Paul.

———. 1969. *Natural Symbols: Explorations in Cosmology*. London: Routledge and Kegan Paul.

Dundes, Alan, ed. 1965. *The Study of Folklore*. Englewood Cliffs, NJ: Prentice-Hall.

Eliade, Mircea. 1975. *Myths, Dreams and Mysteries: The Encounter between Contemporary Faiths and Archaic Realities*. New York: Harper and Row.

Ellul, Jacques. 1964. *The Technological Society*. New York: Random House.

———. 1988. *Anarchy and Christianity*. Grand Rapids: Eerdmans.

Evans-Pritchard, E. E. 1940. *The Nuer: A Description of the Modes of Livelihood and Political Institutions of a Nilotic People.* Oxford: Clarendon Press.

Febvre, L., and H. J. Martin. 1984. *The Coming of the Book: The Impact of Printing, 1450–1800.* Trans. David Gerard. London: Verso Books.

Ferguson, James. 2002. "Global Disconnect: Abjection and the Aftermath of Modernity." In *The Anthropology of Globalization: A Reader*, ed. Jonathan Inda and Renato Rosaldo, 136–53. Oxford: Blackwell.

Finger, Thomas N. 1985. *Christian Theology: An Eschatological Approach.* Nashville: Thomas Nelson.

Fix, Andrew C. 1991. *Prophecy and Reason: The Dutch Collegiants in the Early Enlightenment.* Princeton, NJ: Princeton University Press.

Forde, Daryll, ed. 1954. *African Worlds: Studies in the Cosmological Ideas and Social Values of African Peoples.* London: Oxford University Press.

Foster, George M. 1965. "Peasant Society and the Image of the Limited Good." *American Anthropologist* 67: 293–315.

Foucault, Michel. 1980. *Power/Knowledge: Select Interviews and Other Writings, 1972–1977.* Trans. C. Gordon, L. Marshall, J. Mepham, and K. Soper. New York: Pantheon.

Fox, Richard W., and Jackson Lears. 1983. *The Culture of Consumption: Critical Essays in American History, 1860–1960.* New York: Pantheon.

Frazer, Sir James G. 1922. *The Golden Bough: A Study of Magic and Religion.* Abridged ed. London: Macmillan.

Friedman, Jonathan. 1994. *Cultural Identities and Global Processes.* London: Sage.

Fukuyama, Francis. 1989. "The End of History?" *National Interest* 16: 3–19.

Geertz, Clifford. 1973. *The Interpretation of Cultures: Selected Essays by Clifford Geertz.* New York: Basic Books.

———. 1983. *Local Knowledge: Further Essays in Interpretive Anthropology.* New York: Basic Books.

Gellner, Ernest. 1992. *Postmodernism, Reason and Religion.* London: Routledge and Kegan Paul.

Gergen, Kenneth J. 1994. "The Limits of Pure Critique." In *After Postmodernism: Reconstructing Ideology Critique*, ed. Herbert W. Simons and Michael Billig, 58–78. London: Sage.

Giddens, Anthony. 1990. *The Consequences of Modernity.* Stanford, CA: Stanford University Press.

Goody, Jack. 1987. *The Interface between the Written and the Oral.* Cambridge: Cambridge University Press.

Greider, William. 2003. *The Soul of Capitalism.* New York: Simon & Schuster.

Grint, Keith. 1997. *Fuzzy Management: Contemporary Ideas and Practices at Work.* Oxford: Oxford University Press.

Gross, Joan, David McMurray, and Ted Swedenburg. 2002. "Arab Noise and Ramadan Nights: *Rai*, Rap, and Franco-Maghrebi Identities." In *The Anthropology* of *Globalization: A Reader*, ed. Jonathan Inda and Renato Rosaldo, 198–230. Oxford: Blackwell.

Guinness, Os. 1994a. "Mission Modernity: Seven Checkpoints on Mission in the Modern World." In *Faith and Modernity*, ed. Phillip Sampson, Vinay Samuel, and Chris Sugden, 322–52. Oxford: Regnum Lynx.

———. 1994b. *Fit Bodies, Fat Minds: Why Evangelicals Don't Think and What to Do about It*. Grand Rapids: Baker.

Hall, Edward. 1959. *Silent Language*. Garden City, NY: Doubleday.

———. 1977. *Beyond Culture*. Garden City, NY: Anchor Books.

———. 1983. *Hidden Differences: How to Communicate with the Germans*. Studies in International Communication. Hamburg: Stern.

Harvey, David. 1990. *The Condition of Postmodernity: An Enquiry into the Origins of Culture Change*. Cambridge, MA: Blackwell.

Hauerwas, Stanley, and W. H. Willimon. 1989. *Resident Aliens: Life in the Christian Colony*. Nashville: Abingdon Press.

Hawking, Stephen. 1988. *A Brief History of Time: From the Big Bang to the Black Hole*. New York: Bantam Books.

Herzfeld, Michael. 2001. *Anthropology: Theoretical Practice in Culture and Society*. Malden, MA: UNESCO.

Hiebert, Paul. 1971. *Konduru: Structure and Integration in a South Indian Village*. Minneapolis: University of Minnesota Press.

———. 1989. "Form and Meaning in the Contextualization of the Gospel." In *The Word Among Us: Contextualizing Theology for Mission Today*, ed. Dean S. Gilliland, 101–20. Dallas: Word.

———. 1994. *Anthropological Reflections on Missiological Issues*. Grand Rapids: Baker Academic.

———. 1999. *Missiological Implications of Epistemological Shifts*. Harrisburg, PA: Trinity Press International.

———. 2006. "The Missionary as Mediator of Global Theologizing." In *Globalizing Theology: Belief and Practice in an Era of World Christianity*, ed. Craig Ott and Harold A. Netland, 288–308. Grand Rapids: Baker Academic.

Hiebert, Paul G., R. Daniel Shaw, and Tite Tiénou. 1999. *Understanding Folk Religion: Christian Response to Popular Religious Beliefs and Practices*. Grand Rapids: Baker Academic.

Hobsbawm, E. J. 1959. *Primitive Rebels: Studies in Archaic Forms of Social Movement in the Nineteenth and Twentieth Centuries*. Manchester, UK: Manchester University Press.

Hoebel, E. Adamson. 1954. *The Law of Primitive Man: A Study of Comparative Legal Dynamics*. Cambridge, MA: Harvard University Press.

Hoekema, Anthony A. 1986. *Created in God's Image*. New York: McGraw Hill.

Hofstede, Geert H. 1994. *Cultures and Organizations: Software of the Mind*. London: HarperCollins.

Horton, Robin. 1970. "African Traditional Thought and Western Science." In *Rationality*, ed. Bryan R. Wilson, 131–71. New York: Harper Torchbooks.

Howard, Thomas Albert. 2006. "America in the European Mind." *First Things* 167 (November): 11–14.

Hsiao, Hsin-Huang Michael. 2002. "Coexistence and Synthesis: Cultural Globalization and Localization in Contemporary Taiwan." In *Many Globalizations*, ed. Peter L. Berger and Samuel P. Huntington, 48–67. New York: Oxford University Press.

Hsu, Francis. 1961. "American Core Values and National Character." In *Psychological Anthropology: Approaches to Culture and Personality*, ed. Francis Hsu, 209–30. Homewood, IL: The Dorsey Press.

———. 1963. *Clan, Caste, and Club*. New York: D. Van Nostrand.

Huntington, Samuel P. 1996. *The Clash of Civilizations and the Remaking of World Order*. New York: Simon & Schuster.

Hutcheon, Linda. 1980. *A Poetics of Postmodernism*. New York: Routledge.

Inda, Jonathan, and Renato Rosaldo, eds. 2002. *The Anthropology of Globalization: A Reader*. Oxford: Blackwell.

Johnson, Phillip E. 1995. *Reason in the Balance: The Case against Naturalism in Science, Law and Education*. Downers Grove, IL: InterVarsity.

Jones, Alwyn. 1991. *Logic and Knowledge Representation*. London: Pitman.

Jones, E. Stanley. 1957. *Christian Maturity*. Nashville: Abingdon Press.

———. 1972. *The Unchanging Person and the Unshakable Kingdom*. Nashville: Abingdon Press.

Kant, Immanuel. 1959. *Foundations of the Metaphysics of Morals and What Is Enlightenment?* Indianapolis: Bobbs Merrill.

Kasdorf, Hans. 1980. *Christian Conversion in Context*. Scottdale, PA: Herald Press.

Kavanaugh, James F. 1981. *Following Christ in a Consumer Society: The Spirituality of Cultural Resistance*. Maryknoll, NY: Orbis Books.

Kearney, Michael. 1984. *World View*. Novato, CA: Chandler and Sharp.

Kepler, Johannes. 1858. *Joannis Kepler, Astronomi Opera Omnia*. Ed. Ch. Frisch, 8 vols. Frankfurt: Heyder & Zimmer. Quoted in Burtt 1954, 68.

Kluckhohn, Clyde. 1965. "Recurrent Themes in Myths and Myth Making." In *The Study of Folklore*, ed. Alan Dundes, 158–68. Englewood Cliffs, NJ: Prentice-Hall.

Koester, Craig R. 2005. "Revelation and the *Left Behind* Novels." *Words and World: Theology for Christian Ministry* 25 (Summer): 274–82.

Kraft, Charles H. 1979. *Christianity in Culture: A Study in Dynamic Biblical Theologizing in Cross-Cultural Perspectives*. Maryknoll, NY: Orbis Books.

Kraus, C. Norman. 1974. *The Community of the Spirit*. Grand Rapids: Eerdmans.

———. 1979. *The Authentic Witness: Credibility and Authority*. Grand Rapids: Eerdmans.

Kroeber, A. L. 1948. *Anthropology*. Rev. ed. New York: Harcourt Brace Jovanovich.

Kuhn, Thomas S. 1970. *The Structure of Scientific Revolutions*. 2nd ed. Chicago: University of Chicago Press.

Ladd, George. 1999. "The Gospel of the Kingdom." In *Perspectives on the World Christian Movement*, ed. Ralph D. Winter and Steven C. Hawthorne, 3rd ed., 64–77. Pasadena, CA: William Carey Library.

Larson, Edward J., and Larry Witham. 1998. "Leading Scientists Still Reject God." *Nature* 394 (6691): 313.

Lash, Nicholas. 1996. *The Beginning and the End of "Religion."* Cambridge: Cambridge University Press.

Laudan, Larry. 1977. *Progress and Its Problems: Towards a Theory of Scientific Growth.* Berkeley: University of California Press.

———. 1996. *Beyond Positivism and Relativism: Theory, Method, and Evidence.* Boulder, CO: Westview Press.

Lausanne Committee for World Evangelism. 1980. *The Thailand Report on Secularists: Report of the Consultation of World Evangelization Mini-Consultation on Reaching Secularists.* Wheaton: Lausanne Committee for World Evangelism.

Levi, Edward H. 1949. *An Introduction to Legal Reasoning.* Chicago: University of Chicago Press.

Levi-Strauss, Claude. 1978. *Myth and Meaning: Cracking the Code of Culture.* Toronto: University of Toronto Press.

———. 1984. *Anthropology and Myth.* Oxford: Basil Blackwell.

Lewellen, Ted C. 2002. *The Anthropology of Globalization.* Westport, CT: Bergin and Garvey.

Lewis, C. S. 1960. *A Preface to Paradise Lost.* London: Oxford University Press.

Linder, Robert, and Richard Pirard. 1978. *Twilight of the Saints: Biblical Christianity and Civil Religion in America.* Downers Grove, IL: InterVarsity.

Little, Kenneth. 1954. "The Mende in Sierra Leone." In *African Worlds: Studies in the Cosmological Ideas and Social Values of African Peoples*, ed. Daryll Forde, 111–37. London: Oxford University Press.

Lovejoy, Arthur. 1936. *The Great Chain of Being: A Study of the History of an Idea.* Cambridge, MA: Harvard University Press.

Luriia, A. R. 1976. *Cognitive Development, Its Cultural and Social Foundations.* Trans. M. Lopez-Morillas and I. Solotaroof. Cambridge, MA: Harvard University Press.

Lyotard, Jean-François. 1984. *The Postmodern Condition.* Minneapolis: University of Minnesota Press.

MacMaster, Eve. 2006. "It's Not about the Fish: Reflections on the Book of Jonah." *The Mennonite* (September 5): 12–14.

Malik, Charles. 1987. *A Christian Critique of the University.* Waterloo, ON: North Waterloo Academic Press.

Malinowski, Bronislaw. 1922. *Argonauts of the Western Pacific: An Account of Native Enterprise and Adventure in the Archipelagoes of Melanesian New Guinea.* London: Routledge and Sons.

———. 1926. *Myth in Primitive Psychology.* Westport, CT: Negro Universities Press.

Marshall, Christopher D. 2001. *Beyond Retribution: A New Testament Vision for Justice, Crime, and Punishment*. Grand Rapids: Eerdmans.

Masterman, Margaret. 1970. "The Nature of a Paradigm." In *Criticism and the Growth of Knowledge*, ed. Imre Lakatos and Alan Musgrave, 59–89. Cambridge: Cambridge University Press.

May, Rollo. 1991. *The Cry for Myth*. New York: Dell.

McFarland, H. Neill. 1967. *The Rush Hour of the Gods: A Study of New Religious Movements in Japan*. New York: Macmillan.

McGrath, Alister. 1996. *A Passion for Truth: The Intellectual Coherence of Evangelicalism*. Downers Grove, IL: InterVarsity.

McNeill, Donald, Douglas Morrison, and Henri Nouwen. 1982. *Compassion: A Reflection on the Christian Life*. Garden City, NY: Doubleday.

Meade, Dale R. 2005. "The Meaning of Life as Seen through the Window of Death Rituals Practiced within Colombian Folk Religion." PhD diss., Trinity International University, Deerfield, IL.

Mencken, H. L. 2003. *The Philosophy of Friedrich Nietzsche*. Tucson: Sea Sharp Press. (Orig. pub. 1908.)

Meneses, Eloise Hiebert. 1997. "No Other Foundations: Personal Commitment for the Christian Anthropologist." Unpublished manuscript.

Mezirow, Jack. 1978. "Perspective Transformation." *Adult Education* 28 (2): 100–110.

———. 1991. *Transformative Dimensions of Adult Learning*. San Francisco: Jossey-Bass.

Mitford, Jessica. 1963. *The American Way of Death*. Greenwich, CT: Fawcett Crest.

Montefiore, Hugh. 1992. Introduction to *The Gospel in Contemporary Culture*. Ed. Hugh Montefiore. New York: Mowbray.

Moon, Stephen. 1998. "A Hermeneutical Model of Urban Religious Symbols: The Case of Konya, Turkey." PhD diss., Trinity Evangelical Divinity School, Deerfield, IL.

Moore, Charles A., ed. 1967. *The Indian Mind: Essentials of Indian Philosophy and Culture*. Honolulu: University of Hawaii Press.

Mumford, Lewis. 1934. *Technics and Civilization*. New York: Harcourt, Brace and World.

Naugle, David K. 2002. *Worldview: The History of a Concept*. Grand Rapids: Eerdmans.

Neill, Stephen. 1960. *Christian Holiness*. The Carnahan Lectures for 1958. London: Lutterworth Press.

Netland, Harold. 1991. *Dissonant Voices: Religious Pluralism and the Question of Truth*. Grand Rapids: Eerdmans.

Neuhaus, Richard John. 2000. *Death on a Friday Afternoon: Meditations on the Last Words of Jesus from the Cross*. New York: Basic Books.

———. 2005. "Our American Babylon." *First Things* 158 (December): 23–28.

Newbigin, Lesslie. 1942. *What Is the Gospel?* SCM Study Series 6. Madras: Christian Literature Society.

———. 1954. "Why Study the Old Testament?" *National Christian Review* 74: 71–76.

———. 1963. *The Relevance of Trinitarian Doctrine for Today's Mission*. Richmond: John Knox Press.

———. 1966. *Honest Religion for Secular Man*. Philadelphia: Westminster Press.

———. 1976. "Bible Study on Romans." Bible study presented at the conference "Church in the Inner City," Birmingham, September.

———. 1980. *Your Kingdom Come: Reflections on the Theme of the Melbourne Conference on World Mission and Evangelism 1980*. Leeds, UK: John Paul the Preacher's Press.

———. 1989. *The Gospel in a Pluralist Society*. London: SPCK.

———. 1991. *Truth to Tell*. Grand Rapids: Eerdmans.

———. 1992. "The End of History." *The Gospel and Our Culture* 13: 1–2.

———. 1993. "The Kingdom of God and Our Hopes for the Future." In *Kingdom of God and Human Society*, ed. R. Barbour, 1–12. Edinburgh: T & T Clark.

———. 1995. *Proper Confidence: Faith, Doubt, and Certainty in Christian Discipleship*. Grand Rapids: Eerdmans.

———. 1998. *The Household of God: Lectures on the Nature of the Church*. Carlisle, UK: Paternoster Press.

———. 2003. "The Kingdom of God and the Idea of Progress." In *Signs amid the Rubble: The Purposes of God in Human History*, ed. G. Wainwright, 1–55. Grand Rapids: Eerdmans.

Nott, Kathleen. 1971. *Philosophy and Human Nature*. New York: New York University Press.

Oden, Thomas. 1992. *Agenda for Theology: After Modernity What?* Grand Rapids: Zondervan.

Ong, Walter J. 1969. "World as View and World as Event." *American Anthropologist* 71: 634–47.

Opler, Morris E. 1945. "Themes as Dynamic Forces in Culture." *American Journal of Sociology* 51: 198–206.

Palmer, Parker J. 1983. *To Know as We Are Known: A Spirituality of Education*. San Francisco: Harper and Row.

———. 1993. *To Know as We Are Known: Education as a Spiritual Journey*. San Francisco: HarperSanFrancisco.

Parsons, Talcott, and Edward Shils, eds. 1952. *Toward a General Theory of Action*. Cambridge, MA: Harvard University Press.

Peirce, Charles S. 1955. *Philosophical Writings of Peirce*. Ed. J. Buchler. New York: Dover. (Orig. pub. 1940.)

———. 1958. *Charles S. Peirce: Selected Writings*. New York: Dover.

Pepper, Stephen. 1942. *World Hypotheses*. Berkeley: University of California Press.

Peterson, Eugene H. 1988. *Reversed Thunder: The Revelation of John and the Praying Imagination*. San Francisco: Harper and Row.

————. 1997. *Leap Over a Wall: Earthly Spirituality for Everyday Christians.* San Francisco: HarperSanFrancisco.

Piaget, Jean. 1970. *Structuralism.* New York: Basic Books.

Pickett, J. Waskom. 1933. *Christian Mass Movements in India: A Study with Recommendations.* New York: Abingdon.

Pike, Eunice V. 1980. "The Concept of Limited Good and the Spread of the Gospel." *Missiology: An International Review* 8 (October): 449–54.

Polanyi, Michael. 1962. *Personal Knowledge: Towards a Post-Critical Philosophy.* Chicago: University of Chicago Press.

Postman, Neil. 1985. *Amusing Ourselves to Death: Public Discourse in the Age of Show Business.* New York: Penguin Books.

Rad, Gerhard von. 1962. *Old Testament Theology.* 2 vols. London: SCM.

Radcliffe-Brown, A. R. 1958. *Method in Social Anthropology.* Ed. M. N. Srinivas. Chicago: University of Chicago Press.

Rader, William. 1978. *The Church and Racial Hostility: A History of Interpretation of Ephesians 2:11–12.* Tübingen: Mohr.

Radin, Paul. 1927. *Primitive Man as Philosopher.* New York: Appleton.

Ramachandra, Vinoth. 1996. *Gods That Fail: Modern Idolatry and Christian Mission.* Carlisle, UK: Paternoster Press.

————. 1999. *Faiths in Conflict? Christian Integrity in a Multicultural World.* Secunderabad, India: OM Books.

Rao, Raja. 1967. *Kanthapura.* Oxford: Oxford University Press.

Rapley, John. 2006. "The New Middle Ages." *Foreign Affairs* 85 (May–June): 95–104.

Redfield, Robert. 1968. *The Primitive World and Its Transformations.* Harmondsworth, UK: Penguin Books.

————. 1989. *The Little Community: Peasant Society and Culture.* Chicago: University of Chicago Press.

Rentas, Angelo. 2006. "Intelligent Design." *Trinity Magazine* (Spring): 22–24.

Riessman, Catherine Kohler. 1993. *Narrative Analysis.* Newbury Park, NY: Sage.

Ritzer, George. 2001. *Explorations in the Sociology of Consumption: Fast Foods, Credit Cards and Casinos.* London: Sage.

Rosenau, Pauline Marie. 1992. *Post-Modernism and the Social Sciences: Insights, Inroads, and Intrusions.* Princeton, NJ: Princeton University Press.

Rosenwald, G. C., and R. L. Ochberg. 1992. "Introduction: Life Stories, Cultural Politics, and Self-understanding." In *Storied Lives: The Cultural Politics of Self-understanding,* ed. G. C. Rosenwald and R. L. Ochberg, 1–18. New Haven: Yale University Press.

Rossi, Ino. 1983. *From the Sociology of Symbols to the Sociology of Signs: Toward a Dialectical Sociology.* New York: Columbia University Press.

Russell, Bertrand. 2004. *History of Western Philosophy.* London: Routledge. (Orig. pub. 1946.)

Sanneh, Lamin. 1993. *Encountering the West: Christianity and the Global Cultural Process*. Maryknoll, NY: Orbis Books.

Sapir, Edward. 1949. *Selected Writings in Language, Culture, and Personality*. Ed. David G. Mandelbaum. Berkeley: University of California Press.

Saussure, Ferdinand de. 1966. *Course in General Linguistics*. Ed. Charles Bally and Albert Sechehaye in collaboration with Albert Reidlinger. Trans. with an introduction and notes by Wade Baskin. New York: McGraw-Hill.

Schroeder, Manfred. 1991. *Fractals, Chaos, Power Laws*. New York: W. H. Freeman.

Schuster, Jürgen. 2006. "The Significance of the Kingdom of God in Its Eschatological Tension for the Theology of Mission of Lesslie Newbigin." PhD diss., Trinity International University, Deerfield, IL.

Shenk, Wilbert. 1980. "The Changing Role of the Missionary: From Civilization to Contextualization." In *Missions, Evangelism and Church Growth*, ed. C. Norman Kraus, 33–58. Scottdale, PA: Herald Press.

Simons, Herbert W., and Michael Billig, eds. 1994. *After Postmodernism: Reconstructing Ideology Critique*. London: Sage.

Smart, Barry. 1993. *Postmodernity: Key Ideas*. London: Routledge.

Smith, Huston. 1982. *Beyond the Post-Modern Mind*. New York: Crossroad.

Spradley, James P. 1980. *Participant Observation*. Newbury Park, CA: Sage.

Stanley, Brian, ed. 2001. *Christian Missions and the Enlightenment*. Grand Rapids: Eerdmans; Surrey, UK: Curzon Press.

Stott, John R. W. 1979. *The Message of Ephesians*. Downers Grove, IL: InterVarsity.

Taber, Charles R. 1991. *The World Is Too Much with Us: "Culture" in Modern Protestant Missions*. Macon, GA: Mercer University Press.

———. 2002. "The Gospel as Authentic Meta-narrative." In *A Scandalous Prophet: The Way of Mission after Newbigin*, ed. Thomas S. Faust, George R. Hunsberger, J. Andrew Kirk, and Werner Ustorf, 182–94. Grand Rapids: Eerdmans.

Tiénou, Tite, and Paul G. Hiebert. 2006. "Missional Theology." *Missiology* 34 (April): 219–38.

Tocqueville, Alexis de. 1863. *Democracy in America*. Ed. Francis Bowen. Trans. Henry Reeve. Cambridge: Sever and Francis.

———. 1969. *Democracy in America*. Trans. George Lawrence. New York: Doubleday Anchor Books.

Todd, Emanuel. 1987. *The Causes of Progress: Culture, Authority, and Change*. Oxford: Basil Blackwell.

Toynbee, Arnold. 1947. *A Study of History*. Abridgment of vols. 1–6 by D. C. Somervell. New York: Oxford University Press.

Turner, Harold. 1981. "Religious Movements in Primal (or Tribal) Societies." *Mission Focus* 9: 45–54.

Turner, Victor. 1974. *Dramas, Fields, and Metaphors: Symbolic Action in Human Societies*. Ithaca, NY: Cornell University Press.

Van Engen, Charles. 1997. "Mission Theology in the Light of Postmodern Critique." *International Review of Mission* 86 (October): 437–61.

Waddington, C. H. 1941. *Scientific Attitude*. New York: Penguin Books.

Wallace, A. F. C. 1956. "Revitalization Movements." *American Anthropologist* 58: 264–81.

Wallerstein, Immanuel. 1998. *Utopistics, or, Historical Choices of the Twenty-First Century*. New York: New Press.

Wallis, Jim. 1981. *The Call to Conversion*. San Francisco: HarperSanFrancisco.

Walsh, Brian J. 2006. "From Housing to Homemaking: Worldviews and the Shaping of Home." *Christian Scholar's Review* 35 (2): 237–57.

Walsh, Brian J., and J. Richard Middleton. 1984. *Transforming Vision: Shaping a Christian Worldview*. Downers Grove, IL: InterVarsity.

Warner, W. Lloyd. 1953. *American Life: Dream and Reality*. Chicago: University of Chicago Press.

Weber, Max. 1970. *From Max Weber: Essays in Sociology*. Ed. H. H. Gerth and C. Wright Mills. London: Routledge and Kegan Paul.

Werner, Oswald, and G. M. Schoepfle. 1989. *Systematic Fieldwork: Foundations of Ethnography and Interviewing*. 2 vols. Newbury Park, CA: Sage.

Whitehead, Alfred North. 1938. *Modes of Thought*. New York: Free Press.

Wilson, Bryan R., ed. 1970. *Rationality*. New York: Harper Torchbooks.

Wink, Walter. 1992. *Engaging the Powers: Discernment and Resistance in a World of Domination*. Minneapolis: Fortress Press.

Wolf, Eric. 1955. "Types of Latin American Peasantry: A Preliminary Discussion." *American Anthropologist* 57 (June): 452–71.

Wolff, K. 1989. "From Nothing to Sociology." *Philosophy of the Social Sciences* 19 (3): 321–39.

Wolters, Albert. 1985. *Creation Regained: Biblical Basics for a Reformational Worldview*. Grand Rapids: Eerdmans.

Worsley, Peter. 1968. *The Trumpet Shall Sound: A Study of Cargo Cults in Melanesia*. New York: Schocken Books.

Zadeh, Lofti Asker. 1965. "Fuzzy Sets." *Information and Control* 8: 338–53.

Zahan, Dominique. 1979. *The Religion, Spirituality, and Thought of Traditional Africa*. Trans. Kate Ezra Martin and Lawrence M. Martin. Chicago: University of Chicago Press.

Zehr, Howard. 1990. *Changing Lenses: A New Focus for Crime and Justice*. Scottdale, PA: Herald Press.

Zimmerman, Hans-Jürgen. 1985. *Fuzzy Set Theory and Its Applications*. Boston: Kluwer-Nijhoff.

Index

Page numbers in italics indicate figures.